YALE CLASSICAL STUDIES

YALE CLASSICAL STUDIES

EDITED FOR THE DEPARTMENT OF CLASSICS

by

JOHN J. WINKLER

Assistant Professor of Classics, Stanford University

and

GORDON WILLIAMS

Thatcher Professor of Latin, Yale University

VOLUME XXVII
LATER GREEK LITERATURE

CAMBRIDGE UNIVERSITY PRESS

CAMBRIDGE

LONDON   NEW YORK   NEW ROCHELLE
SYDNEY   MELBOURNE

Published by the Press Syndicate of the University of Cambridge
The Pitt Building, Trumpington Street, Cambridge CB2 1RP
32 East 57th Street, New York, NY 10022, USA
296 Beaconsfield Parade, Middle Park, Melbourne 3206, Australia

© Cambridge University Press 1982

First published 1982

Printed in the United States of America

Library of Congress catalogue card number: 81-10219

British Library Cataloguing in Publication Data
Later Greek literature-(Yale classical studies; v. 27)
1. Greek literature-History and criticism-Addresses, essays, lectures
I. Winkler, John J., 1943 –   II. Williams, Gordon, 1926 –
880.9'001   PA3052
ISBN 0 521 23947 8

Contents

v

Introduction

The present volume of Yale Classical Studies is devoted to essays on later Greek literature. The guiding intent which prompted this collection is indicated by the original advertizement for it, which was circulated informally in 1976: 'A forthcoming volume of *Yale Classical Studies* will be devoted to "The Second Sophistic and Later Greek Literature". We hope that the articles in this volume will highlight the literary excellence of undeservedly neglected authors, and help to attract readers and scholars to the riches of this era, which we might roughly define as reaching from Chariton to the Nonnians. Because so many of these later authors have suffered from a "bad press" and pejorative comparison with their classical predecessors, we will give preference to essays which sensibly correct such distortions. The history and text-history of these authors is, of course, relevant to such projects, but we are looking in most cases for solid general interpretations whose clear-sighted enthusiasm will spark interest and provoke discussion.'

The problem we felt then, that much excellent literature written in Greek under the Roman Empire was being chronically underrated, still exists, and it is still our hope that this volume will indeed draw more readers to the rewards and delights of post-Hellenistic Greek literature. The history of Greek literature is very long indeed, an ongoing story whose origins pre-date literacy and whose end is not in sight. Within the limited area marked off for this volume, many remarkable authors and topics are not dealt with: among the many absences we especially regret to have no essays on Nonnus (though the work of Gordon Braden opens a door to that polymathic/polymythic poet and his aesthetic of boundariless hallucination)[1] or his many successors; nor on Philostratus, the

1. Gordon Braden, 'Nonnos' Typhoon: *Dionysiaca* Books I and II', *Texas Studies in Literature and Language* 15 (1974), 851–79; and on Musaios his *The Classics and English Renaissance Poetry: Three Case Studies*, Yale Studies in English 187 (New Haven 1978).

eminent sophists[2] (Lucian being a special case), Aelian, Quintus of Smyrna, the other novelists,[3] the literary criticism of philosophers,[4] Plutarch, Oppian, and many others who well deserve to be read and over whose works we may place the Apuleian motto, *Lector intende, laetaberis*.

Perhaps the greatest need which this collection helps to make clear is for sustained analyses of the fundamental quality of literature written in the shadow of – or in the light of – a classical past. Most of the essays in this volume make some tentative approach to the issue of 'derivative' or 'imitative' writing, but none provide a concerted treatment of the problem.[5] Old habits of thought die hard: several of our contributors had to work to rid themselves of a residual feeling that anything post-Sophocles was automatically second-rate. We begin to suspect that the basic terms of this judgment express our own literary and cultural pre-conceptions in a way which interferes with our understanding of the achievements of ancient Greek literature in most of its history. The attitude to the past is a variable from culture to culture; the Greeks, more than we, tended to canonize their past in a way which appears to give rigor and security to a fixed tradition but which in fact they could use selectively and obliquely to manipulate the present. The self-subordination of 'later' writers who seem, on a rapid overview, to efface their own originality by continuous half-quotation of their Classics may actually represent a cultural style of greater reserve and politesse, a style of sophisticated double-thinking which we perceive in our own categories as 'derivative' and 'unoriginal'. The recent work of

2. Professor George Kennedy's *A History of Rhetoric* will soon include a third volume on later Greek rhetoric (vol. I, *The Art of Persuasion in Greece*, 1963; vol. II, *The Art of Rhetoric in the Roman World*, 1972).

3. The University of California Press is scheduled to publish new translations of the complete Greek novels.

4. J. Coulter, *The Literary Microcosm: Theories of Interpretation of the Later Neoplatonists*, Columbia Studies in the Classical Tradition 2 (Leyden 1976); Robert D. Lamberton, 'Homer the Theologian: The Iliad and Odyssey as read by the Neoplatonists of Late Antiquity', 2 vols. (Ph.D. diss. Yale 1979).

5. J. Bompaire, *Lucien écrivain: imitation et création* (Paris 1958); Ewan Bowie 'Greeks and their Past in the Second Sophistic', *Past & Present* 46 (1970), 1–41, repr. in M. I. Finley, ed., *Studies in Ancient Society* (London 1974); B. Reardon, *Courants littéraires grecs des II*e *et III*e *siècles après J.-C.* (Paris 1971).

Gregory Nagy[6] goes far towards showing that this cultural pattern of sophisticated variation and half-quotation may be fundamental to Greek literature from its earliest known beginnings in oral epic.

Though so much still waits to be done, we are very happy to present this collection of essays which highlight selected topics in Imperial Greek literature. Nowadays we look to papyrology for occasional revelations of exciting new pieces of ancient literature, but there are masterpieces already on the shelves waiting to be noticed. For some readers this volume will contain 'discoveries' – of the sophistication of popular fiction (Chariton, Heliodorus), of the craft of translation (Fisher), the successful techniques for lecturing on Classical subjects (Anderson on Lucian), delicately lascivious love-letters ('Aristaenetus'), the interplay of literary culture and politics (Bowie, Cameron, Baldwin, Bowersock). Within our period the Second Sophistic, as Philostratus dubbed it, was the single most influential current, but only two of our essays deal with this phenomenon directly, one (Bowie's) in a way which illuminatingly revises the accepted notion of the movement. For this reason we have dropped the phrase 'Second Sophistic' from our original title.

We would like to think Professors Susan Stephens, Ronald Mellor and John Nicols for their valuable technical advice on matters of papyrology and prosopography.

John J. Winkler (Stanford)
Gordon Williams (Yale)

6. G. Nagy, *The Best of the Achaeans: Concepts of the Hero in Archaic Greek Poetry* (Baltimore 1979).

Theme, structure and narrative in Chariton

B. P. REARDON

A hundred years ago Chariton's romance *Chaereas and Callirhoe* seemed a poor thing. It seemed so, certainly, to Rohde,[1] who found plot and characters tame, and did not veil his contempt for the sentimentality of the story, for its unheroic and passive hero and heroine, for the cheapness of its general effect; at the same time he did grant that there was something not unpleasing about its simplicity. Two decades later, papyrological discoveries began to be made which were to lead, if not to a revolution in our estimation of the literary form of the romance, at any rate to such a reversal in our dating of the extant texts as enabled the form to be seen for the first time in a comprehensible literary context and line of development.[2] Chariton profited particularly: from Rohde's date of around A.D. 500 he was brought forward perhaps 400 years – nowadays some would put him a hundred years, or even two hundred, earlier than that; and there is general though not universal agreement that his is the earliest of the extant romance texts.[3] Furthermore, the fact that several papyri of Chariton were found suggests that his story was popular. This advance in knowledge enabled Ben Edwin Perry, fifty years ago, to make of

1. *Der griechische Roman und seine Vorläufer* (Leipzig 1876; 4th ed., Hildesheim 1960, repr. 1974).
2. See particularly Lesky, *Geschichte der griechischen Literatur*[3] (Bern/Munich 1971), 957–72 (older histories of literature, such as Schmid's, are badly out of date). For a discussion of this topic see my forthcoming article in *Aufstieg und Niedergang der römischen Welt* II (*ANRW infra*); and my *Courants littéraires grecs des IIe et IIIe siècles après J.-C.* (Paris 1971) (*CLG infra*), 309–403, to which general reference may be made at this point for the bibliography on the subject. For the period 1950–70, see also G. N. Sandy, 'Recent Scholarship on the Prose Fiction of Classical Antiquity', *CW* 67 (1974), 321–59.
3. The evidence is conveniently summarized in the introduction to a recent German translation, K. Plepelits, *Chariton von Aphrodisias: Kallirhoe* (Stuttgart 1976), 4–9 (for the exceptional view that would place the novel around A.D. 200, see n. 5 below). My own guess at the date of the work would be about A.D. 50; perhaps earlier – a date B.C. is not impossible – but not much later.

Chariton's story the basis of an already fairly well-developed theory of the origins of the form romance and its place in cultural history, a theory fully set out in 1967 in his *magnum opus The Ancient Romances*.[4] *Chaereas and Callirhoe*, Perry maintained, was a ripe specimen of the Hellenistic romance, and on that score alone has considerable interest as evidence for a critical stage in literary history; but in addition, Perry, showing early the independence and pugnaciousness which characterizes his work, stoutly maintained that the story, though of a cheap type, had substantial merit in itself.

By that period there was beginning a reassessment of the romances, or novels, that has been pursued, subsequently, with increasing business. Literary merit has been emphasized, in Longus and Heliodorus for instance; fragments have been edited seriously, if not always well; relationships between romance and the age which produced it began to be considered; it was even proposed that these texts were a manifestation of the religious development of post-classical antiquity.[5] For Chariton himself, associated questions have been studied: the relationship of his story with historiography and with contemporary social usage, its date, its language,[6] in short, the literary provenance and cultural context of a work apparently marking the critical stage of social development that has been mentioned – rather, that is, than the story itself, its literary characteristics.

But more recently *Chaereas and Callirhoe* has attracted specifically literary criticism. Karl-Heinz Gerschmann offers a sustained commentary on the composition of the story; Carl Werner Müller approaches the basic question of the aesthetic nature of the work; it

4. 'Chariton and his Romance from a Literary-Historical Point of View', *AJP* 51 (1930), 93–134; *The Ancient Romances: a Literary-Historical Account of their Origins* (Berkeley 1967).

5. K. Kerényi, *Die griechisch-orientalische Romanliteratur in religionsgeschichtlicher Beleuchtung* (Tübingen 1927); R. Merkelbach, *Roman und Mysterium* (Munich/Berlin 1962). Merkelbach's thesis (it is not Kerényi's) requires a later date for Chariton; see *CLG*, 393ff. and 338 n. 61.

6. *CLG*, 340ff., nn.; add, particularly, F. Zimmermann, 'Kallirhoes Verkauf durch Theron: eine juristisch-philologische Betrachtung zu Chariton', *Aus der byzantinischen Arbeit der DDR* 1 (Berlin 1957), 72–81; A. D. Papanikolaou, *Chariton-Studien* (Göttingen 1973) (language, date); and see *ANRW*. Plepelits, *Chariton*, discusses the 'historiographical' aspect of Chariton. Add, now, the introduction of G. Molinié to his Budé edition of Chariton (Paris 1979).

is seen by others, variously, as the story of Chaereas or as the story of Callirhoe.[7] The most searching analysis by far is the technical study of Tomas Hägg, in the relevant parts of his 1971 study *Narrative Technique in Ancient Greek Romances.*[8] Hägg finds in Chariton's novel much more technical skill even than Perry had suggested. Where Perry offered traditional, as it were 'instinctive' literary criticism, Hägg's is scientific, clinical, so to speak 'professional', operating – as does one kind of criticism of modern literature, whose approach he uses – with percentages, statistics and graphs, concerned with tempo and phrases of narrative, scene and summary, narrative time and dramatic time, point of view, internal reference system.[9] It is consequently not Hägg's primary purpose to evaluate, or to discern his author's 'subject' or 'aim', still less any 'message' that he might have. In fact, however, conclusions similar to Perry's do emerge, suggesting that Chariton does know what he is doing, and does it well on the whole – given, of course, certain basic assumptions about the nature of his story.

This paper proposes to pursue such topics as these: to consider the story of *Chaereas and Callirhoe* principally in its literary-critical rather than its literary-historical aspects; to examine what the story is about, how it is put together, how it is told – its theme, structure, narrative method; and to discuss some other aspects of it arising from these considerations. In doing so I shall be referring to things that have already been said, particularly in the last decade or so, and shall try to take account of the most useful of these contributions. There will be nothing revolutionary in what is said here; much has been at least adumbrated by Perry and others; and the rest is a matter of emphasis, of fashion perhaps. We do not really have enough evidence to assert categorically that this story marks a turning-point in literary history. But we do have enough to justify us in treating it, less ambitiously, as an early point of reference for the Greek romance, or novel – extended fictitious

7. Karl-Heinz Gerschmann, 'Chariton-Interpretationen' (diss. Münster 1974); Carl Werner Müller, 'Chariton von Aphrodisias und die Theorie des Romans in der Antike', *Antike und Abendland* 22 (1976), 115–36; Gareth L. Schmeling, *Chariton* (New York 1974); Arthur Heiserman, *The Novel before the Novel* (Chicago 1977), ch. 6: 'Aphrodisian Chastity'. Cf. also Molinié (n. 6), 22–41.
8. Stockholm 1971; abbreviated *infra* as *NT*.
9. Cf. e.g. R. Wellek and A. Warren, *Theory of Literature* (London 1949 etc.).

narrative in prose. Our knowledge of the range of that form has been increased in very recent years by yet more fragments, variously lurid, scabrous, or less spectacular.[10] They are by no means fully explained, of course. But it is worthwhile to look at Chariton again, in a context slightly fuller, and more fully considered, than it once was; to examine with some care the nature and not just the fact of this reference-point. The hinge is worth examining; and Hägg in particular has given us a microscope, to examine it with, that we shall find useful.

Perhaps it will be well to sketch the story. It is not very well known, the text itself has not always been readily available until very recently, and even translations are few and far between.[11] The situation has, however, been to some extent remedied by the appearance of a Budé edition; and this fact, together with the recent work just described, gives some reason for hoping that the time is past when this story and its congeners could be simply disregarded because they were unfamiliar to scholars.

The devastatingly beautiful Callirhoe is the daughter of the famous Hermocrates of Syracuse; Chaereas is the son of an only less prominent Syracusan who is Hermocrates' bitter enemy. The pair fall in love, on the occasion of a festival of Aphrodite. Opposition from their families is overcome by the enthusiastic urgings of the whole town, and Chaereas and Callirhoe are married. But Callirhoe had had other suitors; in their anger they mount a plot which leads Chaereas, out of jealousy, to kick his wife, who falls apparently dead. She is buried richly. The pirate Theron sees the costly funeral, and that night he robs Callirhoe's tomb – just as Callirhoe is recovering from what was really a coma. Theron carries her off to Miletus, sells her to the seigneur of the region, Dionysius, and makes off hastily. Dionysius at once falls in love with her. At this point Callirhoe discovers that she is pregnant by

10. Notably A. Henrichs, *Die Phoinikika des Lollianos* (Bonn 1972); P. J. Parsons, 'A Greek *Satyricon*?' *BICS* 18 (1971), 53–68; H. Maehler, 'Der Metiochos-Parthenope Roman', *ZPE* 23 (1976), 1–20. There have been numerous less remarkable fragments as well.

11. The text used in this paper is that of W. E. Blake (Oxford 1938); for the new Budé, see my review forthcoming in *REG* 94 (1981). A projected Loeb edition has been postponed indefinitely. Translations: W. E. Blake (Oxford 1939); a new version will appear in a volume I am currently assembling. In other languages: P. Grimal, in *Romans grecs et latins* (Paris 1958); add the Budé; and K. Plepelits (n. 3).

her husband; reluctantly, thinking herself separated for ever from Chaereas, she decides to marry Dionysius for the sake of her child.

Meanwhile the tomb-robbery has been discovered, and Chaereas, grief-stricken, has set out in search of Callirhoe, dead though he believes her to be. By good fortune he comes across Theron drifting helplessly, his ship disabled by storms and his crew dead. Theron tells all, and is executed. Chaereas sails to Miletus; there he learns of Callirhoe's marriage to Dionysius; but his ship is attacked and he himself taken prisoner and sold as a slave to Mithridates, the satrap of Caria and neighbour of Dionysius.

In due course Callirhoe bears her child, whom she passes off as Dionysius'. She has by now heard of the arrival and destruction of the Syracusan ship, and is in her turn grief-stricken for Chaereas, whom she thinks now dead. In an attempt to lay his ghost, Dionysius builds a cenotaph for Chaereas. At the dedication ceremony Mithridates is present. As soon as he sees Callirhoe he falls in love with her; returning to Caria, he mounts an intrigue to win her, using for the purpose his prisoner Chaereas, whose identity he has by chance discovered. This intrigue is discovered by Dionysius, who charges Mithridates with malpractice; and the whole situation is reported to the King of Persia, who summons all the parties to Babylon, so that Mithridates can be put on trial.

Here Chariton elaborately mounts a full-dress debate between the rivals Dionysius and Mithridates, over who is, or who is to be, Callirhoe's husband. By now, however, the matter is complicated by the fact that the King, as soon as he catches sight of Callirhoe, inevitably falls in love with her himself. And it is still further complicated by the dramatic appearance, at the critical point of the trial, of none other than Chaereas – to the utter astonishment of all but Mithridates, who has stage-managed the apparition. Chariton here (5.8.2) pulls out all the stops: 'who could describe adequately that scene in court? What dramatist ever staged so sensational a story? You would have thought you were in a theater crowded with passions all tumbling over each other – πάντα ἦν ὁμοῦ, δάκρυα, χαρά, θάμβος, ἔλεος, ἀπιστία, εὐχαί. Χαιρέαν ἐμακάριζον, Μιθριδάτῃ συνέχαιρον, συνελυποῦντο Διονυσίῳ, περὶ Καλλιρόης ἠπόρουν – weeping and rejoicing, astonishment and pity, disbelief and prayers. How happy all were for Chaereas! How glad for Mithridates! For Dionysius how sorrowful! As for

Callirhoe, they did not know *what* to think about her.' And well they might not. They didn't know what to think about Callirhoe; and the King doesn't know what to do about her. This climactic scene issues in a welter of emotions: profound heart-searching in the King, despair in Dionysius, relief in Mithridates; and in the still-separated Chaereas and Callirhoe themselves, heart-rending anguish. But as far as the plot is concerned, it issues in an impasse: the King cannot decide what to do. The impugned pretendant Mithridates has abandoned his hopes, but Dionysius remains and Chaereas remains; and the King, even though in his head he knows he cannot replace his Queen with Callirhoe, or sully his dignity by acting more arbitrarily, cannot bring himself to adjudge Callirhoe to either of her husbands. The author solves the problem by having a sudden rebellion in Egypt, which demands the King's instant attention – much to the King's relief; and which sends Chaereas flying in despair to the rebel side, in order at least to achieve a glorious death and damage his enemies if he can – it is the most whole-hearted of several attempts he has made at suicide. But τύχη has not exhausted her quiver of παράδοξα: Chaereas proves so brilliant a soldier and admiral that he defeats the King. In doing so, he recovers his Callirhoe; and they return to Syracuse, where they live happily ever after.

The conventions that operate here are as clear as those of a Victorian melodrama, and for immediate purposes we need do little more than observe rapidly their principal features. Melodrama, precisely, is the most prominent of them; and with melodrama, sentiment, pathos and simplicity of attitude – these make up the principal characters, those to whom the events happen; the events themselves are spectacular, coincidental, of capital import. Having said this, we should look beyond these features of the story. Such stories stand in a clear relationship with their society and culture – other examples of the kind may be more sophisticated (Longus' story, notably), but do not differ in substance from Chariton's. All offer, in a general way, a spiritual photograph of their time, their Hellenistic-imperial time: isolated individuals seeking, in a wide world and an open society, security and very identity, in love of their fellows – or, in other texts, in love of God.[12]

12. I have developed this interpretation in *CLG*, and more briefly in 'The

So much should be said here, and can be said briefly. The purpose of the present remarks is less general, and concerns this particular story. What is it about? Is it about Chaereas? or about Callirhoe? or about Chaereas and Callirhoe? Or is it really about something wider: about love, or about life, or about people? I shall suggest that this is a matter of perspective, of illusion even; and that is what can lead to different answers to that question. I shall discuss the story in three aspects: first, its overall structure – that is, its plot and the disposition of its major elements; second, its narrative technique – that is, the way in which that plot and those elements are presented to the consumer; and lastly, its theme, as that theme emerges from the plot, narrative, and the writer's attitude to his story and characters.

If we analyse the story into its elements, what are those elements? That will depend on the criterion we adopt: dramatic effect, or mechanical disposition of matter, or logical structure. Perry, following Reitzenstein, saw in the story a Hellenistic drama in five acts:[13] Callirhoe's marriage to Chaereas and to Dionysius; Chaereas' enslavement; the trial; the war; the reunion. The effect of using a dramatic criterion is to turn the spotlight rather on Callirhoe than on Chaereas. A mechanical analysis following the book-divisions – which are Chariton's own[14] – would suggest four stages of development, each given roughly equal time in two books: the adventures of Callirhoe; the adventures of Chaereas; Chaereas and Callirhoe together (in Babylon); and Chaereas again; and although this division cannot be very different from Perry's, Chaereas here seems more important.

But what is the overall impression the story makes on its reader? What is its logical structure, what is its emotional effect? What, that is, is its total aesthetic impact? Here, we shall have to adopt a less mechanical criterion; we shall have to examine both the events of the story and its emotional content, and the relation between

Greek Novel', *Phoenix* 23 (1969), 291–309; see also *CLG*, 321 n. 31, for other studies in general interpretation of the form.

13. *Ancient Romances*, 140ff.

14. Müller, *Chariton*, suggests that the eight books constituted two papyrus rolls, and that the résumé at the beginning of 5 of the contents of 1–4 may indicate later publication of 'Part II'. Chariton probably had compositional reasons for placing this résumé and many others where he did place them, but certainly the résumé at 5 *init.* is unique in covering the previous action comprehensively.

them. And this is the first point at which Hägg's statistical critical tool will have interest for us: the modern theoretical division between 'summary' and 'scene' – between the reporting of what happens and the representation, the mimetic representation, of what happens.

What are the events, then? And what place does Chariton give them? Considered as *what happens*, the story can be analysed as follows:

1. A brief introduction – the marriage of Chaereas and Callirhoe.
2. Separation, beginning with Callirhoe's coma; the fact of this separation is structurally important, since it is the basis of the subsequent plot.
3. The main events – the main things that happen – are the relationships of Callirhoe with Dionysius, Mithridates, and the King. These can be seen as a series of *agones*: the *agon* with Dionysius includes the marriage and the trial; that with Mithridates includes the intrigue and the trial; that with the King includes the trial and the war.
4. Reunion: this, although long, is in itself *structurally* unimportant.

The central structure, then, the body of what happens, is a series of *agones*: Chaereas' rivals.

But is this the aesthetic effect on the reader? Not without qualification. Unquestionably the 'best' part of the story, in the sense of the most striking, memorable, and 'successful', is the trial in Babylon: Dionysius and Mithridates, rivals for Callirhoe's hand, arguing fast and furiously, before a King of Persia who is himself another rival, while all the time Chaereas, her original husband, is sitting helplessly on the sidelines. Chariton puts his best efforts into the scene – I have indicated the nature of the writing at this point: dramatic, spectacular, pathetic. This looks like the climax of the work; and in Perry's discussion, for instance, we read that 'the trial of Dionysius vs. Mithridates overshadows in interest and importance everything that has preceded, and what follows consists in the unravelling of the situation thereby developed . . . It is the culminating point of a suspense which has been gathering momentum for the space of an entire book . . . everything converges towards this climax.'[15]

15. *AJP* 51 (1930), 113.

In fact, this is where the principal illusion lies: an illusion created by the relative fullness with which 'scene', dramatic spectacle, is described by Chariton, and the brevity with which critical events are narrated, with which what actually critically happens is set out. The structure of the story deserves further examination.

The critical events are the *agones*; and what happens 'about' them, as it were, is that (a) they begin – after the separation that creates a vacuum, or a vacancy; (b) they take place, *and the issue of all of them is the same* – they are causally linked the one to the next, and they all issue in the *same result*, namely that *no decision is made*; and (c) they end, when Chaereas recovers Callirhoe *by force*. The trial in Babylon is structurally no different from the other *agones*: as Hägg says, it is a parenthesis.[16] The main problem after the trial, from Callirhoe's point of view, is precisely what the main problem was before the trial: Chaereas versus Dionysius: will Callirhoe have definitely to pass from her first husband to her second? For the earlier stages of the Mithridates episode are merely another parenthesis. After the trial the King has to decide between Chaereas and Dionysius. But the matter of decision between Chaereas and Dionysius could perfectly well have arisen, and in fact in embryo did arise, in Miletus, before anyone ever set foot on the road to Babylon. Structurally, the parentheses, the detours, alter nothing; Mithridates and the King are merely doublets of Dionysius; the only real *agon* is that of Chaereas versus Dionysius, and in respect of it the mounting of the trial is a piece of illusion. The trial, indeed, is the climax of a yet longer series of *agones*, which really begins at the very beginning of the story, with the intrigues of Callirhoe's other suitors – who are Chaereas' earliest rivals. There is a clear progression in the series of rivals, the last of whom is none less than the King of Persia, and this point will have its importance later. For the moment, however, the fact remains that structurally *all* of these *agones* are the same *agon*: Chaereas versus a rival.

This central problem, this central rivalry, arises from Callirhoe's beauty, which engenders love: divine beauty is the motor of the initial movement, and of its complications. The complications are that beauty and love lead to one marriage and consequently (because of Callirhoe's pregnancy) to another. And the problem is only settled by force; war is the real arbiter. Dionysius and

16. *NT*, 265.

9

Chaereas are involved as associates of the powers of Persia and Egypt, and the state quarrel settles the personal issue; the personal issue rises to the level of an affair of state, and is settled *thereby*.[17]

The problem, then, arises from beauty, consists of rivalry for beauty, and is settled by force. The line of events is simple; complications are only apparent. The structural or dynamic function of the whole Babylon episode is not to create a situation but to renew the initial situation, to renew but not to change the movement of the plot; to raise the stakes, as Callirhoe's beauty captivates the highest in the land. And it is precisely because the Babylon episode is inconclusive – a parenthesis – that it can give way to new action, in the shape of τύχη.

But this is only events; and the story consists also of reactions to events. The other pole of the story is emotion. And in this respect, in respect of the emotions that it is the story's whole purpose to generate, Babylon *is* a turning-point. In Babylon, and not till then, Chaereas and Callirhoe are 'reunited' in the sense that they have found each other, have seen each other; each knows the other is alive. Chaereas has long known that Callirhoe is alive; but she has been irrecoverable; Babylon, representing his first real hope of recovering her, is, thus, crucial emotionally for him. As for Callirhoe: she has been quite unsure whether Chaereas is alive, and he has been unobtainable anyway; for her, Babylon represents her first real assurance that he is alive, and the first point at which she can hope – as she does, on leaving Babylon in the King's train, hope that things will take a turn for the better. Babylon is thus emotionally crucial for her too. Thus emotionally Babylon *is* the culmination of the series of *agones*. The weight of the emotion has lain on Callirhoe's side, because it is her side of the story that Chariton shows us more of; and he shows us more of it because it is the more emotionally-charged – she is the one who has the series of lovers, she is the one who has the baby. And she is the emotional

---

17. We may observe that Chaereas, in recovering Callirhoe by force, has become a man of action – no longer passive, ineffective and suicidal, although this is paradoxical since his action began as an attempt at suicide. I exclude this point from my text as not being directly relevant to my argument at this point; but it is worth observing that Chariton has thus observed also the structural weakness which lies in Chaereas' passivity. It is after all the hero – helped, certainly, by τύχη – who solves the problem, and in so doing regains happiness for himself and the heroine.

centre of the story also in that the *male* emotional life in it is distributed over several different men. Here we return to our structural analysis of the series of lovers and *agones*; but this time it is to observe, not an illusion, but a very positive value in the structure. One of the story's major themes is the power of love, and that is seen very clearly in love's power over a series of men, in successively higher place. Political power and status become as nothing when the man, however highly placed, falls in love; he is reduced to the common lot of humanity. And it is Callirhoe in whom the power of this emotion is concentrated – *in* her, and also, by means of the progression of lovers, *on* her.

What Chariton has done, that is, in the overall structure of the story, is to play events against emotion. The story is 'about' both; it has a double focus of interest.

And here we may turn to the analysis made by Hägg, not of the overall structure, but of the manner in which the story is unfolded – its narrative technique.[18] Characteristically, it proceeds by means, first, of rapid narrative summarizing a sequence of events; then, by degrees, the tempo slows; and finally a 'scene' materializes, displaying the actions, thoughts, utterances of an important character at an important juncture of events – Callirhoe, for instance, deliberating whether or not to marry Dionysius. Then the story proceeds – perhaps the subject is changed – and the process is repeated. Events in sequence are played against the crises, in particular the emotional crises, that arise from them. Fundamentally it is the same aesthetic process as we have just observed in respect of the story's overall structure. And here we may note the statistics: practically 90% of Chariton's text is 'scene', and half of that is direct speech; only 10% is 'summary'.[19] So marked is the perspective, the illusion; by so much do the critical moments, and notably their emotional content, predominate over narrative of action. Of course all novelists use such a technique, such illusion, in greater or less degree, with more or less conscious

18. *NT*, esp. chs. 1, 2.

19. I am here compressing a very full and detailed examination (and rounding off figures), but I hope not misrepresenting it (or Chariton). The most useful single reference, here, to Hägg's book would be to the 'Syncrisis' on 'Tempo and Phases of Narrative', pp. 82ff. (with diagrams); but Hägg's summaries cannot dispense the reader from following in detail the exacting analysis conducted in his chapters.

purpose; I am suggesting that conscious purpose is very clear in the case of Chariton, and that the simplicity that Rohde admired is not as artless as he no doubt thought.

The illusion is the more marked in that, for all the rapidity with which he narrates them, Chariton none the less organizes his events with great care. That he does give them a very important place is shown by, among other things, the conscious demonstrations he offers us of his line of events, in the form of a long series of recapitulations: no fewer than 20 of them, some very full and carefully placed at crucial points in the action – just after the trial in Babylon, for instance, or at the beginning of the final book.[20] But the changing of focus is what emerges from Hägg's analysis as the paramount feature of the author's technique. For much of the time Chariton gives Callirhoe centre stage. And stage, scene, is what it is, as he represents (μιμεῖται) her situation and reactions in detail and dramatically, often in monologue, as time after time she comes to a crisis in her affairs. This is indeed a further factor contributing to the emotional predominance, noted above, of Callirhoe in the story. Time and again Chariton uses *her* as his vehicle for discussing the situation, for bringing out its emotional content.[21] Chaereas' side of things is altogether more scantly treated, even when he does something as spectacular as capturing Tyre (like Alexander). Events are played down in the narrative, so they tend to look rather threadbare. But they *are organized*; and when it suits his purpose Chariton demonstrates their *line* with care, and perhaps even (as Hägg suggests) with pride – precisely because it is not events that in his story are made conspicuous.

In this sense, then, 'theme' and 'structure' are not the same thing. Chaereas is as necessary to the *structure* as Callirhoe is, and in this sense the story is about both of them. But the *theme* is really the emotional situation; and in that respect it is Callirhoe who

20. *NT*, 264ff.

21. At 1.3.6 she offers a shrewd guess when she sees the traces of revelling; this heightens the tension. At 1.9.3 (quoted below, p. 17), when she guesses the truth (already known to the reader) on waking up in the tomb, Chariton again uses her to step up the emotional charge of the situation. At 1.11.1–2 and 1.13.10 she knows the pirates are lying to her – and this makes things even more grim. There are many other occasions where her perception of the state of things brings her close to the reader, in an almost confidential relationship, and thus makes him see the story through her eyes.

predominates. Τοσάδε, says Chariton at the very end of his story, περὶ Καλλιρόης συνέγραψα. Possibly Plepelits is right in thinking that Chariton's title for his story was simply *Callirhoe*.[22]

Let us change our own critical focus, here, and look for a moment at what the story may be 'about' in a broader, less concrete sense. Is it 'about' life, or love, or people – as great novels are?

Clearly there is a 'spiritual content', in that what is readily visible to the reader is adventure and emotion – that is, what happens to people, or at any rate these people, and how they feel about what happens to them. And there is a whole gallery of *dramatis personae* – perhaps one should say a whole stageful of them. But events viewed as emanations of character are really rather bleak; Rohde's word for the plot was *armselig*, wretched. The reason is that of the *dramatis personae* nobody who is important enough is nasty enough. Again, Rohde pointed that out long ago; what I would observe here is that Dionysius and the King, notably, are too *civilized* to set the world, or this story, on fire. This is in very striking contrast with the vigour, indeed brutality, of much of older Greek literature (*Agamemnon, Oedipus Tyrannus*). Only the minor characters, and not all of them, have enough punch in their personality to interfere effectively with events – Theron the pirate, Plangon, Phocas, Leonas, Artaxates, the servants of Dionysius and the King. And they cannot *direct* events – when they try to, things end badly; they are not clever New Comedy slaves who can resolve situations successfully. And if Dionysius and the King are too civilized, Chaereas and Callirhoe themselves are even less effective; they are really attitudes, sensitized personality-matter rather than

22. *Chariton*, introduction, pp. 28ff. The usual title *Chaereas and Callirhoe* rests only on the evidence of the unique (late Byzantine) MS. *Callirhoe* is found in a papyrus (but see D. S. Crawford, *Papyri Michaelidae* (Aberdeen 1951), 1; this title could be an abbreviation). But this is a matter of fashion: the form *Jack and Jill* is apparently imperial, but romances were also called e.g. *Ephesiaca*. In pre-romance times plays, for example, were called *Hippolytus*, or *Medea*; Heliodorus' novel was commonly known as *Charicleia* in the Byzantine period. Certainly no interpretation can be built on a title. For the substance of the matter: Schmeling, *Chariton*, 130–41, discusses Chaereas as 'a new kind of hero' undergoing a 'marvelous journey' and *rites de passage* to expiate his guilt. Heiserman, *The Novel before the Novel*, on the other hand, sees the story as being concerned entirely with Callirhoe (whose name he misspells): 'a fantasy of erotic power' is 'in conflict with, and therefore sanctioned by, a fantasy of moral power', and Chariton's story 'reconciles our desire to be Aphrodisian with our desire to be good'.

people with real emotions. It is true that they choose the 'big things': Callirhoe chooses maternity, Chaereas war, and these αἱρέσεις do determine the main lines of the story, its events and emotions. But otherwise they are pale, and even these choices are really 'attitudes' which precipitate action, rather than themselves action – Callirhoe and Chaereas are such people as, faced with such circumstances, will inevitably make a 'pathetic' choice. Chariton is not principally concerned with people's characters, although what he does with some of them – Theron, Artaxates the King's eunuch, and the King himself are good examples – shows ability with people.[23] Events, then, are melodramatic; emotion is really sentiment; the principal people are only half-alive. Perhaps we cannot really maintain that Chariton has, consciously, profound things to say about life, or love, or people, in universal terms.

But he does say something in more limited terms: about life, love (perhaps), people in his Hellenistic world; and he says so in a Hellenistic way, a Hellenistic form. Two things stand out about *Chaereas and Callirhoe*: its technique, and the report it gives us of some aspects, at least, of its author's society. I have already touched on both of these topics – they are closely connected – and here return to them, to develop them further; first, to the matter of Chariton's narrative technique.

The principal technical problem Chariton has to face, as we have seen, is the problem of relating events to scene, to character (in the sense of the *personae* presented in the drama). That is to say that Chariton, or his generation, has in effect to invent narrative fiction – at least, extended narrative fiction, as opposed to the oral *conte*. It has of course some relationship to epic, which is extended and narrative and largely fictitious. But if he is doing an old thing, he is doing it in a new form, the form of prose. Narrative prose has

23. Perry, *AJP* 51 (1930) 115ff., discusses some of these – notably Theron – in some detail, but is pursuing a topic of limited profitability; it is followed further, and given some theoretical basis, by J. Helms, *Character Portrayal in the Romance of Chariton* (The Hague/Paris 1966). What transpires from these studies is that Chariton depicts character dramatically – as could be expected. This topic is brought within the scope of Hägg's study in an addendum by that scholar, 'Some Technical Aspects of the Characterization in Chariton's Romance', *Studi Classici in Onore di Quintino Cataudella* II, Università di Catania, Facoltà di Lettere e Filosofia (1972), 545–56; as in other aspects of his narrative, there is, on examination, considerable but unobtrusive technical subtlety in Chariton's presentation of his characters.

some, but not all, of the characteristics of heroic epic. It is extensible, it is receptive, it can narrate – all of this as opposed to drama, which does not have these characteristics. But it has no fixed constructional base, such as the formulaic hexameter provides. This is a function of its diffusion: it is hard to think that romances were usually purveyed orally to fairly large groups. There may well have been small reading-circles, but presumably a work like *Chaereas and Callirhoe* was essentially a written thing aimed at literate individuals. This, along with social diffusion, would affect its reception, and hence its creation: the result is a freer form, whose narrative conventions had to be shaped. Perry rightly describes the form as 'latter-day epic for Everyman'.[24]

Chariton is writing, however, in the cultural context of the most familiar popular medium of his day, namely dramatic spectacle of one kind or another: Hellenistic drama, or excerpts from the classics, or mime. Hence Perry's further description of the form as Hellenistic drama in prose.[25] There is in fact a fair resemblance, in *Chaereas and Callirhoe*, to 'Scenes from Shakespeare': a monologue by Callirhoe strongly resembles a soliloquy by Lady Macbeth, or a speech like 'The quality of mercy is not strained'; and it is not difficult to imagine a famous actress 'playing' Callirhoe. Only, Chariton insists on the logical thread of events, on the *mythos*. Besides affecting scenes, his story has structure, logical backbone. The question is, the mix. And the illusion of 'subject' and 'treatment', of theme and narrative method, is an aspect of this technical problem; that is why the two cannot be clinically separated; it is a matter of selection and representation.[26]

24. *Ancient Romances*, 48. Müller, *Chariton*, goes so far as to suggest that Chariton's frequent quotations of Homer are not just decoration but part of the very fabric of a story which its author thought of as epic; this is exaggerated.

25. *Ancient Romances*, 72ff.

26. Epic and drama are of course the real aesthetic sources of romance, they are what narrative fiction is 'like' aesthetically. The *form* is that of historiography; this is the most important literary ancestor formally, in that it offers a prose antecedent. But, as Eduard Schwartz said long ago – *Fünf Vorträge über den griechischen Roman* (Berlin 1896/1943) – *degenerate* historiography; the nearer romance is to historiography, the worse for the historiography it is near to. The real problems of historiography – use of sources, narrative method, criteria for analysis, selection of material – are different from the problems of narrative fiction, and the overlap is only partial. It is of course true – the observation is again Perry's – that a historiographical façade can offer to such a story the

Chariton selects and represents, as we have seen, by what is essentially a dramatic technique, the changing of focus; it is perhaps his principal technical device. To continue to report Hägg's examination, this changing of focus, in its turn, is characteristically achieved by 'gliding': 'what we see is a continual gliding motion on a scale extending from great distance and general narrative over medium distance and individualized narrative to a nearness which involves quoting the "exact" words of the persons talking, and, at times, even going a step further to reporting the simultaneous inner mental processes, using more time in the narration than the material narrated "actually" took'; or, *aliter*, Chariton uses 'a continuous time sequence, combined with quick and frequent changes in tempo'.[27] The example that Hägg analyses in detail is the episode (1.12.5–1.13.6) of the sale of Callirhoe by Theron the pirate to Leonas, Dionysius' steward: we see all of Theron's actions over 24 hours, but much of this time is covered in rapid narrative, while certain small parts of it – the discussions between Theron and Leonas – are reported in detail, in direct speech, as it were in close-up.

Another example will serve other purposes as well, here: the episode of the tomb-robbing (1.7–1.9). We are shown, in sequence, Theron, Callirhoe, and Theron again. First, Theron is introduced into the story: his previous career as a brigand is rapidly sketched, in a very few lines; then we see him observing the funeral; and immediately after this his thoughts are brought before us as, that night, he forms the project of robbery: 'why should I risk my life battling with the sea and killing living people and not getting much out of it, when I can get rich from one dead body? Let the die be cast; I won't miss a chance like that of making money. Now, whom shall I recruit for the job? Think, Theron; who would be suitable, of the men you know?' The next day's action consists of his rounding up a suitable gang; again, this is described rapidly, and is at once followed by a detailed representation in direct speech of the colloquy of the assembled villains, who are instructed by Theron to gather that night for the enterprise. The narrative then passes to

---

dimension of academic respectability. To the literature on Chariton's pseudo-historical setting, add now Plepelits, *Chariton*, 15ff., and Molinié, Budé edition, 5ff.

27. *NT*, 38.

Callirhoe, who on that night, in her funeral vault, begins to awaken from her coma.

Her respiration had stopped, but lack of food started it again; with difficulty, and gradually, she began to breathe. Then she began to move her body, limb by limb. Then she opened her eyes and came to her senses like someone waking up from sleep; and thinking Chaereas was sleeping beside her, she called to him. But since neither husband nor maids paid any attention, and everything was lonely and dark, the girl began to shiver and tremble with fear; she could not piece things together. As she stirred into consciousness she happened to touch wreaths and ribbons and make gold and silver objects rattle; and there was a strong smell of spices. So then she remembered the kick, and how it had knocked her down; and reluctantly and fearfully she recognized the funeral vault.

The narrative now glides quickly to the thoughts and reactions of the girl as she realizes that she has been buried alive; and that realization is as it were actualized in the direct speech of her terrified monologue. Then we pass immediately to Theron again; he and his gang are approaching the tomb as Callirhoe has just become aware of the horror of her position; the approach is described rapidly, and once more we pass quickly to a close-up, a long, detailed, animated, dramatic representation of the encounter of the now awakened Callirhoe and the astonished robbers:

When they began to use crowbars and hammer heavily to open the vault, Callirhoe was gripped by a variety of emotions – fear, joy, grief, surprise, hope, disbelief. 'Where is this noise coming from? Is some divinity coming for me – poor creature – as always happens when people are dying? Or is it not a noise but a voice – the voice of the gods below calling me to them? It is more likely that it is tomb-robbers; there, there is an additional misfortune; wealth is of no use to a corpse.' While these thoughts were still passing through her mind, a robber put his head through and came a little way into the vault. Callirhoe, intending to implore his help, threw herself at his knees; he was terrified and jumped back. Shaking with fear, he cried to his fellows 'Let's get out of here! There's some sort of spirit on guard in there who won't let us come in!' Theron laughed scornfully at him and called him a coward and deader than the dead girl. Then he told another man to go in; and when nobody had the courage to do so, he went in himself, holding his sword before him. At the gleam of the metal Callirhoe was afraid she was going to be murdered; she shrank back into the corner of the vault and from there begged him in a small voice 'Have pity on me, whoever you are – I have had no pity from husband or parents! Do not

17

kill me now you have saved me!' Theron took courage, and being an intelligent man realized the truth of the matter.[28]

I have used the term 'close-up'; and indeed what Hägg calls 'gliding' a film director would call 'zooming'; from the panoramic view of the deserted street, the camera zooms in on the lonely and frightened sheriff in *High Noon*. Perhaps the more intimate television is an even better parallel: from events in causal sequence we can pass, in television as in Chariton's novel, to close and intimate examination of the emotions they arouse.

The episode of the tomb-robbery will illustrate also two other characteristic features of Chariton's narrative: the connection of successive episodes by thought – not by mechanical time-sequence – and the distribution of the action among several characters. The passage from Theron to Callirhoe to Theron is a passage determined by a criterion of intellectual continuity: we need to see both aspects of the event to understand it. If we have already observed the Aristotelian feature of *mythos*, we observe here something very close to the Aristotelian feature of διάνοια: intellectual content, coherent sequence of thought. We see too that the line of events can be distributed, in its narration, among the characters who act out its several elements: Theron does his plotting, Callirhoe subsequently does her awakening, Theron subsequently does his tomb-entering – and that is all we are shown: we are not told what Theron did between his plotting and his tomb-entering, because the knowledge of that is not needed. The action is passed, that is, from one character to another: Hägg happily characterizes the technique as a 'relay-race'.[29] It is of course *dianoia* in another aspect; it also helps to economize

---

28. This passage raises the question of how seriously Chariton is treating his story. To modern taste it seems almost farcical; and there are other occasions when we may wonder whether the author's tongue is in his cheek. But overall Chariton seems 'serious' enough – this is not to deny that he is capable of seeing humour as well as pathos in his scenes at times. The whole question of humour in these romances is worth pursuing. My own view of Achilles Tatius' *Leucippe and Clitophon* (?late second century) is that he is certainly in places guying the form, grotesquely. And Longus is overtly detached enough from his story to make us smile at his heroes. But the question is not a simple one: the taste of the period is not altogether ours. A full discussion may be expected in a forthcoming study by Graham Anderson.

29. *NT*, 151.

narrative, and thus contributes substantially to the preponderance of 'scene' in the story.

Let us here 'glide' – imitating Chariton again – to another aspect of his romance, which I will call its 'general characteristics'. In so doing we shall, I believe, discover more fully its 'theme'. We shall, however, see that the movement from its narrative technique is not a very abrupt movement. It will be convenient to start from another of Perry's *dicta*: Chariton, he said, 'writes Greek romance as it should be written'.[30] This looks like one of those intuitive and forthright statements that characterize Perry's work. What did he mean?

Perry liked the *classical* feel of Chariton (perhaps his instinct was not so very different from Rohde's). We have seen *mythos* and *dianoia*, which, while no doubt not exclusively classical literary features, are certainly commonly visible in classical literature, for instance Sophocles; we have seen also that their existence in the story can be attributed to, and expressed in terms of, identifiable and even measurable techniques – recapitulation, scene and summary, relay-race. While we are at it, we should here recall, with Perry, the major classical characteristic of *Chaereas and Callirhoe*: namely, the dramatic irony that the author really does use very effectively (we have just seen that too in the tomb-robbery). It can likewise be pinned down: it is achieved by the convention of authorial omniscience.[31] These features are what Perry was referring to in praising the manner of Chariton's writing. But we should look also at the matter, at the nature of 'Greek romance'. We should consider with imaginative sympathy, if necessary with a temporary disengagement of our 'classical' judgment, another aspect of the story: its Hellenistic-ness, its Hellenistic aspect, and setting, and assumptions.

We may observe, first, that the very action of the story is set squarely in the Hellenistic world, in that it shows the rivalry of two Greeks, Chaereas and Dionysius, resolved (as we have seen) by their involvement in the state affairs of two Oriental empires. But some might say that *Chaereas and Callirhoe* is most notably Hellenistic in displaying a technique more substantial than the content it is meant to carry. There is yet more skill, however, than

30. *AJP* 51 (1930), 129.
31. Hägg, *NT*, 118–19.

has yet been pointed out, and to dismiss it as 'mere technique' is to do the story serious injustice. The use of illusion, for instance, extends beyond the *trompe l'oeil* of subject and perspective; it extends to the passage of time in the story, for Chariton offers very little indication of the 'real' chronological framework – the calendar time taken by events.[32] Deprived, thus, of a firm objective 'handrail' to guide us through events, we turn the more readily to what the author wants to present as important, namely his characters' psychological reactions as set in the emotional *sequence* of events – this is of course an aspect of the gliding-and-close-up technique discussed above. The very basis of the plot – the essential plot-element of separation of hero and heroine – is matter of illusion, for that separation is not as marked as it appears to be (I return to this point below). The relay-race technique does more than economize narrative; it also peoples the story – Chaereas and Callirhoe may be insubstantial, but the characters through whom we learn what happens to them are much less so: their rivals, their rivals' servants. Much of the story is carried by such people, not by the hero and heroine: the tomb-robbery, the sale of Callirhoe, the intrigue which leads to Mithridates' inculpation; and to estimate the effect of this we have only to imagine how baldly these incidents would have been narrated by Xenophon Ephesius. The care for causation is not limited to the major events, the succession of marriages and intrigues, but extends to lesser articulations: Theron is represented as selling Callirhoe extremely hurriedly, and it is this very haste which makes Dionysius realize that she is not a slave and that in consequence he can marry her.[33] If the transitions, the 'glidings' are smoothly managed, so are the changes of subject – by a subordination, a participle, an element of vocabulary.[34] Not only such narrative bridges, but structural bridges too, are built with care: Theron both restores Callirhoe to life and restores Chaereas to the plot[35] – after which he is promptly executed to

32. Hägg, *NT*, 26–7; but in fact all time is accounted for, p. 44. Hägg remarks (p. 210) that Chariton seems not to have paid special attention to temporal structure. This is perhaps instinctive avoidance of realistic precision; or it may be conscious omission (see p. 22 and n. 36).

33. Gerschmann, *Chariton-Interpr.*, 31ff.

34. Hägg, *NT*, esp. pp. 141ff.

35. Hägg, *NT*, 141ff.; Phocas similarly provides a bridge between hero and heroine, 3.7.1–2.

avoid too easy a solution (similarly Shakespeare executes Mercutio to keep him in his place).

There is illusion, then, in all directions: illusion in respect of subject, of theme and climax, of perspective. These several forms of technical skill could without difficulty be documented more fully. Hägg's pages indeed do so document them, and are required reading for any serious student of Chariton; they reveal, dispassionately, what can easily be obscured to the prejudice of a Rohde, or even to the relative enthusiasm of a Perry. The reader who is disposed to notice such skill will find it. It is not, however, the primary intention of this paper to expound such matters systematically, as Hägg does, but rather to take due note of their importance – and having done so, to observe that the presence of marked technical skill is itself one of the distinctive general characteristics of *Chaereas and Callirhoe*, one that itself contributes to its Hellenistic-ness.

Not that technique is exclusively a Hellenistic phenomenon. But some elements of Chariton's do contribute to a typically Hellenistic intention. The geographical separation of hero and heroine is illusory, it has just been suggested. They are close enough, in Miletus and Caria, for the author to maintain a contact between them – in the shape of a shrine of Aphrodite which both can visit, a satrap whose involvement is justified by his proximity, and later a war in which hero and heroine are on contiguous sea and land; Chariton calculates his distances. But some distance is vital to the separation of the pair; and the purpose of this separation is not, as in other such works, separate adventures, but the emotional isolation of each of the principals. And this, with the emotional stop-pulling that it gives rise to, is Hellenistic.

In respect of the manipulation of the emotions, Chariton is indeed at one point as explicit as it is possible to be. At the beginning of the last book, he advertizes its contents: 'you will like this book', he tells his readers, 'because it contains nice things, ἔρωτες δίκαιοι, νόμιμοι γάμοι: no more brigands or slavery or trials or wars – it will clear out the memory of all those nasty things, καθάρσιον . . . ἐστι τῶν ἐν τοῖς πρώτοις σκυθρωπῶν' (8.1.4). It is hard not to think that he is referring to Aristotle (and thus classicizing consciously). But it is not necessarily what Aristotle meant – whatever it is that Aristotle did mean. Chariton seems to

mean that the good will replace the bad, will make you forget it.
Whether he had Aristotle in mind or not, the quality and nature of
the sensibility he posits is not what we think of as classical: it is
sentimental, and it is Hellenistic. Sentimental, and not reticent.
Not that classical tragedy is reticent. It is often strident enough.
But this whipping-up of emotions for the sake of emotions is not
what Sophocles is *about*, in the *Oedipus*, or Euripides in the *Medea*; it
is what Chariton is about.

I do not want to suggest that Chariton's technique is flawless, or
always felicitous. It is not; there are defects in plot and narrative.
Some of them merely represent the cost to Chariton of some
advantage or another. The execution of Theron, for instance: *ben
trovato!*, yes – but how likely is it that Hermocrates would destroy
the only lead he has to his lost daughter? Some, again, are mere
carelessnesses, and relatively trivial. When Chaereas first sets out
from Syracuse to hunt at random for Callirhoe (3.3.8), there
appears to be no difficulty in setting out to sea in mid-winter; but
when, a few pages later (3.5.1), he runs into Theron's ship, brings it
to Syracuse, screws the truth out of the brigand, and sets sail
again – then the enterprise is represented as utterly unthinkable,
ἀδύνατόν.[36] Yet others are instances of waste, simply. The
Montagu and Capulet theme is a very damp squib in this story.

But some of the very shortcomings of the story are distinctively
Hellenistic. Some of the causation, and in major matters, Chariton
motivates by attributing it to *tyche*: the finding of Theron's ship, the
outbreak of the Egyptian rebellion which alone enables the author
to find a dénouement for his story. To do him justice, Chariton
seems acutely conscious of the operation of *tyche* in his story, and
one suspects that he is embarrassed by it;[37] none the less, he does
use this Hellenistic device. Another embarrassment – or such it
seems to be – is the disposition of Callirhoe's child, who is left at the

36. It may be noted (Hägg, *NT*, 26) that this latter occasion is one of the very
few specifications of time in the story.
37. Some examples besides those quoted (3.3.8 Theron, 6.8.1 the rebellion):
1.13.4 it is *tyche* who brings Theron to Dionysius' estate; 2.8.3 though Callirhoe's
pregnancy is explicable enough, *tyche* uses it to overcome her fidelity to
Chaereas – and thus sets up the series of *agones* that constitute the action; 4.5.3
Chaereas' letter to Callirhoe miscarries (in the last two instances the natural
motivation is in fact perfectly adequate); 8.1.2 *tyche* is about to separate Chaereas
and Callirhoe, at Arados, but is overruled for once.

end of the story with Dionysius. This may be, as Perry suggested, the vestige of a legend: there are hints enough that when the boy grows up he will return to Sicily to take his place as the descendant of Hermocrates, which seems appropriate enough to a son of a Dionysius.[38] But if this is legend, it coincides conveniently with the fact that Chariton is embarrassed by his treatment of Dionysius; he has represented him throughout as a noble soul, and as *sympathique*, and cannot bear to leave him out in the cold altogether. Sophocles could have borne it. But in this story, everyone must have a prize (except Theron). Dionysius gets a whole clutch of consolation prizes: military glory, a preeminent position in the King's entourage – and a son. 'And they all go down to the beach and have a lovely time.' It doesn't seem very cathartic to us.

But if Dionysius gets the child, Callirhoe abandons it; and that seems rather ignoble – does her duty, and affection, end with seeing that the child is born, and is properly looked after? There is indeed a good deal of ignobility, to our kind of romantic taste; all of the principal characters do things which hardly fit heroic standards, or even the standards of Victorian melodrama. Dionysius wants Chaereas to die, but is relieved when *his steward* takes the responsibility of attacking his ship (3.9.12). The King of Persia is restrained in his desire for Callirhoe not by any μεγαλοψυχία, but only by the thought of his own position, and of what the Queen would say (6.1.8–12). Callirhoe is quite prepared to consider abortion, and to pass off Chaereas' child as Dionysius'. Chaereas takes Tyre by deceit (7.4.3ff.), and misleads his naval crews when the Egyptian land army is defeated (8.2.5). All of this so clearly forms a pattern that one cannot call these cases 'loose ends' in the story. They are part of the morality of Chariton's world. If the story is epic, its setting is hardly heroic.

This suggests a whole topic, the world-outlook of this Hellenistic world. If it has its own sentiments, it also has its own philosophy, its own theology; and that is far from being clear-cut. Apparently Aphrodite is behind the whole action, as she is behind that of the *Hippolytus*, but her purposes are here altogether less clear – certainly less frank and brutal and uncompromising. She wants to teach Chaereas a lesson, evidently – but Chaereas survives to profit

38. E.g. 2.11.2; 3.8.8; 8.7.12. But see Plepelits, *Chariton*, 30ff., for arguments against Perry.

23

from it. We are told, late in the day, that Chaereas' fault is ingratitude to Aphrodite, shown in his initial jealousy and paid for by his tribulations.[39] We can suppose also that his (and Callirhoe's) redeeming virtue is loyalty to love.[40] That is to say, Aphrodite is thoroughly on the side of the bourgeoisie: stern, but ultimately cosy. And this fits with the characters. There is not even a glimpse of tragedy, not even as much as in the figure of Malvolio in a similarly cosy world; only melodrama.

Whether all this amounts to a 'theology' is another matter. The theology of *Chaereas and Callirhoe* is as vague as much of the theology of the period – that of Isis, for example, who would be all things to all men, a comforter; not so much a perception of forces in life as a projection of wishes. Aphrodite is Love-who-makes-the-world-go-round, and love, beauty and marriage are umbilically linked. Another magazine-convention, another attitude: love and marriage, in the words of a once-popular modern song, go together like a horse and carriage. Aphrodite has underlings: Eros and *tyche*; *tyche* has to be kept in line when at the beginning of the last book she aims to keep our couple separated – this seems too much to Aphrodite. But this hardly amounts to a firm theological system.[41] It is not clearer than Homer's problem about the precedence of Fate over Zeus. *Tyche* is nothing more than a convention: human plans go wrong; and Eros is virtually a doublet of Aphrodite, for the most part. There *is* a divine machinery, of a kind; and Chariton does underline Aphrodite;[42] but he is not underlining anything very substantial. It is not clear that Aphrodite's – that is, Chariton's – intentions did not develop in the course of the story's construction. At the very beginning (1.1.3–4) Eros, stimulated by the difficulty of the Montagu–Capulet situation, resolves to unite the young people; possibly (but not probably) he instructs

39. ἤδη γὰρ αὐτῷ διηλάττετο, πρότερον ὀργισθεῖσα χαλεπῶς διὰ τὴν ἄκαιρον ʒηλοτυπίαν, ὅτι δῶρον παρ' αὐτῆς λαβὼν τὸ κάλλιστον, οἷον οὐδὲ ᾽Αλέξανδρος ὁ Πάρις, ὕβρισεν εἰς τὴν χάριν. ἐπεὶ δὲ καλῶς ἀπελογήσατο τῷ ῎Ερωτι Χαιρέας ἀπὸ δύσεως εἰς ἀνατολὰς διὰ μυρίων παθῶν πλανηθείς, ἠλέησεν αὐτὸν ᾽Αφροδίτη (8.1.3).

40. E.g. (Chaereas) 4.2.1–3; (Callirhoe) 4.7.8; 5.8.6; 6.7.12.

41. As Gerschmann, *Chariton-Interpr.*, suggests, pp. 93ff.

42. Blake, *Index nominum propriorum s.v.* 'Venus', lists over 30 references to her. Helms, *Character Portrayal*, 115ff., sorts them into groups: she is frequently held responsible by Callirhoe for her misfortunes; her aid is invoked by Callirhoe; Callirhoe is compared to her in point of beauty. But there is no more 'theology' than is indicated in the present text.

Callirhoe to worship Aphrodite (1.1.5);[43] and an unnamed deity, ὁ θεός (who could be Aphrodite) contrives that Chaereas and Callirhoe should see each other (1.1.6). At 2.2.8 Aphrodite plans another marriage for Callirhoe, but does not intend it to last. At 2.4.5 Eros is at odds with Dionysius for his σωφροσύνη. At 7.5.3 Callirhoe thinks Aphrodite is offended by her beauty (νεμεσητόν . . . τὸ κάλλος), at 8.1.3, as we have seen, we learn that Aphrodite has been angered by Chaereas' jealousy. All of this may be reconcilable; but it is hardly an explanation of how the world works. It is a reflection, rather, of not very comprehending popular attitudes; an aspect of this story's cultural and social context, not of its intellectual content.

A Hellenistic story in a Hellenistic context: a society of ordinary people. They like cosiness; they are romantic, sentimental, passive, mediocre – Perry has no difficulty in finding suitable adjectives; I should like to recall the adjective 'civilized', not necessarily as a term of praise, but to adjust our angle of vision – civilized, social. The story is full of indications of people's attitudes, of their 'civilization' in the sense that they live in society and reflect the values accepted by that society. They are – that is, Chariton is – thoroughly provincial: he feels the need to show that he knows Athens, and an equal need to affect to despise it[44] – it is the attitude of the provincial Frenchman to Paris. He provides captions from his ordered world: Theron is ὁ πανοῦργος, ὁ κακοήθης, the big bad wolf (e.g. 3.3.12, 17). He is impressed by barbarians as well as scornful of them – the Euphrates is the outer limit of the acceptable world, but at least there is no nonsense about who is boss in Persia (although Chariton does suppose that the δῆμος has a voice there).[45] Chariton's little man knows a seigneur when he sees one: Dionysius is a βασιλικὸς ἀνήρ (2.1.5), and φύσει γίνονται βασιλεῖς (2.3.10); just as he knows that slaves

43. At 1.1.5.2 Gerschmann, *Chariton-Interpr.*, 3, 131, proposes Ἔρωτος (τοῦ πατρὸς Blake) κελεύσαντος προσκυνῆσαι τὴν θεόν. This is palaeographically tempting (see Blake's apparatus), and it is true that Eros has already, early as it is, appeared twice. But Callirhoe is represented as being taken to the festival by her mother, on her first public appearance, and it is not clear how Eros could intrude into this family occasion. The reading would have merit only as an element in a more coherent theological structure than can be found in the story.

44. The pirates think of selling Callirhoe there, but recoil before its litigiousness, 1.11.5–7.

45. 5.1.3; 5.4.1; 6.7.3.

always have an eye to the main chance (6.5.5). And Chariton is sententious with the accumulated wisdom of the world: φύσει εὔελπις ὁ Ἔρως.[46]

Here an important qualification needs to be made. I have described the tone of this romance as 'Hellenistic'; but that is not intended as a derogatory evaluation. It has long been conventional to admire the literary achievements of the 'classical' world, and to be rather condescending towards those of the succeeding period – although much of the philosophy and science, and many of the social mechanisms, that we admire in the ancient world are post-classical. If its literature, in this specimen, seems to reflect a world less elevated than that of a Sophoclean hero, the reason is not necessarily that the Hellenistic world was in all respects of that quality; it is rather that popular attitudes are reflected in such literature much more fully than they commonly are reflected in what has survived of 'classical' literature. If Chariton's world seems undistinguished, we should remember that most people in most societies *are* undistinguished. The realities of life for the inhabitants of fifth-century Athens were surely not very different from the realities observed by Chariton's 'little people'. Their theology was no less vague and confused; we have no reason to suppose that their morality was any more lofty. Aristophanes' heroes would probably recognize Chariton's characters readily enough. And it is no bad thing that a writer should reflect his world. On the contrary, to reflect it as clearly as Chariton does is an achievement worthy of more recognition than it has yet received in the canonical histories of literature.

The scene, then, is Hellenistic; indeed, Chariton's concentration on scene is itself Hellenistic; his interest in personal psychology and its expression recalls Hellenistic statues. He is a photographer of this society; a better one than Xenophon Ephesius, because his art is more flexible; a less sophisticated one than Achilles Tatius, but clearly his audience is less sophisticated too. Plutarch would surely have recognized the feel of literature like this; he is more educated than Chariton, but just as comfortable.

This *is* new; and it did have success; and it merited success; because Chariton shows artistic genius in perceiving the plasticity of this new form. 'Greek romance as it should be written': *Chaereas*

46. 2.6.4: see Blake's *Index sententiarum.*

and Callirhoe is not merely a romantic – non-classical – story written with classical craftsmanship. The formula, attractively simple, is too simple. There is more to it than that: Chariton uses his medium with something of the fluidity of film or television; and he knows very well what he is doing. His technique in this new narrative medium is equal to the task of carrying a story that he conceives essentially in dramatic terms. Others, later – Achilles Tatius, Heliodorus – were to use the form for more specifically narrative purposes.

What Chariton uses medium and technique for is to represent his world rather than to create a new one. And this, at the end, is what his story is 'about': it is about the sentiment of a mass civilization. It is about the situation of his Chaereas and (particularly) Callirhoe. Not about their characters, or their actions, but above all their situation: isolation, and grief – and reunion. Life can bring isolation and grief; but if Fortune is kind, they can be overcome; let us, for our comfort, suppose that Fortune is kind. This is the salient thing, it is what Chariton has to say.[47] Philostratus is very snobbish about Chariton: 'Do you really suppose', he says in an 'Imaginary Letter' (*Ep.* 66) to him, 'that civilized people are going to remember your story when you are gone? You are a nobody even now you're alive; you'll be less than a nobody when you're dead.' The word that I have here translated as 'civilized people' is Ἕλληνες – for that is what Philostratus means by it: cultured people, civilized in his sense. But the Hellenistic, imperial world did not share Philostratus' contempt. And we need not share Rohde's.[48]

47. Hägg, *NT*, 119, comments that 'Chariton's interest does not lie exclusively in the two particular persons whom he has chosen as the hero and heroine of the romance' (he is discussing the effect of Chariton's authorial point of view). Not exclusively – but primarily. Other characters ('every single character is . . . seen from inside') exist to serve the story of the lovers. Their world, it is true, is peopled with characters often more 'real', or realistically drawn, than they themselves are; and we are certainly invited to feel with Dionysius and Artaxates, for example. But the point of the *mythos* which is so carefully underlined is the situation that Chaereas and Callirhoe find themselves in, as the dominant exemplars of their civilization's emotional physiognomy.

48. Versions of this paper have been read at Berkeley and at the Hellenic Society; I am grateful for comments made on those occasions. And I wish here to offer particular thanks to the editor of the present volume, Mr J. J. Winkler, for his remarks on the original version of the paper; he will recognize, and I wish to record, that I owe much to his thoughtful and detailed remarks.

The importance of sophists*

E. L. BOWIE

Studies of the Second Sophistic are necessarily founded upon the
Lives of Philostratus, our source for the term itself: and it is now a
decade since Glen Bowersock's *Greek Sophists in the Roman Empire*
added depth and breadth to Philostratus' picture in an illuminating presentation of their cultural, social and political roles which
has rightly become a standard work. Both Philostratus and
Bowersock seem to present sophists as men who acquire political
authority through their professional status. Philostratus lays out a
mosaic of anecdotes and assessments without much that could be
called historical analysis to give it shape: our attention is drawn to
consular ancestors or descendants, city offices and benefactions,
encounters and friendships with emperors in such a way that we
gain the impression that they all derive from the practice of
sophistic skills. Bowersock's investigation, by contrast, is carefully
articulated and historically argued. Separate consideration is
accorded to the sophists' origins in the city aristocracies of the
Eastern provinces and their benefactions to these cities; to their
acquisition of immunity from offices and liturgies; to their contact
with emperors as ambassadors, friends and holders of equestrian
and senatorial posts. Yet to my eye the perspective in which these
marks of distinction are presented is sometimes distorted, and the
distortion affects the truth or falsehood of Bowersock's insistence
upon the *historical* (as opposed to literary) importance of the
sophists. In the following pages I shall try to show why it seems to
me misleading to offer such formulations as 'The social eminence of
the sophists in their cities and provinces brought their families
swiftly and inevitably into the Roman upper class', or such
stimulating challenges as 'It could be argued without apology that

* I am very grateful to Dr J. L. Moles for helpful comments on a draft of this
article.

29

the Second Sophistic has more importance in Roman History than it has in Greek Literature.'[1]

The crucial fact, amply documented by Bowersock in a couple of pages, is that 'sophists almost always emerged from the notable and wealthy families of their cities'.[2] With three possible exceptions (and each of these can be challenged), no sophist is known to have risen from humble or even modest origins, nor is any claim advanced by Philostratus that a sophistic career pulled a man up into the established city aristocracies.[3] Rather it is apparent that men who turned to sophistic rhetoric were born into families which had long furnished their cities with magistrates, benefactors and diplomats. Once this has been established we learn nothing new or surprising about the sophists when we are told that they too held office in their cities and in the provincial κοινά, lavished spectacular benefactions and represented city or κοινόν on embassies to the emperor. Fortunately for the historian they constitute one sort of city aristocrat whose activity is illuminated by literary texts as well as by epigraphy and the Digest, but this extra illumination should not blind us to the fact that they are going through the same routines as that much larger but more shadowy chorus of city aristocrats of which they are members, and with whom they share the same stage.

The conspicuous advertizement of wealth by the construction of buildings or the provision of single or recurrent distributions is, of course, a characteristic of the city aristocracies where it is hard to see why sophists should differ from others. The benefactions of sophists are but a fraction of the total already known for the Greek East. The millionaire Herodes Atticus finds his closest analogues not among other sophists but among such big spenders of no known sophistic bent as Vibius Salutaris at Ephesus or Opramoas of Rhodiapolis.[4]

1. G. W. Bowersock, *Greek Sophists in the Roman Empire* (Oxford 1969) (hereafter referred to as Bowersock, *Sophists*), 28 and 58. Compare 10, with n. 6, rejecting Wilamowitz's view of the Second Sophistic as an invention of Philostratus, and the reaffirmation of the historical importance of the movement in *Approaches to the Second Sophistic* (University Park, Pennsylvania, for the APA 1974), 2–3.

2. Bowersock, *Sophists*, 21–3.

3. Bowersock, *Sophists*, 21–2 allows three instances of 'low or middle-class origin', for which see Appendix 1.

4. For sophists' benefactions, Bowersock, *Sophists*, 27f. For Vibius Salutaris at Ephesus, F. F. Abbott and A. C. Johnson, *Municipal Administration in the Roman*

In diplomacy and political leadership, however, it might be thought that the sophist's greater skill in public speaking gave him an advantage over his peers, secured him greater authority as a city politician and commended him for more frequent representation on important embassies, embassies which might in turn lead to imperial favour or friendship for the individual.[5] Unfortunately the case of political activity within city or province is hard to judge. From Philostratus and from the extant orations of Dio and Aristides we have abundant evidence of sophists playing a leading part in times of internal crisis or in conflicts between neighbouring and rival cities.[6] It is also apparent and in no way unpredictable that none of these figures achieved unchallenged pre-eminence through his eloquence. Dio in Prusa and Herodes in Athens are hard-pressed by political opponents who lack their professional advantages, and Aristides' rhetorical gifts could not check unwelcome attempts to impose liturgies.[7] But a systematic comparison of the success of sophists with that of others in city politics is unattainable, because we have no source of information about the

Empire (Princeton 1926), 387 no. 71 (= *Inscr. Brit. Mus.* iv.481; B. Laum, *Stiftungen in der griechischen und römischen Antike*, 74; *Inschr. gr. Städte aus Kleinasien*, ll.i (*Ephesos* Ia) no. 27); for Opramoas see especially *IGR* iii.739; for Herodes Atticus the study of P. Graindor, *Un milliardaire antique, Hérode Atticus et sa famille* (Cairo 1930), remains important, but for a brief note of more recent material see G. W. Bowersock and C. P. Jones in *Approaches* (n. 1), 38. A comprehensive study of the benefactions of city aristocrats and others in the Eastern provinces is much needed.

5. As Dr J. L. Moles points out to me, Plut., *Praec. ger. reip.* 814 and Dio, *Orr.* xviii.3 and xlvii.1 might be used as evidence that sophistic rhetoric *was* widely regarded as useful in a Greek political context. For modern views cf. H. I. Marrou, *Hist. educ.*[6], 294 (quoted by B. P. Reardon, *Courants littéraires grecs des IIe et IIIe ʻiècles après J.-C.* (Paris 1971), 135–6 n. 35), 'le prestige artistique . . . reconnu à l'orateur aboutit à investir indirectement celui-ci d'une certaine efficacité politique . . .'. On the other hand the unsuitability of the epideictic style to public life is recognized in Cicero, *De or.* i.81; *Or.* 37–42; Quint. x.1.79; Plut., *De lib. educ.* 7a5–6.

6. Cf. Lollianus at Athens, *VS* i.23 (526); Polemo at Smyrna, *VS* i.25 (531) for internal troubles; Marcus of Byzantium at Megara for inter-city rivalry, *VS* i.24 (529); Dio of Prusa, *Orr.* xxxiii–xxxiv; xxxviii–xli; Aristides, *Orr.* xxiii–xxiv Keil.

7. For Dio cf. C. P. Jones, *The Roman World of Dio Chrysostom* (Cambridge, Mass. 1978), and P. Desideri, *Dione di Prusa: un intellettuale greco nell'impero romano* (Florence 1978); for the troubles of Herodes much is added to the information in Philostratus, *VS* ii.1 (559ff.) by the inscription edited by J. H. Oliver, *Marcus Aurelius: Aspects of Civic and Cultural Policy in the East, Hesperia* Suppl. 13 (1970) with revisions proposed by C. P. Jones, *ZPE* 8 (1971), 161–83. For Aristides see Bowersock, *Sophists*, 36ff.

thousands of families who ran the cities of the Eastern provinces that is comparable to the *Lives* and *Orations*. Epigraphy can furnish names, offices, and evidence of honour bestowed by city or κοινόν; occasionally it attests an unusual benefaction in economic crisis, whether famine or fiscal embarrassment; but only rarely does it reveal the presence of political conflict, and never the ease or difficulty with which a family placed a son in a succession of high offices.[8]

With embassies it is different. The evidence of literary sources, of the Digest, of imperial letters recorded in cities, and of honorific inscriptions attesting activity as a πρεσβευτής can be assembled to give a meaningful account of the procedures and persons involved. The subject has been treated with characteristic insight and finesse by Fergus Millar in *The Emperor in the Roman World*, and it is with hesitation that I offer some measure of disagreement with details of his presentation. Like Bowersock he attaches particular importance to the part played by sophists in embassies to the emperor: 'Once the hearing was gained, all might depend on the favour with which the emperor greeted the oration; hence arose the well-attested role of the orators of the Second Sophistic on embassies before the emperor.'[9] Yet the evidence does not entirely support the thesis that sophists were always especially desirable members of embassies. It is true that a command of rhetoric was of great importance, but that could be assumed in a much wider range of the educated upper classes than rhetors and sophists. The πεπαιδευμένοι who formed their audiences and pupils – such men as Menemachus of Sardis, the addressee of Plutarch's πολιτικὰ

8. For references to political troubles within cities cf. *IGR* iv.914 from Cibyra, honouring Q. Veranius Philagrus as a benefactor and as having καταλύσαντα συνωμοσίαν μεγάλην τὰ μέγιστα λυποῦσαν τὴν πόλιν (this Philagrus may well be an ancestor of the 'Cilician' Philagrus who quarrelled with Herodes, *VS* ii.8) – the date is Claudian; *Inschriften von Magnesia* no. 114 (= *Inschr. gr. St. Kl.* 12 (*Ephesos* II) no. 215) attesting ταραχὴν καὶ θορύβους caused by striking bakers in second-century Ephesus that clearly went beyond the capacities of local politicians and precipitated proconsular intervention; *IGR* iv.444 for a similar situation in Pergamum; and the hint of a political quarrel at Stratonicea in *IGR* iv.1156a. 11ff., the order of Hadrian, clearly in response to the request of an embassy, that one Ti. Claudius Socrates should either repair or sell a house he owned in the city that was falling into disrepair (1 March, A.D. 127).

9. Fergus Millar, *The Emperor in the Roman World* (London 1977), 385. The topic of embassies is touched on *passim*, and they are the central theme of the brilliant chapter 7, 363ff.

παραγγέλματα – will have been as familiar with the ground rules as the star performers, and could surely have met the requirement (which I do not contest) of 'a comportment, diction and choice of words in accordance with the exacting canons of Greco-Roman culture'.[10] But that the speaker should conduct himself in a manner characteristic of sophistic recitals could also be counter-productive. Bowersock includes the embassy of Alexander of Seleucia among his examples of sophistic envoys, but he should perhaps have drawn attention to the fact that Pius' reaction was far from favourable:

> Now the Emperor seemed to be paying too little attention to him, whereupon Alexander raised his voice and said: 'Pay attention to me, Caesar.' The Emperor, who was much irritated with him for using so unceremonious a form of address, retorted: 'I am paying attention, and I know you well. You are the fellow who is always arranging his hair, cleaning his teeth, and polishing his nails, and always smells of myrrh.'[11]

Philostratus narrates an equally adverse reaction by Caracalla to Philiscus when he appeared before him to defend his own immunity from liturgies:

> . . . he gave offence by his gait, he gave offence by the way he stood, his attire seemed far from suitable to the occasion, his voice effeminate, his language indolent and directed to any subject rather than to the matter in hand. All this made the Emperor hostile to Philiscus . . .[12]

Philiscus lost his immunity, and we can see that the *prima donna*-like comportment of the lecture-hall might be unhelpful in a hearing where the emperor, not the sophist, called the tune. It is perhaps worth adding that a speech of Polemo which won Smyrna certain temple privileges was delivered posthumously by another envoy, which shows that in this case, at least, it was not delivery but the argumentation, style, or authority of the composer which seems to have been effective.[13]

There is no disputing that the crucial factor was an envoy's ability to secure favour, noted, for example, in a decree from Cius

---

10. *Ibid.* 385.

11. Philostratus, *VS* ii.5 (570–1) (transl. W. C. Wright), cited Bowersock, *Sophists*, 46.

12. *VS* ii.30 (623) (transl. W. C. Wright).

13. *VS* i.25 (529), which is actually cited by Millar, *Emperor*, 434 to demonstrate that rhetoric was crucial.

in Bithynia honouring a man πάντα καὶ [λέγ]οντα καὶ πρά[ττ]οντα [τὰ συμ]φέροντα τῇ πατρίδι καὶ διὰ τὸ [χ]άριεν παρὰ τῷ Σεβαστῷ.[14] This favour might indeed be secured – or alienated – by rhetoric, but other qualifications could be of comparable or greater importance. Highly eligible is a man who already had some connection with the emperor. He might be as humble as one of the emperor's soldiers, utilized as an envoy by the villagers of Aragua in Phrygia when appealing to the Philips in the years between A.D. 244 and 247.[15] At the other end of the social scale the cases of Ilium and Rhodes were defended before Claudius in the year A.D. 53 by no less a person than the young Nero.[16] Between those extremes there were many sorts of individual who might be expected to start off with an advantage when arguing a case before the emperor. Note first an instance from the very beginning of the Principate, before the period under immediate consideration but illustrating a feature which, like many in the conduct of embassies, did not change significantly in the next four centuries: after Actium the city of Rhosus in Syria chose Octavian's admiral, Seleucus, as a member of an embassy sent to the victor in Asia to offer honours and request confirmation of privileges, and Octavian's reply made it clear how important his link with Seleucus was in determining his attitude to the city.[17] A similar grasp of political realities was shown in the reigns of Claudius and Nero by citizens of Cos, for whom many embassies to the emperors were conducted by Ti. Claudius Cleonymus, brother of Claudius' doctor and secretary C. Stertinius Xenophon and himself honoured with a military tribunate.[18] Claudius' reign also saw an embassy from Alexandria which included one Barbillus, acknowledged by the emperor as his friend.[19] The same acknowledgement

14. *IGR* iii.22.
15. *IGR* iv.598.b5 (= Abbott and Johnson, 476 no. 141 lines 8–9).
16. Tac., *Ann.* xii.58.1; Suet., *Claud.* 25.3; *Nero* 7.2. Of course Nero is not technically an ambassador – those sent by Rhodes are honoured in *IGR* iv.1123 (= Abbott and Johnson, 356 no. 52).
17. *IGLS* iii.718, discussed by Millar, *Emperor*, 410–11, observing 'they naturally chose as an ambassador a man who would have the best claim on Octavian's affection and goodwill'.
18. *IGR* iv.1060 = *Syll.*³ 805, esp. 8–9, καὶ πρεσβεύσαντα πολλάκις ὑπὲρ τῆς πατρίδος πρὸς τοὺς Σεβαστούς. For the positions and authority acquired by Xenophon cf. Millar, *Emperor*, 85–6, and below n. 25.
19. *Corp. Pap. Jud.* no. 153, 105 Βαρβίλλῳ τῷ ἐμῷ ἑτέρῳ. This may be the same

of friendship recurs in a reply to an embassy from Philadelphia sent by Valerian and Gallienus from Antioch on 18 January A.D. 255: P. Aelius Pigres is called ὁ φίλος ἡμῶν.[20] We know of several envoys that they offered hospitality to the emperor or his armies, even if we cannot be sure in each case that the establishment of a link of this sort with the emperor preceded the man's selection by his city for service on an embassy.[21] It may also be relevant that a very large number of envoys attested by honorific inscriptions acted either as priest of Augustus in their city or as archpriest associated with the imperial cult administered by the κοινόν. Their very tenure of these offices marks them out as pre-eminent in local politics, but we can see that an emperor might be expected to hearken most readily to a priest who officiated in the cult of his own divinity.[22] Finally we should reflect upon the phenomenon of repeated embassies. A high proportion of epigraphically attested envoys claim to have acted two, three, or many times on embassies to Rome or the emperors.[23]

as the Claudius Barbillus who became prefect of Egypt in A.D. 55, Tac., *Ann.* xiii.22, as favoured tentatively by Millar, *Emperor*, 87, and if so he is a literary man *perfectusque in omni litterarum genere rarissime* (Sen., *Quaest. nat.* iv.2.13). For a different view and full discussion see H. G. Pflaum, *Les carrières procuratoriennes équestres* i (Paris 1960–1), no. 15.

20. J. Keil and F. Gschnitzer, *Anz. Öst. Ak. Wiss.* 18 (1956), 226 no. 8 (= *Bull. Epigr.* (1958), no. 438, *SEG* xvii.528; revisions by C. P. Jones *ZPE* 14 (1974), 294). Keil suggests Pigres is the son of an Asiarch who appears on coins of Philadelphia under Caracalla. He might just be the man mentioned some 25 years earlier by Philostratus as the only pupil of Cassianus, *VS* ii.33 (627) and therefore perhaps a sophist himself (although Philostratus does not so term him explicitly): the MSS read Περίγητος τοῦ Λυδοῦ but the name is unparalleled, and Valckenaer's change to Πίγρητος is highly probable.

21. From Prusias ad Hypium (*IGR* iii.66.12–14: παραπέμψαντα τοὺς μεγίστους καὶ θειοτάτους αὐτοκράτορας καὶ τὰ ἱερὰ αὐτῶν στρατεύματα), and 60, 62 and 1421, with similar formulae, all Severan; from Thyatira (*IGR* iv. 1247, 6, ὑποδεξάμενον Μ. Αὐρήλιον Ἀντωνεῖνον βασιλέα καὶ τρὶς πρεσβεύσαντα πρὸς τοὺς αὐτοκράτορας προῖκα.).

22. *IGR* i.664 (Dionysopolis); iii.204 (Ancyra); 292 (Isaura); 322 (Apollonia); 526, 527 (Lydae); 589, 590, 596 (Sidyma); 628 (Xanthus); 796 (Perge); iv.783 (Apamea); 1238, 1247 (Thyatira); *MAMA* viii.410, 484 (Aphrodisias); *JRS* 30 (1940), 50 (Beroea); Abbott and Johnson, 451 no. 126 (Sinope); *OGIS* 494 (Miletus); *Ath. Mitt.* 75 (1960), 94 no. 6 (Samos). This is not intended to be a complete list.

23. *IGR* iii.66 (Prusias ad Hypium); 204 (Ancyra); 526, 534 (Lydae); 590 (Sidyma); 628 (Xanthus); 681 (Patara); 778 (Attalea); 796 (Perge); 804 (Aspendus); 857 (Corycus); 982 (Citium); iv.25f (Mytilene, Potamon and Crinagoras); 1031, 1033 (Astypalaea); 1060 (Cos); 1169 (Attalea in Asia); 1247, 1255 (Thyatira); 1756–7 (Sardis); *OGIS* 494 (Miletus); *Insch. von Magnesia* 180;

In some cases the repetition may be explained by a shortage of suitable candidates, but when the larger cities are involved I suspect another factor plays a part: the man already known to the emperor and his staff has a greater change of success.

Since the late Republic, of course, men distinguished in various branches of Greek literary activity had enjoyed special links with Roman dynasts, whether as tutor, court poet or simply cultivated friend.[24] Moreover the prestige of Greek culture was such that even a practitioner of distinction not personally known to a Roman leader might nevertheless expect to command some authority. I shall return to this theme when considering sophistic *ab epistulis*. As far as concerns embassies, however, it is clear that few Greeks, if any, who regularly had the emperor's ear would be at the disposal of their cities for ambassadorial duties, though they might intercede from a higher plane,[25] and that sophistic rhetoric was not the only art that might confer authority. On occasion we find athletes as envoys for their city; more often philosophers; at least twice a poet.[26] Yet in every case we are dealing with members of the upper classes whose station and local political activities would have fitted them to be ambassadors anyway, and it is hard to gauge how important to their eligibility their cultural activity was.

I hope that it may be seen from the foregoing material that many

---

Ath. Mitt. 75 (1960), 94 no. 6 (Samos); *Fouilles de Delphes* iii.4 (1970), nos. 288, 301 (Antigenes), nos. 304, 335 (Aristotimus); *Forschungen in Ephesos* II (1912), 178 no. 69; *JÖAI* 44 (1959), Beibl. 258 no. 3 (Ephesus); Abbott and Johnson, 451 no. 126 (Sinope). This is not intended to be a complete list.

24. See G. W. Bowersock, *Augustus and the Greek World* (Oxford 1965), esp. 30–41, 122–39; *Sophists*, esp. 10; Millar, *Emperor*, 83ff.

25. Thus perhaps Areus of Alexandria, when in 30 B.C. Octavian spared Alexandria first because of Alexander, secondly for its size and beauty and thirdly Ἀρείῳ τῷ ἑταίρῳ χαριζόμενος, Plut., *Ant.* 80.1–3, cf. *Mor.* 207 a–b, Cass. Dio li.16.3–4. More explicitly Claudius asks the senate in A.D. 53 to give immunity to Cos in response to the entreaties (*precibus*) of Xenophon, Tac., *Ann.* xii.61.2.

26. Athletes: *Inschr. von Magnesia* 180; *IGR* iv.1251–2 from Thyatira; cf. L. Robert, *Études Anatoliens* (Paris 1937), 50f., on Hippolochus of Pergamum. Philosophers: Apollophanes of Pergamum, *Ath. Mitt.* 33 (1908), no. 38 (?Augustan); C. Iulius Amynias Isocrates of Samos, *Ath. Mitt.* 75 (1960), 70f. no. 1b (to Augustus); M. Aur. Diodorus Callimedes, *MAMA* viii.499(b), from Aphrodisias. Poets: Crinagoras of Mytilene, *IGR* iv.33; Chaeremon of Tralles, Agathias ii.17 (both in 26 B.C.). Of course many men of letters composed poetry *as well as* practising in that branch of literature on which their reputation was based, e.g. Scopelian, *VS* i.21 (518). We may note also the ἰατρὸς τέλειος καὶ φιλόλογος Ameinias of Lydae, *IGR* iii.534.

factors might affect the choice of an ambassador from the ranks of the aristocracy, and that the indubitably relevant skills of rhetoric were not so monopolized by sophists as to give them an immediate advantage. Some consideration of numbers involved may support this. Some sixteen cases of a sophist or rhetor on embassies to emperors from Greek cities can be documented from the Flavians to the middle of the third century, seven in Philostratus, four in other literary sources and five known from inscriptions. The period from Augustus to Nero, before Philostratus' Second Sophistic, offers another rhetor.[27] For these three hundred years we have attestation of about two hundred embassies. For some we know no more than the names of the ambassadors and the city where they were honoured. A substantial number about which more information is available – some fifty – were primarily congratulatory, and so might not have required the best pleaders available, though such embassies were often concerned to secure retention of city privileges as well as to offer honours to the *princeps*.[28] Of those sixty odd embassies whose business we know to have been of considerable moment, 75% are conducted by men of no known sophistic qualifications. This is not remarkable in smaller cities where sophists might be few or undistinguished, but it is significant that in the case of Ephesus, where the epigraphic and literary records of a major sophistic centre are relatively generous, the non-sophistic envoys outnumber the sophists.[29] Correspondingly, it is only for six of his 43 sophists that Philostratus mentions embassies, although epigraphy can add a seventh.[30] The hazard of epigraphic survival or Philostratus' own very uneven reporting may be distorting the picture, and some sophists will certainly have taken advantage of their immunity from the liturgy of ambassadorial service.[31] But we are still justified in concluding that the typical members of an embassy were aristocrats who were not sophists; that sophists did not play a preponderant part in ambassadorial activity; and that

27. The cases I enumerate are listed in Appendix 2.

28. As perhaps Dio, and arguably Nicomedes in 217/18, in the list in Appendix 2: other embassies in that list may well be in this category too. Cf. Millar, *Emperor*, 410ff.

29. For Ephesus we already know nine ambassadors, listed in Appendix 3.

30. Cf. Appendix 2 nos. (ii), (iv) and (vii), (ix), (x), (xiii). The seventh is Hermocrates, *ibid.* (xi) and (xii).

31. On immunities cf. Bowersock, *Sophists*, 30ff. with the reservations of M. Griffin, *JRS* 61 (1971), 278–80 and V. Nutton, *JRS* 61 (1971), 52–63.

when they do serve on embassies their role as city politicians from distinguished families is as significant as their eminence in sophistic oratory.

One further observation may be justified by the evidence. We know of three cases of sophists or rhetors acting as envoys to Hadrian, but only one for the entire reigns of Pius, Marcus and Commodus.[32] Perhaps the lottery of surviving testimony. But it may reflect an understanding by cities of the different reactions one might expect. Hadrian's enthusiasm for things Greek and his involvement in the arts may have encouraged the belief that he would be impressed by rhetorical virtuosity. Pius was more hard-headed in cultural matters (witness, perhaps, his limitation of the immunities formulated in generous terms by Hadrian) and prone to sarcastic rebuttal of claims on his attention or generosity.[33] We have already seen how the *prima donna* role assumed by Alexander of Seleucia was counter-productive. Marcus does indeed acknowledge learning from Pius the correctness of yielding to those with specialist knowledge τοῖς δύναμίν τινα κεκτημένοις οἷον τὴν φραστικὴν ἢ τὴν ἐξ ἱστορίας νόμων ἢ ἐθῶν ἢ ἄλλων τινῶν πραγμάτων;[34] but it is a considerable step from taking specialist opinion on how something should be expressed (which is what this seems to mean) to giving a privileged hearing to the arguments put forward by a rhetor or sophist: the meagre attestation of sophistic embassies to Pius and Marcus, in a generation when Philostratus' Second Sophistic was at its height, might be attributed to these emperors' lower estimate of the rhetor by comparison with Hadrian or Caracalla. We must remember, of course, that a letter from the sophist Aristides is said to have moved Marcus to tears and to have secured the aid for earthquake stricken Smyrna that the city had appointed an embassy to seek. But we should also take note that nothing is said of the embassy being disbanded, nor of its having comprised a sophist among its number.[35]

32. Cf. Appendix 2 nos. (vi)–(viii) and (ix). It must be admitted that if Polemo had survived to act on the embassy from Smyrna mentioned in *VS* i.25 (529) the tally for the reign of Pius would be two.

33. Note the terms of his refusal of immunity to philosophers, *Dig.* xxvii.1.6.7 and cf. W. Williams, 'Antoninus Pius and the Control of Provincial Embassies', *Historia* 16 (1967), 470ff.

34. *Ad se ipsum* i.16.6, cf. Millar, *Emperor*, 60.

35. *VS* ii.9 (582) referring to Aristides xix.3 as a μονῳδία (the title under which

The large number of rhetors or sophists who were appointed by the emperor to the office of *ab epistulis* is a very different matter. Here it is indisputable that the verbal expertise of the rhetor could be seen as pertinent to the duties of the post and that literary men were favoured in selection for it.[36] But we must be as precise in our analysis of this phenomenon as the evidence allows. In assessing the historical importance of the Philostratean Second Sophistic we must be careful to distinguish declamatory sophists from other literary men, even, as far as possible, from rhetors. Although the terms clearly overlap, it seems that both virtuoso declamation and teaching were expected of a σοφιστής:[37] many men who declaimed might be called simply ῥήτωρ but ῥήτωρ could also be used of teachers, and equally of forensic orators, sometimes but not always distinguished as ἀγοραῖοι ῥήτορες.[38] In the discussion that follows I attempt to distinguish men whom Philostratus thinks are properly sophists from those whom he does not mention at all or those whom he labels differently, and I hope that observing this distinction may cast some light on the developments involved in selection of such men for the post *ab epistulis*.

Bowersock noted twelve 'oriental litterati' in the office between Hadrian and Caracalla.[39] The credentials of some of these are

Aristides xviii is transmitted). Aristides xxi also appears to have an imperial addressee, Commodus (cf. Bowersock, *Sophists*, 46), but if so its invitation to visit the rebuilt city was not taken up.

36. Cf. Bowersock, *Sophists*, 50ff.; Millar, *Emperor*, 83ff., 226–8.

37. Cf. Bowersock, *Sophists*, 12–14, and my remarks in 'Greeks and their Past in the Second Sophistic', *Past and Present* 46 (1970), 5–6, repr. in *Studies in Ancient Society*, ed. M. I. Finley (London 1974), 169. For the imprecision of terminology we may now note that Dionysius of Miletus, called ῥήτορα καὶ σοφιστήν in the inscription on the base of the honorific statue set up by Claudius Eutychus (J. Keil, 'Vertreter der zweiten Sophistik in Ephesos', *JÖAI* 40 (1953), 5–7), is simply called ῥήτωρ on the sarcophagus published in *Anz. Wien* (1969), 136.

38. Cf. the father of Alexander of Seleucia, τοὺς ἀγοραίους λόγους ἱκανώτατος, *VS* ii.5 (570), and τὸ τῶν ἀγοραίων ἔθνος, *VS* ii.20 (614). In the latter passage Philostratus contrasts the forensic orator with the σοφιστής who spends much of his day ξυσπουδάζων μειρακίοις, but ῥήτωρ is also used as late as Pius to describe teachers, cf. *Dig.* xxvii.1.6.7.

39. Bowersock, *Sophists*, 50 referring to Pflaum, *Carrières* ii (Paris 1960), 684 n. 1. That note does indeed list twelve *ab epistulis* and observes that the post *ab epistulis graecis* was 'réservée en general aux grands rhéteurs grecs', but the earliest, Dionysius of Alexandria (cf. below p. 41 with Appendix 4), falls outside the period Hadrian to Caracalla, and Bowersock naturally makes no literary claims for the shadowy —ilius of *ILS* 1452 (Pflaum no. 178, and no. 4 in 684 n. 1). To the ten remaining Bowersock adds Ti. Claudius Vibianus Tertullus (cf. below p. 41 with

questionable, but one or two may be added, so that a figure of twelve can be reached, a high proportion of the sixteen names known, for the period from Trajan to Caracalla. But of these only four are properly sophists: Alexander of Seleucia, Hadrianus of Tyre, Antipater of Hierapolis and Aspasius of Ravenna. A fifth, L. Iulius Vestinus, is indeed called σοφιστής by the *Suda*, but the activity catalogued for him is scholarly – an epitome of the Γλῶσσαι of Pamphilus and a selection of words from Thucydides and Attic orators. If Philostratus had mentioned him at all he would very probably have put him in the secondary role he assigns to Celer, a τεχνογράφος, who was inadequate to the demands of declamation though a good imperial secretary. Cornelianus, to whom Phrynichus dedicated his *Ecloga*, may be the same sort of rhetor: Phrynichus flatters him as ἐν παιδείᾳ μέγιστον ἀξίωμα ἔχοντα and compliments him on introducing high standards of Greek into imperial hearings, and it is reasonable to suspect that his strength lay in choice of words rather than in declamation.[40] Of Maximus we only know that the distinction of his φωνή led to his promotion, and, since he too is ignored by Philostratus in the *Lives*, that distinction is more likely to have been in writing than in declamation.

The τεχνογράφος Celer is almost certainly the *orator graecus* whom the *Historià Augusta* records as tutor to Marcus. The same source offers an Ateius (or Attius) Sanctus as teacher of rhetoric to

Appendix 4) and also mentions T. Aur. Larichus (*Sophists*, 55 with n. 2): but Larichus, known from a letter from Commodus to the Athenian *gerousia* to have been in office *ca* A.D. 186 (J. H. Oliver, *Hesperia* 36 (1967), 332; A. E. Raubitschek, *Hesperia* Suppl. 8 (1949), 289–90) and already known as equestrian from an inscription honouring his wife Ulpia Phila at Xanthus (*TAM* ii.300), has no special claim to be a literary man. But two more figures *could* have been mentioned to strengthen Bowersock's case, L. Iulius Vestinus (who happens to be classified as *ab epistulis* rather than *ab epistulis graecis* by Pflaum, cf. his fasti, *Carrières* II (1961), 1021) and T. Aius Sanctus, who emerged too late for Pflaum's list and is discussed by him as no. 178*bis* in *Carrières* III, 1002–7. Since he was also too late for the list of second-century *ab epistulis* in G. B. Townend, *Historia* 10 (1961), 380–1, and since that list also omits Alexander of Seleucia, I append a list of those men who were either Greeks with the title *ab epistulis* or are specified as *ab epistulis graecis* (and hence presumably of Greek origin), without here entering into details of chronology or the vexed question of when the imperial secretariat was split between Latin and Greek officials (see Appendix 4).

40. Phrynichus, *Ecloga* p. 379 Lobeck ccclvi Rutherford: for other documentation of this discussion see Appendix 4.

Commodus, and this man can now be recognized as T. Aius Sanctus, *ab epistulis graecis* to Marcus. To these five non-sophistic rhetors should be added the Hadrianic *ab epistulis* Heliodorus: his involvement in rhetoric is established by the acid remark of his rival Dionysius of Miletus that Caesar could give him money and honour but could not make him a *rhetor*, and Cassius Dio ascribes his elevation to the prefectship of Egypt to his rhetorical ἐμπειρία, but his omission from the *Lives* and the Historia Augusta's classification of him as a philosopher may justify questioning whether he declaimed.

There remain two men to whom literary activity can independently be ascribed: the γραμματικός Dionysius of Alexandria, and Sempronius Aquila, who *might* be the Aquila noted as a ῥήτωρ εὐδόκιμος and a pupil of Chrestus in the *Lives*. Eudaemon might also be a literary man, especially if identical with the Eudaemon recalled for his δριμύτης by Marcus along with Charax of Pergamum and Demetrius the Platonic philosopher: but the identification is not certain, and the *ab epistulis* differs from other rhetors in that office by holding a number of non-literary posts before being *a bibliothecis* and *ab epistulis*. Bowersock[41] would also ascribe 'some sort of rhetorical or literary proficiency' to Ti. Claudius Vibianus Tertullus, but he too differs from the others in holding the post *a rationibus* after *ab epistulis*: as Millar observes of the post *a rationibus*, 'With one possible exception [*viz.* Tertullus] no literary men or jurists are attested, and instead we have a substantial series of men with full military and equestrian careers.'[42] It would be safer to leave Tertullus, like Larichus and —ilius, as men for whom the present evidence does not document literary activities.

The proportion of rhetors and, after Marcus, of sophists, is indeed impressive, but it requires cautious interpretation. What sort of importance does it attest for the Greek sophists? Is that importance such as to establish the greater historical than literary significance of the Second Sophistic?

One point must be recalled at the outset and kept in mind throughout: the movement of educated Greeks from the upper classes of Eastern cities into the service of Roman dynasts did not

41. *Sophists*, 54.
42. *Emperor*, 105.

begin with the Second Sophistic. The process was already under way in the late Republic. Pompey's friend and historian, Theophanes of Mytilene, and Augustus' tutors and advisers Areus of Alexandria and Athenodorus of Tarsus, are simply the most prominent examples of a class of intellectual Greeks taken up by Romans precisely as purveyors of prestigious Greek culture. The phenomenon is fully and admirably expounded by Bowersock in his *Augustus and the Greek World* and its development into the more formal employment of Greeks as imperial secretaries has been delicately analysed by Millar.[43] It has always been clear why such men were the most likely type of Greek to win dynastic favour. On the cultural plane they could transmit their store of *paideia* or create a literary monument to their patron's deeds. In political terms they were not only in themselves a link with the aristocracies of Greek cities, but were well suited to guiding and formulating a ruler's dealings with them. There is, of course, a difference in status between the Greek who is a friend and informal adviser and the Greek who is appointed to a salaried post *ab epistulis*, but that difference is a function of the development of the institutions of the principate, and does not disqualify us from treating the two as part of a single historical process.

One change that seems to be detectable in this process is in the type of Greek intellectual who attracts Roman attention. Until late in the first century A.D. rhetors are hard to find as advisers or appointees. Instead we encounter philosophers or scholars, many with origin or training in Alexandria. Athenodorus and Nestor of Tarsus, Athenaeus of Seleucia and Areus of Alexandria are all presented in our sources as philosophers. Thrasyllus, friend to Tiberius, was an Alexandrian with Pythagorean as well as astrological interests. One of the first men to hold a post with formal responsibility for Greek diplomacy *may* be his son, Ti. Claudius Balbillus;[44] this man had at any rate Alexandrian training, and seems to have been *ad legationes et res[ponsa graeca?]* under Claudius before becoming prefect of Egypt in A.D. 55. A different sort of Greek intellectual is represented by C. Stertinius

43. Bowersock (n. 24), esp. 30ff.: Millar, *Emperor*, esp. 83ff. Cf. Bowersock, *Sophists*, 43–4 and 58 (where however it is perhaps tendentious to specify rhetors as men who had 'associated in official and unofficial relationships with the leaders of the Roman aristocracy').

44. Cf. evidence and discussions cited in n. 19 above.

Xenophon, who must have come to Claudius' attention by reason of his successful medical practice in Rome before becoming court doctor and being entrusted with Ἑλληνικὰ ἀποκρίματα: Xenophon may well have been a scholar as well as a doctor, but there is no evidence that he was a rhetor.[45]

Even with the rise of sophistic rhetoric, assigned by Philostratus to Nicetes in the reign of Nero, the holders of the office *ab epistulis* seem still to be recruited from other sources, particularly Alexandria. Dionysius of Alexandria, ἐπὶ τῶν ἐπιστολῶν at some time between Nero and Trajan, is termed γραμματικός by the *Suda*, who tells us that he succeeded his philosophy teacher Chaeremon as head of the Alexandrian Museum. L. Iulius Vestinus, whose activity seems to be that of a γραμματικός rather than σοφιστής in Philostratus' sense, was also head of the Alexandrian Museum before moving to control of the libraries in Rome and the posts *a studiis* and *ab epistulis*: his origin is certainly Alexandrian. If Eudaemon, another of Hadrian's *ab epistulis* and the first specifically termed *ab epistulis graecis*, is a literary man at all, it is equally likely that he had Egyptian connections: certainly he starts as a procurator of the *dioecesis Alexandrina* and ends up, in 141/2, as prefect. Only with Celer and Heliodorus do we at last encounter provably rhetorical figures, and as we have seen, Celer is a τεχνογράφος, Heliodorus a philosopher as well as rhetor.[46] This may remind us that the one Greek whom we encounter advising rulers between Augustus and Hadrian did so as a philosopher rather than sophist, Dio of Prusa: and although Dio may have composed sophistic works for Titus, it is the Italian philosopher Musonius who is remembered as Titus' adviser in Greek tradition.[47]

45. Cf. Millar, *Emperor*, 85–6.

46. For documentation see Appendix 4. Recruitment from the Alexandrian museum may be partly explained by the emperor's role, inherited from the Ptolemies, in appointing its head and nominating members, cf. Millar, *Emperor*, esp. 504–6.

47. Dio's *Melancomas* xxix and xxx were presumably written for Titus; Desideri (n. 7) also argues that *Or.* xviii is addressed to Titus. For Musonius cf. Themistius xiii.173c (p. 248.18 Downey). I exclude from consideration the fictional scene in Philostratus' *Apollonius* v.32ff. This leaves us the kingship orations of Dio as our only example of advice that was certainly intended as weighty and serious, even if we cannot tell how seriously it was taken. For discussion and bibliography cf. C. P. Jones, *Roman World*, 16–17 (Melancomas), 115ff. (kingship orations). See further below p. 51 with note 64.

43

The fact that a number of rhetors reached the post *ab epistulis* in the reign of Hadrian, and that the first Philostratean sophist was belatedly appointed by Marcus, cannot be treated as evidence of Greek intellectuals rising to an eminence that such men would not otherwise have attained. Rather we have evidence of a change in the *type* of Greek intellectual who caught the imperial eye, and we can fairly surmise that had there been no sophistic movement these posts would have been filled by literary Greeks of a different sort. In assessing the reasons for the change it is hard not to see both literary and historical explanations as necessary. But the most important factor was surely a literary one, the growth of sophistic rhetoric into the most prestigious literary activity of the age.

That growth had itself historical as well as literary explanations. The prestige of sophistic declamation must at different stages have been augmented by its having been taken up by a number of distinguished Greeks of *provincia Asia*; by the success some of these attained in Rome as declaimers (Nicetes and Isaeus, perhaps Dio) and ambassadors (Scopelianus to Domitian, Polemo to Trajan);[48] by the readiness of culturally conscious emperors to hear and reward declaimers – first Trajan honouring Dio and Polemo, then Hadrian treating the same Polemo as a close associate and promoting rhetors and sophists in many ways.[49] The final seal will surely have been set upon the pre-eminence of sophistic rhetoric among the literary arts by the involvement of the great Herodes Atticus. But it is rarely that the *entire* explanation for a fashion is to be found in its adoption by important people. Something in the practice and content of sophistic declamation satisfied the aspirations of its exponents. In conjecturing what that was we must

48. For Nicetes and Isaeus in Rome cf. Pliny, *Epp.* vi.6.3; ii.3. For Scopelianus and Polemo as envoys cf. Appendix 2.

49. For Trajan's taking Dio into his triumphal chariot cf. *VS* i.7 (488). Philostratus does not actually say the occasion was a triumph, and the precedent of Augustus driving into Alexandria with Areus in his chariot (Plut., *Ant.* 80.1–3) may be taken as corroboration of the story (though a sceptic could see it as its origin). Accordingly I would assume that it has a kernel of truth, though such details as Trajan's much-quoted remark to Dio τί μὲν λέγεις οὐκ οἶδα, φιλῶ δέ σε ὡς ἐμαυτόν may simply be a Greek *topos* going back to Ar., *Ranae* 1169: εὖ νὴ τὸν Ἑρμῆν· ὅτι λέγεις δ'οὐ μανθάνω. For Trajan's gift of free travel to Polemo see *VS* i.25 (532) and, on the whole theme of imperial gifts and honours to intellectuals, Millar, *Emperor*, esp. 491ff. Was the embassy (Appendix 2 no. (iv)) the occasion for Polemo's eliciting this gift?

again take account of historical factors. The men who declaim are among the political leaders of the Greek cities, their declamations train themselves and others for political activity; and where real political power is circumscribed by the dependence of the cities on Rome the fantasy world of declamatory themes allows a Greek aristocrat with a Roman name to play the role of Demosthenes.[50] Yet even when such considerations have been weighed there remains in the balance a residuum of purely literary appeal. Philostratus' sophists and audiences *liked* the Asianic rhythms, the exuberant conceits and the elaborate *enthymemata* that were appropriate to declamatory rhetoric. The combative speech, which as a literary form had fascinated Greeks since the composition of the first few hundred lines of the *Iliad*, posed questions concerning delivery, type and ordering of arguments, selection and arrangement of words, and was capable of absorbing intellectual attention in the way that its close relative, tragedy, seems to have dominated mid fifth-century Athens or the novel dominates modern criticism. The typical circumstances of its delivery allowed a rapport between speaker and audience denied to circulated written texts: speaker could work upon audience, and the audience could, especially in impromptu performances, feel the stimulus of participation in the act of creation.

Much more could be said about both the historical and the literary trends which contributed to the rise of sophistic oratory. But the above, very crude sketch is simply intended to remind us that there *was* an important literary component and to explain why I wish to insist that without it Greek *sophists* would not have been found in the office *ab epistulis*. There are, of course, other factors contributory to their attraction of Roman emperors' attention that are not literary. Already under the Flavians certain families from Asia Minor were securing equestrian posts and access to the Roman senate and magistracies;[51] the escalation of

50. For a fuller exposition of the hypothesis that nostalgia for the glories of classical Greece contributed to the choice of declamatory themes see my article cited in n. 37 above, and cf. a similar interpretation of the enthusiasm for declamation among the Roman aristocracy in the first century A.D. suggested by L. Sussman, *The Elder Seneca, Mnemosyne* Suppl. 51 (Leyden 1978), 14–15.

51. On this important topic the discussions of C. S. Walton, 'Oriental Senators in the Service of Rome', *JRS* 19 (1929), 38ff., and G. W. Bowersock, *Augustus and the Greek World*, 140ff., are still valuable, but for a thorough treatment of the

diplomatic activity as Greek cities vied for titles and privileges brought a still wider range of families into contact with the court; and the phenomenon of the travelling emperor – Trajan on his way to Parthian campaigns and Hadrian indulging in his blend of administrative and cultural tourism – exposed his entourage even more to the tastes of the men and cities that offered him hospitality. In all these forms of contact Athens and Asia Minor bulk larger than Alexandria, and this will have made some contribution to the replacement of Alexandrian by Aegean cultural preferences. Finally the personal element should again be emphasized. Just as the interest of great men like Polemo and Herodes in sophistic rhetoric must have contributed to that art's prestige, so too the friendship attested between Polemo and Hadrian and between Herodes and Marcus will have made access to those emperors easier for other practitioners of the art.[52]

On the hypothesis here advanced, then, the sophistic *ab epistulis* are witnesses both to a change in Greek cultural fashions and to the increasing penetration of the Roman governing class by Greek families in Athens and Asia Minor. Only once, however, did a sophist's achievement of the post *ab epistulis* 'constit⌐ ⌐e first step in an equestrian or ultimately senatorial career'.[53] ⌐e sophistic *ab epistulis*, Alexander died in or shortly after office, Hadrianus perhaps even before he could take it up; Aspasiu⌐ ⌐eturned to teaching in Rome. The exception is Antipater. Yet his whole career illustrates how his sophistic eminence was only effective in conjunction with other factors. His father (not known to us or, apparently, to Philostratus, as a rhetor or sophist) is marked out in the *Lives* as one of the most eminent men in Hierapolis and documented by epigraphy as *advocatus fisci* first of Phrygia, then of all Asia. His grandfather, P. Aelius Zeuxidemus Cassianus, had been Asiarch and, as we now know, *logistes* at Aezani.[54] The

evidence now available cf. H. Halfmann, *Die Senatoren aus dem östlichen Teil des imperium Romanum bis zum Ende des 2 Jh.n.Chr.*, Hypomnemata 58 (Göttingen 1979).

52. On these friendships see Bowersock, *Sophists*, 48–50, and below p. 52f.

53. As Bowersock asserts for the category of 'cultivated Greek': yet even for that wider category the instances are few.

54. Cf. Millar, *Emperor*, 92–3, commenting 'With Aelius Antipater of Hierapolis in Phrygia, we come to an area which was central to the Greek renaissance' (92). 'Central' presumably because he touches on the worlds of sophistic declamation, historiography, imperial tutors and secretaries and the movement of

advance generation by generation to the emperor's court was undoubtedly aided at its last stage, and that stage's precise form determined, by Antipater's rhetorical gifts, a *sine qua non* of his post as tutor to the sons of Severus and a strong commendation for the post *ab epistulis*. But the upward movement had already begun with his father, and rhetoric may have determined *what sort of post* Antipater would achieve rather than whether he would reach such height at all. The elevation to senatorial rank and appointment to the legateship of Bithynia after his post *ab epistulis* distinguishes him not only from the three other sophists in that post but from all but two of the other Greek *ab epistulis*. About the possible (but not certain) *ab epistulis graecis* —ilius we do not know enough to explain why after a number of equestrian posts, two of them *ab epistulis*, he was adlected *inter praetorios*. But the other, T. Aius Sanctus, offers an interesting precedent to Antipater. It seems likely that his role as *orator* to Commodus, which may have been concurrent with his post *ab epistulis graecis* or *procurator rationis privatae*, was crucial in obtaining him senatorial rank on Commodus' accession, rank marked by the office of *praefectus aerarii*, and finally the consulate. Likewise in Antipater's case his tutorial role may have been more important to his promotion to senatorial rank than the actual post *ab epistulis*.[55]

There are indeed examples of *ab epistulis* appointments which were followed by a senior equestrian post: Heliodorus, who later became prefect of Egypt, but whom we do not know to have had other posts which might constitute a 'career'; and Ti. Claudius Vibianus Tertullus, who indeed had a career beginning with *ab epistulis graecis* and ending *praefectus vigilum* but who may not have been, like Heliodorus, a rhetor, far less sophist. Finally Eudaemon did have a career in which *ab epistulis* and *praefectus Aegypti* figures, but he held two posts before that *ab epistulis*.

The post *ab epistulis* should not, therefore, be seen as a regular route for Greek sophists to equestrian or senatorial careers. The

Asiatic families into Roman governing class: but although some of these features he shares with a number of contemporaries, the combination is unique (just as is that offered by Herodes) and if the term 'central' has any notion of 'typical' it should be resisted. The new post at Aezani is attested by a text discovered and copied by C. W. M. Cox which will be published by B. M. Levick and S. Mitchell, to whom I am most grateful for permission to allude to it in this discussion.

55. See Appendix 4 no. (x); Millar, *Emperor*, 105.

reason is not far to seek, and indeed may also be adduced when we consider how few sophists were actually Roman senators: maintenance of a sophistic career required both declamation and teaching, and these could not easily be combined with the demands of a full administrative career (as could, no doubt, the writing of poetry or history).[56] This may explain why only two of Philostratus' sophists, Quirinus of Nicomedia and Heliodorus 'the Arab', held the post of *advocatus fisci* for which one would have thought sophistic skills were tailor-made; and why only one, Dionysius of Miletus, seems to have held a procuratorial post.[57] Again with senatorial careers, it is only Antipater for whom sophistry *led to* such eminence. Herodes, perhaps too exceptional to be a useful indicator, was the son of a rich Greek who was twice *consul suffectus* and is unlikely to have had to make more than a token show in any but one of the few posts which preceded his own appointment as *consul ordinarius* in A.D. 143.[58] These will have absorbed only a small fraction of his time by comparison with political activities in Athens, and together these aspects of his public life clearly did not prevent him devoting considerable time to teaching, declaiming and hearing other sophists. The only other

56. Literary activity of various sorts can be documented for a fair number of Eastern *equites* and senators. For *equites* cf. for example Cn. Pompeius Macer, the son of Theophanes, a writer of epic (Ovid, *Am.* ii.18) and tragic (Stobaeus iv.24.52) poetry, who was entrusted by Augustus with organizing libraries (Suet. *Iul.* 56) and with procuratorial posts in Sicily and Asia (cf. Pflaum, *Carrières* I, 11 ff., III, 957), finally to be numbered among the close friends of Tiberius (καὶ νῦν ἐν τοῖς πρώτοις ἐξετάζεται τῶν Τιβερίου φίλων, Strabo xiii.2.3); or Ti. Claudius Balbillus (cf. above n. 19). For senators e.g. the prolific philosopher Flavius Arrianus, some of those works at least seem to be written concurrently with his administrative career, in which the legateship of Cappadocia from 131/2–136/7 was no sinecure; A. Claudius Charax, consul in A.D. 147, writer of 40 books of Greek (or Greek and Roman) Histories (cf. Jacoby *FGrH* 103; C. Habicht, 'Zwei neue Inschriften aus Pergamum', *Istanbuler Mitteilungen* 9/10 (1959–60), 109f: the consul and historian are certainly identical); Demostratus, a writer on ἁλιευτική and philosophy mentioned by Aelian, *De nat. anim.* xv.19 and perhaps identical with C. Claudius Titianus Demostratus of Ephesus, cf. Halfmann, *Senatoren*, no. 104; or finally Philostratus' contemporary Cassius Dio, consul under Severus, *consul* II *ordinarius* in A.D. 229.

57. Cf. Bowersock, *Sophists*, 56–7. Dionysius was procurator οὐκ ἀφανῶν ἐθνῶν (*VS* i.22 (524)) which suggests that the post was not merely honorific (as seems to have been that ultimately obtained for Appian cf. Fronto *Ad Ant. Pium* 9).

58. *Viz. quaestor, trib. plebis, praetor*: his post overseeing the free cities of Asia may have been more demanding, but will at least have kept him in the centres of sophistic rhetoric. For the evidence cf. *PIR*² c 802.

sophist in the Lives known to have reached the consulate or indeed to have been elevated to senatorial rank was Ti. Claudius Aristocles of Pergamum. Different both from Antipater and from Herodes, Aristocles seems to have been commended both by scholarship and wealth. He wrote rhetorical handbooks as well as declaiming, and his interest in rhetoric as well as his distinction in society will have provoked Phrynichus' decision to dedicate to him parts of his *Proparaskeue Sophistike*. It is from Photius' notice of that work that we know Aristocles to have been adlected to the senate, probably late in the 170s, but there is no evidence in Photius, in Philostratus or in epigraphy, that he held a post *ab epistulis* or any other equestrian office.[59] Although his *paideia* was certainly a commendation I would conjecture that his personal connections and status in Pergamum were more important to his promotion: he was a pupil of Herodes, and a large number of Pergamene families had entered the senate by the 170s A.D.[60] Whatever the reason, it is significant that the extremely abbreviated career, involving adlection (presumably *inter praetorios*) and then perhaps only a suffect consulate, which he need not even hold in Rome, will have made few inroads on his activity as a declamatory *rhetor*.

Many sophists came from families which had already produced consuls; in others a relative reached the *fasces* in the same generation, such as M. Antonius Zeno, a connection of Polemo who held the suffect consulate in A.D. 148. Flavius Damianus married into a family from Ephesus, the Vedii Antonini, which had attained senatorial offices in the second century, and his children predictably rose to the consulate.[61] Other sophistic families,

---

59. See Photius, *Bibl. Cod.* 158, 100 b 26, βασιλικῷ δόγματι τῆς ἐν Ῥώμη μεγάλης βουλῆς ἐγένετο κοινωνός, and for his consulate *Inschr. von Olympia* 462, confirming Philostratus' phrase ἐτέλει . . .ἐς ὑπάτους (*VS* ii.3 (567)). Phrynichus dedicated the first three books of the *Proparaskeue Sophistike* to Aristocles, but the fourth to one Iulianus, ostensibly because of Aristocles' elevation. Since the whole work was dedicated to Commodus as Caesar, the adlection should fall in or shortly after 166–77, and a later rather than earlier date within that range is indicated by Phrynichus' complaints about his age. Aristocles' own works include (as listed by the Suda A 3918 *s.v.* Ἀριστοκλῆς) both a τέχνη ῥητορική and five books περὶ ῥητορικῆς (perhaps duplication by *Suda* or his source?), ἐπιστολαί and μελέται.

60. *VS* ii.3 (567) attests that he heard Herodes. For the senatorial families from Pergamum cf. C. Habicht (n. 56), 129ff.; H. Halfmann, *Senatoren*.

61. On Damianus and the Vedii cf. Bowersock, *Sophists*, 28, and on the identity

eminent though they were, seem to have been so only in a local context and may have lacked the wealth or connections to join the συγκλητικοί. But a sufficient number are senatorial to make the fact that only three sophists were themselves senators striking.[62] The consulate cannot have been a prize that a sophist might reasonably expect to attain, nor can we assert that pursuit of a sophistic career brought a man's family into the Roman upper class. Rather a large number of sophists came from families who had already been raised into that upper class by the efforts of earlier members or by the Roman recognition of a need to give prepotent Greeks a place in the governing hierarchy. A man from such a family who chose to be a sophist was in some measure preferring the intellectual to the practical life. The professional demands of a sophistic career were not compatible with those of the equestrian or senatorial *cursus*, and the latter were surer routes to high office and power. A Greek who had such a career open to him but chose rather to be a sophist had still a chance, but a small chance, of achieving eminence in imperial circles, either by appointment *ab epistulis* or as *advocatus fisci* or by adlection to th' senate. But these political plums were too few to explain wh ; so many upper-class Greeks turned to this activity. The pr mary reason for that remains the prestige attaching to intellectual eminence among the Greek and Roman members of the élite alike and the especial attractions of this type of intellectual activity adumbrated above.

of the first senatorial Vedius cf. my article cited in Appendix 3 no. (vi). For Zeno cf. *CIL* xvi.96, *PIR*² A 883.

62. A fourth man who both taught and declaimed should be added, Quadratus; Philostratus names him as teacher of Varus of Perge (*VS* ii.6 (576)) and describes him as ὁ ὕπατος αὐτοσχεδιάζων τὰς θετικὰς ὑποθέσεις καὶ τὸν Φαβωρίνου τρόπον σοφιστεύων, and he must be the Quadratus described as *rhetor* whom Aristides encountered as *proconsul Asiae*, generally identified with L. Statius Quadratus, *cos. ord.* A.D. 142 (Aristides i. 63–70, cf. xlvii.22; Halfmann, *Senatoren*, 154 no. 67) but with C. Iulius Quadratus Bassus, *cos. suff.* A.D. 139 (and son of the great Trajanic marshal who was suffect in A.D. 105) by C. A. Behr, *Aelius Aristides and the Sacred Tales* (Amsterdam 1968), 84 n. 84. See also Bowersock, *Sophists*, 24–5 and 84–5. Philostratus' notice suggests a limited range of declamation, and it is no doubt important that Philostratus does not catalogue him as a sophist in his own right (though he does admit Favorinus). I suspect that his involvement in sophistic rhetoric was less than that of Herodes or Aristocles, and if he *was* the son of the great C. Iulius Quadratus Bassus he may not have been required to hold many senatorial posts.

One further topic must be considered, that of the emperor's advisers and friends. It relates to that of imperial appointments, since emperors on occasion refer to men in their service as their *amicus* or φίλος without there being evidence to suggest that this is an especially close association.[63] On the other hand, literary sources can attest or claim imperial friendship where no formal status was evident. There is no doubt that in the period of the Second Sophistic Greek intellectuals continued to have special claims to an emperor's friendship, as they had since the later Republic. But it is usually difficult to gauge how much influence such a Greek friend might command outside the areas of his expertise. Dio of Prusa could claim συνηθείας . . . ἴσως δὲ καὶ φιλίας with Trajan and was on occasion favoured by him, but it is hard to show that any of Dio's philosophical ideas had a direct effect on imperial policy, nor was Trajan apparently ready to help him in the problems he faced in Prusa in 111–12.[64] Aristides refers with pride to a close relationship with the emperors involving correspondence, but what he seems to cherish most is the privilege of declaiming before them and their consorts as Odysseus had been allowed to entertain the court of Alcinous.[65] Such an association could be the basis of successful requests for favour, like Aristides' letter appealing for aid to earthquake-stricken Smyrna. But it does not amount to 'powerful influence'. There may have been more to the *summa familiaritas* in which the Augustan history asserts Hadrian held Epictetus, Heliodorus and Favorinus, but here too the sphere in which the friendship operated was surely intellectual rather than political, and the anecdotes about Hadrian's harsh treatment of Heliodorus and Favorinus show how precarious was any influence that the relationship bestowed.[66] Only with Polemo

63. Cf. Millar, *Emperor*, 110ff.; J. A. Crook, *Consilium Principis* (Cambridge 1955).

64. *Or.* xlvii.22. Some relation can be proposed between the kingship speeches and developing conceptions of the principate, but it is easier to see Dio as reflecting current thought than offering original advice, cf. A Momigliano, 'Dio Chrysostomus', *Quarto Contributo* (Rome 1969), 257–69; C. P. Jones, *Roman World*, 115–23; Desideri (*op. cit* n. 7); similarly the Euboean *oratio* (vii) if it *is* to be linked with the contemporary schemes (which is very doubtful, cf. Jones, *Roman World*, 60) is taking up imperial ideas rather than proposing (cf. further P. A. Brunt, *PCPhS* 199 (1973), 9–34).

65. *Or.* xlii.14, referring to A.D. 176.

66. *SHA Hadrian* 16.10. For Hadrian's volatile treatment of his intellectual

and Herodes do we encounter sophists whose friendship with emperors seems likely both to have been close and influential.

For Polemo considerable influence can be argued for, even if it cannot be proved. His appearance among the companions of Hadrian in 123, his choice to dedicate the Olympieion, the emperor's lavish gifts to Smyrna and privileges for himself taken together make plausible even the extravagant claim that Hadrian took his advice in making his will.[67] Yet the total silence of the Augustan History and of the epitome of Cassius Dio on the place of Polemo among Hadrian's friends should perhaps give us pause. Was Polemo's importance as great as the selection of anecdotes offered by Philostratus makes out? Furthermore, how much of his influence derived from his sophistic brilliance and how much from his position at the very highest level of wealth and connections in Greek society? Bowersock notes that his treatment of Pius as proconsul of Asia illustrates his social eminence,[68] and reliance on the emperor's support in local politics is not confined to sophists.[69] In the case of Herodes we can see that the friendship had an intellectual basis (Herodes was one of Marcus' teachers) and also that it operates both in intellectual and personal matters: Marcus takes Herodes' advice on appointments to Athenian chairs, and intervenes on his behalf with Fronto.[70] But although Marcus ultimately found in favour of Herodes in his litigation with other Athenians, the troubled course of this shows the outcome was no foregone conclusion.[71] We lack any testimony that Marcus sought

associates cf. Bowersock, *Sophists*, 35–6, 50–2. The architect Apollodorus could be added, Cassius Dio lxix.4.

67. See Bowersock, *Sophists*, 48–9 and his Appendix II: the story about Hadrian's will, very hard to assess out of context, is made by Philostratus, *VS* i.255 (534): ἐν ταῖς ὑπὲρ τῆς βασιλείας διαθήκαις "καὶ Πολέμων ὁ σοφιστὴς" ἔφη "ξύμβουλος τῆς διανοίας ἐμοὶ ταύτης ἐγένετο . . ." It is clearly crucial what sort of item this related to: perhaps no more than another benefaction to Smyrna (cf. *CIL* x.5963 for a testamentary benefaction to Signia) which might at least explain how the detail was known to Philostratus, but would at the same time restrict the sphere of Polemo's influence.

68. Bowersock, *Sophists*, 48.

69. Thus Hadrian's intervention when Smyrna brought an accusation against Polemo concerning his handling of imperial benefactions, *VS* i.25 (533), has a close parallel in Pius' letter to the Ephesians reprimanding them for lack of appreciation of the services of Vedius Antoninus, *IBM* iii.491 = *Syll.*³ 850 = Abbott and Johnson, 423 no. 101.

70. Cf. Bowersock, *Sophists*, 49.

71. See now *Hesperia* Suppl. 13 (1970).

Herodes' advice on matters of state, although we are told of Herodes' intervention in high politics by writing to the rebel Avidius Cassius Ἡρώδης Κασσίῳ ἐμάνης[72], a move designed to show Herodes' loyalty rather than a significant political act. If Marcus did discuss affairs of state with Herodes it will have been a tribute to his wealth and influence rather than his sophistic skills. But it is hard to believe that such men as Polemo or Herodes had the sort of influence with the emperor enjoyed by great army commanders, some of them Greek.[73]

What, then, has emerged from a review of the representation of sophists on embassies to the emperor, in the office *ab epistulis*, in the Roman senate and among the emperor's close advisers? It should be clear, I hope, that in all rôles except that of *ab epistulis* the sophist should be seen as a species of the genus Greek aristocrat and that his membership of that genus is the greatest factor contributing to his success. In selection for embassies the sophist may have a small advantage over his peers, but as far as concerns entry to the senate and access to the consulate by a standard career, his professional activity may have been a positive obstacle. In appointment to the post *ab epistulis* matters are different. But here the sophist only achieves preponderance in the reign of Marcus, and that, like the movement of rhetors into the office from the reign of Hadrian, is a reflection of the increasing fashionability of display oratory within Greek literary activity and not an example of Greek intellectuals scaling new heights in Roman society. That fashion, to which sophistic appointments *ab epistulis* are witness, must be explained in literary as well as historical terms. Because it was a fashion of an educated Greek élite which already had close connections with the like-minded Roman governing class, its exponents naturally included men of historical importance. But if the fashion had been different (say for composing and reciting dithyrambs), the general course, if not the precise personnel, of Greek intellectuals' relations with Rome would not have been very different. The same cannot be said of the literary importance of the Second Sophistic: the forms and styles developed in many other branches of literature

72. *VS* ii.1 (563).

73. E.g. Trajan's marshal C. Iulius Quadratus Cassus, *cos. suff.* A.D. 105 from Pergamum; Marcus' general and son-in-law Ti. Claudius Pompeianus of Antioch, *cos.* II *ord.* in A.D. 173, cf. *PIR*² c 973.

– e.g. dialogue, epistolography, the novel – constantly betray the influence of sophistic rhetoric, and would have been different had it not been fashionable.[74] Different too would have been the proportion of oratory handed down by the period to the fourth century and then to Byzantium, a proportion which in turn affected these eras' tastes. It might after all be that the Second Sophistic has more importance in Greek literature, than in Roman history.

Appendix 1: Sophists of 'low or middle-class origin'

(i) Secundus of Athens, ὃν ἐκάλουν ἐπίουρόν τινες ὡς τέκτονος παῖδα, Philostratus, *Vitae Sophistarum* i.26 (544), normally translated (as by W. C. Wright, Loeb edition 1921) 'whom some called "Wooden Peg", because he was the son of a carpenter'. This is an extraordinary example of banausic origins in a liberal profession, and it is perhaps even more remarkable that Philostratus retails the information without any social comment other than the witticism of his pupil Herodes, adapting Hesiod, *Op.* 25, to suit a quarrel between them, καὶ κεραμεὺς κεραμεῖ κοτέει καὶ ῥήτορι τέκτων. We should perhaps print both Ἐπίουρον (a nickname) and Τέκτονος, the latter to be taken as the father's name (or *cognomen*, if he had Roman citizenship). It is used as a proper name (admittedly with meaningful reference to carpentry as a family trade) by Homer, *Iliad* v.59, Μηριόνης δὲ Φέρεκλον ἐνήρατο, Τέκτονος υἱὸν | Ἁρμονίδεω, ὃς χερσὶν ἐπίστατο δαίδαλα πάντα | τεύχειν, and appears a few times in Egypt, there again probably developing from a nickname. Cf. *BGU* ix. 1900 (A.D. 196); *Ostr. Bodl.* ii.2111, 2 (iv–v A.D.); *P. Strassb.* 570; *Prosop. Arsin.* 5170 (vi–vii A.D.); and Tectonides, Cramer *An. Ox.* i.443. Since Homer marks Phereclus as much loved by Pallas Athene, and a hero of this name was introduced by Simonides into the crew for Theseus' Cretan expedition (Plutarch, *Theseus* 17), it may have seemed a suitable name for an Athenian family which had connections with carpentry to give to a son, but these connections are more likely to have been ownership of slaves or factories than personal activity as a carpenter. This would in no way diminish the effect of Herodes' joke. (I am very grateful to P. M. Fraser for allowing me access to the material gathered under his direction for the *Lexicon of Greek Proper Names*: a fairly wide but not exhaustive survey has failed to reveal any use of the name outside Egypt in the documentary sources, and this might be thought an argument against its use in an Attic family. But even in Egypt it is rare.)

74. On the ramifications of rhetoric see the major contribution to our understanding of the literature of the period, B. P. Reardon's *Courants littéraires grecs des IIe et IIIe siècles après J.-C.* (Paris 1971).

(ii) Quirinus of Nicomedia, *VS* ii.29 (260), attributing γένος . . . οὔτε εὐδόκιμον οὔτε αὖ κατεγνωσμένον. This surely means little more than that Philostratus knows no distinction that he can ascribe to the family, and is insufficient ground for denying its membership of the curial class.

(iii) Apollonius of Naucratis, *VS* ii.19 (599), saying nothing at all about his origins, but gossiping, καθάπτονται δὲ αὐτοῦ τινες καὶ τὸ σταλῆναι ἐς Μακεδονίαν μισθωτὸν οἰκίας οὐδὲ εὖ πραττούσης. There is no indication, *pace* Bowersock, that this fell early in his career (Lucian seems to have acquiesced in a salaried post only late in life, cf. his *Apologia*) and we must handle carefully a story that even Philostratus rejected. None, therefore, of Philostratus' sophists have proven origins outside the curial class. A better case might be made out for Lucian, but it is easier to be sure that he was a sophist (cf. *Bis accusatus* 27, *Apologia* 15) *pace* Bowersock, *Sophists*, 114, than to extract from the conventions of the *Somnium*, with its tale of a prospective career in sculpture, a clear picture of Lucian's social background.

Appendix 2: Sophists or rhetors as ambassadors

In chronological order:

(i) Potamon of Mytilene, *IGR* iv.33, to Augustus in 26 B.C.

(ii) Scopelianus of Clazomenae, *VS* i.21 (520), to Domitian: Philostratus credits him with many embassies to the emperor but focuses his narrative on the famous one to save Asian viticulture.

(iii) Dio of Prusa (*Or.* xl.13–5, cf. xlv.3) to Trajan (for date cf. Jones, *Roman World*) an embassy which achieved for Prusa the right to enrol 100 new βουλευταί.

(iv) Polemo of Laodicea, *VS* i.21 (521), probably to Trajan for Smyrna when Scopelianus was too old. The embassy was ὑπὲρ τῶν μεγίστων (unspecified).

(v) Rhetors from Tyre and Antioch support envoys from the Greek and Jewish communities of Alexandria to Trajan (*Acta Hermaisci* – H. Musurillo, *Acts of the Pagan Martyrs* (Oxford 1964), no. 8). The incident may be fictional.

(vi) Marcus of Byzantium, *VS* i.24 (530), to Hadrian, whom he impressed: object unstated.

(vii) Polemo of Laodicea, *VS* i.25 (531), to Hadrian, from whom he elicited generous gifts to Smyrna: for these see also *IGR* iv.1431.

(viii) Paulus of Tyre (*Suda* iv.69 *s.v.* Παῦλος) to Hadrian, who gave Tyre the title μητρόπολις.

(ix) Alexander of Seleucia, *VS* ii.5 (570–1), to Pius, cf. above p. 33 with n. 11.

(x) Apollonius of Athens, *VS* ii.20 (601), to Septimius Severus in Rome, probably in A.D. 202: object unstated, but cf. ἔν τε πρεσβείαις ὑπὲρ τῶν μεγίστων ἐπρέσβευσεν.

(xi) Hermocrates of Phocaea, *Altertümer von Pergamon* VIII.3, 76 no. 34, argued by Habicht *ad loc.* to have represented Pergamum, probably *ca* A.D. 200, and hence honoured posthumously as μετὰ πάσης προθυμίας καὶ εὐνοίας [συνδι] | [κή]σαντα καὶ προαγωνισάμ[ενον]. Note that he is termed φιλόσοφος whereas *VS* ii.25 presents him as a declaimer.

(xii) Hermocrates of Phocaea, argued by Habicht *ibid.* to be mentioned in *Forschungen in Ephesos* II (1912), 125 no. 26 because acting for Ephesus and not (as held by Stein, *PIR²*F 285, and Crook, *Consilium Principis*, 165 no. 149a) as a member of Caracalla's *consilium*.

(xiii) Heliodorus the Arab, *VS* ii.32 (625–6), to the emperor in Gaul, presumably Caracalla in A.D. 213.

(xiv) Ti. Claudius Nicomedes, *Altertümer von Pergamon* VIII.3, 71–4 no. 31 (calling him σοφιστής), argued by Habicht *ad loc.* to have represented Pergamum, probably to Macrinus in A.D. 217/18 (cf. *SEG* xvii.505).

(xv) M. Ulpius Isodemus, *Arch. Anz.* 57 [1942], 183 no. 24, honoured at Beroea as τὸν δοκιμώτατον τῶν ῥητόρων ἀρετῆς ἕνεκα καὶ εὐνοίας εἰς τὴν ἐπαρχείαν, argued by L. Robert, *Hellenica* 5 (1948), 34 to be so honoured because he pleaded for the province. ? Late second/early third century.

(xvi) Nicagoras of Athens, *Suda* iii.465 *s.v.* Νικαγόρας, wrote a πρεσβευτικὸς πρὸς Φίλιππον τὸν Ῥωμαίων βασιλέα, so A.D. 244–9. Noticed by *VS* ii.33 (628).

(xvii) P. Aelius Pigres of Philadelphia, *SEG* xvii.528, cf. n.20, envoy to Valerian and Gallienus in Antioch to obtain freedom from contributions to maintenance of ἀρχιερωσύνων and τὰς τῶν πανηγύρεων ἀρχάς: 18 January A.D. 255. *May* be identical with the sophist mentioned in *VS* ii.33 (627) where MSS read Περίγητος (cf. n.20).

Appendix 3: Ambassadors from Ephesus

(i) P. Vedius Antoninus, *JÖAI* 44 (1959), Beibl. 257–8, *IGSK* 13 (*Ephesos* III), no. 728, πρός τε τὴν σύγκλητον καὶ τοὺς αὐτοκράτορας, probably Trajan and Hadrian (cf. article cited under no. (vi)).

(ii) Cascellius Ponticus (or Politicus), *Syll.*³ 833, Abbott and Johnson, 398, no. 78, *IGSK* 15 (*Ephesos* v). no. 1486, from the gerousia to Hadrian, whose reply is dated 27 September A.D. 120.

(iii) (Probably) Ti. Claudius Piso Diophantus, the archiereus who obtained permission for a second neocrate temple, *JÖAI* 44 (1959), Beibl. 265 no. 40, *ca* A.D. 132.

(iv) Flavius Ath—, *Forschungen in Ephesos* II (1912), no. 24, cf. J. Keil, *JÖAI* 27 (1931), Beibl. 18–25, probably to Pius, concerning debts to city from deceased and ex-office-holders.

(v) Cn. Pompeius Hermippus, *Forschungen in Ephesos* II (1912), 178 no. 69, πρεσβεύσαντα πολλάκις πρὸς τοὺς αὐτοκράτορας καὶ τὴν ἱερωτάτην σύγκλητον, middle or late second century?

(vi) P. Vedius Antoninus Sabinus, *ÖAI* 44 (1959), Beibl. 257–8, *IGSK* 13 (*Ephesos* III), no. 728, πρεσβεύσαντα πρός τε τὴν σύγκλητον καὶ τοὺς αὐτοκράτορας περὶ τῶν μεγίστων καὶ ἀεὶ νικήσαντα, probably between 138 and 162 (when he lavished benefactions during L. Verus' ἐπιδημία) hence to Pius and Marcus. Cf. *Proceedings of the Xth International Congress of Classical Archaeology* (1973) (Ankara 1978), 867–74 for this man's identity.

(vii) Iulius Artemas, *Forschungen in Ephesos* II (1912), 164, who undertook embassies to Marcus and Commodus, so A.D. 161–92.

(viii) L. Flavius Hermocrates the sophist, above Appendix 2 no. (xi), *ca* A.D. 200–205.

(ix) *Ignotus, SEG* xvii.505 = J. Keil, *Sitz. Bay. Ak. Wiss.* (1956), 3, honoured for embassies to Severus, Caracalla, and finally Macrinus in A.D. 217/18.

If the *ignotus* of (ix) were a sophist we should still have only two sophists out of nine ambassadors known for the century from Trajan to Macrinus: perhaps Dionysius of Miletus should be added, since some service to Ephesus must lie behind the prestigious honour of burial in a public place within the city (contrary to *Dig.* xlvii.12.3.5) asserted by Philostratus, *VS* i.22 (526), loosely using the term ἐν τῇ ἀγορᾷ and confirmed (not for the *agora* proper) by a recently discovered inscription, *Anz. Wien* (1969), 136 = *Bull. Epig* (1971), no. 574, *IGSK* 12 (*Ephesos* II), no 426.

Appendix 4: Greeks with the title *ab epistulis* or *ab epistulis graecis*

(i) Dionysius of Alexandria — (Between Nero and Trajan) τῶν βιβλιοθηκῶν προΰστη καὶ ἐπὶ τῶν ἐπιστολῶν καὶ πρεσβειῶν ἐγένετο καὶ ἀποκριμάτων, *Suda* Δ 1173 *s.v.* Διονύσιος, calling him γραμματικός.

(ii) L. Iulius Vestinus — ἐπιστάτῃ τοῦ Μουσείου καὶ ἐπὶ τῶν ἐν ῾Ρώμῃ βιβλιοθηκῶν ῾Ρωμαικῶν καὶ ῾Ελληνικῶν καὶ ἐπὶ τῆς παιδείας ῾Αδριανοῦ, ἐπιστολεῖ τοῦ αὐτοῦ αὐτοκράτορος, *IG* xiv.1085 = *IGR* i.136 = *OGIS* 679: called σοφιστής by the *Suda* O 835 *s.v.* Οὐηστῖνος.

(iii) Celer

βασιλικῶν μὲν ἐπιστολῶν ἀγαθὸς προστάτης, *VS* i.22 (524), Aristides, *Or.* 1.57 – probably to Hadrian. Philostratus *loc. cit.* calls him τεχνογράφος, and he is probably the *orator graecus* who was tutor to Marcus, Caninius Celer (*SHA Marcus* 2.4, cf. *Ad se ipsum* viii.25).

(iv) C. Avidius Heliodorus

τὸν τὰς ἐπιστολὰς διαγαγόντα (of Hadrian), Cassius Dio lxix.3.5; became prefect of Egypt ἐξ ἐμπειρίας ῥητορικῆς, *id.* lxxi.22.2; grouped with Epictetus as a philosopher, *SHA Hadr.* 16.10.

(vi) (Valerius) Eudaemon

proc. dioec. Alex., proc. bibl., ab ep. gr. etc., *ILS* 1449, generally agreed to be the prefect of Egypt in 141/2, cf. Pflaum, *Carrières* I (1960), 264–71 no. 110; ? cf. *Ad ipsum* viii.25 and Millar, *Emperor*, 102–3.

(vi) —ilius

ILS 1452, Pflaum, *Carrières*, no. 178 (cf. however Townend, *Historia* 10 (1961), 378, on whose reconstruction his first post *ab epistulis* is to Verus in A.D. 162). After two intervening posts he became *ab epistulis latinis* and was then adlected *inter praetorios*.

(vii) Alexander of Seleucia

Appointed to ἐπιστέλλειν Ἕλλησιν by Marcus in Pannonia, *VS* ii.5 (571), i.e. A.D. 169/70–175.

(viii) Sulpicius (?) Cornelianus

ἀποφανθέντα ὑπὸ τῶν βασιλέων ἐπιστολέα αὐτῶν, Phrynichus, *Ecloga* 418 Lobeck, cccxciii Rutherford, cf. 379L, cclviR; probably the ῥήτωρ who is father to the sophist Metrophanes of Lebadeia, *Suda* M 1010 *s.v.* Μητροφάνης; *ab epistulis* to Marcus and Verus or Marcus and Commodus.

(ix) Ti. Claudius Vibianus Tertullus	*ab epistulis graecis, a rationibus Augustorum, praefectus vigilum, ILS* 1344; the post *ab epistulis* is now dated to some time between A.D. 173 and 175 by a further text from Pergamum, C. Habicht, *Altertümer von Pergamon* VIII.3 (Berlin 1969), no. 28.
(x) T. Aius Sanctus	L. Moretti, *Riv. fil.* 28 (1960), 68f.; Pflaum, *Carrières* III, 1002–7, no. 178bis. *Ab epist. gr.* (Pflaum argues for *ca* A.D. 171–2), *proc. rationis privatae, praef. Aegypti* (A.D. 179 or 180). Probably the *orator*, i.e. teacher of rhetoric to Commodus, transmitted by the MSS of *SHA Commodus* 1.6 as Attius or Ateius Sanctus, which would help to explain why on Commodus' accession he gets the senatorial post *praefectus aerarii* and ultimately the consulate. Cf. Millar, *Emperor*, 105.
(xi) Hadrianus of Tyre	Appointed on his death-bed by Commodus, *VS* ii. 10 (590).
(xii) Aurelius Larichus	*ab epistulis graecis* to Commodus in *ca* 186, *Hesperia* 36 (1967), 332.
(xiii) Maximus of Aegeae	Philostratus, *Apollonius* i.12, ἠξιώθη δὲ καὶ βασιλείων ἐπιστολῶν οὗτος εὐδοκιμῶν τὴν φωνήν, ? late second century (cf. *ANRW* II.xvi.2, 1685 n. 129).
(xiv) Sempronius Aquila ? of Ancyra	*IGR* iii.188, Bosch no. 203; cf. the Aquila from Galatia who is a pupil of Chrestus, *VS* ii.11 (591) and ῥήτωρ εὐδόκιμος.
(xv) Aelius Antipater of Hierapolis	*VS* ii.24 (607), appointed ταῖς βασιλείοις ἐπιστολαῖς by Severus; cf. Galen xiv.218 Kühn, *Forschungen in Ephesos* II (1912), 125 no. 26. Tutor to Geta and Caracalla, adlected to senate, legate of Bithynia.
(xvi) Aspasius of Ravenna	*VS* ii.33 (628).

Lucian: a sophist's sophist

GRAHAM ANDERSON

Lucian is without doubt the most readily accessible of Second Sophistic authors;[1] he exploits a wide cross-section of the movement's resources and capabilities, and he is a better advertizement for its achievements than most of its other surviving practitioners. He is also an author whose appeal is direct, and that has made it tempting to form facile judgments about him, and through him, of his age as a whole. My aim is to look briefly at several characteristic links between the sophist and his movement, and to note some of the pitfalls in passing judgment on either.

I. A sophist's choice of media

Part of Lucian's success undoubtedly lies in his lightness of touch, which often amounts to sleight of hand. He was a rhetorician who did not feel compelled to take the standard priorities of rhetoric very seriously: almost the whole of his output can be related to the elementary exercises, the *progymnasmata*, of the rhetorical schools, and it is the signal service of Bompaire to have explained his output largely in terms of the basic curriculum.[2] But we should also note where Lucian's interests lie within that curriculum: this will supply the key to his literary personality.

1. Quotations from Lucian are cited from Macleod's *OCT* for *Opuscula* 1–68, and from his *LCL* vol. VII for the miniature dialogues; otherwise from Jacobitz' Teubner. J. Bompaire, 'Lucien écrivain, Imitation et création', *BEFAR* 190 (1958) and B. P. Reardon, *Courants littéraires grecs des IIᵉ et IIIᵉ siècles après J.-C.* (Paris 1971), 155–180 are indispensable for Lucian's place in the Second Sophistic. For B. Baldwin's criticisms of the so-called 'mimesis-approach' (in his *Studies in Lucian*, Toronto 1973), see Bompaire's reply in *REG* 88 (1975), 226–9 and *infra*, 78–84. My *Lucian: Theme and Variation in the Second Sophistic*, *Mnemosyne* Suppl. 41 (1976) and 'Lucian's Quotations: Some Short Cuts to Culture', *BICS* 23 (1976), 59–68, attempt to study Lucian's response to two characteristic 'habits' of the movement.

2. Bompaire, *Ecrivain*, *passim*, esp. 239–332 ('Composition rhétorique'); Reardon, *Courants*, 165–70.

The simplest of rhetorical exercises was no more than the re-telling of a story (*mythos* or *diēgēma*); Lucian himself has a predilection for it. Almost all the *laliae* contain at least one if not two self-contained narratives, so that storytelling accounts for most of *Bacchus, Hercules, de Electro, Herodotus, Zeuxis, Prometheus es, Dipsades, Harmonides,* and *Scytha.* To these must be added the two major collections of *novellae, Toxaris* and *Philopseudes*; the extended lying tale *Verae Historiae,* and probably some version (or versions) of the *Onos.* Half of the essay *Quomodo historia conscribenda sit* should also be included (short extracts from bogus historians); and so should the satiric dialogues whose contents form more or less continuous narrative: *Icaromenippus, Necyomantia, Navigium, Symposium, Eunuchus,* and *Alexander.* Almost as elementary is the *chreia,* an exercise constructed round a saying, often a stock quotation or *bon mot.* Most of the miniature dialogues and *Vitarum Auctio* can be related to this starting-point, as can the *Dissertatio cum Hesiodo* and *Iuppiter Confutatus*: Lucian has overworked fewer formulae more obviously than 'But Homer says that you . . .'! Many of the more substantial dialogues are based on a slightly more ambitious exercise, the *syncrisis* or fully worked-out comparison: such pieces as *Piscator, Timon, Gallus, Rhetorum Praeceptor,* and *Anacharsis* are no more than dramatized antitheses. Several other major pieces can be related to the encomium, one of the proper ends of epideictic oratory: this will account for the two encomia proper, *Nigrinus* and *Imagines*; the mock encomia *de Parasito, Muscae Encomium,* and *de Saltatione*; and the *psogoi Adversus Indoctum, Peregrinus, Alexander,* and *Pseudologista.*[3]

It will be seen that Lucian concentrated his talents on developing the exercises at the lower end of the scale. This had a twofold advantage: it enabled him to communicate with the widest possible 'educated' audience, and it offered much more obvious scope for frivolity than the conventional historical subjects of the major formal exercises, the *meletae*; it is scarcely without significance that Lucian had so little interest in Demosthenes. When he moves from story-telling and small dialogue units into more

3. A number of pieces are difficult to classify: *Sacr., Luct., Calumnia* and *Merc. Cond.* are best described as moral essays – one might treat *Saturnalia* as an isolated example of *nomou eisphora* – and a number of pieces admit of more than one classification; it is often difficult to draw the line between narrative and *ecphrasis,* when battles and voyages automatically involve both. But the general tendency is clear.

conventional displays, he tends to cultivate the less usual alternatives: mock-encomia outnumber the real thing, and so do *psogoi*;
while the two examples of encomium as such are as untypical of
their kind as they could be. The *meletē* itself, the acme of rhetorical
exercises in Philostratus' hierarchy, is only represented by the two
Phalaris pieces and two others (*Abdicatus, Tyrannicida*). Assuming
that we have a representative sample of Lucian's output, how can
we characterize it? We can say that he has turned the rhetorical
curriculum upside-down: in an age obsessed with *doxa*, most of his
output verges on 'adoxography' – the elevation of the undignified
just for the fun of it. We are dealing with a fully-fledged sophist who
likes to pose as a sophist's apprentice.

II. A sophist's approach to Satire

But it is neither convenient nor illuminating to label Lucian as 'a
manipulator of the techniques of *progymnasmata*': since the Renaissance the title of satirist has persisted, and it has seldom proved
satisfactory.[4] The problem is best illustrated by a formula such as
G. M. A. Grube's 'the Second Sophistic and its Satirist', which
tends to suggest that Lucian stands further apart from the
movement than is in fact the case.[5] And scholars concerned with
satire as such have treated Lucian with a mixture of indignation
and contempt:

'He has almost wholly abandoned one of the essential virtues of satire,
which is to be topical in subject and realistic, urgent and combative in
style.'[6]

'The *spoudaiogeloion* of Lucian is a spurious satire, because for the most part
the *spoudaion* in his works is a sham seriousness.'[7]

Lucian, it is easy to claim, has no real commitment, and he does
not scourge vice or folly in any new way. Such charges admit of no

4. For Greek Satire, see J. Geffcken, 'Studien zur griechischen Satire', *NJklass
Alt* 27 (1911), 393–411, 469–93; C. A. van Rooy, *Studies in Classical Satire and
Related Literary Theory* (Leyden 1963), 90–116.
5. *The Greek and Roman Critics* (Toronto 1965), 325.
6. So G. Highet, *The Anatomy of Satire* (Princeton 1962), 42f. It has to be said
that any evaluation, moral or literary, of Lucian in relation to Juvenal or
Petronius must take into account the absence of consensus in evaluating their own
respective contributions as satirists.
7. Van Rooy (n. 4), 110.

refutation; but they are the wrong charges, and it would not have taken Lucian long to slip out of them. The second century was the age of the *Halbphilosoph*, the rhetorical writer who concerned himself with moral (and very often religious) commonplace.[8] Lucian has the repertoire and outlook of such a person: he offers epideictic entertainment less as a pseudo-Demosthenes than as a pseudo-Socrates. But he must be judged on the comic results rather than the moral pose: one example will illustrate his use of satirical material. A favourite cliché is the act of moralizing on the follies of mankind from above. Aristophanes had already exploited its comic effect: his Socrates shows Strepsiades a map on which Sparta seems uncomfortably near Athens; and Trygaeus thinks the spectators look bad even from above.[9] Plato and the Cynic tradition had each contributed to the moral development of the topos,[10] and it is a *sine qua non* for the second-century philosophic journalist; Marcus Aurelius informs it with a persistent and personal pathos. Lucian has realized the potential of all these approaches in the *Charon*, where Hermes shows the ferryman the follies of mankind from the top of Ossa-cum-Pelion; but when even Charon purveys Homeric similes to dismiss the arrogance of man,[11] and the humble ferryman turns out to be a virtuoso rhapsode in his own right, it is clear that the common property of Aristophanes, Plato, and the Cyno-Stoic moralists is now safe in sophistic hands. One may choose to say that Lucian's handling falls short of satire – or that it reaches beyond it. He is now concerned only with the fun of Aristophanes (the political problems of the Fifth Century are irrelevant); he develops only the literary imagination of Plato, since the doctrines are already 'recognized';[12] and he varies the kind of popular philosophic clichés which command assent without argument. Anyone who feels that it is a sophist's obligation to be concerned for the human condition wholly misunderstands the sophists' milieu. Although public speakers could make dramatic interventions or lavish benefactions,

8. For the *Halbphilosoph* as a type, cf. Reardon, *Courants*, 199–205; G. R. Stanton, *AJPh* 94 (1973), 350–64.

9. *Nub.* 206–17; *Pax* 821ff.

10. *Phaedo* 109Aff.; for a Cynic application, see R. Helm, *Lucian und Menipp* (Leipzig 1906), 90f.

11. *Charon* 19.

12. For Lucian's 'recognition' of Plato (in the mouth of Chrysippus!), *Pisc.* 22.

the responsibility for the well-being of the Eastern Empire lay elsewhere; and the emperor derived his own spiritual nourishment from the same stock of clichés. One can say that in an age of political, cultural and spiritual stability it took Lucian's eclectic technique to revitalize what everybody had always read and always believed; and it took his skill to combine as many as possible of the literary traditions in which their common heritage was to be found. It is not that he refused to preach to the converted: he simply prefers to play with preachers' themes in front of them. Part of the fun is to pose as a preacher: that is not so much the art of the hypocrite as the art of the joker. He is a *praeceptor morum* in the same ironic way as Ovid is a *praeceptor amoris* – a self-appointed leader without a cause, writing didactic entertainment with irrepressible virtuosity.

Lucian's scheme of moral satire is simple and memorable; and it can be adapted to admit infinite repetition and variation.[13] He himself (or some deputy, such as Truth or Philosophy), will take up an elevated stance (on the Caucasus, for example, or the Acropolis);[14] put up the unfortunate offender to be stripped of his finery; fit him out with an appropriate ball-and-chain; and have him sent off to a house of correction or reform. The scheme can be modified if the victim is beyond reform: and in any case he will come before the judgment-seat via some well-known situation in literature.[15]

From such basic motifs Lucian can branch out into other favourites: some of his victims will have some physical disability;[16] some will require a surprise witness to bring about their execution; some will have some last-minute reprieve; and some will offer an opportunity for proclamation.[17] And there will be some glaring incongruity between their mores and their behaviour, between their hopes and their real prospects – or between any other convenient pair of opposites. So long as Lucian can manage to keep

13. Cf. my *Theme and Variation*, 106–9 and index III *s.v.* Exposure Scenes.
14. *Prom. Cauc.* 1; *Pisc.* 21.
15. Cf. Bompaire, *Ecrivain*, 242–64 ('genre judiciaire'), 365–78 ('thème de l'Hadès').
16. *Pod.* 297–307; *Neky.* 11; *D. Mort.* 22.2–5.
17. E.g. *Katapl.* 27; *Pseudolog.* 25; *Fugit.* 29, cf. *Bis Acc.* 11; *Eun.* 10; *Peregr.* 7–30 (surprise witnesses); *Neky.* 13; *D. Mort.* 30.3; *Icar.* 33 (last-minute reprieves); *Neky.* 20; *Deor. Conc.* 14–18; *Pisc.* 40f.; *Bis Acc.* 12 (proclamations).

the paradoxes moving, the message does not matter very much. He is clearly more interested in punishment than in reform. It is true that Hermes stops Menippus from sawing off a philosopher's beard:[18] he is to use a single stroke instead. That victim got off lightly, and thanks to the inefficiency of Providence, there is a high rate of acquittal and postponement for some of the rest.[19] But Lucian enjoys the plight of his victims: the tyrant Megapenthes is not allowed to drink the Waters of Lethe, since he must remember his past life more bitterly;[20] adulterers are gleefully suspended by their offending member, or pitched and left naked on the top of Haemus;[21] assemblies spend their time devising horrific punishments, or the gods debate whether to consign the philosophers to the pit, to Tartarus, or to the giants;[22] and if Lucian wrote the *Onos*, as I believe, he was in his element when the robbers come round to debating the heroine's horrible fate.[23] Even in the mildest of his 'Platonic' dialogues there is room for bizarrerie of this kind: Mnesippus is to have his hand cut off if he fails to prove that Greek friends are better than Scythian ones![24]

The main achievement of Lucian's satirical output is a long range of variations on the hypocrite and pretender. Few professional types will be mentioned unless they can be presented as ignorant and immoral hypocrites: only the historians can have no charge of immorality brought against them.[25] One topos will cover most of Lucian's criticism of the philosopher: the victim talks about virtue, but devotes himself privately to pleasure. Why did Lucian have such an obsession with this motif? Because it was simple, easy to accept without reflection, and flexible; it could be adapted to suit almost every school; and it could be accommodated to any literary colouring. The philosopher could be presented through the medium of Aristophanes, Plato, Cynic satire, or contemporary life,[26] and he could be allowed to assimilate almost every other

18. *D. Mort.* 20.9.

19. E.g. *D. Mort.* 24 (Sostratus); *Neky.* 13 (Dionysus); *Icar.* 33 (the philosophers).

20. *Katapl.* 28f.   21. *VH* 2.31; *Fugit.* 33.   22. *Pisc.* 2; *Icar.* 33.

23. *Onos* 25; cf. my *Studies in Lucian's Comic Fiction*, *Mnemosyne* Suppl. 43 (1976), 39.

24. *Tox.* 10, cf. 62.   25. Cf. *Theme and Variation*, 77ff.

26. For useful inventories of Lucian's variations on this subject, R. Helm, *Lucian und Menipp*, *passim*; Bompaire, *Ecrivain*, 485ff.; M. Caster, *Lucien et la pensée religieuse de son temps* (Paris 1937), 9–122.

character-type in the process – rich or poor, rhetor or magician, young or old.[27] But most of his examples still turn out as variations on the same paradox: one thing on the outside, another within. It is the opportunity for a grotesque image, rather than the prospect of reform, that brings Lucian back to it so often. Every variation will turn out as another literary hippocentaur in itself.[28] For such a writer a Roman's life, for example, is like a tragedy inside, underneath the purple and gold.[29] Lucian's own will not be much different: the *Apology* for his essay *de Mercede Conductis* is a convenient repertoire of paradox. His accusers, he argues, will point out the inconsistencies between his present way of life and his composition – rivers uphill, world upside down, palinode for the worse. They will compare him to the monkey who threw off his cloak in pursuit of a fig, talking philosophy only with his lips, saying one thing and hiding another in his heart.[30] Lucian defends himself in kind: 'you will find the two lives two octaves apart, . . . as similar as lead and silver, bronze and gold, anemone and rose, monkey and man'.[31] Such illustrations do not merely illustrate his compulsive sophistic habit of accumulating quotations, fables and proverbs; they prove his relish for slipping from one paradox into another.

The association of comic and serious in itself was particularly convenient for a writer of Lucian's interests: that in its turn offered an opportunity for paradox. The term σπουδογέλοιον ('serio-comic') tended to be associated with Cynic diatribe; Lucian himself says that Menippus γελῶν ἅμα ἔδακνεν.[32] But in fact his other and better-known 'models' often aim to blend the two: Plato was able to diversify his serious philosophical enquiry by presenting humorous repartee, and often smiles at the idiosyncrasies of the parties involved;[33] and Aristophanes makes repeated claims to be

27. Cf. *Theme and Variation*, 67–84.

28. For Lucian's use of the image in relation to his own work, cf. *Zeuxis* 12, *Prom. es* 5.

29. *Merc. Cond.* 41.   30. *Apol.* 1.   31. *Apol.* 11.

32. For the history of this combination, see M. Grant, *Ancient Rhetorical Theories of the Laughable*, University of Wisconsin Studies in Language and Literature, 21 (Madison 1924). L. Giangrande's *The Use of Spoudaiogeloion in Greek and Roman Literature* (The Hague/Paris 1972) is unsatisfactory.

33. For Platonic humour see the excellent bibliography in M. Mader, *Das Problem des Lachens und der Komödie bei Platon*, Tübinger Beiträge zur Altertumswissenschaft 47 (1977).

socially and politically useful in the midst of burlesque.[34] Each of
these authors presents a different balance between comic and
serious, and there is no one way to characterize it. But we can
suspect that in Lucian's case *some* serious material may in fact have
been selected merely for its comic (and rhetorical) possibilities, and
that in the end his balance between the two elements is much closer
to that of Aristophanes than to that of Plato. Where he uses Old
Comic material he tends to put it first and last, leaving the middle
for a virtuoso display of moralizing.[35] It is easier to juxtapose one's
authors and sources than to mix them; and in this case he is not
departing from Aristophanes' own practice in the use of *agon* and
parabasis: he is simply putting the more inventive and memorable
parts of his creations in the right place from the audience's point of
view. The listener to *Piscator* will be arrested by a swarm of angry
philosophers mimicking the *parodos* of the *Archarnians*; and he will
be left with a picture of false philosophers dangling on the end of a
fishing-line.[36] By that time he will have forgotten Lucian's
intervening tirade about the hypocrisy of philosophers;[37] it is
much the same as any of his others. When dealing with Plato, on
the other hand, Lucian's procedure is often to extend the
proportion of space available for frivolity. In *Anacharsis*, for
example, it takes him half the dialogue to set the Platonic scene;[38]
in *Nigrinus* the sheer accumulation of Platonic *politesses* comes close
to threatening the balance of the dialogue as a whole.[39] In the
literary pamphlets, comic and serious form a facile *syncrisis*: 'how
not to succeed in extempore rhetoric, and how to do so' (*Rhetorum
Praeceptor*); 'how not to write history, and how to write it' (*Historia*);
or 'how not to revive Attic words and how to do it' (*Lexiphanes*). In
Historia the balance is roughly even; in the other two it is no
surprise to find that the caricature takes up most of Lucian's
attention.

In his invectives, however, one *can* speak of satirical conviction:
here Lucian is waging cultural warfare, and he is a committed
Atticist and philhellene. We should note how often the bellettrist
attacks a cultural sham. The bitterest attack by far is over a single

---

34. See K. J. Dover, *Aristophanic Comedy* (Berkeley and Los Angeles 1972), 51 ff.
35. For the 'mechanics' of Lucian's arrangement of themes, *Theme and
Variation*, 135–66.   36. *Pisc.* 1 ff.; 47–52.
37. *Pisc.* 29–37.   38. *Anach.* 1–19.   39. *Nigr.* 6–12; 35–38.

word, *apophras*: and it is directly connected to a typical sophistic scene, in which Lucian laughed at a stupid declamation (*Pseudologista*). Another is concerned with a bibliophile who hopes to impress perhaps even Marcus Aurelius by the cultural aura of his investments (*Adversus Indoctum*); a third is about an upstart sophist (*Rhetorum Praeceptor*); a fourth about how private Roman patronage will ruin the educated man (*de Mercede Conductis*). The major pamphlets on Peregrinus and Alexander are of course primarily religious: but it is the cultural aspect of religion, rather than mere rationalism as such, that engages Lucian. Peregrinus' suicide is heralded by melodramatic but distasteful harangues at the Olympic games; and Alexander has set himself up as a contemptible Paphlagonian answer to Delphi and Eleusis.

III. Sophistic lies, cheating, falsehood

But Lucian is not so much concerned with vice as interested in its implications: cheating, deception, hypocrisy, and above all lying. All of them had literary probity; all of them allowed the opportunity for fantasy and comic paradox. And they were by no means frowned on by the sophistic movement: the λέξις ἐσχηματισμένη which Philostratus considers the real test of a sophist is in fact an exercise in pretence,[40] and Polemo, like Lucian, was keen on the tag

> ἐχθρὸς γάρ μοι κεῖνος ὁμῶς Ἀίδαο πύλῃσιν,
> ὅς χ᾽ ἕτερον μὲν κεύθῃ ἐνὶ φρεσίν, ἄλλο δὲ εἴπῃ.[41]

The *Alexander* is an extended study of deception in action.[42] However many imprecations Lucian hurls at his enemy, it is clear that he admires the sheer virtuosity of his deceptions, and recounts them with corresponding zest; and of course Alexander's tricks give him the opportunity to present a whole gallery of the gullible.[43] This charlatan does not stop at planting oracles, or disguising information in an oracular style: he has to alter the record when oracles do not turn out correctly,[44] and vary the kind of falsehoods in his own responses. He will issue an oracle full of dramatic

40. *VS* 542.   41. *Il.* 9.312f. (*ibid.*); cf. *Fugit.* 30 (adapted).
42. Not least on Lucian's own part, *Theme and Variation*, 124-7.
43. Cf. Theophrastus' δεισιδαίμων, Bompaire, *Ecrivain*, 498.
44. *Alex.* 27.

intrigue, complete with names and details, for someone who does not exist at all;[45] give out oracles in nonsense languages; or give a completely random response to a genuine question.[46] Lucian is of course equal to the task of countering such falsehoods,[47] submitting one question ('When will Alexander's trickery be caught?'), passing it off as eight under a different name, and 'planting' information which will lead to a false answer.

The *Phalaris* declamations are often dismissed as essays of a kind Lucian avoided in his mature output: a routine pair of sophistic *meletae* on a historical theme. But it is easy to miss the speaker's viewpoint: it is in fact a link between the satirist's pose and the liar's. Of course sacred diplomacy is standard fare in Second Sophist declamation, particularly in Aristides. But Lucian chooses an arch-criminal to boast of his enlightened government, his novel punishment, and his artistic elegance and piety: Phalaris is close to his own heart.[48]

The interview with a charlatan is one of Lucian's best-practised topoi: *Vitarum Auctio* is composed of no fewer than eight such encounters; the *D. Mort.* offer in the region of fifteen; *Gallus* is the most ambitious example, with the shrewd, sophisticated and versatile Pythagoras as the victim. Lucian is particularly interested in the charlatan hedging just as he is about to go on the run: Pythagoras asks Micyllus not to ask him about his taboo on eating beans (because it is bogus);[49] Toxaris is in no hurry to discuss the Scythians' treatment of their fathers (because he does not want to talk about anthropophagy in a dialogue on friendship);[50] Tychiades does not know why only parasites are right to take other people's property, and quickly changes the subject to the other virtues of 'parasitic'![51] Liars, too, are naturally caught out: when the tyrant Megapenthes is accused of murders and sexual violence, he admits to the former, but modestly wants to hide the latter.[52] Or Euphorbus tries a little exaggeration, claiming to have killed Patroclus instead of merely wounding him,[53] while the *Miles gloriosus* Leontichus protests that at least *some* of his typically tall story was true.[54]

45. *Alex.* 50.   46. *Alex.* 51, 53; 50.   47. *Alex.* 54.
48. *Phal.* 1.11f.   49. *Gall.* 18.   50. *Tox.* 9.
51. *Paras.* 22.   52. *Katapl.* 27.   53. *Gall.* 17.
54. *D. Meretr.* 13.6.

Not only is Lucian a connoisseur of charlatans: he likes to beat them at their own game, and go one better.[55] A substantial proportion of his output is concerned with refined fraud of one sort or another, as is clear even from such titles as *Pseudologista*, *Philopseudes*, or *Pseudomantis*. For *pseudos*, as for so much else, he is ready with respectable precedent: he himself names Homer, Ctesias and Iambulus in the preface of *Verae Historiae*; and in *Philopseudes* he adds Herodotus as well.[56] To indulge in lies after their fashion was to link two of his chief interests, *mimesis* and fantasy. Lucian tells his readers how to do it:

λέγοντος γάρ τινος τῶν μεγαλοτόλμων τούτων ποιητῶν, ὡς γένοιτό ποτε τρικέφαλος καὶ ἑξάχειρ ἄνθρωπος, ἂν τὸ πρῶτον ταῦτα ἀπραγμόνως ἀποδέξῃ μὴ ἐξετάσας εἰ δυνατόν, ἀλλὰ πιστεύσας, εὐθὺς ἀκολούθως ἂν ἐπάγοι τὰ λοιπά, ὡς καὶ ὀφθαλμοὺς ὁ αὐτὸς εἶχεν ἓξ καὶ ὦτα ἓξ καὶ φωνὰς τρεῖς ἅμα ἠφίει καὶ ἤσθιε διὰ τριῶν στομάτων καὶ δακτύλους τριάκοντα εἶχεν, οὐχ ὥσπερ ἕκαστος ἡμῶν δέκα ἐν ἀμφοτέραις ταῖς χερσί.

If one of those adventurous poets were to say that there was once a man with three heads and six hands, and you accepted this without enquiring if it were possible and simply believed him, he would follow it up immediately with all the rest – that this same man had six eyes and six ears, spoke with three voices and ate with three mouths, and had thirty fingers, unlike us with our ten on two hands.[57]

And in *Verae Historiae* Lucian has carried out his own instructions.[58] A good example is his own adventure inside the whale: his first concern is to spend time on the credible domestic details of his desert island – a man and a boy marooned inside twenty-seven years before, and eking out a modest living from market-gardening! Only after all this has been unobtrusively established at some length do we hear of the monsters in the whale: Saltfishers, Tritongoats, Tunnyheads and the rest. The details may be carefully arbitrary (the Saltfishers live at the west end – the tail!), or they may be deduced. The Tritongoats are not so unjust as the other races: one is left to infer that because they are part human they are not so evil as the wholly marine compounds.[59] Part of Lucian's technique is undoubtedly his knowing where to stop: he

---

55. Bompaire (n.1), 694–8.
56. *VH* 1.3.; *Philops.* 2.
57. *Herm.* 74.
58. 1.37ff.
59. Thanks to a suggestion of Professor Winkler's, I am now convinced that these creatures, half-man and half-swordfish, had more sinister and obscene preoccupations.

fills in three sides of the whale and the interior: but the eastern part, at the mouth, is largely uninhabited, since it is subject to tidal inundation!

Lucian's narrative technique is well equal to the task of lying πιθανῶς τε καὶ ἐναληθῶς.[60] After his solemn declaration that everything is a lie, he proceeds with a perfectly conventional voyage narrative. It is only after two paragraphs and a routine storm that he and his crew so much as encounter a footprint of Heracles![61] He is also fond of strategic *aposiopesis* in a tall story:

Ὁπότε γὰρ ἐξ Αἰγύπτου ἐπανήειν οἴκαδε . . . καλῶς ἔχειν ἡγησάμην ἐν παράπλῳ πειραθῆναι τοῦ χρηστηρίου καί τι περὶ τῶν μελλόντων συμβουλεύσασθαι τῷ θεῷ –

'On my way back from Egypt . . . I decided to try the oracle on the way past and consult the god about the future . . .'[62]

And in *Alexander* he even provides a novella without a beginning or end:

ὁ γὰρ πέμψας σε τέθηκεν ὑπὸ τοῦ γείτονος Διοκλέους τήμερον, λῃστῶν ἐπαχθέντων Μάγνου καὶ Κέλερος καὶ Βουβάλου, οἳ καὶ ἤδη δέδενται ληφθέντες.

'The man who sent you died today at the hand of his neighbour Diocles, assisted by the bandits Magnus, Celer and Bubalus, who have already been captured and imprisoned.'[63]

Not a little of the charm of Lucian's lies is to be found in their whimsy; when discussing his fellow liars, he makes Aristophanes truthful (like himself!), but presents Ctesias and Herodotus as arch-villains;[64] and faced with the chance of visiting Nephelokok-kugia in person, he is prevented because of the weather![65] Or his Homer gets a number of details wrong, including the number of the Gates of Sleep, but can still oblige with an appropriate inscription in honour of the author himself![66] In particular Lucian is well able to manipulate ordinary statements in order to pass off extraordinary ones. He can point out a wrong detail as unusual, as when he tells us that it is unnatural for the sea to fall apart: but he mentions without comment the bridge which goes across to the other side.[67] *Philopseudes* provides similar opportunities: 'I used to be more incredulous than you about that sort of thing . . . but the

60. *VH* 1.2.
61. *Ibid.* 5–7.
62. *Philops.* 38.
63. *Alex.* 52.
64. *VH* 1.29; 2.32.
65. *VH* 1.29.
66. *VH* 2.34; 2.28.
67. *VH* 2.43.

first time I saw the foreign stranger flying – he was a Hyperborean, he said – I was convinced and won over after holding out for a long time.'[68] Lucian has presented this nonsense as if the nationality of the flyer might be disputed – but not the fact that he flew. A flourish of erudition can bring about the same ends: Charon and Hermes can put Pelion on top of Ossa with no more than a flourish of Homer.[69] Or Lucian himself can make a casual observation:

θέντες (τὴν ναῦν) ἐπὶ τῶν κλάδων, πετάσαντες τὰ ἱστία καθάπερ ἐν θαλάττῃ ἐπλέομεν τοῦ ἀνέμου προωθοῦντος ἐπισυρόμενοι· ἔνθα δὴ καὶ τὸ Ἀντιμάχου τοῦ ποιητοῦ ἔπος ἐπεισῆλθέ με – φησὶν γάρ που κἀκεῖνος·
  Τοῖσιν δ' ὑλήεντα διὰ πλόον ἐρχομένοισιν.

Putting (our ship) on the branches and spreading sail as if on the sea we sailed along, struck by the forward thrust of the wind: it was then that that line of the poet Antimachus occurred to me – for he says somewhere:
  'and as they sailed upon their wooded way'.[70]

Antimachus is thus vindicated, and the fact of Lucian's own voyage is unquestioned. There are even quite *ordinary* goings-on in Scythia: when Lonchates arrives to cut off the enemy king's head, he has to lead up to his task from mundane beginnings, with a routine diplomatic note from the Scythians about grazing rights on the border with the Sauromatae![71]

Lucian is also able to manipulate audience reactions to a story: when Icaromenippus explains that his wings have no wax like those of Icarus, his friend begins to believe that he really has come back from heaven;[72] and when Mnesippus has to listen to Toxaris' tallest story, he concedes:

Πάνυ τραγικά, ὦ Τόξαρι, καὶ μύθοις ὅμοια· καὶ ἵλεως μὲν ὁ Ἀκινάκης καὶ ὁ Ἄνεμος εἴεν, οὓς ὤμοσας· εἰ δ' οὖν (Fritzsche) τις ἀπιστοίη αὐτοῖς, οὐ πάνυ μεμπτὸς εἶναι δόξειεν ἄν.

Most impressive, Toxaris, even fabulous; so help me the gods Scimitar and Wind, the gods you swore by; but if one were to disbelieve them, I do not suppose one would be altogether open to criticism.[73]

One piece in particular vindicates Lucian's role as a sophistic liar. That is the practical joke which Galen reports him as having played.[74] He had forged a treatise under the name of Heraclitus,

---

68. *Philops.* 14.   69. *Charon* 4.   70. *VH* 2.42.
71. *Tox.* 49.   72. *Icar.* 3.   73. *Tox.* 56.
74. G. Strohmaier, 'Übersehenes zur Biographie Lukians', *Philologus* 120 (1976), 117–22.

then duped an eminent literary figure into commenting on it. We may adapt Bompaire's and Reardon's terminology to take account of such *jeux d'esprit*: for Lucian falsehood offers the chance of *création pseudatrice*; it also offers the chance of *pseudos appliqué*.

IV. Sophistic manipulation: Mimesis

Lucian's output has to be read in terms of his models, and he introduces several ironic disclaimers to remind his audiences of the fact:

Ταῦτά σοι καὶ αὐτὸς ἀπειλῶ, οὐ μὰ τὸν Δία τῷ Ἀρχιλόχῳ εἰκάζων ἐμαυτόν – πόθεν; πολλοῦ γε καὶ δέω . . .
I too am threatening you, not of course comparing myself to Archilochus – how could I – I fall far short of him. . . .[75]

πρὸς Φιλίου μή με κορυβαντιᾶν ὑπολάβητε μηδὲ τἀμὰ εἰκάζειν τοῖς ἐκείνου . . .
For heaven's sake don't think I've taken leave of my senses and am comparing myself to (Herodotus) . . .[76]

Since Bompaire's *Lucian écrivain* we have had what amounts to a directory of literary models, not only for Lucian himself but for the Sophistic as a whole. The almost oppressive complexity of his borrowings, and the simplicity of their results, have long been a cause of impatience. Because sophistic writers live in the past, it is easy to assume that they have no right to do so, that they fail to re-create it convincingly, and that they have nothing to add to it; that they can only follow school habits indiscriminately, in this case with mildly amusing results. But it is necessary to come to terms with a sophist's outlook. In fact he is no more hide-bound by traditional literary forms and materials than Hellenistic poets; he can manipulate his models as he pleases to the same end of sophisticated entertainment; and it is perhaps unfair to pass judgment on intellectuals who had no political present or future, but whose past was actively underwritten by the very régime which set limits to their freedom.

Lucian lays claim to several literary specialities: in particular the use of Old Comedy, Plato and Diatribe.[77] In Plato's case there was

75. *Pseudolog.* 2.   76. *Herod.* 6.
77. *Bis. Acc.* 33. Professor Winkler draws my attention to Plut. *Quaest. Conv.* 7.8 (711 b–c) on the practice of reading aloud Platonic dialogues at symposia, with roles distributed between several actors.

no problem: the dialogue was as ideally suited for the recitation conditions as the sophistic λόγος; of diatribe we know little, but again there were no problems with a basically 'conversational' medium. But Aristophanes did present a difficulty: how to adapt situations conceived in visual and dramatic terms for use in public recitation.[78]

It might seem unfair and pedantic to compare Lucian and Aristophanes at all:[79] it is conventional to see the former as a pale shadow of the latter.[80] But in the first instance we have to point out two hidden factors: we have a much smaller sample of Aristophanes than we appear to have of Lucian, and it may be that the repetitions which operate so obviously against the latter would also have told against Aristophanes, had he been represented by a wider range of works. The second hidden factor is that the second-century readership would almost certainly have preferred Menander to Aristophanes: this is the period of the *Comparatio Menandri et Aristophanis*.[81] What Lucian gains in smoothness he undoubtedly loses in boisterousness. Bompaire has already implied that the rhetorical tirades in the Menippean pieces are an unconvincing equivalent to the cut-and-thrust of an Aristophanic *agon*;[82] and references to calls of nature and urgent sexual needs lose their propriety in the second-century salon. One cannot fairly blame Lucian because the ways of pantomime and serious intellectual entertainment had now parted company. But we should look at what he has put in place of such a combination. Aristophanes' blend of Socrates and Old Comedy in the *Clouds* is on his own terms: but we have to learn to see Lucian's blend instead in terms of the imitation of Old Comedy in Plato's *Symposium*:[83] as refined prose dialogue with all its attendant restrictions.

78. See still A. R. Bellinger, 'Lucian's Dramatic Technique', *YCS* I (1928) 3–40. Reardon, *Courants*, 166ff. well stresses Lucian's capacities for the dramatic. But it is not so low on the Sophistic movement's order of priorities as R. makes out; the taste for tragedy was by no means confined to the lost plays of Nicetes or Scopelian; few forms practised by the sophistic could escape its influence.

79. For the borrowings, I. P. Lederberger, 'Lukian und die altattische Komödie' (Progr. Einsiedeln 1905), 14–82: Bompaire, *Ecrivain*, index II *s.v.*

80. E.g., Helm, *LM, passim.*   81. *Mor.* 853aff.

82. Bompaire, *Ecrivain*, 252ff.

83. *Symp.* 189c–193d. Of course anything was tolerated in sophistic invective; one suspects however that such works as Lucian's *Pseudologista* would have been circulated privately.

One example will show how the two entertainers respond to their respective milieux. When Aristophanes' Trygaeus mounts to heaven on the dung-beetle, he has of course to discourage it from being tempted back to earth, by calling on the man in the Piraeus to postpone his call of nature.[84] He has then to call to the operator of the *ekkyklema* to be careful,[85] and inevitably he risks losing control and feeding the beetle himself. Aristophanes, then, is mechanically obscene; and he also breaks the dramatic illusion rather blatantly – there is not much point in keeping it, since the audience can see the apparatus that is carrying the hero up to heaven. Lucian on the other hand conducts his fantasy under quite different conditions. In *Icaromenippus*, instead of far-flung calls in mid-air to the μηχανοποιός, we have a polite and urbane conversation between Menippus and Empedocles;[86] and in the other scene which imitates this passage of the *Peace*, Charon and Hermes are busy moving Ossa on top of Pelion with the minimum of inconvenience: since the audience cannot *see* the actors on the *ekkyklema*, the illusion is intact.[87] Charon does share Trygaeus' fears, and comments that the mountain is a μηχανή, duly alluding to Aristophanes' break in the illusion. Hermes points out that they have done the job ῥαδίως ἅμα καὶ ποιητικῶς.[88] We might add καὶ σοφιστικῶς. No-one need suggest that Aristophanes has been 'improved'. But Lucian's audience could go away without having seen their hero lumbering up to heaven; instead they encountered gods who 'knew their Aristophanes'. What the dialogue has lost in spontaneity it has gained in refinement.

In the course of identifying Lucian's sources it is easy to leave another task undone: we have to stand back and contemplate the relationship between the authors he employs in any one piece. It is often misguided to regard the result as mere pastiche: Second Sophistic authors are able to produce new and often startling relationships within their literary past; and that has to be taken into account. Where there is an obvious Socratic set-piece which Lucian has used as the introduction, he will undermine it by ensuring that the subject-matter which ensues has somehow 'gone wrong': the *Toxaris* is a περὶ φιλίας: but it consists of two blocks of (trivial) stories, one broadly based on the Attic orators, the other

84. *Pax* 164ff.   85. *Ibid.* 174ff.   86. *Icar.* 13f.
87. *Charon* 3ff.   88. *Ibid.* 4.

on Herodotus:[89] both are as much at variance with their philosophic introduction as they are with each other. It is a particular refinement of Lucian's Platonic 'jeu des fausses politesses'[90] for the Scythian to postpone the discussion of (father-eating) Scythian 'friends' till later[91] – and to decline to cut out his Greek friend's tongue after all!

On one occasion Platonic dialogue takes Lucian to court, where he complains that he has been shut up with Eupolis and Aristophanes, and even with the ancient Cynic dog Menippus.[92] What is the result of this mixture, and how successful is it? As usual Lucian has a preference for any incongruous combination, and a number of dialogues can be considered in this light. The simplest case is perhaps *Iuppiter Confutatus*. The frame dialogue clearly depends on the conventions of Comedy: a philosopher is having an interview with Zeus, and the subject itself is dealt with in Aristophanes' *Clouds* (do the Olympian gods exist or not?).[93] But the conventions of the dialogue, and a fair amount of the argument itself, belong to Plato, in particular to the short *Ion*,[94] in which the poet is shown to be nothing more than a link in the chain of inspiration from the listener back to the gods. In Lucian's version Zeus himself is shown to be nothing more than a link in the chain of authority from men back to the Fates. And now that he is one of the partners in the dialogue, he can be put in the position of condemning himself out of his own mouth. These are not the only constituents: Lucian has also brought the dialogue up-to-date, by employing the contrast of Cyno-Stoic and Epicurean arguments; and the fact that these had been current for so many centuries does not detract from their relevance and topicality in the second century. The mixture of sources also continues elsewhere: Lucian does not deal in *Iuppiter Confutatus* with the substance of the *Ion* itself – the problem of inspiration of the poet and rhapsode, and whether they really possess knowledge on their own account. This topic reappears instead in the most unlikely 'Platonic' interview with Hesiod himself,[95] and so the game of contaminations goes on.

There are much more complex examples in which Lucian is no less fluent. In *Verae Historiae* 12–20 a battle is fought between the

89. *Studies in Lucian's Comic Fiction*, 12–24.
90. Bompaire, *Ecrivain*, 312.   91. *Tox.* 62, cf. 10.   92. *Bis Acc.* 33.
93. *Nub.* 365–426.   94. 533dff.; 535eff.   95. *Dissertatio cum Hesiodo*.

forces of the moon and the sun.[96] The levies on each side are as prodigious in kind as they are in size and numbers: Lucian has mobilized his whole repertoire of hippocamps and tragelaphs for the occasion. But this is not just a matter of Gargantuan fantasy; it is a pastiche of several identifiable authors, and there may well be others we miss in the present state of knowledge. The fantastic animals themselves are a blend of two sources: Old Comedy, where such curious compounds are of course a matter of routine, and the *Batrachomuiomachia*, whose miniature mock-Epic is largely concerned with a catalogue of similar compounds. But to these easily assimilable sources Lucian adds the narrative mannerisms of conventional historians. Ctesias or Herodotus could find room for flying snakes from time to time; but here there are also formal military manoeuvres from Xenophon, who is less accommodating; and even a formal peace treaty from Thucydides.[97] This is the most unlikely blend of all: a Thucydidean *Batrachomuiomachia*. But to list the sources is not enough: they interact with each other, and the fantastic elements are disciplined in a way in which Old Comedy is not, while Thucydides in particular can never be quite the same again. What is lost in the blending? If there is any loss of vitality in Lucian's fantasy, there is a gain in smoothness.[98] The reader must decide for himself whether the enlivening of Xenophon compensates for the 'toning down' of Aristophanes; but he must at least ask.

V. A sophist's perspective: past and present

Lucian's virtuosity in the use of past literature has often been taken to imply some lack of involvement with the present. The sophist who sets out to re-create the Ilyssus and the Ceramicus is accused of taking leave of absence from his own time. Such a problem is always complicated by the temptation to pass moral as well as literary judgment on archaism, to dismiss it as a symptom of sterile literary imagination, and feel the need to assert the 'relevance' of

96. For the texture of this passage, see A. Stengel, 'de Luciani Veris Historiis' (diss. Rostock Berlin 1911), 22–30.

97. L. Hermann, *AC* 18 (1949), 359ff.

98. Cf. Lucian's own argument in *Zeuxis* 2: ἁρμονία is as much a part of craftsmanship as is novelty.

an author to his own age. The problem should not have arisen at all in the Second Sophistic: literate aristocracies in Asia Minor relived their past in the present not just with complacency or conviction, but with intensity;[99] and educated authors could and did acquire the linguistic and literary skills necessary to exploit the common ground between the two.

Sometimes, it has to be said, Lucian did not have to try very hard to blend conditions of the Second Century A.D. and the Fifth Century B.C. Take the case of the *Rhetorum Praeceptor*: despite the narrowing of sophistic interests after Isocrates, Lucian's picture shows that not much has changed between Plato's *Phaedrus* and Philostratus; and the allegory of Prodicus, that standard moral paradigm, has now been adapted as an advertizement for sophistic education. At the same time Aristophanes' *Logos*-Debate has now become a contest between two new kinds of *Logoi*: the carefully prepared speech and the impressively improvised nonsense.[100] Again, when Lucian talks about the Parthian Wars he is once more up to the minute. But once more the situation is close to situations in the most distant past.[101] In the Fifth Century itself Thucydides had taken a dim view of his predecessors; and there was now plenty to condemn in the Alexander-historians. To laugh at reporters of the Parthian war was an opportunity to deal with present-day charlatans in a way which applied equally well to the tall-story-tellers of five centuries before. Theophrastus' λογοποιός had won verbal victories by land and sea – in the Stoa. Lucian has only to transfer the scene from Athens to Corinth, when one of his Parthian historians wins a victory in Armenia – on the way from the Kraneion to Lerna.[102] Theophrastus' same rumour-monger had quoted unverifiable sources to the effect that Polyperchon and the king had won a victory, and Cassandrus had been taken prisoner; Lucian's Parthic Historians – equally unverifiable – simply bring the details up-to-date.[103] The λογοποιός had made pathetic laments for Cassandrus; Lucian's dupe offers a similar display for Severianus.[104]

99. See now E. L. Bowie, *Past and Present* 46 (1970), 1–41 (= *Studies in Ancient Society*, ed. M. I. Finley (London 1974), 166–209).

100. *Rhet. Prec.* 9–25.

101. *Contra* Baldwin (n.1), 75–95.

102. Theophrastus *Char.* 8.6, *Quomodo Historia* 29.

103. Theophrastus *Char.* 8.6.   104. *Quomodo Historia* 25f.

Even the sequence which most obviously sets out to imitate a classic is never excluded from having some contemporary relevance. When Lucian faces the philosophers about to stone him, he is obviously imitating Aristophanes' *Acharnians*, and casting himself in the role of Dicaeopolis.[105] But it is worthwhile to note that he also remembers one of his own teachers for taking a similar stand: Demonax had offered to allow the Athenians to stone him, and by so doing disarmed the opposition.[106] We have simply to bear in mind that the art of coping with public disorder had not changed a great deal in seven centuries; and that such situations could be assimilated all the more easily as a result.

It must be stressed that Lucian is not in any way exceptional even in his approach to religion in the second century. He does not embody a one-man crusade of rationalism and outspokenness against the abuses of his day: several of the Greek novelists are just as rationalistic in their approach to the gods and their dupes.[107] And the Middle Platonic *daimones* are a small omission in a corpus which includes *Peregrinus* and *Alexander*; as it so happens, Lucian does not make much of the original *daimon* of Socrates either.[108] And the workings of Providence as felt in the second century are certainly ridiculed (even if they do not receive the attention Caster demanded for them);[109] so is a problem as topical as the decline of oracles in mainland Greece.[110]

It is difficult, or rather unnecessary, to pronounce on the 'relevance' of Lucian's treatment of the hypocritical philosopher.[111] That this figure had been a tiresome cliché since Socrates there can be no doubt; and that fact in itself was surely one of its chief attractions for sophistic rhetoricians, always on the alert

105. *Pisc.* 1–39 (Lederberger, *L. und die altattische Komödie*, 33–6).

106. *Dem.* 11.

107. See my *Eros Sophistes: Ancient Novelists at Play*, American Classical Studies (forthcoming), in particular chs. 3 (Achilles Tatius), 4 (Heliodorus), and 5 (Longus).

108. The lunar *daimon* in *Icar.* 14 might just be taken as a topical allusion to Middle-Platonic *daimones*. Caster, *Pensée*, 223f. wrongly suggests that the necessary literary authority was lacking: Lucian was certainly free to exploit such a text as Pl. *Symp.* 202eff.

109. Caster, *Pensée*, 175ff. claims that Lucian does not exploit the proofs of Providence as evinced in animals; but in fact *Gallus* 27 (human vice contrasted with animal virtues) comes close to it; and what about *Musc. Enc.*?

110. *Icar.* 24 touches on the same problem as Plutarch's *de Defectu Oraculorum*.

111. Bompaire, *Ecrivain*, 485–9.

against the one group who could attack their own basic integrity, not without cause. But such philosophers did undoubtedly exist in the early Empire, and the conflict between worldliness and idealism did generate real divisions. One notes the blind but apparently spontaneous admiration which the Younger Pliny displays for Euphrates;[112] and the evidence, dubious as it may be, for the latter's quarrel with Apollonius of Tyana.[113] Nor did the matter end there: three centuries later Jerome was still able to invest such worn-out clichés with as much vehemence as they had ever had for pagans.[114]

The real world, then, and that of the sophist's imagination could be made to converge and coincide. But that is only half the picture, and the other half must also be noted: if the sophists lived in an illusory past, the essential features of that past were ludicrously up-dated into the present. No literary haven was safe from the incursion of the Sophistic and its mannerisms. Epigraphy has recently brought to light a new example: in *Deorum Concilium* Lucian presents a debate in which Zeus proposes the expulsion of immigrant gods improperly registered. Since Lucian's attempts to portray the religious experience of his own century are held to be so half-hearted, it is usual to relate the scene to textbook common-places and leave the matter there.[115] But an inscription discovered in 1966 in the Roman Market at Athens contains an *epistula* of Marcus Aurelius probably just prior to 176, to the effect that fraudulent registration for priesthoods was to be prevented.[116] The pressure-groups among the gods are not dissimilar to those of Herodes Atticus and his enemies. It is a fatal trap to read the whole of Lucian as a diary of Herodes,[117] but the analogy in this case can be allowed to stand. Whether or not Lucian's dialogue dates from

---

112. *Ep.* 1.10.

113. Apollonius, *Epp.* 1–8, 51, 53.

114. See D. S. Wiesen, *St. Jerome as a Satirist, a Study of Christian Thought and Letters* (Ithaca 1964), 65–112.

115. Caster, *Pensée*, 339–43 (citing Cic., *de Nat. Deor.* 3).

116. See J. R. Oliver, *Marcus Aurelius, Aspects of Civic and Cultural Policy in the East, Hesperia* Suppl. 13 (1970), 76. It is not enough simply to say that here as in *J. Trag.* 7ff. 'Lucian transfers the problems of Greek cities to heaven': his audience or readers would also interpret πλουτίνδην κελεύεις ἀλλὰ μὴ ἀριστίνδην καθίζειν in the light of Solon's reforms.

117. Cf. J. Schwartz, *Biographie de Lucien de Samosate, Collection Latomus* 83 (1965), 32, 133.

as late as the 170s, it is at least comparable, since dissatisfaction had presumably been simmering for some time. In an age which clearly prized its archaic institutions at all costs, this satire was certainly 'relevant'.

Nor should we be in any doubt that Lucian's most timeless characters are in fact second-century sophists at heart: Zeus opens a speech with a tag from Demosthenes, a favourite expedient, as he points out, for extempore orators; and he refuses to destroy the Porch with its indispensable reminders of Marathon and Cynegirus, inevitable inspiration for declaimers.[118] Lucian's underworld is no longer a place for poetic competitions, as it had been in the *Frogs*; it is now a council-chamber for the promulgation of decrees, or for the sophistic debates of Alexander and Hannibal.[119] The latter even points out that although he was not a pupil of professor Aristotle before he made his conquests, at least he has learned Greek down in Hades! Nor does Scythia fail to produce a sophist with a competent ecphrasis at the ready;[120] and Jesus Christ is also a member of the same profession.[121] So is the household cock in Lucian's *Gallus* (as he reluctantly admits): the movement has taken over and transformed the pathetic fallacy.[122]

A typical example of such 'transpositions' of sophistry is Lucian's treatment of Proteus,[123] himself a favourite 'sophistic' figure.[124] Homer's version is in the background, and it is simple enough: Menelaus has to catch the god, but he is something of an illusionist and a sorcerer; the discussion is simply about Menelaus' own fate and that of his fellows.[125] But Lucian makes Proteus instead a rather erudite sophist and charlatan: he tries to divert Menelaus' attention with a favourite school analogy, the polypous; but his pupil still cannot see how the same deity can be fire and water at the same time![126] In the end this is a variant on one of Lucian's favourite jokes, the 'half-burnt figure';[127] but the myth has been brought up-to-date in a significant way.

Lucian has a particular skill in placing classical authors *in person* into his own text, or even each others'. The all-time greats are ready to be summoned at will, and treated on familiar terms:

118. *J. Trag.* 15; 32.

119. *Neky.* 19f.; *D. Mort.* 12, 13, 25.

120. *Tox.* 8.

121. *Peregr.* 13.

122. *Gall.* 18.

123. *D. Mar.* 4.

124. *Dem. Enc.* 23; Philostratus, *Vit. Apol.* 1.4.

125. *Od.* 4.441–592.

126. *D. Mar.* 4.3.

127. *Theme and Variation*, index III *s.v.*

καὶ σὺ βάλλε, ὦ Πλάτων . . . κεκμήκατε, ὦ Ἐπίκουρε καὶ Ἀρίστιππε; καὶ μὴν οὐκ ἐχρῆν . . . Ἀριστότελες, ἐπισπούδασον.
It's your turn to throw now, Plato! . . . Don't tell me you're tired, Epicurus and Aristippus! . . . Hurry up, Aristotle![128]

And Hesiod is perhaps the last person one expects to find as an interlocutor discussing his own works. It is a considerable step from the complacent rhapsode in Plato's *Ion* to the complacent poet cross-referring to his colleague Homer and issuing such an instruction as

ἀνάγνωθι, ὦ οὗτος, τὰ Ἔργα μου καὶ τὰς Ἡμέρας.
I'd advise you to read my *Works and Days*.[129]

Even the gods themselves fall back on curriculum authors, listening to performances from Hesiod's *Theogony* and Pindar's first *Hymn* at dinner; the heroes in the Isles of the Blest have Homer and the lyric poets, with the latter providing live performances.[130]

I conclude this section with two longer illustrations of how Lucian can exploit this perpetual past-cum-present. The weakness of a one-sided approach to this question is nowhere better demonstrated than in the two most characteristic linguistic pamphlets.[131] Baldwin has argued that such works are concerned with the burning issues of the later second century, and stresses the literary coteries to which they must be related; no-one is likely to deny as much. But the '*mimesis* approach' he rejects is an essential complement in both cases. The argument of *Pseudologistes* may be paraphrased as follows:[132]

'I am going to treat you worse than Archilochus would have done, even with the help of Simonides and Hipponax' (1–2).
'But here is Menander's prologue Elenchus to tell the audience all about you' (4).
'Now I am going to tell the rest (with the unacknowledged help of Demosthenes)' (10),
'leaving your tongue and beard to complain about your secret crimes' (25).
'Now here are some worldly-wise tags to make you wish you'd never asked about *apophras*' (32).

---

128. *Pisc.* 1. 129. *Hes.* 6. 130. *Icar.* 27; *VH* 2.15.
131. *Studies in L.'s Comic Fiction*, 3; 41–59.
132. For an analysis in terms of Lucian's habits of arrangement, see *Theme and Variation*, 160f.

Here, for the benefit no doubt of the illiterate sophist, Lucian names some of his authors as he goes along; all of them are firmly in the past, and on nodding terms; and it is only to avoid monotony that he does not summon forth Archilochus and Demosthenes in person as well as *Elenchus*.

The *Lexiphanes* is much more subtle. Baldwin rightly emphasizes its connection with the Ulpianists,[133] but with this approach it is easy to miss an important parallel in the fourth century B.C. – available, as it happens, through the same Athenaeus who supplies information on the Ulpianists themselves.[134] It is very hard to believe that persons with the level of education required to enjoy *Lexiphanes* in the first place would have been unaware of the passage of Straton's *Phoenicides*, in which a cook who issues directions in the language of Epic fails to make himself understood.[135] Lucian has transposed the situation, so that the culinary pedant of classical times has now become the classical pedant of his own. His extraordinary speech is a reminder that Lucian had real skill in any kind of gobbledegook: this is fantasy and falsehood translated into linguistic terms, and there is not much difference between Straton's hyperarchaised sheep and oxen and Lucian's:

καὶ ὄϊν δὲ ὅλον ἱπνοκαῆ εἴχομεν καὶ βοὸς λειπογνώμονος κωλῆν.
And we had a whole sheep barbecued, and hind-quarters of an edentulous ox.[136]

> οὐδ' ἄρα θύεις ῥηξίχθον'; οὐκ, ἔφην ἐγώ.
> βοῦν εὐρυμέτωπον; οὐ θύω βοῦν, ἄθλιε.
> μῆλα θυσιάζεις ἄρα; μὰ Δί' ἐγὼ μὲν οὔ.

'Not I,' I replied. 'No broad-browed ox?' 'I'm sacrificing no oxen, idiot.' 'Then you are immolating wethers?' 'Good Lord no, not I.'[137]

The forged treatise of Heraclitus also illustrates the relationship of past and present in Lucian: a competent forgery of an author eight centuries old is still a matter of topical interest in Galen's discussion of medical forgery.[138]

---

133. Baldwin, *Studies in L.*, 50–3.
134. *Deipnosophistae* 9. 382c.
135. *CAF* III. p. 361 κ.
136. *Lex.* 6, tr. A. M. Harmon, *LCL* v, p. 303.
137. Straton *loc. cit.*, II, 19–21 (tr. D. L. page, *LCL* Select Papyri III, p. 264).
138. Strohmaier (n. 74).

VI. A sophistic personality

Many of the foregoing traits can be illustrated from Lucian's handling of his own character and literary persona. His interest in both falsehood and paradox should be borne in mind when one reads his biographical excursuses. We are asked to believe that he abandoned sculpture for rhetoric after a day, that he abandoned rhetoric for philosophy around the age of forty, that he produced a mixture of prose and verse, that he mixed Comedy, Satyric drama, Eupolis and Aristophanes, and then added Menippus.[139] The whole picture is a pastiche of half-truths. It is of course a blatant and knowing misrepresentation that he wrote in a mixture of prose and verse. In the dialogues there is nothing more than the most perfunctory exchanges of quotations, and that in a very few works, where they are most carefully 'prepared' within the text itself.[140] It is scarcely very convincing either that he wrote σατυρικόν: he did not as far as we know write Satyr-plays, or anything like them, nor are satyrs even very conspicuous as comic characters in the rest of his work.[141] More spurious still is the claim that he abandoned rhetoric for philosophy; still less did he ever abandon law-courts and τυράννων κατηγορίας, which are rife throughout the extant works. And he certainly did not invent satiric dialogue either, although he may have been the first to mass-produce it in sufficient quantity to claim it as his own characteristic product.[142] We can explain most of Lucian's misstatements in terms of the tendencies already discussed: σατυρικόν may well be included simply because of its incongruity – Dialogue wants nothing to do with drunken satyrs. Conversions as such are a sensational enough rhetorical gesture, and they have ample precedent. Lucian's statement may be largely dictated by his *mise en scène* (Cratinus' *Pytine*); or by the wish to picture his own works as a grotesque creation, neither one thing nor another.

But Lucian does reveal himself to a considerable degree. He has

139. For general scepticism, Bompaire, *Ecrivain*, 528–32; Baldwin, *Studies in L.*, 12–20; *Theme and Variation*, 80ff., and also my remarks against the approach of Schwartz's 'Biographie', *AJPh* 97 (1976), 262–75.

140. Bompaire, *Ecrivain*, 560.

141. Cf. *Theme and Variation*, 101f.

142. *Theme and Variation*, 168–72 (comparison with Dio Chrysostom's second *Basilikos* and Plutarch's *Gryllos*).

not left us with the neurotic diaries of Aristides (though the one dream he does offer in *Somnium* is perhaps revealing enough).[43] Nor do we have to strain to read between the lines in Lucian, as we do in Philostratus. He is particularly sensitive about rapid success, especially of fellow orientals;[144] and he is particularly sensitive to criticism or attacks on his own culture.[145] He sees himself as the man of taste, and assumes that his own addressees see him likewise: his most characteristic poses are to be seen in *Pseudologistes* and *Peregrinus*,[146] where he is among that part of the audience who laugh at the pathetic displays of rhetorical melodrama and incompetence.

Lucian clearly enjoyed indulging his own indignation, and expected his audiences to enjoy it too. His frequent self-irony should not be missed: this sophist at least knew perfectly well when he was overdoing things:

ΠΑΡΡΗΣΙΑΔΗΣ: Μισαλαζών εἰμι καὶ μισογόης καὶ μισοψευδὴς καὶ μισότυφος καὶ μισῶ πᾶν τὸ τοιουτῶδες εἶδος τῶν μιαρῶν ἀνθρώπων.
ΦΙΛΟΣΟΦΙΑ: Ἡράκλεις, πολυμισῆ τινα μέτει τὴν τέχνην.
PARRHESIADES:
I am a charlatan-hater and a cheat-hater and a lie-hater and an extravagance-hater and a hater of all those sorts of villany.
PHILOSOPHY:
Goodness, you follow a hateful profession![147]

And he knew that he was protesting too much in *Nigrinus* or *Convivium*:

Οὗτος ἀνὴρ οὐ παύσεται τήμερον πρός με πολλῇ τῇ σκηνῇ καὶ τῇ τραγῳδίᾳ χρώμενος.
This man will never stop trying all his stage-sets and tragedy on me today![148]

Θρύπτῃ ταῦτα, ὦ Λυκῖνε. ἀλλ᾽ οὔτι γε πρὸς ἐμὲ οὕτως ποιεῖν ἐχρῆν, ὃς ἀκριβῶς πολὺ πλέον ἐπιθυμοῦντά σε εἰπεῖν οἶδα ἢ ἐμὲ ἀκοῦσαι.
You know where to take your news, Lycinus: but you didn't have to strike that pose to me, for I know that you are much keener to tell me than I am to listen.[149]

The pose is taken over directly from Pl. *Phaedr.* 228aff.: but Phaedrus is at least only a lover of λόγοι: Lycinus presents

143. *Somnium seu Vita* 5–16.
144. E.g. *Pseudolog.* 19, cf. *Podagra* 265–307; *Rhet. Prec.* 24.
145. *Pseudolog.; pro Lapsu.*   146. *Pseudolog.* 5–7; *Peregr.* 3–7.
147. *Pisc.* 20.   148. *Nigr.* 12.   149. *Conv.* 4.

himself – rightly – as a lover of scandalmongery at all costs. He is accordingly full of mock shame when he reveals the enormity of his rivals' misconduct:

Αἰδοῦμαι μὲν οὖν ὑπὲρ ἀμφοῖν, ὑπέρ τε σοῦ καὶ ὑπὲρ ἐμαυτοῦ· σοῦ μέν, ἀξιοῦντος μνήμῃ καὶ γραφῇ παραδοθῆναι ἄνδρα τρισκατάρατον, ἐμαυτοῦ δέ, σπουδὴν ποιουμένου ἐπὶ τοιαύτῃ ἱστορίᾳ καὶ πράξεσιν ἀνθρώπου, ὃν οὐκ ἀναγιγνώσκεσθαι πρὸς τῶν πεπαιδευμένων ἦν ἄξιον.

I am ashamed for both of us: for you, for countenancing that an absolute villain should be handed down to memory in writing; for me, that I should take trouble over such an account of the doings of a man educated people shouldn't read about.[150]

Ῥητέον δὲ ὅμως, εἰ καὶ ἕωλα δόξω λέγειν, ὡς μὴ αἰτίαν ἔχοιμι μόνος αὐτὰ ἀγνοεῖν.

Tell it I must, however, even if I seem to be going over what is stale, so that I should not be accused of being the only one who does not know.[151]

This is only matched by his uninhibited *Schadenfreude* that the victim should have fallen right into his hands:

καὶ ἔοικε θεῶν τις ἐπὶ χεῖλος ἀγαγεῖν σοι τότε τὸν γέλων ἐπὶ τῇ ἀποφράδι λεχθείσῃ, ὡς αὐτὸς μὲν Σκυθῶν καταφανέστερος γένοιο κομιδῇ ἀπαίδευτος ὢν καὶ τὰ κοινὰ ταῦτα καὶ τὰ ἐν ποσὶν ἀγνοῶν, ἀρχὴν δὲ εὔλογον παράσχοις τῶν κατὰ σοῦ λόγων ἀνδρὶ ἐλευθέρῳ καὶ οἴκοθέν σε ἀκριβῶς εἰδότι καὶ μηδὲν ὑποστελουμένῳ τὸ μὴ οὐχὶ πάντα ἐξειπεῖν.

And it was very likely some god who made you laugh when I mentioned the word ἀποφράς, so that you would appear more obviously than any of the Scythians to be a total ignoramus who didn't know these elementary facts that are common knowledge; and so that you would provide a plausible opening against yourself for a man of independent spirit who knew all about you from home and had no inhibitions about revealing all.[152]

Lucian is also a connoisseur of *diabole* against himself: it gives him satisfaction to quote what Theagenes or Alexander had to say about him (or what he thought they ought to have said);[153] but even this is no equal to the charges of hypocrisy he levels against himself for his volte-face after the pamphlet *de Mercede Conductis*[154] – followed by as much again of defences, before he blithely dismisses the whole business with little more than οὐ φροντὶς Ἱπποκλείδῃ. Even Lucian's volte-faces are contrived to provide ready-made entertainment.

---

150. *Alex.* 2.
151. *Pseudolog.* 3.
152. *Ibid.* 2.
153. *Peregr.* 31; *Alex.* 45.
154. *Apol.* 1–7.

VII. A sophistic ensemble: *Navigium*

I shall attempt to draw a number of these strands together as they occur in a single work. It would perhaps be wrong to describe the *Navigium*[155] as the 'typical' Lucianic dialogue: the author is clever enough not to commit all his resources at any one time. But it certainly does illustrate a typical convergence of 'Lucianic' interests, and to that extent can fairly be described as 'central'. So far as one can see there is no clear connection with Menippus here: Lucian speaks through his own mouthpiece, and the time is the present: he is in his element, as Lycinus, between Athens and the Piraeus. The subject he has chosen is as usual one of the most basic satirical themes, in this case the vanity of human wishes. But as well as being a timeless commonplace, it is relevant to the present. Each of the empty dreams of the three dreamers is in fact found in Aelius Aristides' *Hieroi Logoi*, that curious textbook of sophistic *Zeitgeist*: Aristides dreams that the ship on which he was to sail to Chios goes down; Lycinus forecasts that Adimantus' dreamboat will sink.[156] Aristides shares a pedestal with Alexander the Great, or impresses Vologeses of Parthia with a declamation: Lucian's Samippus captures Alexander's kingdoms in a fantasy-speech.[157] Aristides is of course forever being raised to the skies by the divine favour of Asclepius; Lucian's Timolaus wants to identify himself with the operations – and the advantages – of Providence.[158]

Other contemporary parallels have been drawn: Adimantus' dream of reaching Athens by his own canal is reasonably close to Herodes' actual voyages on the sacred ship, to say nothing of his much-vaunted ambitions of excavating the Isthmus;[159] Samippus' exploits would certainly gain from circulation side by side with Arrian's *Anabasis*.[160] If Lucian was not thinking in terms of Herodes or Arrian, his work certainly saw its fulfilment in their

155. There is now a serviceable commentary by G. Husson, *Le navire ou les souhaits* (Paris 1970).

156. *Or.* 48.17k; *Navig.* 19.

157. *Or.* 50.48k; *Navig.* 28–38.

158. *Navig.* 41–44.

159. Philostratus, *VS* 550; 552. J. Schwartz, *Biographie* (n. 117), 133; Husson *ad Navig.* 24.

160. See my 'Arrian's *Anabasis Alexandri* and Lucian's *Historia* ', *Historia* 29 (1980), 119–24

subsequent gestures: he is either a commentator or a prophet, and in both cases he is 'relevant'; and his picture of Alexander of Abonoteichos also comes very close to a realization of Timolaus' dream of emulating Providence.

The problem of *mimesis* here in *Navigium* is complex, and has not been thoroughly studied, largely because Helm had little interest in a piece not easy to connect with Menippus.[161] I have shown elsewhere why I think Lucian had the *Republic* itself in mind: this is his περὶ πολιτείας gone wrong, with allusion to Adimantus and the ring of Gyges to jog the memory.[162] He will often contaminate a major and a subsidiary source: in this case several of Theophrastus' characters supply minor touches within the broad framework of Plato.[163]

The ἀλαζών boasts about his overseas trade when he has nothing in the bank and has not even travelled outside Attica; he has jewelled cups and gives lavish gifts to the citizens. This is close to both of Adimantus' day-dreams: he wishes himself a huge merchantman with expensive cargoes, then digs up treasure which will provide him with expensive goblets and allow him to become an ostentatious philanthropist.[164] Other details of the same portrait would supply the next portion of Lucian: the ἀλαζών campaigns with Alexander and has three letters of Antipater inviting him to Macedonia: this would provide the mainspring of Samippus' adventure.[165] The juxtaposition of these items in both authors is important in itself, all the more so when Lucian seems to have cross-fertilized his material with distinctive details from several other portraits:[166] Theophrastus' μικροφιλότιμος sends all sorts of little presents to his friends abroad – pickled olives to Byzantium, Spartan hounds to Cyzicus, honey from Hymettus to Rhodes. In *Navigium* Adimantus is to do all this in reverse, sending his friends in Athens the various delicacies from overseas – Nile saltfish, myrrh from Canopus, or an Ibis from Memphis (but

---

161. *Lucian und Menipp*, 338.

162. *Mnemos.* 30 (1977), 363f..

163. Cf. Bompaire, *Ecrivain*, 206 rightly compares the ἀλαζών to the *Miles gloriosus* in *D. Meretr.* but seems hesitant about seeing an ἀλαζών *marin* in *Navig.* (205 n. 4).

164. *Char.* 23.2; *Navig.* 14f; 20–5.

165. *Char.* 23.3f; *Navig.* 28–38.

166. *Char.* 21 (accepting Ussher's transposition); *Navig.* 15.

Lucian's victim thinks big – he is to send one of the Pyramids as well!). The δειλός provides further colouring: he is scared at sailing or military manoeuvres. In *Navigium* Lycinus himself keeps up this pose throughout his friends' day-dreams: he is scared of Adimantus' shipwreck, and keeps wanting to opt out of Samippus' dream-campaign. And the most distinctive jokes in *Navigium* belong together in Theophrastus: some men win victories by land and sea – in the Stoa![167] Lucian's Samippus wins his mock victory between the Piraeus and Athens, and Adimantus has his shipwreck on the same route.[168] The λογοποιός misses his dinner while verbally capturing cities; Lucian rearranges this slightly, and gives Samippus an imaginary banquet in Babylon to celebrate his imaginary capture of the city.[169] What is the effect of all this? Once more urbane incongruity, with the *mise en scène* for Platonic sublimity used as a container for the meanest of Hellenistic *homunculi*!

Specific parallels apart, the *Navigium* also develops several characteristic situations in the rhetorical schools: it was evidently a favourite pastime to allow a pompous rival to embark on a rule of three, then cap his miserable bombast with the fourth stroke. Cestius Pius launched on three *adynata: Si Thraex essem, Fusius essem; si pantomimus essem, Bathyllus essem; si equus, Melissio;* thereupon Cassius Severus interrupted: *si cloaca esses, Maxima esses.*[170] One of Lucian's own teachers, Demonax, had played the trick on an unnamed sophist from Sidon who began: Ἐὰν Ἀριστοτέλης με καλῇ ἐπὶ τὸ Λύκειον, ἕψομαι· ἂν Πλάτων ἐπὶ τὴν Ἀκαδημίαν, ἀφίξομαι· ἂν Ζήνων, ἐπὶ τῇ Ποικίλη διατρίψω. But when he then offered to follow the silence of Pythagoras, Demonax deflated him with a timely καλεῖ σε Πυθαγόρας.[171] In *Navigium* Lucian has presented his own variation on this situation:

'If only I had a ship'
'If only I were Alexander'
'If only I were God . . .'
'If only you would all be quiet'.

There is also a hint of another situation that may have been commonplace in Alexander-declamations. Seneca records a case where Arellius Fuscus brought a pupil down to earth when he was

167. *Char.* 25; *Navig.* 14–19, 30–7.   168. *Char.* 8.12; *Navig.* 35, 14.
169. *Char.* 8.13; *Navig.* 39.   170. Sen. *Contr.* 3 *praef.* 16.   171. *Dem.* 14.

carried away in the middle of a *suasoria* on Alexander's debate before Babylon; Fuscus made Alexander stab him – with an appropriate Virgilian tag! So here Lycinus arranges for Samippus to be wounded in the imaginary onslaught before taking the city.[172]

The other literary features already discussed – lies, falsehood, paradox – are also an essential part of the texture of *Navigium*. It may be seen as a clever juxtaposition of two types of lying: the fictitious voyage described in wholly realistic terms, and the three impossible voyages – all in ascending order. (And each one is exposed for the paradox it is by Lycinus' subsequent remarks.) The whole ensemble is a reminder of Lucian's capacity and inclination to combine his techniques and interests wherever possible.

VIII. Conclusion: A 'sophistic' joker in a sophist's world?

Why, then, should one read Lucian? One cannot arrive at an adequate view of the Second Sophistic, or of Greek Satirical tradition, without him. But that is no comment on his literary quality. One must be resigned to judging him less on the originality of his achievements than some of his audiences did. He should be read rather for the academic quality of his wit: he is the *pepaideumenos* with *jeu d'esprit* – a professor of *pseudos*, paradox and parody, and an earnest pamphleteer only for *paideia* itself, and his own reputation. He is the sophisticated and detached virtuoso *praeceptor* of whatever nonsense it is his whim to teach.

One single piece of belles-lettres written within the past few years will serve to show that the taste for Lucian's elegant wit has not yet disappeared: it would be hard to parallel his most characteristic pose more closely than the following, either in language or in content:

The news that you send me, *viz.*: that your silly London gazette *The Times* has publicly declared me to be none other than our worthy Regius Professor of History, has diverted us in Oxon not more hugely than you in London, all men recognising at once both the impossibility and absurdity of it; that professor and I, chancing to meet of late at the Ordinary, forgot our mutual differences . . . and made merry together over this exquisite new piece of folly.[173]

172. *Suas.* 4.5, cf. *Navig.* 37.
173. *The Letters of Mercurius* (London 1970), 67 (from *The Spectator*, 21 March 1970).

The question of Mercurius' identification with the said professor does not affect the parallel, though it adds an appropriate suspicion of *pseudos*. Such a situation might well have occurred when the truth came out about Lucian's forgery of Heraclitus. Here once more we have the *pepaideumenos*, never happier than when he is exchanging pleasantries about an erudite pseudepigraph with one of his peers; and the whole situation is expressed in the educated language of several centuries before. It is not far from this to the beginning of Lucian's *Eunuchus*:

ΠΑΜΦΙΛΟΣ: Πόθεν, ὦ Λυκῖνε, ἢ τί γελῶν ἡμῖν ἀφῖξαι; ἀεὶ μὲν γὰρ φαιδρὸς ὢν τυγχάνεις· τουτὶ δὲ πλέον τοῦ συνήθους εἶναί μοι δοκεῖ, ἐφ' ὅτῳ μηδὲ κατέχειν δυνατὸς εἶ τὸν γέλωτα.

ΛΥΚΙΝΟΣ: Ἐξ ἀγορᾶς μὲν ἥκω σοι, ὦ Πάμφιλε, τοῦ γέλωτος δὲ αὐτίκα κοινωνὸν ποιήσομαί σε, ἢν ἀκούσῃς . . .

PAMPHILUS:
Where have you come from, Lycinus, and what are you laughing at? But of course you are always cheerful; but this is more than your usual, since you are unable to suppress your laughter.

LYCINUS:
I have just come from the agora, Pamphilus, and you will soon be laughing too when you hear . . .[174]

For so transparent a writer, Lucian has proved surprisingly difficult to characterize neatly without considerable explanation. Various labels, or pairs of labels, such as 'sophist and satirist' or 'satirist and bellettrist', are not entirely satisfactory. Their failure is due in large measure to their emphasis on genre: and to describe Lucian as a 'writer of dialogue' is a solecism only equal to that of denying him the title sophist, a term so flexible and subjective in second-century usage that it cannot fail to stick. How then *is* Lucian to be characterized? Two labels, I think, do justice to his individual temperament and his relation with the Second Sophistic, and both he would have approved. We can fall back on the title 'sophist's apprentice', for a writer who plays with the raw materials of rhetoric and turns the sophist's lecture-room upside down at every opportunity, or we can say that his manipulations of sophistic material and techniques come closest to realizing the real literary potential of this uniquely well-equipped literary movement: we can call him a sophist's sophist.

174. *Eun.* 1.

The mendacity of Kalasiris and the narrative strategy of Heliodoros' *Aithiopika*

JOHN J. WINKLER

Two persistent problems which otherwise enthusiastic readers of the *Aithiopika* have raised are the apparent contradictions, first in Kalasiris' character, and second in his narrative. The troubling aspect of Kalasiris' character, as some readers feel it, is the tension between his oft-alleged wisdom, piety, virtual sanctity on the one hand, and his outrageous mendacity on the other. Kalasiris is boldly and repeatedly deceitful, cozening anyone – and there are many – who might stand in the way of his success in getting Charikleia and her lover to Aithiopia. The second problem could be said to stem from the first: one particular lie which Kalasiris seems to tell in his long narrative to Knemon is that after exiling himself from Memphis he happened to arrive in Delphi and while there happened to discover that Charikleia was actually the princess of Aithiopia. But he later mentions that he had in fact already visited Aithiopia and undertaken at the queen's request to search for her long-lost daughter. This inconsistency, fundamental to his entire story and motivation, is usually regarded as a simple contradiction in the narrative which Heliodoros should have avoided.[1] I want to suggest that this contradiction is not a mere oversight or poorly planned effect but more like a deliberate narrative strategy on Kalasiris' part, and hence an aspect of the larger problem of his honorable mendacity.

My focus then is on Kalasiris the crafty narrator, who fools

1. The 'contradiction' was first discovered by V. Hefti, 'Zur Erzählungstechnik in Heliodors Aethiopica' (diss. Basel/Wien 1950), and is reported in Bryan Reardon, *Courants littéraires grecs des IIe et IIIe siècles après J.-C.* (Paris 1971), 390–2. Reardon's is the basic work to consult on the Greek novels and cites the standard bibliography, which will be omitted here. On Kalasiris, see G. Sandy, 'Characterisation and Philosophical Decor in Heliodorus' *Aethiopica*'. On matters of more remote background (love literature and story telling in general) Rohde's *Der griechische Roman*[5] (Hildesheim/New York 1974), chapters 1–2, has still not been superseded.

various audiences, and yet seems in some sense to maintain his integrity and lofty morality in the service of divine providence. I take these two problems to be important ones because Kalasiris, who is the narrator (with some interruption) of Books II.24 through v.33, employs the same sophistication and narrative skills as Heliodoros does in his role as narrator of the rest of the novel, and the analysis of Kalasiris' religiosity and craftiness is simply a test case for our understanding of Heliodoros' religious and narrative strategies in general.

Heliodoros' principal narrative excellence (in the judgment of enthusiastic critics since the Renaissance) is his disposition of material so as to arouse interest in the careful reader by the giving or withholding of information.[2] The two kinds of effect which depend on the careful manipulation of information from author to reader are surprise and suspense, which are differentiated precisely by the degree of information given the reader. Suspense is an effect of knowledge, surprise of ignorance. What creates suspense in a narrative is the foreknowledge of a perilous event that may be averted; the simple closing of a library door on time can be an incredibly tense event when the audience is fully aware, as the clock ticks away, that the event (ominous in context) is scheduled to happen.[3] Surprise on the other hand is an effect dependent upon ignorance, such as the unexpected appearance of a murderer in the bathroom while the heroine is taking her shower. To revert from modern popular entertainment to ancient, we may compare the parental recognitions in *Daphnis and Chloe*, which are surprising because unforeseen, with those in Heliodoros, which are suspense-

2. The views of Amyot, Tasso, and Scaliger are reported in A. K. Forcione, *Cervantes, Aristotle, and the Persiles* (Princeton 1970). Amyot in his preface to his translation says that Heliodoros 'maintains [the audience's] attention through the ingenious relating of his story, for they do not understand what they have read at the beginning of Book I until they see the end of the fifth; and when they have arrived at that point they find themselves even more eager to see the end than they have been to see the beginning. Thus the reader's mind remains constantly in suspense until he comes to the conclusion.' The extraordinary menace and power of the opening scene is described by Michael Psellos as like the head of a serpent so coiled that it is lying in the center of its own windings, ready to spring forth with great force. (Psellos, and other pre-Renaissance testimony, is accessible in A. Colonna's edition of the *Aithiopika*.) Norbert Miller, *Der empfindsame Erzähler* (Munich 1968) well analyzes the respectful attention paid to Heliodoros by eighteenth-century novelists.

3. Hitchcock's *Shadow of a Doubt* (Universal 1943).

ful, having been carefully planned from the moment in Book IV when we learn the truth of Charikleia's parentage.[4]

Generally speaking, whereas the other Greek novelists do contrive some surprises, though very little suspense, Heliodoros regularly manipulates points of view so as to contrast and highlight states of relative knowledge and ignorance. These are calculated to produce neither pure suspense nor pure surprise, but rather states of partial knowledge: provocative uncertainties, riddling oracles, puzzles and ambiguities. All these forms of relative knowledge and ignorance are cases of *incomplete cognition*, a phrase which I will use to analyze several conscious strategies of the author, and which I regard as the fundamental principle of Heliodoros' narrative technique. The focal point in this game of knowledge and ignorance must always be the reader, who is by turns puzzled and enlightened in a shifting chiaroscuro of irony, half-truths and recognitions. If it were true that the reader at any point in the narrative were pointlessly puzzled, that would be a serious charge against the author. But I maintain that this is not the case in the *Aithiopika*, and that the novel's plotting not only withstands close scrutiny but invites it. I will show this by analyzing the general principles of Heliodoros' narrative technique, mainly from examples in Book I (section I), his use of duplicity as an intellectual and moral theme (section II), and finally Kalasiris' narrative strategy (section III).

I. Omniscience, irrelevance, and detection

We have a name for the narrative format of novels which begin as Heliodoros' *Aithiopika* does: they are called 'omniscient author' novels. The term implies that the narrator of the story knows all there is to know about the characters and events. This may broadly and roughly be contrasted with the 'documentary' format, in

4. Criticism of Heliodoros for 'revealing the secret' too soon are quite off the mark (as in J. C. Dunlop, *The History of Fiction* (London 1876), 22). Our knowledge of Queen Persinna's exposure of her white child makes possible many situations of suspense and irony. Further, it gives us a firm grasp on the essence of Heliodoros' plotting, *viz.*, that adventures and locales do not succeed each other randomly (as in the novels of Xenophon of Ephesos and Achilles Tatius) but are organized in a linear and irreversible progression to a unique goal, represented by the land of Aithiopia.

which some pretence is made that the narrator has discovered what
really happened, whether by personal observation of the events, by
interviewing characters who took part in the story, by finding a
document which sets down the tale, or a combination of these
reportorial methods.

Nowadays we are so used to the omniscient author as a familiar
narrator's voice that we may fail to appreciate just how unusual it
was for a novel to begin, 'The day began to smile, and the sun had
gilded the summits of the mountains, when certain men armed like
thieves were peering over the ridge of a hill, near one of the many
mouths – this one the Herakleotic – where the Nile flows at last
into the ocean.'[5] By ancient conventions this prologue-less beginning is startlingly abrupt, an opening which could well prompt the
reader to wonder, 'Who is speaking, and from what point of view?'
The novels of Longos, Achilles Tatius, Chariton, and Antonius
Diogenes begin (like most literary compositions) by identifying the
author and the circumstances of discovery (Diogenes, A.T.) or
composition (Longos, Chariton) of the story.[6] But with the
Aithiopika we have to deal with a narrator who is not only
omniscient but by ancient standards quite peculiarly and provoca-
tively absent. Yet in a sense we learn to identify that narrator as a
certain kind of mind, one characterized by three principles or
habits of organizing and presenting the story. I will present these

5. The translations in this paper are my revisions of either the anonymous 1717
translation published in London or Walter Lamb's (London/New York 1961).
The Greek text is that edited by R. M. Rattenbury and T. W. Lumb (2nd ed.,
Paris 1960).

6. The one known exception – Xenophon of Ephesos – confirms the principle
in an indirect way. His simple introduction ('There was in Ephesos a man among
the most prominent citizens whose name was Lykomedes') is modelled on the
opening of Xenophon's *Anabasis* – a *faux-naïf* suppression of the writer's usual
statement of identity and point of view. As Lucian remarks of later writers who
aped the opening of the *Anabasis* but without Xenophon's real sophistication,
akephalous histories (which skip the preface and go right to the events,
ἀπροοιμίαστα καὶ εὐθὺς ἐπὶ τῶν πραγμάτων, *De hist. conscrib.* 23) ought somehow
to imply all that would ordinarily be made explicit in a conventional proem (οὐκ
εἰδότες ὡς δυνάμει τινὰ προοίμιά ἐστι λεληθότα τοὺς πολλούς, *ibid.*). The opening
of Xenophon of Ephesos' *Ephesiaka* is a 'virtual proem' inasmuch as he provides us
with a cast of characters, the dramatis personae, suitably described and
commented on, and a set of simple motivating forces (pride, love, jealousy, divine
anger) which will keep the plot rolling. The story is so clearly in the author's
control – and modelled upon classic precedent – that no uneasiness is felt in the
absence of a personal statement by 'Xenophon'.

three principles in this first section as a general sketch of Heliodoros' narrative technique. They are (1) the aporetic measuring of characters' ignorance ('Little did they know . . .'), (2) the discovered relevance of seemingly incidental details or digressions ('So *that* was why . . .'), and (3) the postponement of wanted information ('But the answer to that would have to wait for . . .').

It is the narrator himself who provokes us to wonder from what point of view the opening tableau is narrated, not only by the absence of a conventional prologue, but by the aporetic style of his exposition. The formula for these *aporiai* is a binary one: sense data, usually visual,[7] followed by the brigands' conjecture or bafflement. Thus, looking out to sea they spy nothing that might be preyed upon, but closer to shore they notice a moored cargo ship. They infer that it is heavily laden because they can see – even at a distance, καὶ τοῖς πόρρωθεν – that the water is lapping up to her third line. Yet they are nonplussed by the absence of any men on board, sailors or passengers. They see corpses littered in various attitudes all over the beach and overturned banquet tables; from this they draw the limited conclusion that there had been an unexpected fight, but beyond that they are deeply puzzled. The fact that 'some are in the last throes of death and their limbs still twitching was a plain indication that the bloody action was only lately over'; but the vanquished have no victors, a defeat was plain but no spoils taken away. The meaning and correct interpretation of this theatrical tableau eludes them (οὐδὲ συνιέναι τὴν σκηνὴν ἐδύναντο).[8] Throughout the scene the narrator tells us what the bandits saw, what they inferred, and what left them confused.[9]

---

7. W. Bühler, *WS* 89 (1976), 177–85. The pretense of a strictly visual, impersonal camera-eye view of things gives way, of course, to the unsuppressible sense of a narrator-in-charge, particularly in the gnomic comments (1.2.9, 4.3, etc.) and in the occasional οἶμαι (1.8.1, 11.22.1, v.5.3, v11.8.2, ix.9.5, x.6.5), but the ἐγώ implied in that οἶμαι is never exposed.

8. J. W. H. Walden, 'Stage Terms in Heliodorus's *Aethiopica*', *HSCP* 5 (1894), 1–43.

9. The scene is well-lit, fully visible, quite clear to see, but the mind looking on is in the dark. At the risk of sounding Pythagorean, I will list the key elements of this scene in two opposing categories, references to optical phenomena and references to interpretive responses of the characters:

Vision: 1.1, καταυγάζοντος, ὀφθαλμοῖς, ὄψεις, θέᾳ; 1.2, τοῖς πόρρωθεν; 1.4, τὰ φαινόμενα σύμβολα; 1.7, θεωροὺς; 2.1, θέαμα; 2.3, κατεφαίνετο, ἀντέλαμπεν,

The process of careful detection, including decipherment and reading small signs as tokens of a larger pattern, is one of Heliodoros' favorite modes of presentation. Helm compares this technique to that of a modern *Kriminalroman*:[10] there are *corpora delicti* (so to speak) but no murderer. The brigands, from whose limited perspective the reader takes in the scene, are only second-rate detectives. They can figure out that since the tables on the beach were still full of food the attack must have been a sudden one in the middle of a meal. From the position of one of the bodies half-hidden under an overturned table they surmise that he had tried to take cover and had thought himself secure from view but was wrong in that belief.

The scene of the crime is even more like a detective story than the audience at first reading can guess, for one sentence is a Clue. After the survey of methods of death (bludgeoning with cups, cleavers, rocks and shells snatched from the beach, firebrands, etc.), the narrator remarks, speaking from the bandits' observation, 'But most were killed by some archer's arrows' (οἱ δὲ πλεῖστοι βελῶν ἔργον καὶ τοξείας γεγενημένοι). I have intensified the clue-quality of the sentence by the ominous 'some archer'; the Greek is more general and impersonal – 'most deaths had been the work of missiles and archery'. It is not until the 'solution' (v.32) that we learn the meaning of this phrase – Charikleia, dressed in her robes as priestess of Artemis, had been shooting into the melee from the

ὀφθαλμοῖς, ὄψις, ὁρᾶν, ἑώρων; 2.5, ὄψεως ὥσπερ πρηστῆρος, ἔδοξε (a trick of perspective), πρὸς τὸν ἥλιον ἀνταυγαζούσης; 2.6, ὁρώμενον; 2.7, ὁρῶντες; 2.8, σκιᾶς τοῖς ὀφθαλμοῖς παρεμπεσούσης, ἀνένευσε καὶ ἰδοῦσα ἐπένευσε, ὄψεως; 3.1, κατὰ πρόσωπον, ἀνένευσε, ἰδοῦσα, ὄψιν; 3.6, ὁρῶντες; 4.3, ἐφαίνετο, ὄψις. Interpretive reaction: 1.2, συμβάλλειν; 1.3, κατηγορούντων; 1.7, οὐδὲ συνιέναι; 1.8, ἀποροῦντες; 2.1, ἀπορώτερον, ἀναπείθουσα; 2.4, Theagenes' query; 2.6, ἡ τῶν γινομένων ἄγνοια, ταῦτα ἐγίνωσκον, τὰ ὄντα δὲ οὔπω ἐγίνωσκον; 2.7, πρὸς ἑτέρας ἐννοίας τὴν γνώμην μετέβαλλον, τὴν τῶν ἀληθῶν γνῶσιν; 3.1, ἑώκεσαν, ὡς ἔοικεν; 3.2, οὐδὲν συνιέναι ἔχοντες; 3.5, ὑπὸ τῆς τῶν ὁρωμένων ἀγνοίας; 3.6, εἴκαζον; 4.1, οὐδὲν συνιεῖσα, συμβαλοῦσα; 4.2, συνείς, προσδοκήσας.

The contrasts between the two groups include light/dark, knowledge/uncertainty, and picture/explanation. Perhaps the most basic contrast underlying this scene is the definiteness of spatial location and time of the day as opposed to the indefiniteness of 'location' in the plot. It is a beginning which has all the signs of being an end, and the reader is very far from being able to place the scene in the novel's spatio-temporal framework, that is, to know just where it is in the middle.

1   R. Helm, *Der antike Roman* (Berlin 1948; Göttingen 1956), 40.

safety of the ship's deck. If she is thus identified as the murderer of most (οἱ πλεῖστοι), it is ironic that the bandits treat her as the least likely suspect: they plunder the cargo and pay no attention to the woman and the wounded man she is nursing, leaving them 'under no other guard but their own weakness' (ἰσχυρὰν αὐτοῖς φυλακὴν τὴν ἀσθένειαν αὐτῶν ἐπιστήσαντες). And yet, in detective story fashion, they had actually noticed that she was still carrying an unstrung bow and a quiver on her shoulder and had even conjectured, in a moment of panic when she leaped up from the rock where she was sitting, that she might be a goddess or a frenzied priestess 'inspired with divine fury to execute that great slaughter plain to see' (οἱ δὲ ἱέρειαν ὑπό του θεῶν ἐκμεμηνυῖαν καὶ τὸν ὁρώμενον πολὺν φόνον ἐργασαμένην).[11] Though the brigands suspect her of the deed as long as she seems to be a goddess or priestess, they abandon the hypothesis that she might be the guilty party. And so do we. Interestingly enough, it is only at this moment in the scene that the narrator utters a sentence which might be read as an intrusive 'Little did they know': καὶ οἱ μὲν ταῦτα ἐγίνωσκον, τὰ ὄντα δὲ οὔπω ἐγίνωσκον. Even this phrase may be read in two ways – either as the narrator's personal intrusion, commenting on the bandits' ignorance, or as a more sophisticated indirect statement of what the brigands were thinking, 'So much we know, but the truth we do not yet know.' This sleight of hand directs our attention away from the truth (that Charikleia is the murderous archer). It is almost as if, in order to achieve this, Heliodoros is willing to *seem* to abandon his very objective, self-effacing tone and speak instead as the popular story-teller, rather like a Chariton, who chats with the reader as the plot moves along. All the other references of the narrator to the incomplete cognition of the characters in this scene are quite relentless reports of what their eyes and mind were objectively able to comprehend.

11. There might be a parallelism between the three elements of Charikleia's appearance which the brigands notice and the three conjectures they make: (a) clang of arrows – Artemis; (b) gold clothes gleaming – native Isis; (c) flowing, unbound hair – frenzied priestess. It is the second element which seems uncertain. This reference to 'native Isis' is one of the signs that the novel is written from and for a Hellenocentric point of view: a reference by name to Neith, the arrow goddess whose home city was Sais near Naukratis, would have had to be glossed. Of course this does not prevent Heliodoros from contriving non-Hellenic viewpoints, as when Kalasiris refers to 'someone or other named Lykourgos' (II.27.1).

We must revise, then, our understanding of the term 'omniscient author' as applied to Heliodoros, for the contrast between omniscient author and documentary author does not hold in his case. Heliodoros combines the superior authority of an omniscient narrator, who has immediate access to all relevant knowledge, with the critical discrimination of a documentary narrator, who verifies the reliable accuracy of every sentence, every observation. What interests Heliodoros most in the opening tableau is the *process of interpretation*, particularly in the forms of misapprehension and failed understanding. Though we must think of the narrator as one who knows 'the truth' which the bandits fail to grasp, yet he does not advertize his knowledge or even his presence but conceals himself behind the splendid bafflement of that panorama and its tiny predators, whose failure to understand it is the clearest fact of all.

We must ask now what are the limits of Heliodoros' ruthless objectivity. We could imagine a yet more radical isolation of the pure perceptual field apart from all mental constructs, but that would be the technique of the *nouveau roman*, not of the ancient. Heliodoros, on the contrary, assumes that the ordinary principles of common sense and empirical truths are still valid, as when the brigands conclude that the ship is fully loaded because the water laps up to the third line. This is important: Heliodoros does not require us to suspend judgment or bracket all empirical knowledge, and particularly not the expectation that this is a romance. In solving this scene not only the laws of nature but the conventions of the genre will hold good. Yet he is requiring that we hold on to those expectations in a more conscious and critical way, perceiving them for what they are – not data of the text but patterns of probable foreknowledge brought to the text by the literate reader. These generic expectations of what the limits are within which the problem will be resolved are analogous to Kant's categories of the mind 'operating' on sense data, literally making sense of them. Generic expectations are, according to a familiar modern comparison, like the rules of a game,[12] which tell us what range of moves is

---

12. Neatly qualified by Joseph H. Greenberg, 'Is Language Like a Chess Game?', in his *Language, Culture, and Communication* (Stanford 1971), 330–52. 'In a chess game we know the rules. . . . But language is more like a game in which we are trying to deduce the rules by watching the games' (p. 344).

possible and meaningful but not which move will be made in any particular situation. The opening tableau leaves us both certain *that* this is a romance and quite uncertain as to *how*. My thesis will be that Heliodoros' techniques of displaying incomplete cognition are designed to heighten our awareness of the game-like structure of intelligibility involved in reading a romance, and that Kalasiris is the major representative of one who know how to play this game.

The second principle of the Heliodoran narrator's mind or style is his demand that every item be significant. The opening chapters are in many ways very pictorial,[13] but it would be wrong to call them an *ekphrasis*, insofar as that term often connotes the elaboration of a descriptive passage for its own sake rather than to provide information, plot development or any functional connection. Heliodoros utterly eschews irrelevance, though he sometimes allows the deceptive appearance of irrelevance. It may be that he intends us to be tempted to understand the opening scene of the *Aithiopika* as a novel kind of *ekphrasis*, in contrast with the novels of Longos and Achilles Tatius, which begin by describing paintings which are only tenuously and obliquely related to the general thematics of the ensuing stories. Heliodoros' opening tableau looks like one of those paintings, but so far from being marginal it is a critical scene from the very center of the *Aithiopika*'s plot. Another intended contrast may be the occurrence of a crocodile at Achilles Tatius IV.19 and Heliodoros VI.1. Achilles Tatius, master of the inconsequential filigree, had described the crocodile at length in a manner which as usual had nothing to do with the plot ('And I saw another creature of the Nile . . .'), but in Heliodoros the beast slips like a shadow along the ground, hardly visible much less described at length, and more importantly its passage is functional. Knemon's fright at barely glimpsing it starts a conversation about an

13. Indeed one of the closest analogs to the Heliodoran tone is the voice often adopted by Philostratos describing a painting, raising questions, musing on the possible meanings of the visible details. One of his paintings, the murder of Kassandra (II.10), closely resembles the banquet-turned-battle in Heliodoros' opening tableau (bodies everywhere, blood mixed with wine, men still breathing, tables filled with food, cups fallen from the hands of drinkers, various manners of death, a maiden in the midst of it looking at a weapon poised to bring her death – as Charikleia has her dagger ready for suicide). Certainly Philostratos' interrogation of the meaning of what he sees is closer to Heliodoros than is the unproblematic descriptions of temple art which open the novels of Longos and Achilles Tatius.

earlier show of cowardice and leads to the revelation of the name Thisbe. I think it likely that the pattern of describing exotic beasts in some detail was so well established that any reader would have noticed the absence of *ekphrasis* at this point.[14] A variation occurs at x.27 where the marvellous appearance of giraffe is described. This seems at first to be a typical irrelevant digression such as romances allowed and even cultivated. However what seems to be a digression becomes functional when the animals assembled for sacrifice are frightened by the strange giraffe and give Theagenes an opportunity to perform an impressive rodeo stunt which wins the hearts of his captors. Heliodoros particularly likes to present casual conversations which unexpectedly lead to important revelations (1.8.5–6, II.10.4–5, 23.6–24.3, VI.3.1–4).[15] Perhaps the most significant instance is IV.16: Kalasiris is hastening to the Delphic oracle to seek a solution to a problem when an accidental encounter with a Phoenician merchant answers his prayer before he had even uttered it. 'God is very sharp-witted', remarks Kalasiris at that point (IV.16.3).

The asides between Kalasiris and Knemon which retard the long flashback to Delphi are sometimes thought to be irrelevant digressions, but consider what is probably the chief candidate for such a charge – the tale of Egyptian Homer's birth (III.14). In form it is a digression on a digression, explaining why Kalasiris, when he explained the marks by which a true god is recognized in human form, called Homer 'Egyptian'. Knemon makes a demand which we may make our own for the entire novel: that not a single word slip by without scrutiny for its precise meaning (μὴ παραδραμεῖν σε τοῦ λόγου τὴν ἀκρίβειαν), and he compels Kalasiris to tell the hitherto unheard story that Homer was an Egyptian by birth. The ensuing tale of Hermes' fathering Homer by the wife of a Hermetic prophet might seem irrelevant to the *Aithiopika*, but the pattern of a genetic fluke (his hairy thigh, like that other son of Hermes, Pan) bringing on charges of bastardy and resulting in exile and wandering is in fact a neat parallel for Charikleia's own story. As

14. H. Rommel, *Die naturwissenschaftlich-paradoxographischen Exkurse bei Philostratos, Heliodoros und Achilleus Tatios* (Stuttgart 1923).

15. And casually introduced persons who become significant actors: the brigand chief and his henchman (1.3.4), the Naukratite merchant Nausikles (II.8.5), a daring pirate (V.25.1), a soldier of Mitranes (VII.1.2). At first mention these all seem to be forgettable walk-on parts.

Heliodoros continually draws on Homeric material for his novel, so his heroine, by a witty conceit, is living out a destiny essentially like Homer's own. We may even say of this double digression what Charikles says of his own digression: 'So there, my friend, you have the explanation of my traveling thither, but there is something parenthetical to my tale, or rather, to speak more truly, the principal point of it, which I would have you know' (. . . ἢν δέ σε βούλομαι παρενθήκην γνῶναι τοῦ διηγήματος, μᾶλλον δὲ ἀληθέστερον εἰπεῖν, αὐτὸ δὴ τὸ κεφάλαιον . . ., II.30.1). This technique of significant displacement, which makes the incidental necessary and the random relevant, is fundamental to Heliodoros' style of thinking, and we will see it deployed even more strikingly in section II below.

A third basic feature of Heliodoros' narrative technique, which is evident in the opening scene and carried through the rest of the book, is postponement. I will here analyze only its use in the first book. If we consider Book I in the light of the conventions of narrative information – the initial identification of characters, relations and motives – we can say that the book is structured around four major postponements of that information. Each of these postponements is so timed as to provoke the reader to a greater awareness of the conventions of reading fiction, which are (1) an intelligible language shared by author, reader and characters, (2) a plot, (3) a smattering of conventional motifs and familiar themes, and (4) a certain identification with the fortunes of the heroes.

(1) Part of the mystery of the opening tableau is that the reader has questions ('Who are these characters?', 'What is their story?') which would normally be answered when the actors begin to speak. We can tolerate a certain amount of preliminary scene-setting whose meaning is not entirely perspicuous, but we expect the characters' speeches at least to provide the information which is necessary for us to situate ourselves in the story. The first conversation does not do this (1.2.4); it is an intimate exchange between the seated maiden and the wounded young man (both as yet unnamed) which tells us that they are devoted to each other unto death, and therefore probably romance heroes. We have more justified hopes of being informed about the situation when the bandits advance upon the maiden, for they are strangers like

ourselves and stand in the same need of explanation. Her speech to them displays a courageous character,[16] but it is not particularly informative. This would normally be followed by questions and answers, but just as we are ready to learn who she is the narrator tells us that they understood not a word she said (1.3.2) but instead rushed past her to gather booty. And so the novel remains a curious dumb show until the protagonists are assigned a translator (1.8.5). Heliodoros' Greek is hard even by ancient standards, which means that the brigands' noncomprehension of Greek is simply the extreme case of what every reader is experiencing, that is, a certain struggle to comprehend and sort out not only the plot but the very *language* of the plot.

I believe Heliodoros is unique in ancient literature for his continual attention to problems of language and communication.[17] He repeatedly describes situations in which ignorance of a language blocks communication (1.4.1f., 11.33.1) or in which knowing a foreign language makes communication possible (11.21.5, x.31.1, 39.1, 40.1). To navigate one's way through this conspicuously polyglot world it is very helpful to know at least two languages, and several characters do: Knemon (1.7.3, 19.3, 21.3, 11.18.3), Kalasiris (vi.12.3, 14.1), Hydaspes (ix.25.3). Professional interpreters are essential (vii.19.3, viii.17.2, ix.1.5). One can use another person's ignorance of a language to avoid being understood (v.8.4, x.9.6). The point of this constant awareness might be simply a striving for naturalism if it were not for two facts: Heliodoros uses knowledge and ignorance of a language in a dramatic and significant way to underscore the cross-purposes, complications and dénouements of his plot. To this end, the references to linguistic knowledge and ignorance are particularly frequent in the first and last books. The best example occurs at the

16. More specifically, that melodramatic display of resolve which was often exhibited in tragedy, hence the verb for her speaking is ἐπετραγῴδει. If Euripides is the grandfather of the Greek romance, Heliodoros is his favorite grandchild, and Koraes rightly calls him φιλευριπίδης.

17. Hippothoos knows the Cappadocian language (Xen. Eph. iii.1.2). Chariton's Persians and Egyptians all speak Greek to each other, even though at one point the author notices that this is not to be assumed (vii.2.2). References to translators and knowledge of foreign languages crop up everywhere in ancient literature from Homer on (cf. T. W. Allen, W. R. Halladay and E. E. Sikes, *The Homeric Hymns* (Oxford 1936), *ad Ven.* 113) but I think nowhere with such sustained attention as in Heliodoros.

conclusion of Book I: Thyamis, shouting in Egyptian, is led through the darkness of the cave by following the voice of a woman speaking in Greek. Of course we are not told what they were saying since her identity must not be revealed to the reader. But had they understood each other's language in this striking bilingual duet of voices seeking each other out, the murder which is its culmination would have been averted (1.30.7). Secondly, Heliodoros not only describes a world like the real one in which many languages are actually spoken, but cultivates scenes in which a dim and partial awareness of a foreign language is displayed, ranging from the minimal knowledge of a foreign name (II.12.4)[18] to quasi-competence (II.30.1, VIII.13.5, 15.3, X.15.1, 35.2, 38.2). This purblind consciousness of what a language, a speech, or a text means is another form of incomplete cognition and rightly takes its place in the Heliodoran universe of steadily expanding meaning. In the same category come other scenes of failed communication, not because the language is foreign, but because one character is partly deaf (v.18.4–6) or totally absorbed in his thoughts (II.21.3). These two motifs are combined at v.1.5, where Kalasiris does not notice the entry of Nausikles: 'I didn't notice (says Kalasiris), perhaps because I've become a bit hard of hearing at my age; old age, you see, especially affects the ears; or perhaps I was just concentrating on my narrative.' This remark closes the long session of story-telling which extends from II.24 to v.1 with an ambiguous double explanation. (Heliodoros uses this 'either/or' construction to mark significant transitions in his narrative; they are the subject of section II below.)

To return to Charikleia's tragic speech at 1.3.1, the news that this speech is just so much garbled gibberish to the brigands who hear it is a special kind of literary shock. Heliodoros associates our disappointment at not learning more of the truth with the brigands' ignorance of the language in which the novel is written. This is an effect of defamiliarization: our ordinary comprehension

---

18. Thermouthis falls asleep, grieving for his murdered mistress Thisbe, and muttering her name: 'He went back to the mouth of the cave and coming to the body of the slain woman he knelt down and placed his head on her breast, saying "Oh Thisbe" – repeating the word often and nothing more, until shortening the name bit by bit and gradually losing consciousness he fell insensibly asleep' (II 14.5). We had earlier been told that the name 'Thisbe' is the one word of Greek which Thermouthis has learned (II.12.4).

of the language of the text becomes suddenly a thing of some wonder rather than an unquestioned habit. Our natural assumption is that, because we understand the language which the author and his first speaking character use, so will all the characters automatically have the same faculty, inasmuch as they have their literary being, their mode of existence, in a Greek novel. But from now on, knowing Greek must be felt as an achievement rather than a premise, and our comprehension of Greek characterizes us from that moment on as readers, and the brigands as non-readers, of this novel.

(2) Later, alone in a tent (1.8), Charikleia and Theagenes speak vaguely of their past sufferings and Apollo's persecution. The interpreter assigned to protect them, Knemon, is the first stranger who can communicate with them in the same language. However, for the next ten chapters they listen to his story and then fall asleep without telling him their own. This is a second major postponement, and it reveals much about Heliodoros' ideas of narrative, both in itself and in relation to the still-postponed plot of Charikleia.

The tale of Knemon which thwarts our desire is a complex one with multiple narrators, hidden motives, betrayal and double-dealing, false accusations and shocking revelations. It is almost as if the protagonists of the *Aithiopika* were taking time out from their adventures to read a different novel. The balance at this point may be precarious for the reader who is still trying to locate the basic terms of this narrative: who are the central and who the incidental characters?[19] But even the reader who knows that Charikleia is indeed the heroine should wonder why the author delays her story while she listens to a completely unconnected novella. In fact, however, Knemon's tale is of special interest as a demonstration model of an alternate narrative strategy. We may even say that the importance of Knemon's novella lies principally in the fact that the

19. We may even ask a question which many readers have probably forgotten: how soon is the reader of the *Aithiopika* sure that Charikleia and Theagenes are in fact the protagonists? In the time when the novel was referred to by the title *Charikleia*, the reader would have known at 1.8.3–4, when the names Theagenes and Charikleia are first used. But if a reader came upon the book under the title *Aithiopika* and before its reputation was established, he or she might continue to wonder (as I did on first reading) how to distinguish the main characters from the minor ones.

powerful narrative intellect which we can sense behind the opening tableau here enters a simpler persona and works within the narrower conventions of a naive raconteur in order to make clear what kind of story the *Aithiopika* is *not*.

The distinctive feature about the conventions of Knemon's tale is that they are instantly intelligible. There is no Heliodoran irony about the meaning of this narrative event. In fact Knemon sounds rather like Xenophon of Ephesos: ἦν μοι πατὴρ 'Αρίστιππος, τὸ γένος 'Αθηναῖος . . ., 'My father was Aristippos, an Athenian by birth . . .', though by the third sentence he has noticeably reverted to Heliodoros' characteristic luxuriousness of language (a sentence of 75 words, exquisite compounds such as ὑπερθεραπεύουσα, clausular balance, expressions which are by turn sententious and prolix). The characters are not only clearly named and put into relation to each other (father, stepmother, maid, etc.) but assigned fixed moral characters, particularly the insidiously wicked Demainete (1.9.2). This is a narrative shorthand which allows the quick development of plots; Knemon says as much – καὶ τὰ μὲν ἄλλα τί δεῖ μηκύνοντα ἐνοχλεῖν; 'And as for the other (signs by which she showed her true character), what need for me to tire you with a lengthy recital?' (1.9.4). This ploy serves to accommodate the coexistence of two opposite narrative structures, allowing Knemon to speak both as an omniscient narrator who declares at once the inner reality of his characters (Demainete's wickedness), and as a documentary narrator who relates only what he experienced. These two structures are effectively combined so that we follow Knemon's story both as a well-made tale by an author who has designed the plot and also as a personal account by the man who lived it. Knemon's references to what happened outside his immediate knowledge (Demainete's plotting) are easily integrated with the documentary stance; the implicit qualification accompanying all such information is, 'as I later learned'. The narrator exploits the best features of both narrative stances: he communicates a masterly sense of control over the story by references which alert the audience to transitions and remind us of the beginning and end: 'in the end it came to this: . . .' (1.10.1); 'She, for she was not yet sated, devised a second plot against me, as follows: . . .' (1.11.2); 'But Demainete, hateful to heaven, did not continue to escape punishment. The manner thereof you shall hear

anon' (1.14.1–2). And on the other hand the narrator in his role as
experiencing-I recaptures the immediacy of dramatic moments as
if they were happening now, in a way no third-person narrator
could (1.12.2–3) without straining credulity.

The relation of Knemon's tale to the major plot is much more
than mere retardation or postponement – important as that is:

(a) Insofar as it is a tale with a perfectly intelligible beginning,
an unproblematic narrative from its very first words, it has been
designed and positioned to emphasize the ambiguity and unans-
wered questions of the opening tableau. Knemon's tale shows that
Heliodoros is perfectly capable of writing an old-fashioned novel in
a direct narrative mode, one which tells a story from the beginning,
and that in the *Aithiopika* he is writing against that mode.

(b) Knemon's tale is a model of the ordinary *chronological*
intelligibility of all plotted stories, no matter what form they may
take. No matter what point in the plot the narrator chooses to
begin from, he must sooner or later assemble the parts so that
meaningful chronological order is understood. Knemon's tale is,
particularly at the beginning, an instance of this ideal narrative
intelligibility, what every narrative must in some sense be
reducible to. Photius' report of the *Aithiopika* (*Bibl.* cod. 73)
re-assembles the plot in chronological order, so that in his words it
sounds like a straightforward series of adventures rather than the
epistemologically self-conscious work it is. Knemon's tale represents not only what pre-Heliodoran novels were or happened to be,
but an inherent demand for meaningfulness which any fiction,
including his own, must somehow obey.

(c) Knemon's narrative moves in counterpoint to the main plot
of the *Aithiopika*, for whereas the novel as a whole begins in cunning
obscurity and gradually moves (by means of 'discovering' a
narrator, namely, Kalasiris) to a unified and reasonably straightforward pattern, Knemon's novella begins with ingenuous simplicity but becomes more and more complex in narrative structure,
and then does not end cleanly and clearly but has a number of
partial endings and unexpected resumptions.[20]

20. Complexity: In the second phase of the novella, Demainete's maid Thisbe
the clever arranger of intrigues in which each character has a different notion of
the truth. As arch-manipulator she successfully tells different lies to Demainete,
Arsinoe and Aristippos and contrives a double bed-trick: Demainete taking the

(d) Knemon's particular story also reproduces the problem of Charikleia's story. He is exiled from his native land by a move to vindicate a mother's chastity, just as Charikleia was. The overarching question of the *Aithiopika* turns out to be whether (and how) Charikleia will return to her homeland. This question very slowly and sinuously winds toward its answer in the final book. The same question governs Knemon's plot. He has come to Egypt to find Thisbe because only she can explain what really happened, and only with her evidence can he bring about the restoration of his father's property and citizenship (II.9.3–4). So it is the same question of the child's return from exile to its parent and homeland and the ensuing vindication of the parent's honor which is fully and luxuriously answered in the case of Charikleia but left hanging in the case of Knemon. Knemon's story is a variation of Charikleia's, just as Homer's invented etymological biography is patterned on Charikleia's history.

(e) Finally, Heliodoros places the two narrtives in an explicit relation of equivalence, as in the two pans of a balance scale. Knemon's tale and Charikleia's are *exchanged* in a bargain struck between Kalasiris and Knemon. They enter an agreement to tell each other their histories (II.21.5–7), an agreement which they treat from the start as a binding contract of reciprocal exchange (ἐν μέρει, II.21.7). This mutual obligation requires that the first to ask is the first to be answered, and that Kalasiris must therefore tell his complete story before Knemon is required even to reveal his name.[21] These terms become clear when several times they are nearly violated (II.21.5, 26.3, III.1.1–2, V.2.3). This series of

place of Thisbe, who is taking the place of Arsinoe. Thisbe is also the source of the story, the ultimate narrator. The reader gets so wrapped up in her involuted but carefully planned web that it comes as a small shock when Charias, the intermediate narrator, says 'you' to Knemon (I.17.2) – so completely do we forget the framing narrative situation. When the story comes to an end we experience in a rush the multiple transition from Thisbe to Charias to Knemon to Heliodoros, a Chinese box of narrators.

Incomplete endings: I.14.2, Knemon tries to stop for sleep; I.18.1, Knemon actually stops for sleep; II.11, 'the rest I am unable to recount'; VI.2–3, Knemon repeats his entire story, Nausikles refrains from filling in his part of it; VI.8, Nausikles reveals himself as Thisbe's lover and Knemon agrees to return with him to Athens. We never learn whether Nausikles' testimony, in place of Thisbe's, was sufficient to clear Aristippos.

21. The same contract, without self-conscious testing of the convention, at Xen. Eph. III.1.4f., 2.15.

postponements comes to an end at VI.2.2 when Knemon has both
occasion (the name of Thisbe again) and opportunity (a journey)
to tell his story. 'It is your turn now, Knemon, to give us the story
which you have so often promised to relate to me, and which will
acquaint us with your own adventures, but which you have
hitherto put off each time with various dodges' (σὸς ὁ λόγος, ὦ
Κνήμων, ὃν πολλάκις μοι διελθεῖν γνῶσίν τε τῶν κατὰ σεαυτὸν
παρασχεῖν ἐπαγγειλάμενος εἰς δεῦρό τε ποικίλαις ἀεὶ διαδύσεσιν
ὑπερθέμενος ἐν καιρῷ λέγοις ἂν τὸ παρόν). This is followed by a
synopsis of Knemon's tale as we already know it from the first,
well-framed narrative situation (1.9–17) and the later additions
(Knemon's further narrative, II.8.4–9; Thisbe's letter, II.10).
Knemon's fulfillment of his part of the bargain comes late and, as
far as we the readers of the *Aithiopika* are concerned, is perfunctory;
but this should not conceal the structural relation which is posited
between the two narratives. The histories of Kalasiris and of
Knemon are contractually bound to each other as an equivalent
exchange.[22]

(3) The third major postponement encountered in Book 1 is
another narrative. Summoned before the brigands' council,
Charikleia accepts an offer of marriage from their captain (himself
a priest's son in exile) and in doing so tells them the story of her
birth and the recent events which led to the puzzling banquet-and-
battle scene on the beach (1.22). Part of her story is that she is still
within, but near the end of, a year's service to Artemis, and she asks
that her marriage wait upon her official retirement from that office
in a ceremony which must take place at any established altar or

22. The metaphor of mercantile value assigned to the transaction is made
explicit at II.23.3–4. The most valuable object which Kalasiris can give to
Knemon in return for the appearance of Theagenes and Charikleia in person is his
tale of their romance. This second bargain struck is not identical with the first, and
it will make a difference (see below, pp. 146–7) whether Kalasiris is thought of as
telling his own story (the original contract) or Charikleia's (the second request).
    A scene which duplicates the theme of exchange is Kalasiris' payment of a
precious engraved ring to Nausikles for the return of Charikleia (V.12–15). In
both cases the receiver is in some sense duped, appreciating the superficial glamor
of the gem/tale but not fathoming how it was produced; and in both cases the
object exchanged for the heroine is one whose boundaries are cleverly blended
with its content and whose most marvelous quality is not the material itself but the
interaction of container and content (V.14.4). Kalasiris' religious charade is
performed in the name of Hermes, the presiding genius of the *Aithiopika* (see nn. 25
and 51).

temple of Apollo. Her story thus serves immediately to postpone (εἰς ὑπερβολήν, 1.25.6) the proposed marriage, and a few chapters later we realize that it has also postponed our learning who Charikleia really is. The tale was a lie – told in the service of chastity, or as Charikleia puts it 'an account adjusted to the occasion and serving a useful purpose' (λόγων ἐπικαιρίων καὶ πρός τι χρειῶδες εἰρημένων, 1.25.3). Theagenes understands that her calling him her brother has saved his life and that her tale of wanderings (πλάνη) has led them astray (πλάνην τῷ ὄντι τοῖς ἀκούουσιν ἐπάγοντα, 1.25.6); thus Heliodoros informs us that those parts of her story were not true. She then recommends that in view of the dangers which surround them they hold to his lie (πλάσμα) as a sort of jiujitsu feint or wrestling trick (πάλαισμα) and not trust even Knemon with the truth. The effect of her cunning and caution is that we will be given no opportunity to learn what we want to know in order to begin appreciating her situation as part of an intelligible plot.

Her account is not only a lie, it is nearly a parody of the Greek romance as a genre, conflating typical motifs from several novels, as a sort of least common denominator of what such a story could be expected to be.[23] It is as if for Heliodoros the measure of the brigands' gullibility is their willingness to believe in the plot of a Greek romance. A reader who like the brigands accepted her word at face value or like Thyamis was 'enchanted as if he had been listening to a Seiren' (1.23.2) should feel a little put out when Charikleia not only admits she was lying but remarks on the rustic simplicity of persons like Thyamis who are easily misled and mollified by words complaisant to their desire (1.26.3). The parallel. is a designed one – Thyamis the easily beguiled lover is to Charikleia's lie as the fond and romantic reader is to the conventional Greek romance. The plot of her lie presents no thoughtful difference, no challenge of any kind to the reader who knows Xenophon, Chariton and Achilles Tatius. It is a 'compliant story, one which matches pace with the expectations' of the reader,

23. γένος μέν ἐσμεν Ἴωνες, Ἐφεσίων δὲ τὰ πρῶτα γεγονότες ∼ ἦν ἐν Ἐφέσῳ ἀνὴρ τῶν τὰ πρῶτα ἐκεῖ δυναμένων, Xen. Eph. 1.1.1; ὁλκὰς οὖν ἐπληροῦτο χρυσοῦ τε καὶ ἀργύρου καὶ ἐσθήτων ∼ ναῦς μεγάλη . . . πολλὴ μὲν ἐσθὴς καὶ ποι-κίλη, πολὺς δὲ ἄργυρος καὶ χρυσός, Xen. Eph. 1.10.4; γήρᾳ τε προηκόντων ∼ ἐσχάτῳ γήρᾳ, Chariton III.5.4; the crowd of citizens is frequent throughout Xen. Eph. and Chariton; the storm at sea ∼ Achilles Tatius III.1–3.

as Charikleia says of her strategy in spinning a fiction for Thyamis (λόγος εἴκων καὶ πρὸς τὸ βούλημα συντρέχων, 1.26.3).

Each of the three major postponements so far in Book 1 which prevent our getting a grasp on this plot defines one of the three fundamental parameters within which Heliodoros is composing his novel: language, narrative sequence, and conventional romantic motifs. These three obstacles are paradoxically the three premises which the reader would bring to the text: that it makes sense in Greek, that it tells a story, that it is in the tradition of the romance. All of these turn out to be true, but only after Heliodoros has made us conscious that they are assumptions which we employ in making sense of the text.

(4) The conclusion of Book 1 is in a sense another postponement, and a drastic one. The death of the heroine is the end of her story, and cuts short the better part of our curiosity as to her identity and history. This is designed to shock (or, if we don't believe that she died, at least to make explicit) another one of our fundamental operational principles, namely, our identification with the fortunes of the protagonists. The mysterious emptiness of the conclusion to Book 1 is increased by its formal balance with the opening scene, which was designedly paradoxical and puzzling. The same band of brigands are again looting and again bypassing Charikleia. The lighting has changed – from dawn to dusk – and the lovers have reversed roles, Theagenes from apparently dead to inactive, Charikleia from inactive to apparently dead. All this, however, is action without a narrative context within which it makes sense. If it makes sense at all, it does so as some kind of closure – death, sunset and captivity all promoting the sense of an ending. It is as if we had been reading a book rather casually while half our mind was engaged elsewhere and we suddenly realize that it is over before we know what is happening.

To summarize the argument so far: the three principles of Heliodoros' narrative technique are (1) the precise, often aporetic, measurement of degrees of incomplete cognition, (2) the insistence that every part of the text have a relevance to the whole, sometimes discovered after the fact; and (3) the suspension of attention by postponement of expected information, which occurs four times in Book 1, each time so arranged as to provoke the reader to a greater awareness of one of the conventions of reading fiction, which are

(3a) an intelligible language, (3b) a sequential plot, (3c) familiar motifs, and (3d) identification with the heroes. Of these, (3b) receives very elaborate illustration in the long interpolated tale of Knemon, which has a complex relation of contrast and equivalence with Kalasiris' narrative and with the *Aithiopika* as a whole.

One answer to the question of what kind of meaning is to be found in the *Aithiopika* is – sentential. The three principles of narrative technique which we have isolated as significant in this novel are exactly the categories which guide our comprehension of any complex, periodic sentence. Heliodoros' sentences are often mobiles of intricately articulated and well-balanced cola, such as test and refine our powers of attention. A random example:

Πετόσιρις ἀδελφὸς ἦν αὐτῷ κατὰ τὴν Μέμφιν· οὗτος ἐπιβουλῇ τὴν ἱερωσύνην τῆς προφητείας παρὰ τὸ πάτριον τὸν Θύαμιν παρελόμενος νεώτερος αὐτὸς ὤν, τὸν προγενέστερον ἐξάρχειν ληστρικοῦ πυνθανόμενος, δεδιὼς μὴ καιροῦ λαβόμενος ἐπέλθοι ποτὲ ἢ καὶ χρόνος τὴν ἐπιβουλὴν φωράσειεν, ἅμα δὲ καὶ δι' ὑποψίας εἶναι παρὰ τοῖς πολλοῖς αἰσθανόμενος ὡς ἀνῃρηκὼς τὸν Θύαμιν οὐ φαινόμενον, χρήματα πάμπολλα καὶ βοσκήματα τοῖς ζῶντα προσκομίσασιν εἰς τὰς κώμας τὰς ληστρικὰς διαπέμπων ἐπεκήρυξεν. (1.33.2)

Simply to read such a sentence is already to employ the mind in making assessments of the relevance, subordination, and completeness of each phrase as it contributes to the intelligible unity of the whole. If the narrative structure of the *Aithiopika* be compared to a long sentence, Book 1 is like an introductory clause about whose meaning we must suspend judgment until much more of the sentence is uttered. Heliodoros has given his novel a narrative movement of discovered coherence analogous to that of reading any sentence.[24] The *Aithiopika* belongs to that class of literature which does not naively assume the conventions of some genre but pricks us to the highest awareness of literature as self-referential, as an act of language whose limits and whose accomplishments are

24. It is interesting to see this critical insight expressed not only among the avant-garde ('. . . the fundamental premise that a homologous relation exists between the sentence and extended narrative discourse . . .', Roland Barthes, *Communications* 8 (1966), 3) but also in traditional philological journals: O. Mazal, 'Die Satzstruktur in den Aithiopika des Heliodor von Emesa', *WS* 71 (1958), 116–31 speaks of the *Gestaltungswille* of an author being apparent not only in the overarching design of the work but in each well-constructed period.

those of language itself.[25] Heliodoros plays with the fundamental features of language so as to make us aware that literature is (among other things) a textual game, and is like a sentence in that within its structure our foreknowledge of admissible possibilities is being continually refined and particularized. This is the deepest sense in which the narrative technique of Heliodoros is one of incomplete cognition: the passage to a solution that is *predictable within certain limits* is the same as the movement of any sentence from subject through dependent clauses to a concluding verb. So it is that in each of my own sentences the reader knows within ever tighter limits as the thought progresses what words can bring this sentence to a successful and meaningful

II. Duplicity, amphiboly, and the need for interpretation

In this section I will address the issue of Kalasiris' mendacity and morality, but the approach to that central topic will necessarily be gradual because the issues of interpretation are complex. This is the point – that interpretation itself is a complex and difficult process, and Heliodoros often describes the problems which characters have in interpreting what they see or read. He constructs several scenes as debates about the meaning of a dream or oracle and elsewhere exploits to great effect amphibolies (either/or's) which pose alternative explanations for a single event. It is by way of these interpretative scenes and amphibolies that we will set up the terms to make plausible the claim that Kalasiris' duplicity is morally good.

I begin with Charikleia's dream of losing her right eye (II.16),

---

25. The accomplishments of language are catalogued by Plato at *Kratylos* 407e–408d, and it reads like a list of the major themes in the *Aithiopika*. Hermogenes, who is charged (like Kalasiris' Egyptian Homer) with being or not being a son of Hermes, asks the etymological riddle of the name of Hermes, to which Socrates in a series of puns replies that Hermes stands for translation, communication, theft, verbal deceit, and sharp business practices, in short all the functions of λόγος, and that Pan too is an emblem of language's essential duplicity in that he has two natures (διφυής) – smooth/hairy, divine/mortal, true/false. Language here means any system of signs which can be used to tell a lie; if something cannot be used to tell a lie, it cannot be used to tell the truth, it cannot in fact be used to tell at all.

Ironically, the Gymnosophists, who are forbidden to lie (X.14.1), dwell in the temple of Pan (X.4.1).

which most commentators have thought is an otiose premonition of danger, one which has either no fulfillment or a trivial one.[26] However, as we have seen, loose ends and irrelevancies are fundamentally antithetical to Heliodoros' technique. Charikleia's mysterious dream is unsolved at the time, but it points forward to a significant turn in the plot, namely, the death of the narrator, Kalasiris.

Asleep in the treasure cave, Charikleia sees a violent man approach her with a sword and cut out her right eye (II.16). She wakes with a scream; her first response is to feel her face and realize that the dream was not literally true. Her next thought is the wish that it had been literally true (ὕπαρ) rather than symbolically true (ὄναρ), 'for I greatly fear that this dream points to you (Theagenes) whom I regard as my eye, my soul, my all' (II.16). Knemon quiets that romantic alarm by providing an alternative explanation: since eyes refer to parents, loss to death, and the right side to males, the total dream must mean that Charikleia's father will die.[27] But since neither Theagenes nor the king of Aithiopia dies, and the dream is not mentioned again in the novel, critics have concluded that the episode is a meaningless scare.

There is however a solution to the dream, one which is clearly marked by every sign *except* a tediously explicit 'So *this* was the meaning of that dream in the cave!' Charikleia has many 'fathers' in this novel: an Ephesian aristocrat, according to her early lie (I.22); Charikles, 'her supposed father' (ὁ νομιζόμενος πατήρ, III.6.1, IV.11.2); Hydaspes, her natural father; and the man who is most often called her father during the course of this novel, Kalasiris. Of these the only one who dies is Kalasiris, and it is his death which her dream foretells. The evidence for this is extensive and I will cite only a few of the key passages in which the equation is established. Kalasiris is introduced to us as a father bereft of his

26. No meaning: T. R. Goethals, 'The Aethiopica of Heliodorus' (diss. Columbia 1959), 187f., John Morgan, 'A Commentary on the Ninth and Tenth Books of Heliodoros' Aithiopika' (diss. Oxford 1978), 228, 'a red herring'. Trivial: K. Kerenyi, *Die griechisch-orientalische Romanliteratur*[2] (Darmstadt 1962), 51–3, F. Weinstock, *Eos* 35 (1934), 46 – both take the dream to refer to the next day's capture of the pair and their separation.

27. This is standard oneirocritical symbolism, found for instance in Artemidoros' *Dream Analysis* 1.26. In the same chapter Artemidoros discusses dreams of blindness as signifying that travellers will not return to their homeland (33.5f. Pack).

children (II.22.4); these children are identified as Charikleia and Theagenes (II.23.1–2); it comes as a surprise that the two children whom Kalasiris mentions at II.24.6 are Thyamis and Petosiris rather than Charikleia and Theagenes. Throughout their adventures Kalasiris acts as and is regarded as their father.[28] When he dies the relationship is dwelt on at length, the word 'father' being repeated again and again.

> The sacristan consoles them, 'However, you may be pardoned, since you have been bereft, as you say, of your father, your protector and your only hope' (VII.11), Kybele similarly speaks to them of Kalasiris 'who had been in the place of a father to you' (ἐν πατρὸς ὑμῖν χώρᾳ γεγονώς, VII.12). Theagenes emphasizes the reality of the relationship when he says, 'We have lost not only our natural parents but Kalasiris, our reputed *and actual* father' (τὸν δοκοῦντα καὶ ὄντα πατέρα μετὰ τῶν ἄλλων προσαπολωλεκότες, VII.13). Left alone Charikleia and Theagenes lament their new misfortunes and the loss of Kalasiris their father, emphasizing the word (τὸ γὰρ χρηστότατον ὄνομα καλεῖν ἀπεστέρημαι πατέρα, τοῦ δαίμονος πανταχόθεν μοι τὴν τοῦ πατρὸς προσηγορίαν περικόψαι φιλονεικήσαντος, VII.14). Then Charikleia lists all three of her 'fathers' – Hydaspes, τὸν μὲν φύσει γεννήσαντα οὐκ ἔγνωκα, Charikles, τὸν δὲ θέμενον Χαρικλέα, οἴμοι, προδέδωκα, and finally Kalasiris, τὸν δὲ διαδεξάμενον καὶ τρέφοντα καὶ περισώζοντα ἀπολώλεκα, whom she asserts she will call 'father' even against the will of fate, ἀλλ' ἰδού σοι, τροφεῦ καὶ σῶτερ, προσθήσω δὲ καὶ πάτερ, κἂν ὁ δαίμων μὴ βούληται, VII.14.

As if these indications of the dream's fulfillment were not enough, Heliodoros adds a few references to blindness (VII.12.2) and to impaired sight (VII.14.3).

To understand the deeper significance of Charikleia's dream and its fulfillment we must remind ourselves how important a fact it was for a maiden to have a father. In the course of her life Charikleia, like every maiden, was socially defined by reference to a male protector: Sisimithres (from her birth to the age of seven),

---

28. He cares for Theagenes as for a child (ἅτε μοι λοιπὸν ὡς παῖδος ὑπερφροντίζειν προηρημένος, IV.3.4) and takes the place of Charikles as Charikleia's guardian and father (οὐχὶ πατήρ εἰμί σοι . . .; IV.5.7, σῷζε πάτερ, IV.18.1). The characters they meet on their journey all regard Kalasiris as the lovers' father (e.g., V.20.2, 26.3f., 28.1; V.15.1, which is evidently the background to the mention of information withheld at V.16.5). Details on this and other verbal questions may now be explored much more conveniently by using the *Alphabetical Keyword-in-Context Concordance to the Greek Novelists*, published by the Thesaurus Linguae Graecae (Irvine, California 1979).

Charikles (from seven to sixteen), and Kalasiris (her seventeenth year).[29] This group of protecting men, her *kyrioi*, occupy in turn that necessary role of maiden's sponsor and safeguard which would ordinarily be exercised by her natural father.[30] With the death of Kalasiris she has lost not merely one of her fathers but any father at all; heretofore she had merely changed fathers, one taking up where his predecessor left off. When no other protecting father immediately replaces Kalasiris in Charikleia's life, her dream has very significantly been fulfilled.

Consider next Thyamis' dream (1.18), which is also debated immediately on waking. He sees in his dream the temple of Isis at Memphis, altars streaming with blood and crowds clamoring in the porches, and the goddess herself presents Charikleia to him with the words 'You will have her and not have her; you will do her wrong and you will slay the foreign woman but she will not be slain.' Thyamis ponders the text and image, turning them one way and another to grasp at their significance. Eventually he decides that the goddess' sentence must be interpreted as both elliptical and metaphorical: he supplements the first part ('You will have her *as a wife* and you will no longer have her *as a maiden*') and

29. Our society has lost now a good deal of that extraordinary pressure which once dictated an unmarried woman's total symbolic dependence on a male figure, whether a father or some other man *in loco patris*. Charikleia, for instance, is represented as deeply reluctant to speak in the presence of a group of strange men (1.21.3). The less insightful characters all assume that this is a valuable social practice (e.g., Knemon at VI.7.7). But the logical outcome of such protective practices is spiritual annihilation of the protected, a sort of foot-binding of the free will, and in the case of choosing a husband (a father's right, as Charikles and Hydaspes think) what feels to Charikleia like rape. See further the end of section II, pp. 131–2. 136–7..

30. In a sense the whole novel is built around the birth rite whereby a mother presents her newborn child to its father for approval and recognition. Because Persinna hesitated at that moment, out of fear that she would be considered adulterous and her child killed or dishonored, a series of intermediaries – foster-fathers – is required to conduct Charikleia away from Aithiopia to Greece and then in the fullness of time back again to the motherland (ἡ ἐνεγκοῦσα, as Heliodoros so often and strikingly calls it), so that she may be recognized by her father as his new-born child, and at the same time as a newly-wed wife and a newly-installed priestess. Interestingly, these three foster-fathers are themselves chaste priests, two are widowers and well on in years, one is young and celibate, and this gives them a certain absolution from sexual suspicion which as unrelated men they would certainly have come under – at least this is Heliodoros' point of view, IV.18.4f., V.4.5. Kalasiris in particular is quite maternal, like a mother bird at II.22.4.

understands 'slaying' as a metaphor for sexual penetration, a 'wound' from which she will not die.

His dream however has a true fulfillment which is different from the interpretation he reached. At the end of Book I Thyamis is surrounded by flowing blood and corpses in flickering light and recognizes the scene from his last night's dream. He then makes up his mind that no one else will have Charikleia and rushes off to the underground cave where she has been placed and there kills a woman in the dark. His dream-oracle turns out to have that Delphic quality of not only eluding interpretation but actually inducing the horror it hints at. The horror in this case is an illusion (he kills the maid Thisbe, not the heroine Charikleia), and this illusion is the real fulfillment of the prophecy: 'You will do her (Charikleia) wrong (by intending to kill her), and you will slay the foreign woman (Thisbe) and she (Charikleia) will not be slain.'

Now Heliodoros quite carefully notes Thyamis' inadequacy in producing a satisfactory meaning for the dream: 'Tiring at length of this (perplexity and interpretive effort), he forced the solution to suit his own wish. . . . This was the sense in which he construed his dream, according to the exegesis of his own desire.' (ἤδη δὲ ἀπειρηκὼς ἕλκει πρὸς τὴν ἑαυτοῦ βούλησιν τὴν ἐπίλυσιν. . . . τὸ μὲν ὄναρ τοῦτον ἔφραζε τὸν τρόπον, οὕτως αὐτῷ τῆς ἐπιθυμίας ἐξηγουμένης, 1.18.) Thyamis' exegetical shortcomings are serious; he does violence to the text (ἕλκει), he lets his need and desire for a particular meaning project that meaning onto the dream, and above all lacks the patient attentiveness and the ability to suspend the demand for immediate completion which every reader of a long and sophisticated novel must have.

A similar remark on inadequate exegesis is made by Kalasiris at the end of Book II:

When the god had thus pronounced his oracle, a deep perplexity possessed the company gathered there, who were at a loss to construe what was the meaning of it. Each of them strained (ἔσπα) the message to a different sense, making some conjecture to suit his own will; but none at that time could apprehend the truth of it, for oracles and dreams in general are decided (interpreted, κρίνονται) by their outcomes. And besides, the Delphians were in a flutter of excitement to see the procession, which had been magnificently equipped, and they would not trouble themselves to search out the exact meaning of the oracle (πρὸς τὸ ἀκριβὲς ἀνιχνεύειν). (II.36)[31]

The Greek allows a pun to connect 'meaning' and 'desire': the people are unable to explain what the oracle *means* (ὅ τι βούλοιτο), so they force it in various directions according to individual *will* (ὡς ἕκαστος εἶχε βουλήσεως).[32]

Why does Heliodoros pay attention to various kinds of misinterpretation, failed communication, and especially the role of private desire in forcing a text to mean what the interpreter wants rather than what it wants? The answer is that the originating event, Charikleia's conception and birth, is a marvel which cannot adequately and plausibly be conveyed in ordinary terms. Hence it requires a web of international intrigue, multiple agents with cross-purposes shuttling back and forth over several countries for seventeen years, to create at last a context in which the king of Aithiopia (and his people) can accept with full understanding the sentence that Persinna wanted to say to him at the moment of Charikleia's birth, 'This child, though white, is your daughter.' Charikleia herself is the message or communication of the queen to the king, at the time a failed communication,[33] wrapped in her own story and sent away as a challenge to the higher powers to make the child's birth believable. The problem posed by Persinna to the higher divinities (and to Heliodoros) is whether they can construct a plot which will satisfyingly lead a sophisticated reader of normal resistance to take a profound enjoyment in an incredible romance. As Persinna puts it in her embroidered message, 'for no one would believe me if I told them this extraordinary turn of

31. 'Following the tracks of accuracy' is one of Heliodoros' best metaphors for thinking carefully and drawing conclusions from the signs and tokens which the truth leaves in its trail: he uses it to describe Hydaspes' missing the point (x.33.1), and plays with the idea in a misreading of Homer concerning the traces left by the feet and shins of the gods: the real oddity of that Homeric passage is not the pretended ambiguity of ῥεῖ' but rather the sense in which shins (κνημάων) can be said to leave tracks. I suspect that a pun is intended on the name of Knemon, who is supposedly being taught to read such traces more accurately and 'from a more mystical point of view' (III.13.1).

32. This ordinary Greek idiom expresses the intentionality of a speaker aiming at an idea, trying to communicate a thought, as in our expression 'I mean to say'.

33. When Sisimithres passes Charikleia on into the protection of Charikles he is prevented from completing the account of her birth (II.31.5), an interruption which reproduces the relation of Persinna to Hydaspes.

events', (οὐ γὰρ πιστεύσειν οὐδένα λεγούσῃ τὴν περιπέτειαν, IV.8).[34]

The deepest anxiety which informs this novel is the fear of *misinterpretation*. Persinna's case is exemplary and of course central. The entire revelation of Charikleia's conception is a story of acts of knowledge which are at the same time acts of desire, culminating in a decision to postpone uttering a simple but astonishing sentence and to commit the child and the thought instead to writing. Charikleia's conception began with Hydaspes' dream (ὄναρ), which commands him to have sex with his wife while they are taking a noon-day rest. It is a full ten years since Hydaspes first knew (ἐγνώρισεν) Persinna as wife. At the moment of climax Persinna instantly perceives that she is pregnant (ἠσθόμην τε παραχρῆμα κυοφορήσασα τὴν καταβολήν). When Charikleia is born white Persinna understands the cause (τὴν αἰτίαν ἐγνώριζον) but feels equally sure that she will not be understood and so consigns her daughter/message to fine needlepoint, hoping that the ministering letters will not remain mute and unread/unfulfilled (τὸ γράμμα διάκονον . . . τάχα μὲν κωφὰ καὶ ἀνήνυτα). Fear of misinterpretation is Persinna's motive for withholding her daughter/knowledge from Hydaspes and for launching her child/text rather into the uncertain world of coincidence and happenstance where ignorance and ambiguity are the rule (τὸ γὰρ ἄδηλον τῆς τύχης ἀνθρώποις ἄγνωστον, IV.8).

This tale of desire, knowledge, and fear of misinterpretation lies hidden for seventeen years until at last Charikleia is recognized and her swathe read by the first person crafty and knowing enough to do so – Kalasiris. The success of Charikleia's return to her beginning and of the novel to its end depends on maintaining a level of intelligence equal to Kalasiris', particularly in the ability to recognize what is missing, to wait for what could complete an incompletely understood oracle or dream or event. Therefore Heliodoros deliberately presents characters like Thyamis who are significantly unable to comprehend such messages, whose desire in one fashion or another intervenes as exegete of the text. Poised somewhere between the perfect interpreter (Kalasiris) and the

34. Heliodoros seems to know his Aristotelian poetics, as noted by Kerenyi (n. 26), 22 and A. Heiserman, *The Novel Before the Novel* (Chicago/London 1977), 197f. Heiserman's chapter on Heliodoros is excellent.

inadequate interpreter (Thyamis, the Delphians, *et alii*) stands the actual reader, who must be taught how to read the *Aithiopika*.

As a recurrent reminder of the difficulty of reading and interpreting any signs, be they oracles, events, or letters on a page, Heliodoros inserts explicit questions about the ambiguous nature of various events. The first of these amphibolies occurs just at the moment of Thyamis' dream:

Meanwhile Thyamis (for so was the captain of the thieves called), having slept soundly the greatest part of the night, was waked of a sudden by an odd sort of dream, that employed his thoughts some hours in considering its solution. For about the time that cocks begin to crow (whatever the cause of that act may be, whether – as some say – the bird by natural perception of the sun's return is moved to proclaim the god's welcome to our hemisphere, or whether, because of the day's warmth and an eager desire to feed and be officious, he cries aloud a message peculiar to himself, to rouse his fellow domestics for work), I say about the time of cock-crowing the captain had from the gods a vision of this nature. . . . (1.18).

The contrasting explanations are roughly those of spiritual providence and material desire. Cock-crowing is in either case a meaningful song, but it makes a great difference whether the message be interpreted as a religious hymn to the sunrise or as a command to eat and work.[35] The occurrence side by side of this amphiboly and Thyamis' effort to interpret his dream, both raising an opposition between impatient mortal desire (ἐπιθυμίας, 1.18.3, 19.1) and divinely providential meaning, must be ascribed to the author's πρόνοια and not to τύχη.

The same is true of the amphibolous interpretation provided for Kalasiris' death:

He laid himself down to sleep, and – whether it was that through the greatness of his joy his pores of respiration were excessively stretched and slackened and so his aged body of a sudden was unstrung, or that in fact

35. The cock is an appropriate token of the amphiboly which Heliodoros will so often exploit between natural and supernatural explanations, for on the naturalistic side its crowing at sunrise was traditionally and commonsensically said to be the effect of warmth and dryness (Theophrastos, *ap.* Ailian *NA* III.38) and on the supernatural side its foreknowledge of the sun's rise made it (to believers) not only Helios' special creature (Proklos, περὶ ἀγωγῆς ed. Kroll, quoted by Hopfner in *RE* Suppl. IV (1924), 14) but a living ouija board – a grain of corn was laid on each letter of the alphabet in the sand and a cock allowed to peck at will (Riess, *RE* I (1894), 1363).

(εἴτε καί) the gods granted this as a thing he asked for – at the crowing of the cocks he was known to be dead. (VII.11.4)

This ambiguity is couched in the same general terms as that preceding Thyamis' dream – material causes or providential explanation. Both Charikleia's dream and Thyamis' are placed early in the novel as prominent examples of the kind of image or text which is incomplete and requires interpretation. Thyamis' dream, forcefully and passionately misconstrued by him, soon finds its real meaning. Charikleia's, however, is drastically postponed. When its solution does occur the scene is marked as a companion to Thyamis' dream: the temple of Isis at Memphis, clamoring crowds and torchlight, cock-crows – these are the contents and circumstance of Thyamis' dream and they are the very scene of Kalasiris' death.

I take the narrator's digression on cock-crowing to be significantly placed, but how shall we describe its effect? Does it suggest that there is a philosophical or religious underpinning to the melodrama? And – a far more important question – if there be such an ideological framework is it philosophically or religiously *meant*? A good approach to these questions, which will lead on to Kalasiris' duplicity, is to consider the amphibolies which Heliodoros has scattered through the *Aithiopika*. To anticipate the results of that survey, the answer I would give to the former question is that in the *Aithiopika* the only theology to be found is a vague and shifting set of contrasts between provident/malevolent or provident/indifferent. The answer to the latter is that these references are not meant philosophically or religiously but rather as reflexive allusions to the novel's own structure of progressive and problematic intelligibility.

The eighteen amphibolies in the novel, which I will label by the letters (a) through (r), fall into four groups. The first group contains those which leave the question open or (more often) seem to weight the scales in favor of the more supernatural alternative, by placing it second and adding an intensive καί. I have already quoted (a) the cock-crow at Thyamis' dream (1.18), and (b) the death of Kalasiris (VII.11.4). (c) Theagenes decides to try to stop a runaway bull, 'whether moved by his own masculine spirit or in fact (εἴτε καί) by an impulse from some one of the gods' (X.28.4). (d) At Charikleia's arraignment for murder a maid cries out that she is innocent, 'whether she felt a pang of kindness towards Charikleia bred of their companionship and shared routine or in fact (εἴτε καί) it was the will of heaven' (VIII.9.2). (e) Thermouthis dies in his sleep – 'by the bite of an asp, possibly by the will of fate' (II.20.2). (f) Hydaspes regards Charikleia either as possessed by some god or simply out of her wits through excess of joy (X.22.4, similar to the effects of excessive joy on Kalasiris, VII.11.4, and also on the Aithiopian populace, X.39.1). (g) At twilight the sea grew suddenly rough, 'possibly it took this turn from the time of day, or perhaps in fact (τάχα δέ που καί) it was transformed by the will of some Tyche' (V.27.1). (h) The wind dies down, 'as though it were setting with the sun, or to speak more truly were bent on serving the purposes of our pursuers' (V.23.2). These elegant touches of uncertainty put the narrator at an enigmatic distance. We might translate their force into the clichés of popular, intrusive narrative style as follows: 'But what guiding hand was at work in these events, dear Reader? Is Charikleia a plaything of sportive fortune, or merely a mortal body in a world of natural law, or is she in fact a favored child of providence? Read on!'

> Charikleia and Theagenes themselves spend a good deal of time putting this very question to themselves, most extensively at VII.10f. Theagenes assumes that providence has just done them a good turn, but Charikleia (who is as usual – ἔστι γὰρ χρῆμα σοφώτατον, V.26.2 – more clever than her lover) tries to keep an open mind (ἀμφιβάλλειν, VII.10.2): either the gods favor them, as the recent rescue might show, or the gods hate them, as their persistent run of bad luck indicates, or possibly (putting those two points of view together) god is a professional magician performing impossible feats with their lives. This last possibility is both blasphemous (says Theagenes immediately, VIII.11.1) and true (compare θαυματοποιία τίς ἐστι δαίμονος, VIII.10.2, with αἰσθανώμεθα τοῦ θείου θαυματουργήματος, X.39.3). Depending on one's views of discipline and love one might place IV.1.2 either with this group of amphibolies or the next.

The second group of interpretive dilemmas contains those which are so phrased as to suggest that a providential explanation is unlikely or even foolish. (i) Two very long and complex physical explanations are given of why the dike around Syene collapsed, followed by the laconic 'or one might attribute the deed to divine assistance' (IX.8.2). (j) After explaining that Homer kept his native land a secret out of shame at his exile and rejection from the priesthood, Kalasiris adds, 'or else it was a clever trick whereby Homer in concealing his real country might woo every city to take him as their own' (III.14.4).[36] (k) A similarly cynical note is struck in the double explanation of the name Hypata: 'a metropolis with a glorious name – as the citizens themselves would have it – derived from its ruling and being exalted (ὑπατεύειν) over the rest, but as others think from its mere (περ) position at the base of Mt Oita (ὑπὸ τῇ Οἴτῃ)' (II.34.2). Like Thyamis, the Hypatans interpret an ambiguous (and minimal) text in a sense favorable to their interests, and Kalasiris (who relates this) implies that they are deceiving themselves, that they are precisely reading an exalted meaning into an ordinary word with a plain physical meaning.[37] This amphiboly comes just before the Delphians' significant non-comprehension of the oracle at II.36. (l) Most cynical of all are Heliodoros' alternatives for Thyamis' attempted murder of Charikleia in the treasure-cave. Heliodoros remarks that barbarians in desperate straits always kill their beloved ones 'either falsely believing (ἀπατώμενον) that they will rejoin their loved ones after death, or wishing to rescue them from an enemy's violence' (1.30.6). The supernatural motive is expressly labelled an empty hope and those who act on it are deceived. The hint here of a

36. This motif is also employed at II.34.5, where Charikles explains the claim of Theagenes to be a descendant of Achilles. Other tribes than the Ainianes falsely claimed Achilles as their ancestor to add his glory to themselves. The connection of this passage with the Hermetic Homer story is very close: Homer is here first called Egyptian, and the claim of Theagenes involves a quibble on the Homeric text (similar to III.13.3) as to the meaning of Phthia then and now. Notice how Heliodoros is not content simply to make Theagenes a Phthian and so justify his descent from Achilles without any further ado but makes an issue of it, basing romantic heroism (Theagenes looks Achillean, II.34.4) on a scholarly dubiety. The claim's thematic connection with the Homer joke at III.14.4 and proximity to the Hypatans' equally dubious (and cynically treated) claim to interpret the name of their own city (see the next amphiboly) casts the whole Achilles comparison in a profound shadow of skepticism; the rite too of Neoptolemos, which is what formally brings the lovers into first contact, then takes on a certain High Anglican quality of protested antiquity. Some of Heliodoros' characters seem to have that viewpoint which W. Levitan describes, in his brilliant article 'Plexed Artistry: Aratean Acrostics', *Glyph* 5 (1979), 55–68, as 'the sensibility of the near miss'.

37. The brigands have the same sensitivity to nice points of usage which may affect their honor and self-esteem: Thyamis summons his men to divide the booty, 'which he called by the more dignified name "spoils of war"' (λάφυρα τὰ σκῦλα σεμνότερον ὀνομάζων, 1.19.1), in the very sentence which describes how he construed his dream to fit his own desire.

metaphysical opinion – denial of personal survival after death – is the opposite of the implication at III.5.4–5 where Charikleia and Theagenes fall in love at first glance, in such a way as to

confirm belief in the soul's divinity and its kinship with the powers on high. For at the moment of meeting the young pair looked and loved, as though the soul of each at the first encounter recognized its fellow and leaped towards that which deserved to belong to it . . . as if they had had some previous knowledge or sight which they were recalling to memory.

The hint of Platonic *anamnesis* is muted but unmistakable. The specific contrast of these two passages simply brings into sharper focus the general problem of a text which alternately raises and twits our hopes that a superstructure of providence – Someone up there who likes Charikleia – will be meaningful in this book.[38]

(m) The positive and negative terminals of this alternating current are nearly brought into contact during the description of the siege of Syene. Egyptian theology with its deification of the Nile is outlined in two passages (IX.9 and 22). The former passage contains its own ambiguities (several levels of esoteric and mystical meaning involving physics, mythology, and Deeper Significance) but seems at the time to be treated seriously. At least the narrator refuses out of holy reverence to dwell on the mysteries any further (IX.10.1). The subject is resumed at IX.22 where the priests of Syene show Hydaspes the Nilometer and explain the numerological equation of the Nile with the year. Hydaspes' reply is fairly terse, reminding them that all they have said of the Nile's favor to them applies first to the Aithiopians, and he refers to the Nile as 'this river, or god according to you'. This flippant dismissal is another example of the cynical bent which Heliodoros gives to *some* of his alternatives, and so flatly contradicts his 'own' attitude at IX.10.1 ('Thus far may our account of this matter meet with divine approval; but the deeper secrets of the mysteries must be paid the respect of strict silence') that we must ask whether the author has failed to make a connection or have we.

The answer, I will argue, is that both groups of alter-

---

38. The theology of the *Aithiopika* is not a coherent system, as J. Morgan has shown (APA panel on the novels as *Mysterientexte*, Vancouver 1978). The same could be done for Heliodoros' references to an afterlife, which are strictly designed to fit the occasion (in addition to those cited in the text see II.24.6, VII.11.9, VIII.11.10).

natives – those weighted toward the supernatural and those weighted toward the natural – are meaningful and have complementary functions in the context of a melodramatic narrative whose characteristic feature is the alternation between hope and despair. When the narrator pauses to reflect on the significance of an event, on the larger interpretative scheme within which it will make sense, he poses both an optimistic view and a pessimistic view, inclining now to one, now to the other. That the real meaning of these ambiguous alternatives is to express the nature of the novel itself as melodrama is supported by two further groups of such amphibolies which pertain to aesthetics and to Kalasiris.

Three amphibolies are employed to celebrate what we might call an aesthetic of Mind-Boggling Variety. (n) At vii.6.4 'whatever divinity or whatever tyche oversees human affairs' is invoked as responsible for the stage-entrance of Kalasiris into an already complex tableau. This entire scene (vii.6–8) is a culminating showpiece of conflicting emotions, of pain and joy, concluding with the death of Kalasiris. (o) Knemon overhears the voice of a woman who identifies herself as Thisbe, his dead mistress (v.3–4). As the cocks crow, he stumbles to his room and swoons. Heliodoros then remarks on the two explanations of Knemon's situation: some divinity makes jest and sport of human affairs, mingling pain into what ere long will bring us joy, or else it is simply a fact of human nature itself that joy in its purity cannot be experienced. Reflections such as these on the crazy-quilt of Life and whether a friendly designer or a brute force is behind it have the value of self-advertizements for the author, since the novelist will be most successful on his own terms if we regard his story as one of impossible odds and plausible resolutions, that is, an elegant mediation between the hopelessness of a world governed by malevolent or indifferent tyche and the confidence of a world mysteriously orchestrated by providence.

(p) At the close of the novel (x.38.3–4) the entire Aithiopian audience applaud the dénouement, even though it has been conducted in a language foreign to them, namely Greek: 'The spoken words, on the whole, they could not comprehend, but they conjectured the facts from what had previously transpired concerning Charikleia; or else it might be that they were led to surmise the truth by the influence of some divine power that had designed the whole of this dramatic scene, and by whose means extreme contraries were now composed into a harmony, etc.' This final amphiboly in the *Aithiopika* is about how to explain the audience's appreciation of a scene they ought not to be able to understand. It corresponds to the opening scene of failed communication between the black brigands and the white maiden.

The double explanation offered for the Aithiopians' transcendence of the language barrier is very ironic – either they guessed the right answer correctly and *en masse* by a natural process of the mind, or they were enlightened by God the Author of this novel. In either case what is being explained is the Aithiopians' role as audience to a Romance, and that from a cognitive point of view. The central aesthetic structure is described as a hard-won balance between centrifugal Variety and centripetal Unity: '. . . by whose means extreme contraries were now composed into a harmony. Joy and grief were intertwined, tears were mingled with laughter, and the most baleful proceedings were converted into festivity' (x.38.4). This is the same response which Kalasiris feels when he reads Persinna's embroidered message, a mini-novel. I have explained above how that message is a tale of partial recognitions and incomplete communication; the capstone of that series is the reader's (Kalasiris') understanding and recognition of its meaning: 'When I had read these words, Knemon, I recognized (ὡς ἀνέγνων ἐγνώριζον) and admired the wise dispensation of the gods. Filled with mingled feelings of pleasure and pain, I went through the singular experience of weeping and rejoicing at the same moment' (IV.9.1). The singular experience of this novel for us is its analysis, through romance-readers like Kalasiris, of comprehending a romance. Heliodoros' sophistication lies not merely in his mastery as a narrator but in his presentation of narrators and audiences caught in the fact of understanding or missing the romantic pattern.

This third group of amphibolies, centering on the aesthetics of the romance, explains the underlying compatibility of the first two groups – the sublime and the cynical. Our epistemological progress through the labyrinthine ways of this plot takes us along stretches where the light at the end of the tunnel disappears and then again glimmers closer than we thought. By reminding us both of providential and of naturalistic hypotheses, Heliodoros keeps alive the questions of how and on what terms the plot will resolve itself. Particularly effective are the *detailed material explanations* of what in other romances might be simple miracles or wondrous but unexplained coincidences. The very suggestion that the protagonists' escapes and successes may be the result not of divine protection but of the laws of physical nature – analyzed in close detail in a few instances – calls into question the naive but fundamental pretense which is the presupposition of the other novels, namely, that an identifiable god has inaugurated and throughout controls the varying fortunes of the protagonists. The *Aithiopika* is a palimpsest, written on the tablet of naive romance, and one of its fascinating reinterpretations of the underlying conventions is the tentative exploration of a naturalistic explanation of the romantic plot. Heliodoros has raised the question of supernatural control and, like a devil's advocate, has provided counter-evidence against such a belief by interpreting various events in terms of physical law or naturalistic psychology.

The most extended example of such naturalism is found in the fourth group of amphibolies, those uttered by Kalasiris. (q) When Charikles asks Kalasiris to diagnose his daughter's indisposition, which Kalasiris has just vividly described to Knemon and us as Love-at-first-sight, he replies that it must be the evil eye. Charikles tries to reject this as popular superstition, and Kalasiris launches into a quite long scientific analysis of the evil-eye phenomenon in the human and animal realms (III.7–8). His explanation combines physics and psychology, pores and passions, in a display piece of anti-romantic analysis.[39] Kalasiris then is the spokesperson for both views – the lovers' souls share in the divine nature at the moment of mutual recognition *or* Charikleia's orifices were infiltrated by an effluence which popular lore calls the evil eye. Both views make sense in their respective contexts, the romantic extravaganza for the sentimental Knemon, the learned disquisition for the father to be fooled. Kalasiris quite naturally adopts both tones which Heliodoros employs in his other amphibolies, the sublime and the naturalistic. What ought to be a contradiction on the level of serious ideology is perfectly normal practice for a

39. Ironically Kalasiris adduces love-at-first-sight as an analogy to confirm his hypothesis of the evil eye.

narrator: Kalasiris is simply the best single representative of the mind of the author himself.

(r) Kalasiris, at the point in his narrative when Theagenes comes to consult him as a love-magician (III.16), expounds to Knemon the true meaning of Egyptian lore. It is a double knowledge, or rather two quite different cognitive practices which have the same name – a legitimate astral foreknowledge of things to come, which is beneficial to mankind and a prerogative of the priestly class, and a bastard sciolism which confusedly and ineffectually tries to raise spirits of the dead and use herbs and spells as love-magic. Of the several contrasts drawn between the two knowledges – aristocratic/plebeian, celestial/earthly, male/female, divine/pseudo-demonic – the most important for our analysis is that of pander to unbridled pleasure (ἡδονῶν ἀκολάστων ὑπηρέτις) *vs* unworldly mystic, for Theagenes and Charikles consult him as if he were the former and he accommodates his outward behavior to their expectations.

Kalasiris' explanation of the two cognitive systems which pass under the same name of 'Egyptian wisdom' (ἡ Αἰγυπτίων σοφία) is in effect a presentation of two views or interpretations of his own activity at Delphi covering Books II.24 through IV.21 (recurring at X.36.4). Heliodoros traces the precise path of misconception: 'When Theagenes heard mention of "Egyptian" and "prophet", he was at once filled with delight . . .' (III.11.3); 'I surmised that, having heard at the banquet that I was an Egyptian and a prophet, he had come to obtain my assistance in his love-affair' (III.16.2). If Theagenes or Charikles had been as crafty about the exact meaning and implication of words as Heliodoros (mainly through Kalasiris) is teaching us to be, they would not have leaped to the conclusion that 'Egyptian prophet' means 'erotic pharmacologist'. As it is, both approach him with a *preconception* of his role and express to him their desire that he make Charikleia fall in love (Charikles: καὶ γάρ σε καὶ διά τι χρήσιμον ἐμὸν ἀκροατὴν γενέσθαι τῶν συμβεβηκότων πάλαι ἐβουλόμην, II.29.2; πρὸς ταῦτα δὴ σὲ βοηθὸν ἐπικαλοῦμαι. . . . σοφίαν τινὰ καὶ ἴυγγα κίνησον ἐπ' αὐτὴν Αἰγυπτίαν, II.33.6; οἶσθα ὡς ἐπὶ τοῦτό σε καὶ παρεκάλεσα, III.9; veiled at III.19.3 and IV.6.2; Theagenes: συνεργὸν πρὸς τὸν ἔρωτα ληψόμενος, III.16.2; οὐκ ἐσφαλμένος . . . ὧν προσεδόκησε, III.17.3).

Kalasiris' role throughout is not that of meddler or manipulator but of observer, waiting for his partial knowledge to be completed in the gods' own good time. The gods make various things fall into Kalasiris' hands: 'I was glad that the young man was at my door and bade him enter, with the thought that a beginning for my plans in hand was presenting itself to me of its own accord (ταὐτόματον),' III.16.2; 'I was making my way towards the temple of Apollo, intending to entreat the god for an oracle to guide my escape with the young couple. But in truth divinity is sharper than any mind and comes to the aid, all unbidden, of those who are acting according to his will, often anticipating a request of his own benevolence,' IV.16.2–3. Kalasiris sums up his approach when he finally reveals his mind to Charikleia: 'for a long time now, as you know, I have been dwelling here, and from the beginning paying all proper attention to you, keeping the facts silent, waiting to seize the right moment . . . ,' IV.13.1. If we read the whole of Kalasiris' narrative, the general impression is that of a shrewd but very passive observer, one who knows a good deal more than those he is watching and who uses opportunities that are presented to him, but not one who *makes* things happen. One of the opportunities thrust on him is the pressing requests of Charikles to arouse his daughter's dormant sexuality and when she is sick to cure her. (These two requests are nearly the same thing for Charikles: 'May Charikleia too feel one day a lover's longing! Then I should be satisfied that she was in good health and not sick' III.9.) In all the scenes where Kalasiris describes how he complied with these requests there is a clear consciousness of playing not just *a* role but *their* role, living up to their presuppositions about his knowledge and power, and an equally clear sense that behind his masked performance the integrity of his knowledge and purpose is intact. In the play-acting scenes of witchcraft (III.17.1, 18.3, IV.5.2–4, 6.3–5, 7.1–2, 7.12–13, 10.1–12.1, 14.1, 15.2–3) Kalasiris is improvising with the material which the gods have put in his way, quite uncertain of how it will turn out, waiting for the kairotic moment when knowledge will be fully clear and action appropriate. 'I realized then that it was the right time (καιρόν) to play the magician for him and to seem to divine what I already knew' III.17.1.

When I was left alone with her I began what you might call a piece of play-acting business. I burnt the incense and, after muttering some pretended prayers with my lips, I shook the laurel briskly over Charikleia, up and down, from head to foot; then, letting my mouth gape in a sleepy sort of way – really like an old crone – I finally came to a slow halt, having deluged the both of us with a great deal of nonsense. She kept shaking her head, with a wry sort of smile, to signify that I was hopelessly adrift, with no inkling of her sickness. (IV.5.3–4)

What Kalasiris actually does know through all this – both by inspiration and by observation – will be examined in the next section. For the moment let us conclude the discussion of Kalasiris as love-magician with the main point of contrast. The lower Egyptian magic works by violence, forcing unwilling persons to experience desire, forcing the reluctant dead to return (VI.15), whereas the higher wisdom seeks to accommodate itself to the divine will wherever possible. Charikles, and to a much lesser extent Theagenes, want to force Charikleia to feel a love she does not (in Theagenes' case, may not) want. The standard vocabulary for the effects of love-magic is couched in terms of compelling, overmastering, conquering: 'She is indeed somewhat austere and stubbornly resists subjection to the sway of love . . . but art can find a way to force (βιάζεσθαι) even nature', III.17.5. 'You must cease insulting me and my art, by which she has already been captured and compelled (ἥλωκεν καὶ κατηνάγκασται) to love you and prays that, like some god, you might come before her eyes', IV.6.4. 'It was clear enough that she would not withstand even my first onset, without any harassing action by my stronger forces', IV.7.2.[40] Kalasiris however is in fact acting in precisely the opposite way – so far from doing any violence to Charikleia, his negotiations with her are characterized by the gentlest tact and understanding, allowing her full freedom at every stage (III.7.1, 19, IV.5.4–6.2, 7.8, 10.1–13.5). Though her supposed father Charikles is concerned for her and treats her tenderly, he nurtures a fixed plan to wed her to his nephew and will in time force the issue (πρὸς βίαν, IV.13.2),

---

40. I cannot resist referring the reader to the story of that very Charikleian heroine, Sosipatra, in Eunapios 466ff. Boissonade (400ff. Wright). She was a radiant and beautiful child who was trained from the age of five by two mysterious old men ('her truer guardians and parents'), after which she was prescient and telepathic. She chose her own husband, and later dealt with a kinsman who tried to use love-magic on her. This is a bout of spells and counter-spells from which she emerges victorious. She also surpassed her husband in wisdom, as Charikleia does Theagenes.

whereas Kalasiris offers her an opportunity to make her own choice (IV.11.1, 13.2). The contrast then between the higher and lower Egyptian lores is a basic structuring principle behind Kalasiris' Delphic narrative, and it characterizes him as a passive observer who appears to comply with the will of others who want to force Charikleia to experience *eros*. His role is to protect her from this rape of her will.

This contrast between Charikleia's free choice to accept a love because she feels it and judges it honorable and the selection of a spouse for her by her fathers (Charikles, Hydaspes) carries through to the final book, where even her mother assumes that Charikleia will of course submit to the parental decision in this matter (x.21.3). The candidate is at hand (x.24.1f., 33.2). The extraordinary pressure laid on young women not to affirm and declare their own sexual feelings or choices shapes the action of the last book from the recognition of Charikleia (ending at x.17). The question from there on is 'Who is that man you were travelling with, whom you said was your brother?' (x.18.1f.). Charikleia tries to answer the question, blushing – ὅστις δέ ἐστιν ἀληθῶς αὐτὸς ἂν λέγοι βέλτιον, ἀνήρ τε γάρ ἐστιν ἐμοῦ τε τῆς γυναικὸς εὐθαρσέστερον ἐξαγορεύειν οὐκ αἰσχυνθήσεται, 'Truly he could better answer the question, who he is, for he is a man/husband and will not be disgraced to speak out more boldly than me a woman/his wife' (x.18.2). This remarkable sentence is both an answer to the question, and a statement of the principle (woman's silence, as in 1.21.3–22.1) which leads to its misinterpretation. Hydaspes 'does not grasp the sense of what she said', that is, does not see the forbidden answer in the modest self-denigration. She tries to tell him again at x.19.2 and 20.2 (the latter, I think, a hint at suicide, like the tale at Paus. VII.21), with the same results. The force of convention is stated most clearly at x.22.1, which Charikleia experiences as a condemnation of her sexuality. When pressed by circumstances to acknowledge explicitly that she has run away with a lover she uses metaphors of nakedness and unveiling (x.29.5). At x.33.4 she finally does so, but the shamefaced author allows it to be private. The shock is alleviated by the dramaturgy, for when it is announced (by Persinna) that Theagenes is her bridegroom (νυμφίος, x.38.2), the people raise such a shout of approval that the king has no time to wonder about the proprieties. Sisimithres immediately turns this fact into the final flourish of proof that the gods designed this melodrama for their own good purposes (τὸν νυμφίον τῆς κόρης τουτονὶ τὸν ξένον νεανίαν ἀναφήναντες, x.39.2), and the pageant sweeps on to its stately conclusion.

Another interpretation of Heliodoros' amphibolies has been

advanced by John Morgan,[41] who maintains that they are a well-known literary device by which historians generate the impression that they are telling the strict truth. In a display of detailed factual information an historian's occasional admission of ignorance on one point lends credence to the accuracy of the rest. It is not only historians who may do this but any narrator speaking in what I called the documentary, as opposed to the omniscient, mode – e.g. *Od.* IX.237–239, Lucian, *Tox.* 17. The pose in question is that of any realistic narrator of actual facts in contrast to the story-teller who is free to make things up as he goes along. Heliodoros aims for this sense of historiographic or documentary verisimilitude in order to make our experience of the *Aithiopika* more intense than that of Chariton's *Kallirhoe*. His motto is, Truth is stronger than fiction.

This is quite true as far as it goes, but there are two points which must be made to sharpen and extend Morgan's insight . First, we must note the distinct effects of two different classes of expression – expressions of uncertainty, including amphibolies as one form, and supernatural/natural alternatives. Some amphibolies are simply documentary (Herodotos 1.61.2; Heliodoros VIII.9.3) and are virtually equivalent to the phrase ταῦτα οὐκ ἔχω ἀτρεκέως διακρῖναι (Hdt. VII.54.3 *et saepe*). The set of issues raised by such expressions of uncertainty are indeed part of the historiographic pose which Morgan has in mind. A whole different set of issues however is raised by competing explanations when one of them is supernatural, issues such as rationalism, belief, tradition, criteria of probability, theories of divinity and its operation in human affairs. All these, which we may call the rationalistic problem, are also found expressed as double explanations in many genres besides historiography: epic – *Od.* VII.263, A.R. 1.804*, Vergil, *Aen.* IX.243–46, Q.S. XI.184f.; mock-epic – *Culex* 193; tragedy – Eur., *Hek.* 488–491, *Helen* 137–42; philosophy – Pl., *Rep.* 330 e, *Phaidros* 229 b–230 a; fiction – A.T. VIII.6.13, *Herpyllis* 55–60. Historians naturally have many occasions to deal with conflicting accounts of extraordinary events, but when they contrast supernatural and natural explanations it is not *qua* historian that they do so but as

---

41. *Op. cit.* (n. 26), lxi–lxxix, 69, 73, 95f., 470f., 596, and in his 'History, Romance and Realism in the *Aithiopika* of Heliodoros' (forthcoming).

intelligent narrators of events to which some persons have attached a theological meaning.[42] They share this role with geographers, antiquarians, philosophers, and people in the street.[43] To take an extreme example, the issues of interpretation central to Heliodoros have more in common with Petronius, *Sat.* 137 (mantic hocus-pocus with an observer's detection of a natural explanation)[44] than with Herodotos II.103.2 (alternative motives for Egyptian soldiers settling in Kolchis).

Secondly, we must make a distinction between merely using a phrase and meaning it. Literature composed on the shoulders of a great tradition is capable of being mindless repetition or highly mindful rethinking. It is one thing, for instance, to write in Ionic after the manner of Herodotos by culling phrases from his *Histories*; it is quite another to try to think and perceive as Herodotos did (see Lucian, *Herod.* 1, *Syria dea*). Heliodoros to be sure employs his share of borrowed phrases used for ornament alone – ὀλλύντων καὶ ὀλλυμένων of a fierce battle (1.22.5, 30.3); Thucydidean neuter participles, τοῦ θυμοῦ τὸ φλεγμαῖνον, VII.21.4, τὸ πεπτωκὸς τοῦ τείχους, IX.8.1 – but in the case of the amphibolies *with rationalizing content* he is not just using a well-known device of realistic narration but posing a problem, setting up terms with which we may think about this particular literary construct. The sort of thought provoked by the rationalizing amphibolies is not merely 'Perhaps these events really happened, since the narrator does not know all the answers', but even more 'What does this novelist have up his sleeve when he goes out of his way to cast doubt on the providential control of his plot?' (see pp. 127–8 above).

42. I find one lonely example of a Heliodoran amphiboly, spectacular and mutedly cynical, at Polyb. x. 11 and 14. Scipio promises his men both handsome remuneration and a sign from Poseidon, vouched for by the god himself in a dream, to encourage them to fight bravely at New Carthage; he then times his attack to coincide with the beginning of ebb-tide, which empties the lagoon with phenomenal speed, and the soldiers walk through the shallow water, convinced that the god is fighting on their side. Thucydides too is famously pungent on the divine meanings read into things (II.54, VII.50.4).

43. Plutarch is perhaps a good example of a general enquirer rather than a historian proper. His religious attitudes are excellently analyzed in F. E. Brenk, *In Mist Apparelled: Religious Themes in Plutarch's 'Moralia' and 'Lives'* (Lugduni Batavorum 1977).

44. Or Lucian, *Philops.* 13–15 (a Hyperborean magus casts a powerful love spell on a woman whom the narrator thereafter identifies as a willing partner whose love is readily available without any spell).

Heliodoros' irony and sophistication in the use of historio-graphic and rationalistic devices such as the amphiboly stands out clearly when we compare him with a 'real' historian of about the same time who merely juggles narrative clichés from the common stock available to all later writers. Herodian's *History* is an extensive repertoire of inherited tropes, and might indeed have been on Heliodoros' reading list, for they use very many of the same items – Thucydidean neuters,[45] the stage-management of jealous tyche,[46] the private grief motif,[47] the barbarian gnome,[48] *dual explanations*,[49] the slightly cynical verb ἐκθειάζω[50] – but uses them only randomly and decoratively, and never like Heliodoros to mark the structure of a systematic intellectual project.

If Heliodoros had really wanted to create an historiographic verisimilitude he would have spoken in the first person as Herodian, Polybios and Herodotos do. Notice in particular that Herodotos, the most fabulous and romantic narrator, as well as one of the most shrewd and intelligent, is quite intrusive, even when he

45. τὸ πνιγῶδες τοῦ ἀέρος, vi.6.2. See F. J. Stein, 'Dexippus et Herodianus rerum scriptores quatenus Thucydidem secuti sint' (diss. Bonn 1957); G. Kettler, 'Nonnullae ad Herodianum . . . adnotationes' (Erlangen 1882), 22f.

46. 1.8.3.

47. ὠλοφύροντο κοινῇ μὲν πάντες τὰ δημόσια, ἕκαστος δὲ ἰδίᾳ τὰ αὑτοῦ, 1.14.3.

48. φύσει γὰρ τὸ βάρβαρον φιλοχρήματον . . ., 1.6.9; ἐρᾷ δὲ τὸ βάρβαρον καὶ ἐπὶ ταῖς τυχούσαις ἀφορμαῖς ῥᾷστα κινεῖσθαι, 1.3.5, *et saepe*. cp. Hld. 1.30.6.

49. Both of the 'historiographic' type which simply admits ignorance (vi.6.1, vii.10.5) and the amphiboly which pits supernatural and natural explanations against each other (1.9.5, viii.3.9). A sort of link between the two is formed by the type in which Herodian wonders whether a proffered claim is truth or fiction (v.3.10, iv.12.5, vii.1.8).

50. Sometimes the verb in Herodian means 'regard as divine' or 'give a divine explanation to' with no judgment implied on the truth of the belief (1.14.6 [ἐπιστώσατο does not imply Herodian's assent], ii.4.2, iv.2), but the cases are more striking where he uses it with a touch of irony (Commodus' 'divine' beauty, 1.7.5, Ganymede's 'divine' dismemberment, torn apart in a struggle between his brother and his lover, 1.11.2). The attitude is most fully expressed in his discussion of the Emesan black conical rock in the temple of Helios: διοπετῆ τε αὐτὸν εἶναι σεμνολογοῦσιν, ἐξοχάς τέ τινας βραχείας καὶ τύπους δεικνύουσιν, εἰκόνα τε ἡλίου ἀνέργαστον εἶναι θέλουσιν, οὕτω βλέπειν ἐθέλοντες, v.3.5. The language of interpretive desire is quite Heliodoran here. Heliodoros uses ἐκθειάζω of some characters' hyperboles (ii.33.5 from Charikles' point of view, viii.2.1, x.29.1). Its use at ix.9.4 is certainly colored by the preceding θεοπλαστοῦσι and σεμνηγοροῦντες, ix.9.3. I regard the effect of even a single cynical analysis in an otherwise pious text as infectious rather than inoculating. (The correlative concept, 'give a human explanation to divine things', is found at Plu., *de Isid.* 360a: ἐξανθρωπίζειν τὰ θεῖα.)

is pointing out his suspension of judgment, and when he discusses contrasting versions (v.85–7, for instance), he does not leave the reader in doubt about his own opinions. The provocative absence of this identifiable persona, however, is of the essence of the *Aithiopika* as an impersonal, structured ascent of problematic language resolving itself.

Heliodoros presents events as texts, that is, as incomplete until read and interpreted, and as quite likely to be misread and misinterpreted by the reader with presuppositions. If the author intrudes too much he may spoil the reader's discovery that there are problems, the discovery that available categories are too narrow to enclose the richness and wonder of this plot, and the discovery that the exegete's desire must be chastely held in suspense or else the deepest beauty of the text will forever elude.

We have reached then a solution to the first of our problems, that of Kalasiris' moral duplicity. It is only by trying to fix him under a certain preconception of the priest and truth-teller that the problem arises. In fact Kalasiris in his very play-acting as love magus liberates Charikleia to make her own choice and saves her from the raping intentions of others. His hypocrisy is both a cover to conceal and a means to effect the most moral attitude in the book – his loving care for Charikleia. It is as an actor in the gods' complicated plot at Delphi that Kalasiris appears duplicitous, but the justification of his behavior is not that he acts basely in the service of a higher cause, rather *duplicity itself* is the proper moral attitude, duplicity in the sense of carefully weighing alternatives and respecting the volition of all the characters. In his incredible passivity and reluctance to intervene Kalasiris observes the conflict of interests, he actually furthers the unfortunate purposes of Charikles and the purblind purposes of Theagenes and uses them as a wrestler uses an opponent's weight (καθάπερ πάλαισμα τὸ πλάσμα, 1.26.5) to enhance the options of his beloved Charikleia.[51] He is the best guardian, the protector most respectful of her person, and he is the reader whom *Charikleia* the novel and Charikleia the heroine require, for only an accurate and patient intelligence can

51. The wrestling metaphor is finally played out at x.31f.: Theagenes has a refined and exquisite knowledge of this Hermetic technique (τήν τε ἐναγώνιον Ἑρμοῦ τέχνην ἠκριβωκώς, x.31.5) and he uses it craftily, feinting and pretending (κατασοφίσασθαι . . . ἐσκήπτετο . . . ἐσχηματίζετο, x.31.5–6).

both perceive alternative explanations and bide its time for the perfect moment when a delicate balance between them can be resolved. Against the others who read her symptoms and tell her story in ways accommodated to their own will, forcing her into someone else's plot, Kalasiris alone has the necessary doubleness of mind to read the events around her, and so he alone can adequately cooperate in the slow emergence of an unexpected sense – her plot – which is complex and hard to fathom.

The *Aithiopika* is certainly a moral fiction, not just a novel about moral characters but a novel in which being morally perfect requires being an intelligent actor and reader. Kalasiris' duplicity needs no excuse, it simply needs careful analysis. I refer the reader again to the series of encounters between Kalasiris and Charikleia (III.7.1, 19, IV.5.4–6.2, 7.8, 10.1–13.5), in which her whole person – her mind, feelings, aspirations and choices – are accorded a respect no other character offers her. And it is exactly because he can suspend judgment about her identity and the meaning of the oracles around her that Kalasiris can eventually perceive who she really is. His suspension of judgment about her is the intellectual equivalent of his refusal to violate her will. In this sense the *Aithiopika* is a moral fiction, and Kalasiris is its duplicitous saint.

III. What Kalasiris knew

But some readers have asserted that Kalasiris does not suspend judgment: he knew all along that Charikleia was Persinna's daughter, that her homeland was Aithiopia, and that she would return there safely. For he had visited Aithiopia on his travels, had been told by Queen Persinna the story of her long-lost daughter and had been informed by the gods that she was living in Delphi (IV.12). We may focus the discussion of what Kalasiris knows on his claim that he only partially understands the important oracle (II.35.5) which is (apparently) a not-very-enigmatic summary of the plot:

> τὴν χάριν ἐν πρώτοις αὐτὰρ κλέος ὕστατ' ἔχουσαν
> φράζεσθ', ὦ Δελφοί, τόν τε θεᾶς γενέτην·
> οἳ νηὸν προλιπόντες ἐμὸν καὶ κῦμα τεμόντες
> ἵξοντ' ἠελίου πρὸς χθόνα κυανέην,
> τῇ περ ἀριστοβίων μέγ' ἀέθλιον ἐξάψονται
> λευκὸν ἐπὶ κροτάφων στέμμα μελαινομένων.

Notice, O Delphians, her whose first is *charis* and whose last is *kleos*, and also him born of a goddess (θεᾶς γενέτην); leaving my nave and cleaving the wave they will come to the dark land of the sun, and there they will find the great prize for their virtuous lives – a white garland on brows turned black.

The Delphians may be pardoned for being puzzled at this saying since they do not know that this is a romance, but the reader has no such excuse and certainly understands at least that Charikleia and Theagenes will come successfully to Aithiopia, which is both the land from which Charikleia's black guardian brought her (already known from II.32.1–2) and the title of the book, after an adventurous but virtuous career. Yet thrice Kalasiris claims to Knemon that that crucial oracle remained a puzzle to him (III.5.7, II.4, IV.4.5–5.1), one which required much thought and on whose solution much depended. Our question, more exactly put, will be 'Does Kalasiris really not understand (as he claims) that the oracle refers to Charikleia's Aithiopian origin and destiny, an understanding which every romance-loving reader reaches at once and which Kalasiris ought to have had since he had come from Aithiopia looking for Charikleia?' Is his claiming not to understand the oracle a lie, or is it perhaps an innocent fraud like his hocus-pocus with incense and laurel leaves (IV.5), or is it a slip on Heliodoros' part, or is it the truth?

I shall argue in this section that Kalasiris' assertion that he is puzzled as to the oracle's real meaning is a truthful statement, and more importantly one which is meant to sharpen the option between reading the *Aithiopika* in a naively romantic way *as Knemon does* or in a subtler and more attentive way, which is the pattern set by Kalasiris. Kalasiris' narrative to Knemon (II.24–V.3) is, on one level, about the way in which conventional assumptions, such as those which lead the reader to feel confident at once of the meaning of that oracle, are short-sighted and misleading. One of the discoveries which can and should be made by the reader of Kalasiris' narrative is that the oracle's interpretation is a problem. This discovery, I admit, is a difficult one, first, because the obvious romance pattern imposes itself so easily (exile–trials–reward), and second, because Kalasiris, though he says repeatedly that he is somewhat puzzled by this and similar texts, does not clearly say why. The reader therefore is left with the option either of taking the oracle to mean what it obviously means (and Kalasiris' claim of incomplete cognition to be decorative mystification) or of reading Kalasiris' mind. The *Aithiopika* is still an impressive novel if read in the former way, as it always has been. But Heliodoros has designed it with the latter reading in mind, a reading which is more difficult, not easily available to the reader who would rather drift with Xenophon than struggle to think with Thucydides.

A bare summary of the points in the following argument runs thus: (1) the narrative of Kalasiris to Knemon is a model, partly ironic, of how authors and readers play the game of literature together; (2) Knemon is an aggressively romantic reader and as such adequate only to the conventional elements in the plot; (3) Kalasiris is a very subtle narrator of *two* complex plots – (a) the love story of Charikleia and Theagenes and (b) his own discoveries both that Charikleia is the Aithiopian princess whom he is incidentally looking for, and that the gods intend her to reach the dark land of Aithiopia rather than the dark land of Hades (the ambiguous image of blacks); (4) three minor motives support Kalasiris' mysteriosophic pose: (a) his vow of silence, (b) his teasing of Knemon, and (c) his use of Odyssean duplicity as one of the ordinary excellences of literary discourse; (5) in the final pages of the novel (x.39–41) Heliodoros reformulates (in a new language) what the whole plot means, in a way which corresponds to Kalasiris' primary quest for divine wisdom (of which (3b) is a by-product) rather than to Knemon's desire for a smashing romance (which is the understanding of (3a) parodied in (2)).

In Kalasiris' narrative to Knemon (II.24–v.3) Heliodoros gives us a view – I would say, partly a paradigm and partly a parody – of the literary event. The text of, say, a romance is not just a dead letter or inscribed memorial but a semantic performance in which both author and reader have active parts to play. They are contestants in a sort of 'game for two players', and Heliodoros here offers us a model, often ironic, of the correlative crafts of constructing and appreciating a novel. It is not sufficient to call Kalasiris' narrative a flashback, as if it were no more than the absent first stages of the plot into whose *medias res* we have been plunged. As Heliodoros presents it this is not just a romance but a romance-in-frame. The subject in the foreground is Kalasiris' act of 'romancing' in the presence of Knemon. Since both persons, speaking from their present (narrating) time, constantly interrupt the smooth course of the account taking place in past (narrated) time, the conventional impression of a thing-like plot, whose events are independent of the listening audience and usually of the narrator too, cannot gel. Our attention is continually being diverted from the story to its teller and hearer, whether by substantial interruptions or by the simple vocative ὦ Κνήμων. Kalasiris' narrative is at least as much about the roles of narrator and audience (that is, by an obvious extrapolation, author and reader) as it is about a particular pair of lovers. And the question of Kalasiris' mendacity can only be properly addressed if his role as romancer is understood.

Inasmuch as Kalasiris' narrative to Knemon is about the performance of literature, as well as being the narrative of a love story, it is operating on two levels. There is a temptation for the eagerly curious part of our own minds to regard only the plot of Charikleia and Theagenes as of importance, the interchanges between Kalasiris and Knemon being treated as humorous or suspenseful punctuation. But this attitude is exactly that of Knemon, who is eager to be treated to the full spectacle of what we would nowadays call a wide-screen, technicolor romance. The ironic presentation of Knemon should be a major caution against dealing with Kalasiris' narrative as if it were simply a flashback to the long-awaited beginning of this great love story. Rather Kalasiris' narrative is essentially double, not to say duplicitous, in being both that long-desired story of Charikleia and a series of readings, responses, and interpretations of it by Knemon. One of the effects of his interventions is to shape the narrative so that it becomes Charikleia's story more than Kalasiris would have it be.

Let us look first at the character of Knemon. Kalasiris addresses him shortly after he begins to narrate as ὦ ξένε (II.25.5) and ὦ νεανία (II.26.1), for it is only at II.26.3 that Knemon's interruption leads to the revelation of his own name. From then on he is addressed by name frequently, so that the reader can never for long lose awareness of the fact that Kalasiris is speaking to one particular listener, a listener who actively approves or disapproves, questions, delays, shouts his excitement, and generally by his unrestrained conduct makes a nuisance of himself. There are four stretches in Kalasiris' narrative (each ranging from five to nine

Budé pages)[52] where the reader for a time might be lulled into forgetting Knemon's presence; but each of these is followed by a rather more extensive or significant development of Knemon's character as listener.

Knemon is characterized in ways which have the effect, first, of identifying his response with our own as readers, and second, of parodying his over-eagerness and emotionalism in such a way that we disassociate ourselves from him. In the first category come Knemon's appreciative remarks on Kalasiris' performance (II.26.3, III.15.1), his interested questions about points of detail (III.12.1, 14.1 [referring back to II.34.5 and III.13.3], V.17), his vexation, curtly expressed, at the elaborate triple-box of narrators leading up to the solution of Charikleia's real identity, a solution which is however postponed once again (II.32.3). Knemon's active participation in Kalasiris' narrating makes him what we might call, reversing Wolfgang Iser's term, *der explizite Leser*.[53] Most of all do we identify with Knemon when he recognizes the names which Kalasiris mentions from his past and present history – Nausikles and Thisbe (II.24.1), Theagenes and Charikleia (II.23.2), and Thyamis (II.25.7). For since we possess the same information as Knemon, his recognition of these names duplicates what we experience at each of those moments, and we might even call Knemon's startled reaction a sort of stage direction or rubric for the appropriate reader's response. Further, since Knemon's own story is known and, as far as we can tell, finished, he is able to be Kalasiris' audience (for the story which *we* want to hear) with almost no overlapping or confusion of his different roles as audience and as actor or narrator. Having been before both actor and narrator, he is now pure auditor; his knowledge and ignorance of the heroine and hero is identical with ours, and he will not surprise us by taking further part in their narrative as an actor. He is precisely as concerned and interested in them as are we (based on a similarly short acquaintance) and he listens to Kalasiris tell the

52. From II.26.3 (Kalasiris learns Knemon's name) to II.32.3 (closure of the triple-box of narrators); III.5.7 to 10.3 (followed by Kalasiris' double digression and the characterization of Knemon as a simple reader, III.12.1–15.1); III.17 to IV.3.4 (followed by Knemon's alarm and relief at Theagenes' race, IV.3.4–4.3); IV.4.4 to 8.1 (the account of recovering the swathe). After this the game between Kalasiris and Knemon is essentially over.

53. *Der implizite Leser* (Munich 1972; **English translation, Baltimore 1974**).

story of their earlier adventures with a curiosity and romantic excitement such as we might bring to a work of this genre.

But Knemon is gradually distanced from us by the broadly drawn comedy of his hyper-romantic sensibility. There is a noticeable escalation of enthusiasm from the opening passage, where he is slightly impatient with Kalasiris' delay in launching at once into his story (II.22.5, 23.5, 24.4), to his insistence on an unabridged version of the Delphic procession in honor of Neoptolemos, including a verbatim quotation of the complete hymn to Thetis (III.1.1–3, 2.3), to his acknowledgement that he is indeed insatiable in his lust for love, whether physical or literary: 'I never found my appetite flag either in enjoying the act of romance or in hearing stories about it. But when Theagenes and Charikleia are the subject, who might be so hardy or iron-hearted as not to be quite spellbound with the history of their amours, though it held the year round. And therefore pray go on' (IV.4.3). At these moments Knemon is characterized by his contrast to Kalasiris: first he is eager to begin the narrative at once, whereas Kalasiris insists on ceremoniously arranging the place (II.21.6), washing themselves and arranging comfortable couches (II.22.2), food and libations (II.22.5); but while the story is in progress Knemon finds postponements desirable and demands minute elaboration of descriptive scenes when Kalasiris would prefer to speak more pointedly (III.1.1–2). Knemon is magnetically drawn to the luscious and spectacular, perhaps not in itself a fault were he not also characterized as uncritical and self-indulgent in this taste. The contrast with Kalasiris' orderliness in keeping his mind always on the point of the story (διηγήσομαι δέ σοι τἀμαυτοῦ πρότερον ἐπιτεμών, οὐ σοφιστεύων ὡς αὐτὸς οἴει τὴν ἀφήγησιν ἀλλ' εὔτακτόν σοι καὶ προσεχῆ τῶν ἑξῆς παρασκευάζων τὴν ἀκρόασιν, II.24.5) is decisive in shaping our impression of Knemon as uncritically absorbed in the moment rather than thoughtful about the design of the whole. He enjoys riding the story like an emotional roller-coaster: 'No wonder (said Knemon) that the spectators on the spot were anxious when I am myself in fear now for Theagenes; so I beg you to go on and tell me quickly whether he was declared the winner' (IV.3.4). 'You have brought me back to life (said Knemon) by telling of his victory and his kiss; but what happened next?' (IV.4.2). Notice especially that his absorption in the narrative *as if he were present at the events* is precisely an obliteration of the difference between narrating time and narrated time. Knemon reduces this necessary doubleness which every literary narrative maintains (that is, of two time streams: the events as they *happened* over a certain span of time and the events as they are *told* over another span of time, quite different usually in extent and tempo) to a singleness, as if it (the history) could be apprehended as a thing in itself rather than as a telling and recounting of things. Knemon, once his romantic desires are pricked by the names 'Theagenes and Charikleia' (II.23.2), forgets the present: Kalasiris reminds him of the passage of time from high noon to evening (III.4.9) and far into the night (IV.4.2), time to which Knemon is oblivious. He lives in the narrative of Kalasiris as if it were a present reality, even exclaiming at one point about the vividness of the picture in his mind's eye as if it were immediately visible (III.4.7, an old comic gag, cf. Plautus, *Pseud.* 35f.).

In these respects Knemon seems to illustrate the comedy of misreading, rather like the bourgeois couple from the audience in *The Knight of the Burning Pestle* who are invited onto the stage to help construct the play. His role as *lector non scrupulosus* is consistent with his characterization throughout the novel: Charikleia suspects that he is untrustworthy and is glad when he will no longer accompany them (I.26.5–6, VI.7.8); Theagenes speaks scornfully of his easy fear of stage bogies (II.7.3), his feebleness of resolution (II.18.3), and his penchant for melodramatizing a situation (II.11.2–3). Even Nausikles and Kalasiris jeer at his cowardice (VI.1.3), and Heliodoros supports these judgments by his description of Knemon as easily frightened (II.13.2–3, contrasted with Theagenes) and prone to emotional paroxysms (VI.7.3). Indeed his own tale shows him in the role of victim and dupe, never a schemer. The connection between his general cowardice and his romantic misreading is very neatly drawn in the scene which follows Kalasiris' narrative (V.2.3), for here he is shown banging against objects in the darkness as he hurries frightenedly away from the room where he has just overheard 'Thisbe'. What Heliodoros earlier called 'the exegesis of desire' (I.19.1) is here presented as an exegesis based on fear: Knemon interprets the speaker's references to her slavery, to her imprisonment among brigands, and to the man she loves and depends on in light of his overriding fixation on Thisbe. His paranoia inserts Charikleia's references to Theagenes into the preconceived framework of Thisbe's relation to Knemon, and thus he systematically understands everything she says in a way which expresses and heightens his own fear. There is a fine cleverness in the final words of her speech: ἀλλὰ σῴζοιό γε μόνον καὶ θεάσαιό ποτε Θίσβην τὴν σήν· τοῦτο γάρ με καλέσεις καὶ μὴ βουλόμενος (v.2.10) – Charikleia means that Theagenes will call her Θίσβη even though he would rather call her 'Charikleia', Knemon takes her to mean that he (Knemon) will call her τὴν ἐμήν even though he would rather run away! As a sign that we are near one of the central nodes of Heliodoros' complex web, the cocks crow (v.3.2), as they did for Thyamis' dream (1.18.3) and Kalasiris' death (VII.11.4) and nowhere else in the book. Charikleia of course is acting out a role, and it is Knemon's special failing to respond to literature as if it were life (II.11.2–3). He cannot sustain the critical distance which drama and novels require as representations of reality, rather than reality itself, and without that ability to perceive and maintain an ongoing duplicity Knemon will certainly never appreciate the crafty narrative of Kalasiris except as a romantic extravanganza.

That Kalasiris' narrative is, or rather becomes, a romantic extravaganza is not in doubt. But it is another of Heliodoros' duplicities that we are brought to regard the gorgeous pageantry at Delphi, the long, lush description of Theagenes and Charikleia, and the exquisite slow motion of their first love glance as decorative enhancements demanded by Knemon, somewhat off the point as Kalasiris sees it, and for which he is therefore absolved of full responsibility. One of the principal uses which Knemon's comic-audience role serves is to allow Heliodoros to indulge a taste (*our* taste) for sentimental scenes of elaborate beauty and yet to maintain the fiction that the narrator's real *raison de raconter* is the detection and discovery of how a divine plan is riddled in these events. As long as we can think of the romantic and emotional pyrotechnics as existing precisely for Knemon, as Kalasiris' indulgence to him rather than as the narrator's endorsed choice of presentation, we can maintain our pose (with Kalasiris) of restraint and wisdom. Effective sentimentality is surely one of the most difficult literary effects to bring off, and it is significant that Heliodoros has chosen to present the *beginning* of the plot – the most treacherously romantic part of such a story (the love at first sight of an incredibly beautiful hero and heroine) – in suspension between two points of view, Knemon's naive taste for romantic candy and the more crafty pose of Kalasiris. Kalasiris is caught in the dilemma of every Serious Artist – he must pander to the taste of the common folk if his more Significant Message is to find a hearing.

For Kalasiris' lofty-mindedness is also a pose. It is not that only Knemon's style of reading is treated ironically, Kalasiris too is a poseur. His mysteriosophic attitude is delineated in a systematic contrast with Knemon. Thus over against Knemon's eagerness to plunge into the story (an eagerness trebled when he discovers that it will concern his romantic idols, Theagenes and Charikleia) we find Kalasiris' reluctance to speak readily, his Protean postponements (II.24.4), his insistence that the tale, though it must be told (II.21.6), be told 'in order and with attention to the way things follow and fit' (εὔτακτον . . . καὶ προσεχῆ τῶν ἑξῆς, II.24.5). What is important to establish in the first place is not the reality of Kalasiris' cryptic perceptions but the image of him as a careful and scrupulously thoughtful narrator who weighs the relevance of each item before including it in his tale. This restraint is twice the ground for rejecting information that might otherwise have been included – once ironically, when Kalasiris passes over the fact that he had been to Aithiopia ('for it contributes nothing to the story you asked for', συντελεῖ γὰρ οὐδὲν εἰς τὴν παρὰ σοῦ ζήτησιν, II.26.1), and once unsuccessfully, when he gives in to Knemon's petulant, Athenian lust for the spectacular ('I would rather keep you on target, restricting you to the relevant parts of my narrative and such as will answer the question you originally asked', ἐπὶ τὰ καιριώτερά σε τῆς ἀφηγήσεως καὶ ὧν ἐπεζήτεις ἐξ ἀρχῆς συνελαύνων, III.1.2). The essential contrast between this narrator's view of his performance and this auditor's expectations is that Kalasiris comes across as aware of the complexity and mystery of these events, as if their real point and their actual coherence might be missed, whereas Knemon appears as enthralled by the superficial glitter of immediate delights, as one whose appreciation is without *approfondissement*. To be sure he asks some questions, but these serve to highlight Kalasiris' vast knowledge and lofty perspective (a pose, remember) over against Knemon's viewpoint as one of οἱ πολλοί (III.12.2–3). Knemon's questions here give him a diminished and ironic participation in Kalasiris' major quest for exactitude (τοῦ λόγου τὴν ἀκρίβειαν, III.14.1, with Kalasiris' disclaimer ἀλλ' οὐδὲ ἀκριβῶς οὐδὲν ἔτι τῶν ἑξῆς χρησθέντων συνέβαλλον, III.5.7), just as Kalasiris displays some of the romantic affection for the lovers which so dominates Knemon's reaction to the tale.

Both in and out of his narrative Kalasiris is reluctant to bare his thoughts ('many times Nausikles pressured me to disclose the sacred secret of my tale but each time I found a new excuse to thwart him', ὃν πολλάκις γε δι' ὄχλου γινόμενον μυηθῆναι τὴν ἀφήγησιν ἄλλως ἄλλοτε διεκρουσάμην, II.23.6, with II.35.3); not only does he keep his own counsel, the little information he does give out is often duplicitous (the learned explanation of the evil eye, III.7.8, is a façade covering his knowledge of Charikleia's love, III.5). His duplicitous poses in the narrative are matched by the tones of irony in his role as narrator: 'elevating his mind to a more mystical perspective' (III.13.1), Kalasiris then explains that Homer was either the child of Hermes by an Egyptian woman or he lied about his birth in order to enhance his reputation and presumably his income (another function of Hermes) (III.14).

What is this priest-narrator's duplicity in the service of? Not just the furtherance of Charikleia's and Theagenes' love-affair, not just Queen Persinna's request to find her missing daughter, but his own pursuit of wisdom, a goal which includes the other two as integral, subordinate parts. His motive for leaving Memphis was double – to avoid succumbing to the erotic power of the courtesan Rhodopis (II.25.1–4) and to avoid the sight of his two sons fighting each other (II.25.5–6). Both of these frightful events are *possibilities* rather than actualities, possibilities which Kalasiris' reading of the divine pattern in the stars and so forth has discovered (προαγορευθέντων μοι πρὸς τοῦ θείου δυσχερῶν, II.25.3, ἡ ἄρρητός μοι πολλάκις ἐκ θεῶν σοφία . . . προηγόρευε, II.25.5). His positive motive for going to Meroe and Delphi rather than anywhere else is also his divine wisdom (II.26.1, IV.12.1). Kalasiris is a man above all obedient to the divine plan and devoted to ferreting out the gods' intentions as they are disclosed to him in stages of ever greater definiteness. When asked by Knemon to give an account of himself, Kalasiris agrees to do so, and we may call this story which he intends to tell 'My Priestly Life: Adventures in the Service of

Gradual Revelation'. But at the moment when Knemon realizes that this tale will touch on Charikleia and her lover *he focuses his attention* (and ours) *on the love-story alone.* This narrowed aspect of Kalasiris' history is in a sense another story, which we may entitle 'How Charikleia and Theagenes Fell in Love and Eloped to Points South'. Knemon originally asked for the former, then re-asked for the latter, and he continually construes all that Kalasiris has to say only within the framework of his desire for a sentimental romance. The reader of the *Aithiopika* watches Knemon following Kalasiris' narrative, accommodating it to his taste and misconstruing it. We are easily led (for reasons given above on p. 141) to identify with Knemon and to adopt his basic understanding of what Kalasiris' story is. But in doing so we miss, as Knemon does, the irony, the subtlety and the duplicity of Kalasiris' account of how he pursued divine wisdom, how he unraveled its tangled skein, and in the process furthered the love of Charikleia and Theagenes as a sort of interesting sub-plot.[54] This is not the view usually taken of Kalasiris' narrative, so I shall now retell the story 'from a more mystical perspective' (III.13.1) as a divine detective story, an adventure in unriddling the uncertain traces of god's intentions.

Kalasiris' σοφία, by which he has foreknowledge of important developments in the future, is not a clear and complete knowledge but an incomplete cognition. It allows both a latitude for eluding a possible future (Rhodopis) and a certain indeterminacy, of which oracular riddles are the best example. They do not unambiguously picture the future but hint at the general outline of things to come. The entire narrative of Kalasiris from II.35 to IV.13.3 is structured around the progressive certification of a Delphic prediction. By his

54. There are three journeys made for the seeking out of wisdom which result in the seeker's association with Charikleia as a sort of 'bonus': Charikles' journey to Katadoupa (καθ' ἱστορίαν τῶν καταρρακτῶν τοῦ Νείλου, II.29.5), Kalasiris' journey to Aithiopia (ἐπιθυμίᾳ τῆς παρ' ἐκείνοις σοφίας, IV.12.1), and Kalasiris' journey to Delphi, whose intellectual attractiveness, described at II.26.1, is his *primary* reason for going there: 'And so I came to Delphi intending to accomplish the request she had vowed me to, though this was not the reason why I took my journey to these parts so seriously but rather by the supplement of the gods it has been the greatest profit I made on my wandering' (IV.13.1). Charikles too made an unexpected profit, his free acquiring of the ambassador's jewels when he agreed to care for Charikleia (II.30.3f). This secondary profit in gems, which a merchant like Nausikles will regard as primary, is analogous to the romance of Charikleia, which is both subordinate to the higher plans of wisdom and yet very distracting to readers whose hearts are set on a love story.

wisdom Kalasiris learns from the gods, at Queen Persinna's request, that her long-lost daughter is still alive and is at Delphi. He does not learn her name, rank or more detailed history, only that she is living somewhere in Delphi. When he arrives there, in primary pursuit still of divine wisdom but secondarily (as he says at IV.13.1) hoping that the gods will continue to guide him in locating the queen's daughter, he waits until some sign indicates which Delphian maiden is the white Aithiopian. The break comes when Charikles tells him that his foster daughter was given him in trust by an Aithiopian ambassador. This makes Charikleia the chief suspect, though the case for her identity is not yet airtight. At this point comes the oracle which links Charikleia to Theagenes and a voyage to a dark land. There are two aspects of this new clue which Kalasiris finds puzzling. First, why have the gods introduced a new character (Theagenes) into the plot of Charikleia's life, and second, is the dark land Aithiopia? The former is answered when by careful observation Kalasiris detects the love interest in the eyes of the young pair on first beholding each other:

These effects, naturally enough, escaped the notice of the multitude, since everyone was absorbed in one or another interest or consideration of his own; . . . but I was occupied solely with my observation of the young pair, ever since, Knemon, the oracle was chanted concerning Theagenes as he sacrificed in the temple; and I had been moved by hearing their names to speculate on what would befall them. But I could still not make out any accurate meaning for the succeeding lines. (III.5.7)

That night Apollo and Artemis entrust the young pair to Kalasiris' care on a voyage to Egypt and then to a land of the gods' choosing (III.11.5). Kalasiris then has his commission to escort *both* of them, though he is not perfectly sure that Charikleia is the young woman he is looking for and he is gravely suspicious that the land of the gods' choosing may be Hades.

This linkage of Aithiopia and Hades, quite clearly expressed elsewhere in the novel but significantly not made explicit by Kalasiris when it would illuminate his train of thought for Knemon and the reader, must be briefly documented.[55] The initial

55. For further examples see my 'Lollianos and the Desperadoes', *JHS* 100 (1980), 161–4. Other references to haunting or revenants in Heliodoros at II.5.2, 11.3, VI.14f. The author's attitude to this superstition depends (as do all his 'beliefs') on the occasion: he can encourage us to view ghost-raising as either silly or wicked depending on the needs of the story at that moment.

confrontation of Charikleia and the black Egyptian brigands takes place on a battlefield littered with corpses. The grisly possibility is raised that the brigands are ghosts haunting the scene of their untimely sorrow, and it is precisely their black and unkempt look which triggers this interpretation (1.3.1). The equation is virtually explicit at IV.14.2–15.1, where Kalasiris presumably takes the dream of dusky and shadowy phantoms to whose land Charikleia is taken as referring to Aithiopia, while Charikles understands it to mean that she will soon die and go to Hades. The most explicit form of the equation is another dream interpretation in which ironically the *explanandum* is Aithiopia, Hades the *explanans* (VIII.11.3–5). Theagenes takes his perfectly literal dream message and gives to each term a translated significance.[56] As we saw in the case of Charikleia's dream of blindness, Heliodoros takes a special pleasure in playing with problems of interpretation and particularly in postponing solutions, which, when they come, are not announced *as* solutions. This displacement occurs also in Kalasiris' narrative, which is framed as a plot of detection but whose clues and deductions are not explained to us. The uncertainty which Kalasiris several times says he feels about the meaning of the oracle's final lines is a real one, which has been prepared from the opening scene, and which creates an undercurrent of abiding danger about Charikleia's destiny.

Though Kalasiris accepts the gods' new commission to bring Theagenes as well as Charikleia back to Egypt with him, he still does not understand the *point* of the love story, i.e., why the wisdom of the gods has ordained it, and neither do we until the final chapters. This is a real question. Romance readers will assume that a love story is what is expected, but Kalasiris represents a different point of view. To him the emergence of a love interest is a puzzling and unlooked-for development: 'I rejoiced at having found something which I had not expected' (III.15.3). Still, he is a patient and open-minded reader of events, able to revise and refine his understanding of what it is that the gods are having him do: he had originally left Memphis to avoid seeing the conflict of his sons, but the gods arranged this exile 'not more for that reason, it seems, than for the discovery of Charikleia' (III.16.5). By careful watching (ἐκ

---

56. Similarly Persinna interprets her dream metaphorically when its truth is literal (X.3.1).

πολλοῦ παρατηρῶν, IV.3.2) and silent waiting (ἀλλ᾽ ὅμως ἐσιώπων, τὸ μέλλον ἀπεκδεχόμενος, II.35.3) Kalasiris reaches a point where he has guessed with virtually complete certainty that Charikleia is the white Aithiopian princess and must only confirm that by acquiring the baby clothes in which Charikleia was set out:

> But as to the problem of what land they were to be conducted to I could see but one solution – to get hold of, if somehow I could, the swathe which was exposed with Charikleia, and on which was embroidered the narrative (διήγημα) about her, as Charikles said he had been told; for it was probable (εἰκός) that both her fatherland and the maiden's parents, whose identity I had already begun to suspect, could be learned conclusively (ἐκμαθεῖν) from that source and perhaps it was to there that they were being conducted by destiny. (IV.5.1)

Having gulled so many people for so long a time Kalasiris at least reveals 'everything as it was' to the one person who matters, Charikleia herself (IV.12.1). He explains to her not only the story of her true birth but the choice she must make about whether to elope with Theagenes, since that is the course of action which the oracle and dream have indicated: 'And with that I reminded her of the oracle's words and explained to her their meaning: Charikleia was not ignorant of them, as they were sung and scrutinized by many' (παρὰ πολλῶν καὶ ᾀδόμενος καὶ ζητούμενος, IV.13.3).

At this moment Kalasiris learns that what had seemed to be two different divine plots were actually *two ways of saying the same thing*. His Aithiopian commission was to send back the lost princess, whoever she might turn out to be; his Apolline commission was to guard the young lovers on their way to a dark land, wherever that might be. These are now seen to be two incomplete descriptions of the same plot, though they came from opposite ends of the earth. What was indefinite in the one is definite in the other. This movement of revelation is parallel to the announcement that Apollo in Delphi and Helios in Aithiopia are the same divine force, which is the penultimate religious theme of the novel (X.36.3).

> Incidental to this analysis of Kalasiris' discovery there are three other points which might be made to make the shape of his narrative fully intelligible. (1) When Kalasiris accepted his Aithiopian commission, the queen bound him to silence on solemn oath. 'She conjured me to compliance, repeatedly invoking the Sun, an oath no man of religion would dare to transgress' (IV.13.1). While at Delphi Kalasiris maintained an air of innocence and casualness about what he was really

looking for: he did not announce that he was seeking a white Aithiopian maiden to all and sundry. In narrating his story to Knemon, Kalasiris is not deviating from the way the events appeared at the time. It had then the form of a detective story, with the right interpretation of clues withheld from all but the investigator. (2) Knemon teases Kalasiris by not telling him straight out where Theagenes and Charikleia are, saying with an air of mystery that they will appear. This withholding of information is strictly according to narrative contract (as explained above, pp. 109–10). Kalasiris must first complete his part of the bargain, which was to tell the story of his adventures – not the story of Theagenes and Charikleia. The agreement was struck before Knemon knew that Kalasiris was involved with them. Technically speaking, Knemon's ζήτησις was just about Kalasiris' misfortunes. Perhaps this is why Kalasiris says, 'I will omit the events between Memphis and Delphi, young man, for they contribute nothing to your ζήτησις' (II.26.1). There is more razor-edged repartee between these two players at III.4.9–10. Since Knemon has checked Kalasiris' request to know where the lovers are, playing strictly by the rules, Kalasiris in return finesses Knemon by postponing the information about Charikleia's origin, again in strict accordance with what the rules allow, since his original enquiry did not concern her. (3) The Odyssean background of the *Aithiopika* may put us in mind of how subtle and necessary an art lying is. Verbal control by misdirection and half-truth are still a prominent part of Greek socialization. The lies of Odysseus even to Athena and Laertes illustrate that one of the excellences of speech is its use to conceal the speaker and play with the auditor. Kalasiris' tincture of hypocrisy is a bright, pleasing performance, authentically Hellenic in its craftiness and reluctance to trumpet the truth.[57]

There are hints of a deeper cosmic meaning underlying the romantic exile and return of the Aithiopian princess. The following calendrical coincidences are not fortuitous: (a) Charikleia was conceived by divine command on a summer's day at noon (τὸ μεσημβρινόν . . . ὕπνου θερινοῦ, IV.8.4) and her return coincides with the summer solstice (κατὰ τροπὰς τὰς θερινάς, IX.9.2). (b) The Nile's sources are at the Aithiopian–Libyan border, where east meets south (καθ' ὃ μέρος τὸ κλίμα τὸ ἀνατολικὸν ἀπολῆγον ἀρχὴν τῇ μεσημβρίᾳ δίδωσιν); according to its unique nature (ἡ ἰδιάζουσα φύσις) it increases in the summer because at the summer solstice the 'annual' winds drive clouds from north to south (ἐπὶ τὴν μεσημβρίαν) (II.28.1–3). (c) The annual changes in the Nile's movement are called its 'growth' (αὔξησις, IX.9.2, 22.3, 5) and

57. See P. Walcot, 'Odysseus and the Art of Lying', *Ancient Society* 8 (1977), 1–19.

'return' or 'subsidence' (ὑπονόστησις, IX.22.3, 5). (d) The unique diversion of the Nile around Syene features both a subtle increase of its waters at midnight (κατὰ μέσας που νύκτας ... αὐξομένου ... τοῦ ὕδατος, IX.8.2) and the revelation at daybreak that the water has returned to its natural bed (τὸ ἡμέρας φῶς ... τοῦ ὕδατος ἀθρόον ὑπονοστήσαντος, IX.8.4). (e) This artificial 'return' of the river allows the people of Syene more gladly to celebrate the Neiloa, the summer solstice festival of the river's manifest increase (ὅτε ἀρχὴν τῆς αὐξήσεως ὁ ποταμὸς ἐμφαίνει τελουμένην, IX.9.2), an event to which they attach mystical significance (θεοπλαστοῦσι ... σεμνηγοροῦντες ... ἐκθειάζουσιν, IX.9.3) on several mirroring levels simultaneously – agricultural, scientific, mythically romantic, and Something Deeper (IX.9.3–10.1). From these elements the clever reader[58] can begin to conjecture cosmic patterns – Charikleia's journey north and return south reproducing, in harmony or counterpoint, the river's growing up (αὔξησις) and returning home; significant turning points (τροπαί) of the day (dawn, noon, sunset, midnight) and the year (the solstices) marking patterns of the sun's motion across the sky and Charikleia's across the earth, and so forth. But these are only tantalizing hints, a Jamesian figure in her carpet, which elude precise formulation.

The real religious message of the novel, though it is not religiously *meant*, is the declaration by Sisimithres at X.39 that the gods have fashioned the entire plot of Charikleia's life *in order to* convince the Aithiopian people to abolish their paternal rite of human sacrifice (τὰ πάτρια, X.7.1). Let me develop these two points: that the novel concludes with a new religious significance read into the romantic events, and that this religious significance is not religiously meant.

The gods, it seems, wanted the otherwise blameless Aithiopians to accept a fundamental change in religious custom and to this end they could find no better means than a romance, one whose beauty and intricacy would astonish, charm, and successfully persuade them to abolish human sacrifice once and for all. This is the interpretation which Sisimithres gives at X.39:

Hydaspes then enquired of Sisimithres: 'What is to be done, my wise

58. Like the anonymous sophisticate (τις τῶν ἀστειοτέρων, II.28.1) who provoked the first discourse on the Nile.

friend? To deny the gods their sacrifice is impious; to butcher those whom they have bestowed on us is unholy: we must think carefully what is to be done.' Sisimithres replied, speaking not now in Greek but in Aithiopian, so as to be understood by everyone: 'O King, exceeding joy, it would seem, overshadows the minds of even the most sagacious men. You at least ought to have realized long ago that the gods are not welcoming this sacrifice that is underway. For they have now manifested the fortunate Charikleia as your daughter, snatching her from the very altar, and they have sent here from midmost Greece her guardian Charikles, as if *ex machina*, and further they struck the horses and bulls held ready at the altars with that alarm and disorder, by which they meant us to understand that what is regarded as the highest ritual would be abruptly halted, and now, as the colophon (κορωνίς) of their good deeds and as it were a drama's torch, they have presented this foreign youth as the bridegroom of the maiden. Come, let us recognize the divine wonder-working and become collaborators in the gods' will: let us limit ourselves to the holier offerings, and proscribe the sacrifice of human beings unto all future ages.'

The many threads of the complex spiderweb in Book x have nearly converged when Hydaspes puts his simple question – what is to be done? Sisimithres' answer is not just a piece of advice but an interpretation, a reading, of the events in Book x. Four astonishing developments (he could have listed more) are too many to attribute to random chance and merely human motivation, especially when each of them can be read as an omen opposing human sacrifice. He summarizes, that is, the course of Book x, with its two movements (the recognition of Charikleia, 1–17, and the fortunes of Theagenes as he waits for Charikleia to announce that they are vowed to each other as man and wife, 18—38), but does so from a new point of view. The female victim was saved from sacrifice by the revelation that she was not a foreigner; the male victim is also protected from that fate by an auspicious reading of the animals' alarm. As if these two anti-sacrificial signs were not enough, both omens have been confirmed by a specifically theatrical turn – the appearance of Charikles *ex machina* and of Theagenes as the bridegroom escorted by torches in the finale of a play.[59] This pattern of omen/melodrama, omen/melodrama, says

59. This perhaps answers Morgan's objection (*Commentary*, [n. 26] *ad loc.*) that we would expect the article with δράματος. Theagenes is revealed as the bridegroom in *a* drama, a general dramatic sort of effect, not as the bridegroom in this drama or any specific play. W. G. Arnott's argument is essentially correct on

Sisimithres, is too novelistic, entirely too coincidental not to have been the result of, not merely divine planning (βούλημα), but divine play-writing (σκηνοποιία).

The reason intelligent observers did not detect the pattern is that their otherwise wise minds were overshadowed by excessive emotion, which is to say they were following the events of Book x to see how Charikleia and Theagenes would be saved, as any reader of a naive romance would do. From 'a more mystical point of view', the rescue and happy final state of Theagenes and Charikleia are not the telos of this action. It is not the abolition of human sacrifice which makes possible the successful conclusion to the romance, it is the romance itself (complex plot, recognition, coincidences, tableaux and daring exploits) which facilitates the abolition of human sacrifice. The whole seventeen years of romantic incidents were contrived not for their own sake but to make a point. This is why the gods staged such a spectacle, this is the goal towards which even Kalasiris' directives from the gods were aimed, though he did not live to see it realized. If we had not been assuming that this was a romance we might have seen the point long ago (καὶ πάλαι).[60]

Sismithres represents that higher point of view on the action, much the same as Kalasiris' mysteriosophic pose. He has like Kalasiris intimations of what telos the gods seem to have in mind, but will not force their hand ahead of time by second-guessing them. His announcement that the story was all along designed for a different point altogether, which subtle minds unclouded by intense emotional involvement in the play could see, is both a sophisticated *jeu* with the conventions of reading a romance and a trick itself from popular melodrama. For it is a cliché, and an effective one, from the popular stage that 'the Real Truth was

this passage (*Hermes* 93 (1965), 253–55), though I should emphasize that weddings are often the finale of a comedy and, given Sisimithres' equation of bridegroom and torch, the sort of dramatic prop in question must be thought of as a wedding torch.

60. There is an analogous moment in A. Christie, *Murder on the Orient Express* (London 1934) when the detective points out that the presence of twelve people on the same train, all of whom had a perfectly good reason for killing the murdered man, is too great a coincidence. Indeed it is, but the reader had all along been assuming that that fact was part of the *form* of the mystery story rather than a fact to be questioned or explained. Sisimithres' explanation that all the events of Book x are too theatrically satisfying, just a little too neat for merely human purposes to achieve, is of the same order as Hercule Poirot's.

More Astonishing than we realized'.[61] The sophistication of Heliodoros' use of this cliché is that he makes it refer to the form itself of his novel, for what we learn at the end (or almost the end) is that where we thought Heliodoros was writing a romance, the Real Truth is that Heliodoros is telling the story of how the gods devised a romance. He is not a romancer but a mere scribe of the divine melodramatist.

The fact that all readers have continued to regard the *Aithiopika* as a romance and Heliodoros as its author is explained by my second point, that the religious re-signification of the plot is not religiously meant, but is rather part of Heliodoros' playful exploration of popular narrative and its audience. As Knemon was the ironic audience-figure in Kalasiris' narrative, so the Aithiopian populace plays that role in Book x. Most of the events are presented to them as a drama in a foreign language (Greek), which is nonetheless clear enough for them to follow in the main. The semantic entertainment of Book x consists in our watching the Aithiopians as audience of the Charikleia-mime,[62] beginning with the non-verbal message of Hydaspes' victory: 'The special messengers . . . waved palm branches in their hands as they passed on horseback through the more important parts of the city, publishing the victory by their appearance alone' (μόνῳ τῷ σχήματι δημοσιεύοντες, x.3.2). Each of the major scenes is not only presented in Greek to us but is to be thought of as a pantomime independent of words, performed for the Aithiopians: the brazier (x.9.3–5, note the response of the crowd, βοὴν μίαν ἄσημον μὲν καὶ ἄναρθρον, δηλωτικὴν δὲ τοῦ θαύματος ἐπήχησαν), the picture (ἄλλων πρὸς ἄλλους, ὅσοι καὶ κατὰ μικρὸν συνίεσαν τὰ λεγόμενα καὶ πραττόμενα, διαδηλούντων καὶ πρὸς τὸ ἀπηκριβωμένον τῆς ὁμοιότητος σὺν περιχαρείᾳ ἐκπλαγέντων, x.15.1), the reunion (τὸν δῆμον . . . πρὸς τὴν σκηνοποιίαν τῆς τύχης . . . , x.16.3), the rodeo stunt (τὰ μὲν δὴ πρῶτα φυγὴν εἶναι τοῦ Θεαγένους τὸ γινόμενον οἱ παρόντες ὑπελάμβανον . . . προιόντος δὲ τοῦ ἐγχειρήματος ὅτι μὴ ἀποδειλίασις ἦν μηδὲ ἀπόδρασις τοῦ

---

61. Apuleius, *Metamorphoses* x.11f., analyzed as a mime by H. Wiemken, *Der griechische Mimus* (Bremen 1972).

62. Admittedly more sophisticated than the Chariton-mime (*P. Oxy.* 413, D. L. Page, *Greek Literary Papyri*, no. 76), but they share crowds of black foreigners shouting a strange language, a great king, and a heroine in danger.

σφαγιασθῆναι μετεδιδάσκοντο, x.28.5), the wrestling match (x.32.3), Charikles' hauling off Theagenes (ἐσείσθησαν πρὸς τὰ γινόμενα σύμπαντες, τὰ μὲν ῥήματα οἱ συνιέντες, τὰ ὁρώμενα δὲ οἱ λοιποὶ θαυμάζοντες, x.35.2), and the finale (x.38.3). We are audience to a scene which includes an audience who perceive and understand the action in a different mode. Just as in the long narrative of Kalasiris, we are once more treated not only to a romantic melodrama but to the attendant by-play of two minds interpreting the scene – a higher mysteriosophic point of view and a lower, demotic response to the mere thrill of it all. Heliodoros clearly loves both sophisticated self-consciousness in literary irony and popular literature in its most time-tested clichés. It is the interplay of these two interests which gives the *Aithiopika* its special character, and certainly not the particular content of its Religious Truths (sun worship, abolition of human sacrifice, the providence of the gods for beautiful people). It is not Heliodoros' religiously held belief, nor meant to be ours, that an occasional human sacrifice is contrary to the actual divine will. The gods might contrive a romance to prove this point but no human believer ever would. The religious beliefs in the *Aithiopika* are so unobjectionable (killing people is wrong) and so malleable (the sun is a high god) that it would be hard to imagine an average ancient reader who would need to be convinced. Indeed Heliodoros must place his action in a fabulous land at the earth's ends where utopia and dystopia ambiguously meet in order to provide us with an audience who are dead set on the heroine's death and whose conversion to her favor by the theatrical force of the romance itself we can somewhat ironically watch.[63]

The two commonest misinterpretations of the *Aithiopika* are that it is (simply) a romance and that it is meant to recommend some religious beliefs. The involution of its plot, however, is not just a difficulty in chronology to be sorted out but rather puts in question

63. Ironically because human sacrifice is not the real danger but only the necessary stage villain for romance: 'The human sacrifice, usually of a virginal female, is astonishingly persistent as the crucial episode of romance: we meet it in the sixth book of *The Faerie Queen*, and it is still going strong in the late prose romances of William Morris' (N. Frye, *The Secular Scripture: a Study of the Structure of Romance* (Cambridge, Mass./London 1976), 81. Hence the neatness of contriving that the populace renounce human sacrifice because they have been so thrilled at the performance of an excellent stage romance.

the perception and interpretation of the events, most notably by the addition of hyperintelligent (Kalasiris, Sisimithres) and subintelligent (Knemon, the Aithiopian mob) perspectives. The romantic plot is the raw material, the sense data, as it were, for these minds to operate on: each makes of it what his categories allow. It is mere convention, theatrical convention, that the 'higher' perspective is privileged and seems to prevail in the end. It is not that Heliodoros is any kind of believer but merely that he must employ beliefs to illustrate the comedy of composing a romance. There has to be some Noble Message or other at the end, any one will do.

I think I hear a laugh on the closing page, and I will close by mentioning what I think it is. In the midst of their desperate straits the lovers had agreed on a pair of code words to identify themselves – λαμπάς and φοῖνιξ (v.5.2). They have chosen these symbols from their own first meetings when Charikleia gave Theagenes a ceremonial torch (λαμπάδιον, iii.4.6, δᾴς, iii.5.3) at the games of Neoptolemos and a branch of palm (φοίνικος ἔρνος, iv.1.2, φοῖνιξ, iv.4.2) for winning the Pythian footrace (she was also carrying a ritual λαμπάδιον on the latter occasion, iv.1.2). No author plants code words unless he means to use them later, and in due course one of them serves its purpose: 'Oh Pythian', she said to him softly, 'have you not remembered the torch?' (vii.7.7). The torch recurs as a wedding torch in Sisimithres' final revelation of the Meaning of it all (ὥσπερ λαμπάδιον δράματος, x.39.2). Has the φοῖνιξ been forgotten entirely? Perhaps not. Theagenes in the same phrase is called the κορωνίς, the final flourish of the scribe's pen which closes the book, as well as a theatrical wedding torch, and it is in the author's own final flourish that he identifies himself as Φοῖνιξ, a Phoenician (x.41.4).[64]

64. This may in some part explain the order of the final words, 'a small masterpiece of style in the way it builds up to the statement of the author's name in the very last word' (Morgan, [n. 26], 627). ἀνὴρ Φοῖνιξ Ἐμισηνός, τῶν ἀφ' Ἡλίου γένος, Θεοδοσίου παῖς Ἡλιόδωρος. Φοῖνιξ and Ἡλιόδωρος are both given special prominence by their unusual position. The ordinary form of naming is personal name – name of father – name of city – name of people (in authors: Herodotos, Thucydides, Dionysios of Halikarnassos 1.8.4). Heliodoros' self-reference reverses that normal order so as gradually to unfold the secret of his identity, each phrase becoming more specific than the last. When 'Heliodoros' is finally named as the elusive individual who has been so long hidden behind this book, there is a curious satisfaction in the name, as if it were the solution to some larger riddle as well as the immediate paronomasia of Ἡλίου and Θεοδοσίου.

τύχη or πρόνοια? There are many ways to play the game of literature, and a sophisticated player is now and then caught alluding to his private sense of being an author ('Oh Jamesy let me up out of this', says Molly Bloom) and to the ironies of communication. This is an unavoidable dimension of an author's consciousness at least since the invention of writing, and we find it in writers from Aratos to Nabokov.[65] Heliodoros is such an author, and the *Aithiopika* is an act of pure play, yet a play which rehearses vital processes by which we must live in reality – interpretation, reading, and making a provisional sense of things.[66]

65. See Levitan (n. 36). An example of Levitan's 'sensibility of the near miss' is perhaps the closing scene in which Charikles, watching the young couple leave the set crowned with white mitres, remembers (once again!) that oracle and quotes its closing lines, '. . . a white crown on brows turned black'. But does μελαινομένων, the final word, really mean anything? They both still look white; Charikleia has become black in the sense that her Aithiopian generation has been acknowledged, but this is inapplicable to Theagenes. It is at least odd not only that the word was used once (anything might be forgiven, even in a work consecrated to Detection and an image of accuracy), but that it should be so highlighted and actually quoted here strikes me as a palpable 'near miss', like the discord which closes Charles Ives' Second Symphony.

66. This paper was first given as a talk at the International Conference on the Ancient Novel at Bangor, July 1976, and has been improved in its fuller form by comments from Gerald Sandy, Terry Comito, John Morgan.

The Emperor Julian on his predecessors

G. W. BOWERSOCK

The emperor Julian's satire on the emperors that preceded him is well worth reading, though not for the jokes. Julian was an essentially humourless man, whose efforts at wit quickly degenerated into raillery or bitterness. He was aware of this weakness in himself; and when, in December 362 at Antioch, the festive season of the Saturnalia called for an appropriate entertainment, Julian had to confess he lacked the talent: γελοῖον δὲ οὐδὲν οὐδὲ τερπνὸν οἶδα ἐγώ.[1] To an unnamed interlocutor who objected politely, he insisted that he had no natural affinity for jest, parody, or laughter: πέφυκα γὰρ οὐδαμῶς ἐπιτήδειος οὔτε σκώπτειν οὔτε γελοιάζειν.[2] By introducing in this way the work which is generally known as the *Caesars*, Julian disarmed his readers.[3] Despite Lucian and Menippus, whose dialogues provided the models for Julian's satire,[4] we must not look for humour here, but rather for insight into the author himself. Of Julian and his abundant writings it may justly be said, as it once was of Lucilius: *quo fit ut omnis/votiva pateat veluti descripta tabella/vita*.[5]

The title of the *Caesars* in the manuscript is Συμπόσιον ἢ Κρόνια,

---

1. *Caes.* 306a; possibly a quotation from comedy (an iambic trimeter, with omission of δέ and elision at οἶδ' ἐγώ). For the location and date of composition see Chr. Lacombrade, 'Notes sur les Césars de l'empereur Julien', *Pallas* 11 (1962 [1964]), 47–67.

2. *Caes.* 306b.

3. Cf. *Misop.* 340b. Cf. G. W. Bowersock, *Julian the Apostate* (London/Cambridge, Mass. 1978), 14.

4. Cf. M. D. Gallardo, 'Los simposios de Luciano, Ateneo, Metodio y Juliano', *Cuadernos de filología clásica* 4 (1972), 239–96.

5. Hor., *Serm.* II.1, 32–4. We should not, however, join von Borries in asserting (*RE* 19, col. 72) that Dionysus in the *Caesars* represents Julian and Silenus Maximus of Ephesus. I have not seen N. A. S. Levine, 'The Caesares of Julian: an historical study' (diss. Columbia, 1968). B. Baldwin, 'The *Caesares* of Julian', *Klio* 60(1978), 449–66 appeared after this paper was written: despite differences in matters of detail it will be evident that I agree with Baldwin's overall view of the *Caesares* as a highly personal document.

alluding by the first term to the imaginary banquet of the gods which constitutes the setting of the satire, and specifying by the second term the *Saturnalia* (Κρόνια), which occasioned the work.[6] Romulus invites all the gods and all the emperors to dine with him. The banquet takes place in heaven just below the moon in the upper air – which is best suited to the bodies which the emperors have received after death. In the first phase of the symposium the various Caesars, beginning with Caesar himself and extending down to the sons of Constantine and the usurper Magnentius, each make an appearance to the accompaniment of rude remarks from Silenus, who attempts to amuse Dionysus, beside whom he is seated and with whom he is in love.[7] Later Alexander the Great is added to the group of emperors as a particular favour to Heracles, and Hermes proceeds to an interrogation of the superior emperors (Alexander included among them) to determine by vote of the gods who is best. The winner of the competition turns out to be Marcus Aurelius.[8]

This satiric symposium provides Julian with an opportunity not only to discuss matters that interest him but also indirectly to delineate the kind of emperor he would wish to be.[9] He spreads out his ideals and his prejudices before the reader; he reveals incidentally his knowledge of Roman history. Written just over two years after the *De Caesaribus* by Sex. Aurelius Victor, whom Julian knew and promoted in his service, and some seven years before the historical survey of Eutropius, who had been a member of Julian's Persian expedition, the *Caesars* offers an unusual perspective on fourth-century traditions about earlier emperors. The work is an arresting record of the outlook and knowledge of one of the most notable emperors of late antiquity. Julian's unrelenting effort to reinstate the pagan cults, unwelcome as it was (even to many pagans), was in its way heroic. From the *Caesars* we can see, as he saw it, the past he so much regretted.

6. The *Suda* names two different works by Julian, *Caesars* and *Kronia*. But it seems likely that this is an error and that the extant work is precisely the *Kronia* mentioned by Julian himself at 157c (on the sun).

7. *Caes.* 308c.

8. *Caes.* 335c. Cf. Chr. Lacombrade, 'L'empereur Julien, émule de Marc-Aurèle', *Pallas* 14 (1967), 9–22.

9. See J. M. Alonso-Nuñez, 'Politica y filosofia en los Cesares de Juliano', *Hispania antiqua* 4 (1974), 315–20.

Above all Julian desiderated in a monarch the twin virtues of military expertise and philosophical sagacity. After the parade of emperors, as the competition among the top candidates is about to begin, Julian makes Kronos turn to Zeus and observe that Hermes had so far brought forward no philosopher as a prime candidate.[10] Alexander, Caesar, Augustus, and Trajan certainly deserved consideration, but so did Marcus Aurelius. Julian's presentation of the imperial virtues may be compared with Ammianus' characterization of Valentinian. The ultimate tribute is this: *si reliqua temperasset, vixerat ut Traianus et Marcus.*[11] As Sir Ronald Syme has commented, 'These two names epitomize the good ruler: the warrior and the sage.'[12]

While esteeming assiduous cultivation of the mind, Julian denigrated cultivation of the body.[13] His own ostentatious asceticism is reflected in the words he assigned to Marcus near the end of the competition. Almost guiltily Marcus confesses that he took food and drink in his lifetime because his body made a few demands he could not ignore.[14] The severe regimen which Julian imposed on himself led him to expect comparable self-control in others,[15] and his expectations could in turn produce explosive situations that proved more harmful than edifying. The deterioration of his relations with the people of Antioch had deeply disturbed Julian, and one may perhaps hear an echo of his private concern in the censure that Silenus is made to produce on the appearance of Probus. Physicians mix honey with their bitter medicines, Silenus observed. Probus had been too austere, harsh, and unyielding, so that his fate, though unjust, was not unnatural: πέπονθας οὖν ἄδικα μέν, εἰκότα δὲ ὅμως.[16] Little did Julian realize that these words would serve well as his own epitaph six months later.

Julian's portrait of Alexander, whom he much admired, betrays a similar obsession with the problem of excessive severity. Alexander says that if he did anything πικρόν, he did so only to those who deserved it – either by obstructing him or (significantly) by

---

10. *Caes.* 317b–c.   11. Amm. Marc. 30.9.1.
12. R. Syme, *Emperors and Biography* (Oxford 1971), 92.
13. Bowersock, *Julian*, 14–15.   14. *Caes.* 333d.
15. Despite the protestations to the contrary by Claudius Mamertinus, Julian's panegyrist: *Pan.* 12.2.   16. *Caes.* 314c.

failing to use their opportunities.[17] Even so Alexander is made to admit that he had occasionally repented of what he had done. Repentance (μεταμέλεια) he calls a saviour (σώτειρα δαίμων).[18] It was not easy for Julian to endure the unpopularity he brought upon himself at Antioch: the whole of his *Misopogon* is an enraged outcry against the ingratitude of the Antiochenes. His strict code of behaviour had led to the difficulties in human relations that he exposed in Probus and Alexander. His unwillingness to compromise in order to achieve the popularity he craved is dramatically evoked near the end of the *Caesars* when Caesar himself is taxed by Silenus with pandering to the people without winning their affection. Indignantly and incredulously Caesar objects, 'Am I not loved by the people who punished Brutus and Cassius?' No, replied Silenus with malice. For committing the murder the two tyrannicides were rewarded with provincial governorships.[19]

The self-denying character of Julian impelled him to nearly total abstinence from sexual relations. No ancient writer, however hostile, was able to charge him with sexual misconduct.[20] But the strong demands which the emperor made on himself did not eradicate and probably encouraged his prurient interest in the subject. The *Caesars* betrays a taste for erotica that goes well beyond the requirements of the Menippean genre. Silenus' infatuation with Dionysus may reasonably be judged traditional,[21] and it would have been difficult not to allude to Tiberius' adventures on Capri.[22] But it is striking that on his first appearance Trajan is characterized exclusively as a warrior and a paederast.[23] One would scarcely guess that he was destined to re-appear as one of the finalists in the heavenly competition. And Hadrian, the great philhellene whose devotion to the Greeks might have appealed to Julian as it did to Plutarch two centuries earlier, is presented as a homosexual sophist in a vain search for the beloved Antinous.[24]

17. *Caes.* 325b. On Julian's regard for Alexander, cf. 253a (to Themistius).
18. *Caes. loc. cit.*
19. *Caes.* 332b: διὰ τοῦτο μὲν γὰρ αὐτοὺς ὁ δῆμος ἐψηφίσατο εἶναι ὑπάτους. It has not generally been recognized that ὑπάτους here means 'governors', not 'consuls'. Spanheim, however, translated correctly 'proconsuls'. In this point Julian has not erred.
20. As observed by Amm. Marc. at 25.4.3.   21. *Caes.* 308c.
22. *Caes.* 310a.   23. *Caes.* 311c.
24. *Caes.* 311d. On Hadrian and Plutarch, cf. C. P. Jones, *Plutarch and Rome* (1971), 28, 56.

Julian's interest in sexual behaviour arose from his fanatical loathing of it, and in the person of Constantine he could bring together his hatred of Christianity with his suppressed prurience. The result is the most memorable passage in the entire *Caesars*, as Constantine, ignominiously defeated in the competition and lacking a divine patron to succour him, repairs to the arms ol Licentiousness personified (Τρυφή). This improper lady introduces him to Incontinence ('Ασωτία), who is found cohabiting with Jesus. Promising immediate purification, Jesus invites all seducers, murderers, and other wrong-doers to come to him.[25]

Julian's portrait of Constantine is breathtaking in its bitterness. Its linkage of Christianity and harlotry offers a glimpse into personal obsessions such as few writers in antiquity have ever allowed. The reverse of Julian's image of Constantine is his deeply respectful presentation of his pagan grandfather Constantius I, who seemed more closely related to him than Constantine, his father's half-brother.[26] In connection with Constantius I Julian carefully maintains and celebrates the alleged descent of his family from Claudius Gothicus: ἐπένευσαν αὐτοῦ τῷ γένει τὴν ἀρχήν.[27] It has long been observed that this ancestry of the house of Constantius seems to have been invented by Constantine to give legitimacy to his claim to the purple precisely in the year 310. A panegyrist at Treviri in that year declared: *quod plerique adhuc fortasse nesciunt, sed qui te amant plurimum sciunt: ab illo enim divo Claudio manat in te avita cognatio.*[28] This fraudulent claim, which the *Historia Augusta* also perpetuates,[29] served Julian as well as Constantine; and he had already used it before in hymning the virtues of Constantius II, at a time when he had not felt free to reveal openly

25. *Caes.* 336a–b.
26. *Caes.* 315a (τὸν ἐμὸν πάππον Κωνστάντιον) and 336b. The notion that Constantius I was sympathetic to Christians or even himself a believer is peculiar to Christian sources, notably Lactantius in the *de mortibus persecutorum* and Eusebius in the *vita Constantini*. Pagans did not entertain such a view of Diocletian's Caesar.
27. *Caes.* 313d, cf. 336b. On the claim of descent, R. Syme, 'The Ancestry of Constantine', *Bonner-Historia-Augusta-Colloquium* 1971 (1974), 237–53. A. Alföldi stresses Julian's commemoration of this ancestry in 'Die verlorene Enmannsche Kaisergeschichte und die *Caesares* des Iulianus Apostata', *Bonner Historia-Augusta-Colloquium* 1966/7 (1968), 1–8, especially 3.   28. *Pan. Lat.* 2.1–2.
29. *HA Claud.* 13.1–3, allegedly written before 1 May 305 (when Constantius was still Caesar).

his pent-up hatred of the murderer of his father and his family.[30] It may well be that Julian had no reason to suspect the descent from Claudius, for – as we now shall see – his knowledge of Roman history was not very profound.

In an imaginative work like the *Caesars* no one could expect Julian to have worked from historical sources in the manner of a Cassius Dio. What he reports about the emperors was in all probability drawn from reserves of knowledge built up after years of reading and tuition. Obviously those features of an emperor's character or administration that impressed Julian for whatever reason, conscious or unconscious, turn up in the *Caesars* as ingredients in the satire. This is not a systematic study of Roman history, but omissions and errors can be telling nevertheless.

The parade of emperors in the first part of the *Caesars* looks as if it is supposed to be complete. It is not only that Julian seems to go out of his way to register, however briefly, such evanescent figures as Galba, Otho, Vitellius, Pertinax, and Macrinus. But in introducing the banquet he says explicitly of Romulus, who is the host: πάντας ἐκάλει τοὺς θεοὺς καὶ δὴ καὶ αὐτοὺς τοὺς Καίσαρας.[31] The implication is that he has invited all the gods and all the emperors too. Down to the rulers of the late second century Julian's list is remarkably complete, in fact more than complete. After Nero comes a crowd of emperors of all kinds: Βίνδικες Γάλβαι Ὄθωνες Βιτέλλιοι.[32] What is Julius Vindex doing in that list? Spanheim, in his great commentary on the *Caesars*, noted that Julian seemed to be following the supposed authors of the *Historia Augusta* in including men raised up unsuccessfully to the purple by the army.[33] The *Historia Augusta*, however, correctly links Vindex with other military nominees for the throne such as Antonius Saturninus, Pescennius Niger, and Clodius Albinus.[34] What Julian does in the *Caesars* is not comparable. He unequivocally and erroneously registers Vindex as an emperor.

Of the short-lived emperors of 193, Julian mentions Pertinax and omits Didius Julianus. This gap in his imperial list is perhaps

30. Jul. 6d–7a; 51c. 31. *Caes.* 307b. 32. *Caes.* 310d.
33. *HA Pesc. Nig.* 9.2; *Sev. Alex.* 1.7. I have used the 1728 edition of Spanheim's translation and commentary, published at Amsterdam; and I give references to this. On Vindex, p. 58.
34. See the texts cited from the *HA* in n. 33.

unimportant; it certainly does not betray ignorance of any substantial tract of Roman history. The same cannot be said, however, of the presentation of third-century emperors. Severus Alexander is succeeded directly by Valerian and Gallienus.[35] Julian unaccountably omits Maximin, the Gordians, Philip, and Decius as well as several more transitory rulers in that turbulent epoch. Spanheim was puzzled: 'On pourrait trouver étrange, que Julien ne fasse comparoître ici aucun de ces Césars, qui ont regné entre Alexandre Sévère et ce Gallien ou Valérien son père.'[36] Apart from the brevity of several of the reigns of this period, 'je n'en vois point de cause'. This gap in Julian's list is very remarkable. It not only enlarges on the gap between the Gordians and the Valerians in the sequence of biographies in the *Historia Augusta*. It seems also to reflect an attitude not unlike that assumed by the biographer of Severus Alexander. Writing here under the name of Lampridius, the author declares in the context of Alexander's death, *Hactenus imperium p. R. eum principem habuit, qui diutius imperaret post eum certatim inruentibus et aliis semenstribus, aliis annuis, plerisque per biennium ad summum per triennium imperantibus usque ad eos principes, qui latius imperium tetenderunt, Aurelianum dico et deinceps. de quibus, si vita suppeditaverit, ea, quae comperta fuerint, publicabimus.*[37] Julian does not, of course, pass immediately from Severus Alexander to Aurelian, but he does show a neglect of the middle decade of the third century that one may suspect was not peculiar to him. He makes no excuses as the author of the *Historia Augusta* does. Julian's easy transition to Valerian and Gallienus suggests that he was unaware of leaving any emperor out.[38]

The omission of all Roman emperors between Alexander and Valerian is compounded by the absence of the emperor Tacitus (not to mention Florianus, who might like Didius Julianus have more easily disappeared in the crowd of names). To be sure, little was known of the emperor Tacitus, as the biography in the *Historia*

35. *Caes.* 313b: ἐπὶ τούτῳ παρῆλθεν εἴσω Γαλλιῆνος μετὰ τοῦ πατρός.
36. Spanheim (n. 33), p. 90.
37. *HA Sev. Alex.* 64.1–2.
38. Ἐπὶ τούτῳ (n. 35). So large an omission, far greater than the gap from Philip to Valerian in the *HA*, makes it virtually impossible that Julian could have made any use of the so-called *Kaisergeschichte*, which Enmann postulated as a source for fourth-century Latin historians. Cf. Alföldi's treatment of this possibility (n. 27 above).

Augusta makes plain.[39] But his existence and rule was as well established as that of Aurelian, who preceded him, and of Probus, who succeeded him. What is more, all of the emperors missed by Julian are duly registered in their places by Sex. Aurelius Victor in his survey of the Caesars to the year 360. Victor was a man whom Julian had known personally at Sirmium and whom he had promoted and favoured.[40] But it is obvious that if Julian had read Victor's work (with its adroit conclusion designed to please both Constantius II and Julian), it had made no impression whatever.

Julian reports a detail for the emperor Probus that is nowhere else attested: ἄδικα δὲ πεπονθὼς ὑπὸ τῶν ἄθεων.[41] As Lacombrade has acutely noted in his Budé edition, ἄθεοι in the writings of Julian can only mean Christians.[42] He therefore infers that the soldiers who killed Probus were, according to Julian, Christian. That is probably going too far. All we learn from the *Caesars* is that Probus was unjustly treated by the Christians (ἄθεοι), but that is surprising enough. The sharp-eyed Spanheim missed this difficulty because he was under the impression that Julian wrote ἄδικα δὲ πεπονθώς, ὑπὸ τῶν θεῶν ἐτιμᾶτο κτλ.[43] But the manuscripts are univocal, and Julian's remark must stand. It would be nothing less than astonishing if a pagan–Christian confrontation under Probus had failed to find some echo in fourth-century sources. Julian's memory seems to have played him false. Another Probus, governor of Lower Pannonia under Diocletian in the early fourth century, ran into difficulties with a certain Bishop Irenaeus, who was spreading the doctrine of *Exodus* 22.20, *qui diis et non Deo sacrificat eradicabitur.*[44] Irenaeus was brought before Probus at Sirmium and executed. The emperor Probus, it will be recalled, had been dispatched by his soldiers also at Sirmium. It may be conjectured that Julian has simply confused the two Probi and thus transferred the governor's tribulations to the emperor.

Perhaps the most startling feature of Julian's parade of Caesars is the lack of concord between his own assessments of certain eminent

39. On this biography and its subject, see R. Syme, *Emperors*, 237–47.
40. Amm. Marc. 21.10.6. Julian appointed Victor governor of Pannonia Secunda.
41. *Caes.* 314b.
42. Budé edition of Jul., *Oeuvres complètes* II.2 (1964), 13.
43. Spanheim (n. 33), p. 102.
44. H. Musurillo, *Acts of the Christian Martyrs* (1972), 294–301.

emperors and those of his contemporaries. He not only seems unaware, as we have seen, of rulers well known to Aurelius Victor (or Eutropius), but his judgments are so different from theirs in several instances as to reinforce the notion that he had small acquaintance with either their work or the historiographical tradition to which they belonged. The pertinent instances are Titus, Antoninus Pius, Severus Alexander, and (to a lesser degree) Septimius Severus.

In general Titus enjoyed a good press in late antiquity. Suetonius had certainly preserved details of Titus' private life that do not altogether do him credit. His taste for Berenice and his skill in forgery were known, but overall the reign was counted a successful one; and Titus became a paradigm for subsequent monarchs.[45] In the famous eulogy of Julian's character, Ammianus cited Titus, Trajan, Antoninus Pius, and Marcus Aurelius for comparison.[46] In *prudentia* Julian was judged a second Titus. The *Caesars*, however, would lead one to believe that Julian would not have been much pleased by the compliment. Zeus is made to say of Vespasian's sons, τὸν πρεσβύτερον μὲν παίζειν κέλευε μετὰ τῆς 'Αφροδίτης τῆς πανδήμου.[47] That was no way to treat a paradigm of *prudentia*. Spanheim was perplexed: 'Il est certain que Julien pouvait dire quelque chose de plus avantageux en faveur de Titus, les délices de son siècle, si célèbre par sa Douceur et par sa Clémence.'[48]

Aurelius Victor, two years earlier, had written a lyrical account of Titus and singled out his pre-eminence *litteris clementiaque ac muneribus*.[49] His biographical notice ends: *Huius sane mors adeo provinciis luctui fuit, uti generis humani delicias appellantes orbatum orbem deflerent.*[50] At the end of the 360s Eutropius wrote with still greater warmth of Titus, *vir omnium virtutum genere mirabilis adeo, ut amor et*

45. Suet., *Tit.* 7 (Berenice), 3 (forgery). But he was *amor ac deliciae generis humani* (1). Before he became emperor he was less well regarded (also in 1), cf. Dio 66.18.1.

46. Amm. Marc. 16.1.2.   47. *Caes.* 311a.

48. Spanheim (n. 33), p. 62. Cf. J. F. Gilliam, 'Titus in Julian's Caesares', *AJP* 88 (1967), 203–8, reviving Cantoclerus' suggestion, known to Spanheim, that Julian is alluding to the phrase *amor ac deliciae generis humani*. Such a proposal is based on the supposition that Julian would not write about an emperor in a way that is 'quite out of keeping with a well-established tradition' (Gilliam, p. 204). Yet that is just what he does.

49. Aur. Vict., *De Caes.* 10.1.   50. *ibid.* 10.6.

deliciae humani generis diceretur, facundissimus, bellicosissimus moderatissi-mus . . . tantus luctus eo mortuo publicus fuit ut omnes tamquam in propria doluerint orbitate.[51] The harmony of fourth-century praise was eloquently sustained in the verses of Ausonius' *Caesars: unum dixisti moriens te crimen habere;/set nulli de te, nec tibi credidimus.*[52] Julian is utterly remote from all this. He may have been familiar with Cassius Dio's opinion that Titus' reputation as emperor might have deteriorated if he had lived longer (he died ἐν ἀκμῇ τῆς δόξης),[53] but in general Dio's judgment of the reign is certainly positive. Julian has nothing in common with the fourth-century tradition, even as it appeared among his friends and associates, nor with whatever sources gave rise to that tradition. So glaring a discrepancy is more likely to be due to ignorance or, at best, indifference than to any deliberate eccentricity, for it would have suited Julian perfectly well to include Titus (like Augustus or Trajan) among the finalists – only to be rejected as unworthy of the prize.

Ammianus' praise of Julian included the words *clemens ut Antoninus,*[54] and it is evident that this emperor was almost universally considered a model of gentleness and clemency. Of Valentinian Ammianus wrote, *ut Antoninus Pius erat serenus et clemens.*[55] Aurelius Victor had been similarly admiring: *Hunc fere nulla vitiorum labes commaculavit.*[56] Eutropius likewise: *vir insignis et qui merito Numae Pompilio conferatur . . . vixit ingenti honestate privatus, maiore in imperio, nulli acerbus, cunctis benignus . . . Pius propter clemen-tiam dictus est.*[57] Ausonius writes in the same vein: *ille vocatu/consultis-que Pius, nomen habens meriti.*[58] The *Historia Augusta* treats Antoninus Pius respectfully. Although most of Cassius Dio's account of the reign has been lost, it is clear that his overall judgment was no different from that of the Latin authors: ὁ γὰρ Ἀντωνῖνος ὁμολογεῖται παρὰ πάντων καλός τε καὶ ἀγαθὸς γενέσθαι.[59] It therefore comes as a surprise to find Julian introducing this paragon with the barbed characterization σώφρων, οὐ τὰ ἐς Ἀφροδίτην, ἀλλὰ τὰ ἐς τὴν πολιτείαν and to hear Silenus condemn him for σμικρολογία.[60] Once more Julian's knowledge seems

51. Eutrop. 7.21–2.
52. Aus., *Caes.* 47–8.
53. Dio 66.18.5.
54. Amm. Marc. 16.1.4.
55. Amm. Marc. 30.8.12.
56. Aur. Vict., *De Caes.* 15.1.
57. Eutrop. 8.8.2–4.
58. Aus., *Caes.* 65–6.
59. Dio 69.15.3.
60. *Caes.* 312a.

totally devoid of contact with the Latin historiographical tradition of his own age and even with earlier Greek tradition. Once more he lays emphasis on τὰ 'Αφροδίσια. Again there is no reason to think that Julian is attempting a bold and wholly original reassessment.

The case of Severus Alexander is no less surprising. He has an undesirable seat at the symposium (ἐν ἐσχάτοις που καθῆστο), and Silenus addresses him as a fool and an idiot: Ὦ μῶρε καὶ μέγα νήπιε.[61] He is upbraided for the influence of his mother and for his own lack of generosity. The only relief in this bleak presentation is the suggestion that he perished unjustly. For readers of Julian it is nothing less than amazing that Norman Baynes could have imagined that the panegyric of Severus Alexander in the *Historia Augusta* was meant as an oblique tribute to the emperor Julian and was composed during his reign.[62] The biography of Severus Alexander in the *HA* is the central piece in the entire work: it is a long and rapturous account of the reign. No one who knew Julian's opinion of the emperor would have attempted flattery by a comparison of the two rulers. Yet the judgment of the biographer in the *Historia Augusta* is essentially consonant with that of the Latin tradition as it can be seen in Victor and Eutropius. Victor states unequivocally *rempublicam reliquit firmatum undique*.[63] Eutropius is similarly admiring of Severus Alexander's performance both in Rome and abroad.[64] We may assume that these authors reproduce the traditional view of fourth-century Latin historiography. Their source, probably the so-called *Kaisergeschichte* of Enmann, was likewise familiar to the author of the *Historia Augusta*. All this was alien to Julian.[65] Eutropius observed of Severus Alexander: *Romae*

61. *Caes.* 313a.
62. N. H. Baynes, *The Historia Augusta. Its Date and Purpose* (Oxford 1926). Cf. R. Syme, *Emperors*, 99, pointing to Julian's low opinion of Severus Alexander.
63. Aur. Vict., *De Caes.* 24.7.
64. Eutrop. 8.23.
65. On this issue, see T. D. Barnes, 'The Lost Kaisergeschichte and the Latin Historical Tradition', *Bonner Historia-Augusta-Colloquium* 1968/69 (1970), 13–43. Eutrop. 10.16 notes Julian's weakness in Latin erudition. This situation makes an occasional parallel with Victor, Eutropius, the *Epit. de Caes.*, or the *HA* inadequate support for a link with the *Kaisergeschichte*. Alföldi (n. 27 above) helpfully compares Julian's allusion to Gallienus as an effeminate with *HA*, Trig. Tyr. 12.11. But this characterization reflects Julian's preoccupation with erotica in regard to an emperor whom the new Flavians would naturally have denigrated in their effort to claim Gallienus' successor, Claudius, as their glorious ancestor. Gallienus the effeminate presumably entered the tradition with the propaganda

quoque favorabilis fuit:[66] Julian had never even set foot in Rome. In Greek historiography Severus Alexander had been hospitably received by Herodian, whose detailed narration is equally at variance with Julian's view.

The tradition about Septimius Severus was more mixed, and not without reason. Some incidents of cruelty were ineradicably on his record.[67] But even so the fourth-century Latin tradition treated him gently. *Felix ac prudens, armis praecipue*, said Aurelius Victor;[68] and Eutropius, admitting that Septimius was *natura saevus*, acknowledged his *bellica gloria* and his dedication to literature and philosophy.[69] Ausonius commended him for *virtus* and *ingenium*, and Claudian praised him along with the unimpeachable Nerva and the 'tranquil' Antoninus Pius.[70] For Julian, however, Septimius Severus is no more than an embodiment of harshness and cruelty: ἀνὴρ πικρίας γέμων, κολαστικός.[71]

The foregoing examples document Julian's distance from the standard historiographical tradition, most conspicuously in Latin texts of the fourth century. But insofar as one can tell, his opinions were not much closer to the Greek historians either. If his portrait of Titus reminds one slightly of Dio's observation, it is still quite unlike Dio's overall assessment. And certainly Julian's Pius bears no resemblance to the little we have of Dio's account; his judgment of Severus Alexander is far removed from that of Herodian. It is pertinent to observe that Ammianus, who must have had at least as detailed an acquaintance with the Greek historians as Julian, is largely in agreement with the Latin tradition of his time. It would be reasonable to assume that Greek and Latin sources were not all that far apart in their assessments. In any case, Julian must have paid no attention to the recent work by his own man, Aurelius Victor. That much is clear. Julian's report of Roman imperial history was not very accurate, and for the third century it was woefully inadequate. Even for satiric purposes Philip the Arab or

of the second Flavian dynasty. The absence of this characterization in Victor, Eutropius, and the Epitome can only mean that it was *not* present in the *Kaisergeschichte*.

66. Eutrop. 8.23.   67. Cf. R. Syme, *Emperors*, 93.
68. Aur. Vict., *De Caes.* 20.14.
69. Eutrop. 8.18.3 (*natura saevus*); 8.19.1 (*bellica gloria*).
70. Aus., *Caes.* 87–8; Claud., *De VI cons. Honori* 421.
71. *Caes.* 312d.

Decius deserved to make an appearance. Silenus would have had rich material for his acerbic wit.

If we should wish to hazard a guess as to one author whose works on historical subjects had actually made a substantial impression on Julian, Plutarch would be the best candidate. The only parts of the *Caesars* that are noticeably full in historical allusion are the speeches of Alexander the Great, Julius Caesar, and Augustus in the final competition. The pairing of the pieces by Alexander and Caesar, presented so that one answers the other, corresponds exactly to the pairing of the biographies of those two in Plutarch's parallel lives. The speeches reproduce material to be found there.[72] The explanation of the comparable fullness in Augustus' speech may likewise by Julian's familiarity with Plutarch's biography – now lost but the first in his series of imperial lives. It is at least striking that the speeches of the other contestants (Trajan, Marcus, and Constantine) are much shorter and less detailed. It looks as if Julian simply did not know so much about those later emperors. Plutarch, of course, had not written their biographies.

One may perhaps go a step further. In view of Julian's ignoring of the Latin historiographical tradition, it would be unwise to assume, as scholars from Spanheim on have often done, that certain items in the presentation of the early emperors are necessarily drawn from Suetonius.[73] Julian probably never read Suetonius. The instances in which he appears to echo remarks in the Suetonian lives, not only of Augustus, but also of Tiberius, might be more plausibly linked to Plutarch's biographies of the same emperors. There is, at any rate, a much greater likelihood that Julian had once read and remembered those lives of the emperors, now unfortunately lost to us.[74]

Julian's account of his predecessors is, as one might have expected, highly personal. His own observations and ideals dominate the miniature portraits he gives us in the *Caesars*. But,

---

72. Cf. the parallels cited in Lacombrade's Budé edition (n. 42) for the speeches of Caesar (320a–322a) and of Alexander (322b–325c). See also Lacombrade's preface, p. 8: 'Pour la vie d'Alexandre et de César, Julien a surtout suivi Plutarque.'

73. Cf. Lacombrade in the Budé edition (n. 42), p. 8: 'Pour les princes des dynasties julio-claudienne et flavienne, il a fait appel à Suétone.' See also Lacombrade's parallels at 309a–310a.

74. On these lost biographies by Plutarch, see Jones (n. 24), 72–80.

more remarkably, in the domain of Roman history, he reveals an intellectual isolation from his contemporaries, especially those writing in Latin, that is reminiscent of his general lack of interest in Rome and Italy. Julian's acquaintance with the careers of his predecessors was conspicuously imperfect. He was even unaware of who some of them were. In the history of the past he sought only models for himself, and he acknowledged ultimately only Alexander the Great and Marcus Aurelius. Alexander was not, in any reasonable sense, a predecessor; therefore Julian could see himself as the best of all the emperors of Rome apart from Marcus. This was doubtless reassuring; and since Julian believed that even Marcus had committed ἁμαρτήματα in regard to his son and his wife,[75] it is unlikely that he thought himself much inferior to his admired and philosophic predecessor. In short, the *Caesars* can be seen as a work not only of self-revelation but in the end, like the *Misopogon*, of self-justification.

75. *Caes.* 312a. At 334b Julian explains that Marcus was wrong to have had his wife deified and to have entrusted the succession to his son.

Greek translations of Latin literature in the fourth century A.D.[1]

ELIZABETH A. FISHER

Horace's familiar aphorism *Graecia capta ferum victorem cepit* (*Epistles* 2.1.156) neatly summarizes two obvious and important aspects of Graeco-Roman relations in antiquity: the Greeks[2] accepted Roman political supremacy, but the Romans acknowledged, even welcomed, Greek cultural pre-eminence. The numerous histories and handbooks of Latin literature bear out Horace's observation with countless examples of Roman dependence upon Greek models, commencing with Livius Andronicus' Latin translation of the *Odyssey* (third century B.C.). We know, moreover, that outside strictly literary circles many cultivated Romans were thoroughly hellenized. Among the acquaintances of Pliny, for example, Terentius Junior, a retired Roman administrator, was fluent in Greek and so well read that 'one would think he lived in Athens' (Pliny, *Epistles* 7.25); the Greek compositions of Arrius Antoninus prompted Pliny to exclaim, 'Can a Roman really write such

1. I wish to acknowledge with gratitude the help I have received from a number of people at various stages of this project. I am grateful to Glen W. Bowersock for his guidance as I first investigated Greek translation of Latin literature; to the Center for Hellenic Studies, Washington, D.C., for the resources and leisure with which to pursue this topic as a Junior Fellow in 1974–5; to Bernard M. W. Knox and the Junior Fellows at the Center for Hellenic Studies for their insights and suggestions; to the participants at the First Annual Byzantine Studies Conference (Cleveland, Ohio, 1975) and at the Fourth Annual Byzantine Studies Conference (Ann Arbor, Michigan, 1978) for searching questions and helpful additions; to my seminar in Greek translations of Latin literature at the University of Minnesota in the spring of 1976 for lively and informative discussions; to the staff of Dumbarton Oaks Research Library, Washington, D.C., for access to the collection; and to Robert A. Hadley for rigorous criticism, stimulating insights, and timely encouragement. Finally, I am grateful to John Winkler for his helpful insights and suggestions throughout the manuscript, and especially for the citations to Pliny and Artemidorus in the introduction and for perceptive comments on the *Fourth Eclogue* translation.

2. By 'Greeks' I mean Greek speakers educated in and identifying themselves with Hellenic culture. Their first language need not have been Greek, but was not Latin.

Greek? Athens herself, I am sure, could not be as Attic' (*Epistles* 4.3). Greek speakers, on the other hand, apparently avoided acquaintance with Latin culture. No cultivated Greek has been pronounced by his contemporaries 'as Latin as Rome', and several generations of scholarly enquiry into the attitudes of Greeks toward Rome[3] have discouraged us from ever expecting to find such a person. That Greek speakers were indifferent to any language and literature but their own has become virtual dogma.[4] In this paper I hope to demonstrate that this view ignores significant evidence to the contrary.

There is some ancient evidence of Greek–Latin bilingualism as a practical tool among Greek as well as Latin speakers. Artemidorus' catalogue of dreams includes the information that a Greek who dreams of learning the Roman alphabet and a Roman who dreams of learning the Greek alphabet can expect the same outcome, namely, immersion in that foreign culture (*Oneirokritika* 1.53). In this passage, the Greek-speaking student of Latin is regarded as no

---

3. See, for example, Harald Fuchs, *Der geistige Widerstand gegen Rom in der antiken Welt* (Berlin 1938); Jonas Palm, *Rom, Römertum und Imperium in der griechischen Literatur der Kaiserzeit*, Acta Reg. Societatis Humaniorum Litterarum Lundensis 57 (Lund 1959); Bettie Forte, *Rome and the Romans as the Greeks Saw Them* (Rome 1972). For studies concerned especially with language, see, for example, Émile Egger, 'De l'étude de la langue latine chez les Grecs dans l'antiquité', *Mémoires d'histoire ancienne et de philologie* (Paris 1863), 259–76; Ludwig Hahn, *Rom und Romanismus im griechisch-römischen Osten* (Leipzig 1906); Ludwig Hahn, 'Zum Sprachenkampf im römischen Reich bis auf die Zeit Justinians', *Philologus* Suppl. 10 (Leipzig 1907), 675–715; Ludwig Hahn, 'Zum Gebrauch der lateinischen Sprache in Konstantinopel', *Festgabe für Martin Schanz zur 70. Geburtstagfeier* (Wurzburg 1912), 173–83; Henrik Zilliacus, *Zum Kampf der Weltsprachen im ost-römischen Reich* (Helsinki 1935); Carl R. Trahman, 'The Latin Language and Literature in the Greek World' (diss. Univ. of Cincinnati 1942); A. H. M. Jones, 'The Greeks under the Roman Empire', *Dumbarton Oaks Papers* 17 (1963), 3–19; Gilbert Dagron, 'Aux origines de la civilisation byzantine: langue de culture et langue d'État', *Revue Historique* 291 (1969), 23–56; Arnaldo Momigliano, 'The Fault of the Greeks', *Daedalus* 104.2 (Spring 1975), 9–19. J. P. V. D. Balsdon, *Romans and Aliens* (London 1979) discusses the Latin language among Greek speakers on pp. 123–8, 131–5; owing to its very recent appearance, I have not cited Balsdon's book elsewhere in this article.

4. A. H. M. Jones (n. 3), 3; Momigliano (n. 3), 15; Gustave Bardy, *La question des langues dans l'Église ancienne* (Paris 1948), 153; Paul Peeters, *Le trefonds oriental de l'hagiographie byzantine*, Subsidia Hagiographica 26 (Brussels 1950), 72; Paul Peeters, 'Érudits et polyglottes d'autrefois', *Bulletin de la classe des lettres de l'Académie royale de Belgique*, 5th ser., 21 (1935), 123–44, reprinted in *Recherches d'histoire et de philologie orientales*, Subsidia Hagiographica 27 (Brussels 1951), Vol. II, 10.

more peculiar or extraordinary than the Latin-speaking student of Greek, although Artemidorus does acknowledge some distinction when he mentions a Greek who became a slave after he dreamed of learning Latin – predictably, since 'a slave is never taught Greek'. Latin was, in fact, the language of Roman domination in the army, in law, and in the imperial administration; trade demanded some knowledge of Latin as well.[5] The practical incentives for Greek speakers to learn Latin increased during the third and fourth centuries. In A.D. 212 Caracalla extended Roman citizenship to all free inhabitants of the Empire in the *Constitutio Antoniniana*. Chiefly, this legislation symbolized the unity of the Roman Empire and its peoples,[6] but it also meant that Greeks were subject to Roman law and that the language of Roman law, Latin, became an important practical tool in the Greek-speaking world. With the establishment in the East of an imperial residence by Diocletian at Nicomedia and an imperial capital by Constantine at Constantinople, careers in law, in the civil bureaucracy, and among the translators of the imperial chancery beckoned to those fluent in both Latin and Greek. At the same time, episcopal chanceries in Alexandria, Constantinople, and Antioch required translators to handle correspondence with the Church in the West, and ecumenical councils also needed translators.[7] In fact, Greek speakers of the fourth century learned Latin so eagerly that Libanius feared the demise of Hellenism and of Greek studies, neglected in the faddish rage for Latin.[8]

That Greek speakers used Latin in practical areas of life does not compel us to conclude that any cultured Greek speaker read Latin literature or even knew of its existence. There are traces, however, of acquaintance with Latin literature among educated Greeks. Plutarch, for example, who states that he himself learned Latin, expresses admiration for particular features of Latin literary style

---

5. For a full discussion of the question, see Trahman (n. 3), *passim* and, more readily available, Zilliacus, 59–163; a brief sketch available in A. H. M. Jones, *The Later Roman Empire 284–602* (Oxford 1964), 988–91.

6. A. N. Sherwin-White, *The Roman Citizenship*[2] (Oxford 1973), 380–94, 451–60.

7. Bardy (n. 4), 234; Dom E. Dekkers, 'Les traductions grecques des écrits patristiques latins', *Sacris Erudiri* 5 (1953), 217–19.

8. Libanius, *Or.* 1.214, 234; 2.44; 48. 22; *Ep.* 566. Richard Foerster, ed., *Libanii Opera* (Teubner 1903–27).

(*Demosthenes* 2); Pliny remarks upon certain Greeks who learned Latin in order to read and set to music his hendecasyllables (*Epistles* 7.4) – looking for a patron, no doubt! The Greek epic poets Quintus of Smyrna, Tryphiodorus, and Nonnus seem to show direct acquaintance with Latin literature, particularly with Vergil and Ovid.[9] There were also Greek translations of Latin literary works,[10] and these must be considered apart from the official translations, like Augustus' *Res Gestae*,[11] which were produced and promulgated by the imperial chancery for the Greek-speaking subjects of the Empire. Translations from Latin literature into Greek appeared only because there was an audience eager to read the literature of Rome but unable to read its language. Although many of these literary translations have perished,[12] a number survive from the fourth century A.D.

These translations may contribute in various ways to our understanding of Greek speakers' knowledge of the Latin language and their attitudes toward Latin literature. If the translator is a Greek, his translation provides direct evidence of a Greek speaker's competence (or incompetence) in dealing with Latin vocabulary, syntax, and idiom. Whatever the translator's cultural background, we would like to know what circumstances fostered a fluency in Latin and in Greek along with a desire to promulgate Latin literature among Greek speakers. The literature which a translator selected indicates what he considered attractive and/or valuable to

9. Alan Cameron, 'Wandering Poets: A Literary Movement in Byzantine Egypt', *Historia* 14 (1965), 494–6; Gennaro d'Ippolito, *Studi Nonniani* (Palermo 1964), 69–76; argued by James Diggle, *Euripides Phaethon* (Cambridge 1970), Appendix A: 'Ovid and Nonnos', with references to earlier literature.

10. There are several excellent studies devoted to Greek translations from Latin. C. F. Weber's *De Latine Scriptis Quae Graeci Veteres in Linguam Suam Transtulerunt* (Cassell 1835–52) is a comprehensive, comparative treatment of Greek translations and Latin originals, but it is based on the limited evidence available at Weber's own time. Viktor Reichmann's *Römische Literatur in griechischer Übersetzung, Philologus* Suppl. 34.3 (1943) is a detailed philological examination of six translations dating from the first to the sixth century A.D.; Bardy (n. 4) and Dekkers (n. 7) have confined their excellent investigations to the role of translation in the early Christian Church.

11. See Reichmann (n. 10), 19–27, for an analysis of this translation.

12. See Reichmann (n. 10) 1–16, Weber (n. 10) and Trahman (n. 3) *passim*. Especially well known and often cited are Polybius' translation of the *Aeneid* (first century A.D.), Zenobius' translation of Sallust's *Histories, Jugurtha*, and *Catiline* (second century A.D.), and Julius Africanus' translation of Tertullian's *Apologeticus*. Of these, only a translation of Tertullian survives (see VI below).

a Greek-speaking audience. If the translation appeared together with the original Latin text, it is, I think, reasonable to assume that the translator expected his readers to be interested in the original language of the work as well as its contents. The style of a translation suggests the translator's attitude toward his work and also his reader's reaction to it. In antiquity, as today, two general styles of translation were recognized: 'literal' and 'free', or, in St Jerome's terms, *verbum e verbo* and *sensum de sensu* (*Epistle* 57).[13] Sebastian Brock has admirably described the distinct psychological effect which each translation style has upon the reader: the *verbum e verbo* translation brings the reader to the original, while the *sensum de sensu* brings the original to the reader.[14] These two ancient categories of translation will be useful to keep in mind while examining the following examples of fourth-century Greek translations from Latin literature: (1) Vergil's *Fourth Eclogue* and Constantine's *Oration to the Assembly of the Saints*, (2) juxtalinear translations: Vergil and Cicero, (3) Paeanius' translation of Eutropius' *Breviarium*, (4) the Greek version of Jerome's *Vita Hilarionis*, (5) Eusebius' translation of the Edict of Toleration, (6) Eusebius and the Greek version of Tertullian's *Apologeticus*, (7) Latin literary influence on Greek technical treatises, and (8) problematic translations.

I. Vergil's *Fourth Eclogue* and Constantine's *Oration to the Assembly of the Saints*

A polished translation of Vergil's *Fourth Eclogue* is included in the *Oratio ad Sanctorum Coetum*, a document appended to the Eusebian *Vita Constantini* as an example of Constantine's rhetorical style. The question of authorship, both of the *Vita Constantini* and of its documents, has provoked a long scholarly debate;[15] for the purposes of this discussion, suffice it to say that the *VC* and the

13. Cicero and Horace also mention these two styles of translation, which are demonstrated from the Hellenistic world as well. See Sebastian Brock, 'Aspects of Translation Technique in Antiquity', *Greek, Roman and Byzantine Studies* 20 (1979), 69–87, esp. 69–71.

14. Brock, 73.

15. For a survey of modern scholarship on this problem, see Friedhelm Winkelmann, 'Zur Geschichte des Authentizitätsproblems der Vita Constantini', *Klio* 40 (1962), 187–243, esp. p. 188 n. 1.

Oratio are very likely what they purport to be – a tract of Eusebius and a speech of Constantine.[16] According to Eusebius (*VC* 4.32), Constantine composed a Latin text of this oration (now lost), and his chancery staff translated the Greek version which accompanies the *VC*. To render Constantine's quotations from the *Fourth Eclogue*, the chancery translator evidently incorporated an already existing, rather free Greek translation of the poem; the presence of a separate translator for the Eclogue is betrayed by incongruities in the Greek oration between the Eclogue and its exegesis, which Constantine had based on the Latin original of the poem.[17] The opening lines of Vergil's *Fourth Eclogue* and the section of Constantine's oration incorporating them will illustrate the character of the Greek Eclogue translation.[18]

> Sicelides Musae, paulo maiora canamus!
> non omnis arbusta iuuant humilesque myricae;
> si canimus siluas, siluae sint consule dignae.
>
> Vltima Cumaei uenit iam carminis aetas;
> magnus ab integro saeclorum nascitur ordo.   5
> iam redit et uirgo, redeunt Saturnia regna,
> iam noua progenies caelo demittitur alto.
> tu modo nascenti puero, quo ferrea primum
> desinet ac toto surget gens aurea mundo,
> casta faue Lucina: tuus iam regnat Apollo.   10
> teque adeo decus hoc aeui, te consule, inibit,
> Pollio, et incipient magni procedere menses;
> te duce, si qua manent sceleris uestigia nostri,
> inrita perpetua soluent formidine terras.
>
> *Ecloga* IV. 1–14

16. See N. H. Baynes, *Constantine the Great and the Christian Church*[2] (London 1972), 51–6; Pierre Courcelle, 'Les exégèses chrétiennes de la Quatrième Eclogue', *Revue des études anciennes* 59 (1957), 296 n. 1; Ciro Monteleone, *L'Egloga Quarta da Virgilio a Costantino: critica del testo e ideologia* (Manduria 1975), 75.

17. Alfons Kurfess, 'Observatiunculae ad P. Vergilii Maronis Eclogae Quartae Interpretationem et Versionem Graecam', *Mnemosyne* n.s. 40 (1912), 277–84.

18. Latin text is that of R. A. B. Mynors, *P. Vergili Maronis Opera* (Oxford 1969). Greek text is that of Ivar A. Heikel, *Eusebius Werke* vol. 1: *Über das Leben Constantins . . .*, Die griechischen christlichen Schriftsteller 7 (Leipzig 1902); in those passages where Heikel prefers a conjecture to the reading of the manuscripts, I have cited those readings as well. Numbers in parentheses refer to corresponding lines of the Latin text. Additional collations of *Oratio* are available in Ivar A. Heikel, *Kritische Beiträge zu den Constantin-Schriften des Eusebius*, Texte und Untersuchungen, 36.4 (1911).

... τοῦτον Τιβέριος διεδέξατο, καθ᾿ ὃν χρόνον ἡ τοῦ
σωτῆρος ἐξέλαμψε παρουσία, καὶ τὸ τῆς ἁγιωτάτης
θρησκείας ἐπεκράτησε μυστήριον ἥ τε νέα τοῦ δήμου
διαδοχὴ συνέστη, περὶ ἧς οἶμαι λέγειν τὸν ἐξοχώτατον
5 τῶν κατὰ Ἰταλίαν ποιητῶν·
   Ἔνθεν ἔπειτα νέα πληθὺς ἀνδρῶν ἐφαάνθη.　　　　　1 (7)
καὶ πάλιν ἐν ἑτέρῳ τινὶ τῶν Βουκολικῶν τόπῳ·
   Σικελίδες Μοῦσαι, μεγάλην φάτιν ὑμνήσωμεν.　　　　2 (1)
τί τούτου φανερώτερον; προστίθησι γάρ·
10　Ἤλυθε Κυμαίου μαντεύματος εἰς τέλος ὀμφή,　　　　　3 (4)
Κυμαίαν αἰνιττόμενος δηλαδὴ τὴν Σίβυλλαν. καὶ
οὐκ ἠρκέσθη τούτοις, ἀλλὰ περαιτέρω προεχώρησεν,
ὡς τῆς χρείας τὴν αὐτοῦ μαρτυρίαν ἐπιποθούσης·
τί λέγων [αὖθις];
15　Αὖθις (οὗτος Mss.) ἄρ᾿ αἰώνων ἱερὸς στίχος ὄρνυται ἡμῖν·　4 (5)
   Ἥκει παρθένος αὖθις, ἄγουσ᾿ ἐρατὸν βασιλῆα.　　　　5 (6)
τίς οὖν ἂν (ἄρα Mss.) εἴη παρθένος ἡ ἐπανήκουσα;
ἆρ᾿ οὐχ ἡ πλήρης τε καὶ ἔγκυος γενομένη τοῦ θείου
πνεύματος; καὶ τί τὸ κωλῦον τὴν ἔγκυον τοῦ θείου
20 πνεύματος κόρην εἶναι ἀεὶ καὶ διαμένειν παρθένον;
ἐπανήξει δὲ ἐκ δευτέρου, ὅταν καὶ ὁ θεὸς ἐκ
δευτέρου τὴν οἰκουμένην παραγενόμενος ἐπικουφίσῃ.
καὶ προστίθησιν ὁ ποιητής·
   Τὸν δὲ νεωστὶ πάϊν τεχθέντα, φαεσφόρε μήνη,　　　　6 (8)
25　Ἀντὶ σιδηρείης χρυσῆν γενεὴν ὀπάσαντα,　　　　　　7 (9)
   Προσκύνει.　　　　　　　　　　　　　　　　　　　8 (10)
   Τοῦδε γὰρ ἄρχοντος τὰ μὲν ἕλκεα πάντα βρότεια　　9 (13)
   ⟨Ἴαται⟩, (Wilamowitz; καὶ Mss.) στοναχαὶ δὲ　　10 (14)
      (τε Mss.) κατευνάζονται ἀλιτρῶν.
30 συνίεμεν δὴ φανερῶς τε ἅμα καὶ ἀποκρύφως δι᾿
ἀλληγοριῶν τα⟨ῦτα⟩ (Heikel; τὰ Mss.) λεχθέντα, τοῖς
μὲν βαθύτερον ἐξετάζουσι τὴν τῶν ἐπῶν δύναμιν
ὑπ᾿ ὄψιν ἀγουμένης τῆς τοῦ Χριστοῦ θεότητος, ὅπως
δὲ μή τις τῶν δυναστευόντων ἐν τῇ βασιλευούσῃ πόλει
35 ἐγκαλεῖν ἔχῃ τῷ ποιητῇ, ὡς παρὰ τοὺς πατρῴους νόμους
συγγράφοντι ἐκβάλλοντί τε τὰ πάλαι ὑπὸ τῶν προγόνων
περὶ τῶν θεῶν νομιζόμενα ἐπικαλύπτεται τὴν ἀλήθειαν.
            ΤΩΙ ΤΩΝ ΑΓΙΩΝ ΣΥΛΛΟΓΩΙ 19

Constantine's purpose in quoting the *Fourth Eclogue* can be
gleaned from his commentary on it. First, Constantine expected his
audience to recognize Vergil by reputation, without even mentioning his name (lines 4–5); he also expected them to be familiar with
the text of the Eclogue itself, since he acknowledges that he is

quoting lines out of their familiar sequence (line 7). Second, Constantine asserts that the Eclogue is actually an allegorical prediction (lines 30–33) of the birth of Christ (lines 17–20), disguised by Vergil under a cloak of politically expedient pagan references in order to avoid penalties from the reigning dynasts (lines 33–37). These two features of the Eclogue – its enduring literary fame and its 'hidden' Christian meaning – suggest why Constantine quoted and quarried it so extensively. The Eclogue is a very emblem of Constantine's own Empire, at once preserving the ancient traditions of pagan Rome and incorporating the 'new' religion, Christianity. For Constantine, the *Fourth Eclogue* is a powerful tool for shaping his public image.

It is not surprising, therefore, that Constantine suppresses two sets of passages which conflict with his Christian imperial reading of the Eclogue. He truncates line 10 and removes Vergil's reference to the pagan god Apollo (*tuus iam regnat Apollo*), undesirable not only because Apollo had no place in the Christian New Age, but also because Apollo/*sol invictus* enjoyed a prominent (and here potentially embarrassing) role as protector of Constantine's own reign.[19] He does not quote lines 2–3 and 11–12, referring to the consul Pollio, during whose term of office Vergil's wonder child was to be born. Instead, Constantine mentions the reign of Tiberius (commentary, lines 1–4) as the time in which Jesus established the Christian version of the New Age and the New (apostolic) Society (*Luke* 3.1). Constantine chooses to measure sacred history in terms of emperors (like himself) rather than consuls.

Like Constantine, the anonymous Greek translator of the *Fourth Eclogue* appreciated the poem as a literary masterpiece and interpreted it as a Christian prophecy. The translator has capably preserved Vergil's dactylic hexameters[20] and has also reproduced

---

19. A. A. Vasiliev, *History of the Byzantine Empire 325–1453*[2] (Madison 1958), 49; Hans Lietzmann, *A History of the Early Church*, III, trans. Bertram Woolf (New York 1953), 150–2.

20. Several devices – or licenses – enable the translator to maintain the meter without straying too widely from the sense of the original. For example, in line 4 an unaccented diphthong is shortened before an initial vowel in the manner of Homer and tragic lyric (see Herbert Weir Smyth, *Greek Grammar* [Cambridge, Mass. 1966], §148 D 1); a spondaic fifth foot appears in line 2 and a feminine fourth-foot caesura in line 6.

his elevated tone by using distinctively epic vocabulary (ὀμφή line 4, πληθὺς ἀνδρῶν line 7, ὁπάσαντα line 9)[21] and forms (ἐφαάνθη line 7, πάϊν line 8, φαεσφόρε line 8).[22] Yet, in spite of this evident respect for Vergil, the translator has treated the original quite freely, sometimes omitting entire phrases (*caelo . . . alto* line 7, *ultima aetas* line 4, *toto mundo* line 9, *primum* line 8, *si qua manent* line 13, *perpetua* line 14) and adding some small words for which there is no equivalent in the Latin: ἡμῖν line 5, and πάντα line 13. Most of these changes are, in terms of the metrical translator's difficult task, negligible. The marvel of the translation lies in its transformation of the poem's meaning from pagan to Christian by redefining and refocusing elements present in the original. This process is both thorough and consistent; in most cases, however, it requires no more than the alteration of a phrase or a shift of emphasis onto an idea which was only incidental to the meaning of the original Latin sentence.

In the first line quoted by Constantine (line 7), the translator resolves the ambiguity of *progenies* (either a single person or a group of people) with the collective νέα πληθὺς ἀνδρῶν, which represents the new society, the assembly of Christians, rather than the founder himself. Since this assembly could not be said to proceed from heaven, *caelo demittitur alto* shrinks and fades to the helpfully ambiguous verb ἐφαάνθη. The translator believed that the Eclogue predicted the advent of Christianity, and he emphasizes the poem's prophetic character by rendering the neutral phrase *paulo maiora canamus* (line 1) with μεγάλην φάτιν ὑμνήσωμεν, which focuses the sentence upon the noun object φάτιν ('report' or 'oracle'). ὀμφή (line 4) for *carminis aetas* re-emphasizes this view of the poem as prophecy; εἰς τέλος (with Ἤλυθε, line 4) for *ultima* (with *aetas*) implies that the prophecy has now come to fulfillment. Lines 5–6 are more overtly Christianized. ἱερός for *magnus* (line 5) makes explicit the sacred implications of the poem, and (παρθένος) . . . ἄγουσ' ἐρατὸν βασιλῆα for *redeunt Saturnia regna* (line 6) conforms to Christian theology by emphasizing the virgin's active role in establishing the new order and also by substituting an unnamed

21. Alfons Kurfess, 'Die griechische Übersetzung der vierten Ekloge Vergils', *Mnemosyne* 5 (1937), 286.

22. For philological discussion of the Greek version of the Eclogue, see Reichmann (n. 10), 58–61, and B. Baldwin, *AJP* 97 (1976), 361–8.

king for 'Saturn's reign'. The motif of a virgin producing a king links the Greek Eclogue with the Gospel accounts of the Nativity in Matthew 1:18–2:11 and in Luke 1:26–35.[23] Lines 8–10 betray similar adjustments. The new-born child actively establishes the golden age (πάϊν . . . ὀπάσαντα) instead of merely coinciding with its appearance (*quo ferrea . . . aurea mundo*), and the pagan deity Lucina (line 10) becomes simply the moon (φαεσφόρε μήνη line 8), exhorted to reverence the child (προσκύνει for *fave*, line 10). προσκύνει recalls the vocabulary of Matt. 2:11 (προσεκύνησαν αὐτῷ); the star of Bethlehem mentioned by Matthew (2:2, 9–10) serves the divine child just as the moon in the Greek Eclogue is encouraged to do. Lines 13–14 of the Greek version show the most alteration and, unfortunately, the most textual corruption. The genitive absolute τοῦδε . . . ἄρχοντος is similar in form to the ablative absolute *te duce*, but radically different in reference, because Vergil's Pollio (*te*) is replaced by the child-king in the Greek version. *Sceleris vestigia nostri* and *perpetua . . . formidine* become τὰ . . . ἕλκεα πάντα βρότεια and στοναχαί . . . ἀλιτρῶν, a possible reference to Jesus' mission of healing.

Constantine's exegesis of the Eclogue in his commentary and this free Greek translation of the poem share several points of interpretation in common. Both treat *progenies* (line 7) as the Christian community (commentary lines 3–5), both interpret *redit . . . virgo* (line 6) as a reference to the mother's continued virginity after conception (Ἥκει . . . αὖθις line 6, commentary lines 19–20), and both suppress any reference to Pollio. These similarities suggest that Constantine and the translator of the Greek *Fourth Eclogue* drew upon the same exegetical interpretation of the poem. Monteleone argues that Constantine was himself responsible for propagating, or perhaps for originating, this interpretation of the Eclogue, and suggests that the Greek Eclogue translation also came from Constantine's court as an element of imperial propaganda.[24]

23. Monteleone (n. 16), 80.

24. Monteleone (n. 16), 17–18, 89–91. As Trahman (n. 3) observes (p. 118), Constantine's interpretation of the *Fourth Eclogue* established Vergil's reputation in the East as a Christian prophet. See Paul Peeters, 'Une légende de Virgile dans l'hagiographie grecque', *Mélanges Paul Thomas* (Bruges 1930), 546–54, repr. in his *Recherches* I (cited n. 4 above), 214–21.

II. Juxtalinear translations: Vergil and Cicero

Among the many papyrus and parchment fragments recovered from Roman Egypt, some few preserve Latin literary works. Latin texts of Vergil, Cicero, Sallust, Terence, Juvenal, Lucan, and Livy range in date from the first to the sixth century A.D.; since approximately one quarter of these texts include Greek glosses or pronunciation marks, and since Latin–Greek selective glossaries to Vergil also survive, it is evident that Greek speakers used some of these Latin texts.[25] Latin texts of Cicero and Vergil also occur with juxtalinear Greek translations; these were apparently intended for Greek students learning Latin word by word and line by line, in the manner traditionally used for studying Homer.[26] Because Vergil and Cicero provided texts for elementary Latin instruction in the small, provincial towns which have yielded papyrus remains, it is reasonable to infer that juxtalinear translations of their works were also known to educated persons in the great metropolitan centers of the East.[27]

Three examples of juxtalinear translations from the fourth or early fifth century will be discussed here: the fragments on papyrus of Cicero's *First Catilinarian Oration* (*P. Vindob.* 30) and of Vergil's *Aeneid* (*P. Ryl.* 478), and a section of the *Aeneid* preserved on parchment (*Palimps. Ambros.*) which, to quote Cavenaile, '. . . semble se situer à un niveau plus élevé'.[28] To illustrate the Cicero translation, I quote the first fragment from it:[29]

P. Vindob. 30. 885 a *recto*

Provenance?	4th–5th century
[sacris]	μυσ[τη]ριοις
[ac devota sit]	και εκαθ[ωσι]ω[μενη
[nescio]	ουκ οιδα

25. R. E. Gaebel, 'The Greek Word Lists to Vergil and Cicero', *Bulletin of the John Rylands Library* 52 (1969–70), 284–7.

26. For a full discussion, see Gaebel (n. 25), 284–325. Most of the texts are available in Robert Cavenaile, *Corpus Papyrorum Latinarum* (Wiesbaden 1958).

27. E. G. Turner, *Greek Papyri: An Introduction* (Princeton 1968), 43–5, and Gaebel, 284. 28. Cavenaile (n. 26), 23.

29. Juxtalinear text from Hans Gerstinger, 'Ein neuer lateinischer Papyrus aus der Sammlung, Papyrus Erzherzog Rainer', *Wiener Studien* 55 (1937), 102. Cicero text from Albert Curtis Clark, *M. Tulli Ciceronis Orationes* (Oxford 1905). At the suggestion of John Winkler and Susan Stephens, I have supplemented Gerstinger's text in line 14, restoring *iam* and νυν to conform with the received text of Cicero.

	[quod eam]	οτι ταυτην
5	[necesse]	ανανκαιον
	[esse]	ειναι
	[putas]	λογι[ʒη]
	[in consulis]	εις το του υπα[του
	[corpore]	σωμα
10	[defigere]	καταπ̣η̣σσ̣ι̣ν̣
	[nunc vero]	νυ[ν δε]
	[quae tua est]	ποια η ση εστιν
	[ista vita]	αυτη η ʒοη
	[sic enim iam]	ου[τως γαρ νυν
15	[tecum]	μετα σο[υ
	[loquor]	λαλω
	[non ut odio]	ουκ ως μισι
	[permotus]	κινιθις
	[esse videar]	[ει]ν̣α̣[ι δοκω]

. . . .

This represents *In Catilinam* 1.6.16:

> . . . sacris ac devota sit nescio, quod eam necesse putas
> esse in consulis corpore defigere. Nunc vero quae tua est
> ista vita? Sic enim iam tecum loquar, non ut odio permotus
> esse videar . . .

Juxtaposed lines provide a word-by-word translation in Greek of the Latin text. This format is itself a teaching device, since a single line sometimes consists of several adjacent words which form a short, cohesive grammatical unit (e.g. lines 2, 12, and 17). Where word order deviates from the received Latin text (cf. lines 5–7 *necesse esse putas* and Clark's *necesse putas esse*), the new arrangement clarifies the structure of the subordinate clause *quod . . . defigere*.[30] The choice of individual Greek words also serves as a teaching device. καταπησσιν (line 10 = καταπήσσειν) is an etymological equivalent of *defigere*, and illustrates the parallel meaning and function of κατα- and *de-*, of -πήσσειν and *-figere*.[31] Although the

30. Several fragments of this papyrus text survive in good condition, enabling the editor to reconstruct with confidence the Latin half of the fragment quoted here. The other fragments demonstrate that word order in the Latin and in the Greek halves of the text correspond exactly; the Greek word order in this passage may thus be used to indicate the minor rearrangement of words in the Latin text which is discussed here. This is the only section of the papyrus which offers word order different from that in Clark's edition.

31. For the orthography of καταπησσιν, see below, p. 187. Etymological equivalents as a feature of translation are discussed by Brock (n. 13), 84–5.

tense of a Greek verb usually reflects that of the corresponding
Latin verb, translating the Latin perfect *permotus* (line 18) with the
Greek aorist κινιθις (= κινηθείς) teaches the Greek reader that the
perfect tense has broader connotations in Latin than in Greek.

In summary, this translation is literal because it is utilitarian.
Gerstinger considers it the work of a teacher, and he reconstructs
the original as a large (40 × 30 cm.) papyrus codex probably
containing the entire *First Catilinarian Oration*.[32]

The Rylands Vergil (*P. Ryl.* 478) is a badly damaged papyrus in
five fragments, which dates from the fourth century.[33]

P. Ryl. 478 a *recto* (lines 28–48)[34]

Provenance?	4th century
. . . .	. . . .
[hic tamen ille]	εντανθα ομω[ς εκεινος]
urbem Patabi	την πολ[ιν Πατου]ι̣ι̣[ου]
30 sedesque locavit	και εδρας ιδρυσεν
*Teu*crorum et genti	των τρωων και το
nomen dedit	ονομα δεδωκεν
arm*que fixit*	και οπλα επηξεν
Troia n[[.]]u*nc*	Τ[ρωικα
35 placid*a* com*p*[o]*s*[tus	]
pace qu`*i*˝ e*scit*	[ ]
nos tua progen[ies	]
caeli quibus	[ ]
abnuis arcem	[ ]
40 navibus a[[r]]miss*i*[s]	νηων απολλυμενω[ν]
infándum unius	αθεμιτως μιας
ob iram pr[odim}*ur*	δι οργην προδιδομεθα
adque I*talis*	και των [Ι]ταλιωνων
longe d*isiungimur*	μακραν διαζευγνυμεθα
45 hic pieta*tis ho*[nos]	αυτη της ευσεβιας τι̣[μη]
s[ic] *nos* [i]n sceptra	ουτως ημας ες τα βασιλια̣
*re*ponis	αποτιθη
olli s*u*bridens	εκινη υπομηδιων
. . .	. . .

(In this Latin text, italic letters appear instead of pointed letters.)

32. Gerstinger (n. 29), 100–2.

33. Fully described and discussed by Reichmann (n. 10), 33–7. *P. Fouad* I. 5, of
the late fourth or early fifth century, resembles the Rylands Vergil, except that it is
shorter and it alters Vergil's original word order with greater frequency. It is
published in Cavenaile (n. 26), 20–3.

34. Juxtalinear text from Cavenaile (n. 26), 7–15. Vergil text from Mynors.

This represents *Aeneid* 1. 247–53:

> hic tamen ille urbem Pataui sedesque locauit
> Teucrorum et genti nomen dedit armaque fixit
> Troia, nunc placida compostus pace quiescit:
> 250 nos, tua progenies, caeli quibus adnuis arcem,
> nauibus (infandum!) amissis unius ob iram
> prodimur atque Italis longe disiungimur oris.
> hic pietatis honos? sic nos in sceptra reponis?'
> Olli subridens . . .

In dividing the lines of this juxtalinear text, the translator has attempted either to group together adjacent words belonging to the same grammatical unit (lines 29, 37, 40 and 45) or to end a hexameter at the end of a line (lines 30, 33, 36, 39, 44, and 47). In theory this method of dividing lines could aid the student both in construing the Latin and in scanning it. In practice, however, it creates problems both for translating (in lines where unrelated 'leftover' words clump together – cf. 31, 34, and 41) and for scanning (in line 42, where a hexameter ends between an adverbial phrase and its verb). The Latin text follows traditional word order with two exceptions: in line 41, *infandum* has shifted outside the ablative absolute, perhaps to aid the reader;[35] and in line 44, *oris* has disappeared, perhaps through an oversight. The Greek translation explains Latin words by supplying etymological equivalents (*prodimur*: προδιδομεθα line 42, *disiungimur*: διαζευγνυμεθα line 44) and by substituting familiar proper nouns for more obscure ones (τρωων for *Teucrorum*, line 31). The translation parallels purely Latin idioms and constructions with equivalent expressions in Greek (e.g., *in sceptra*: ες τα βασιλια line 46; and ablative absolute: genitive absolute, line 40). It teaches readers the wide semantic range of the Latin perfect tense by translating it variously with a Greek perfect (line 32), present (line 40), and aorist (lines 30, 33). Although there are a few Latin misspellings (*Patabi* for *Patavi* in line 29, and *a[[r]]missis* in line 40; both may result from an aural/oral confusion), the Latin text is carefully written and, according to Reichmann, bears evidence of two correcting hands; apices and long marks indicate Latin

---

35. Since the line still scans in the papyrus version, the shift of *infandum* may have occurred earlier in the textual tradition and represent a genuine variant reading.

pronunciation for the Greek reader.[36] The Greek text shows itacism (βασιλια for βασίλεια line 46), which reflects fourth-century pronunciation and is not uncommon in Greek papyri.[37]

Both these translations on papyrus are designed for practical rather than literary purpose. A juxtalinear Vergil translation with artistic as well as pedagogical merits has survived in a parchment palimpsest from the late fourth or early fifth century. I supply a few lines to illustrate the character of this translation.[38]

Palimps. Ambros.

Syria/Egypt   4th/5th century
Folio 113 *recto*
  ηδη ο πατηρ Αινειας
  και ηδη η Τρωικη
  νεοτης
  συνερχονται
5 και τω εστρωμενω
  επανακλεινεται; κοιτ[ω]
  διδοασιν οι θεραποντες: τ[αις χερσιν]
  υδατα
  και Δημητραν: κανισκιο[ις]
10 διευλουτουσιν
  και κεκαρμενοις φερουσιν
  χειρεκμαγεια μαλλο[ις]

Folio 113 *recto*
  Iam pater Aeneas et iam Troiana iuventus
700 Conveniu[nt] stratoque super discumbitur ostro.
  Dant famuli manibus lymphas Cereremque canistris
  Expediunt tonsisque ferunt mantelia villis.

In Mynor's edition, these lines read:

  iam pater Aeneas et iam Troiana iuuentus
700 conueniunt, stratoque super discumbitur ostro.

36. Reichmann (n. 10), 33–4.

37. Orsolina Montevecchi, *La papirologia* (Turin 1973), 74. See Reichmann (n. 10), 34, for a complete list of confusions in the Rylands Vergil.

38. Text from Iohannes Galbiati, 'Vergilius Latine et Graece in Palimpsesto Codice Arabico', *Aevum* 1 (1927), 61 and 68–9. Although Galbiati describes the juxtalinear arrangement of the text and supplies an illustrative plate as well (p. 51 and following p. 56), his transcriptions obscure the format of the text. Galbiati prints the Greek translation twice, both in juxtalinear and in hexameter line arrangements, but the Latin appears only in hexameter line arrangement. Cavenaile reprints only Galbiati's hexameter form lines (pp. 23ff.). This interesting text needs re-editing!

dant manibus famuli lymphas Cereremque canistris
expediunt tonsisque ferunt mantelia uillis.
Aeneid 1. 699–702

The same scribe apparently wrote both the Latin and the Greek texts in a fine and careful hand. The Latin text maintains the traditional word order with one exception: *dant famuli manibus* replaces *dant manibus famuli* (line 701). The palimpsest reading may be a deliberate alteration to aid the Greek reader, since it brings together verb and subject; alternatively, it may be a genuine variant of the tradition, since it scans regularly.

The translation shares some pedagogical characteristics with the juxtalinear translations on papyrus. Word order in the Greek translation exactly reproduces that of the Latin text, Greek etymological equivalents explain Latin vocabulary (συνερχονται line 4 for *conveniunt* line 700; διευλουτουσιν line 10 for *expediunt* line 702), and Greek proper names explain Latin ones (Δημητραν line 9 for *Cererem* line 701). In several respects, however, the palimpsest translation achieves a higher literary plane than the other juxtalinear translations. None of their phonetic spellings appear in Galbiati's transcription of the palimpsest. Its line arrangement is careful and consistent: one hexameter line from Vergil fills three lines of the juxtalinear text with the exception of line 600, fol. 117v, in two lines. Since the beginning of each hexameter is indicated by a horizontal stroke in the margin,[39] and the end of each hexameter occurs regularly at the end of every third line, the format sets forth the metrical structure of the Latin text for the reader. The Greek translation pays some attention to the sounds of the Latin text: κανισκιο[ις] (line 9), which echoes *canistris* (line 701) very effectively, is emphasized by the subsequent alliteration of κεκαρμενοις . . . χειρεκμαγεια (lines 11 and 12). The rather formal and academic tone of the Greek translation is evident in sections of the palimpsest not quoted here. The Homeric word ευπλοκαμος (for *crinitus*, fol. 120r) belongs to the diction of poetry, and the peculiar accusative plural τας νευς (for *navis*, fol. 115v) may be an unsuccessful attempt to use obsolete dialect forms rather than simply a careless error. The fact that this translation appears not on papyrus but on parchment may well indicate a well-to-do clientèle, since in Egypt

---

39. Gaebel (n. 25), 321.

at least parchment was scarcer and more expensive than papyrus.[40]

Although the three translations of Latin classical authors examined here all demonstrate a similar juxtalinear format and pedagogical method, they suggest different levels of competence and literary sophistication on the part of the translators or their prospective readers. The two papyrus translations are simply aids to understanding the syntax and vocabulary of their corresponding Latin texts; the Ambrosian Palimpsest, on the other hand, emphasizes the metrical structure of the Latin text and enhances the literary appeal of the Greek translation with poetic vocabulary, alliteration, and classical orthography.[41] And yet the juxtalinear translations, whether plain or embroidered, are clearly utilitarian. Their purpose is very different from the free and artistic recreation of a poetic work in Constantine's Vergilian Eclogue. Between these two extremes, the fourth century knew yet other translations which are literal or literary in varying degrees.

III. Paeanius' translation of Eutropius' *Breviarium*

We turn next to a translation which happens to contain examples of both the free literary and the literal translation style. The *Breviarium* of Eutropius, completed *ca* A.D. 369,[42] appeared in Paeanius' Greek translation before A.D. 380.[43] 'An elegant summary for gentlemen who had not the patience to plow through Livy',[44] the *Breviarium* satisfied the fourth century's desire for a

---

40. Montevecchi (n. 37), 20–1. The status of papyrus outside Egypt in relation to parchment is more difficult to determine, and while it is certainly possible that this palimpsest was written outside of Egypt (in Syria), the mere fact of its being parchment does not necessarily require such a conclusion, see E. G. Turner, *The Typology of the Early Codex* (Pennsylvania 1977), 40–1.

41. It resembles, however, the fifth-century palimpsest fragment of a juxtalinear *Georgics* translation described by Elinor M. Husselman, 'A Palimpsest Fragment from Egypt', *Studi in onore di Aristide Calderini e Roberto Paribeni* (Milan 1957), 453–9.

42. Otto Seeck, *Symmachi Opera*, Monumenta Germaniae Historica, Auctorum Antiquissimorum 6.1 (Berlin 1883), p. cxxxiii; André Chastagnol, 'Emprunts de l'histoire Augusti aux "Caesares" d'Aurelius Victor', *Revue de philologie* 41 (1967), 85.

43. H. Droysen, *Eutropii Breviarium cum Versionibus et Continuationibus*, Monumenta Germaniae Historica, Auctores Antiquissimi 2 (Berlin 1879), p. xxi.

44. Jones, *Empire*, 1010.

résumé of Roman history which was comprehensive, concise, and convenient. The narrative follows events from Rome's foundation until the death of Jovian (A.D. 364) in a straightforward manner with frequent references to significant dates; moreover, it takes a neutral religious stance, neither partisan nor offensive to the pagans or to the Christians.[45] These features of the *Breviarium* would recommend Paeanius' translation to a Greek audience as readily as they would attract a Latin audience to the original. Not only did schools need a textbook suitable for instructing younger pupils, but there were also potential readers among those members of the court and imperial administration who might wish to study the imperial past. The Greek *Breviarium* offered them the additional attraction of a pleasing and graceful prose style.[46]

For purposes of comparison, I quote the first few sentences of Eutropius' *Breviarium* and of Paeanius' translation:[47]

I.I.I   Romanum imperium, quo neque ab exordio ullum fere minus neque incrementis toto orbe amplius humana potest memoria recordari, a Romulo exordium habet, qui Reae Silviae Vestalis virginis filius et quantum putatus est Martis cum Remo fratre
2   uno partu editus est. is cum inter pastores latrocinaretur,   5 decem et octo annos natus urbem exiguam in Palatino monte constituit, XI Kal. Maias, Olympiadis sextae anno tertio, post Troiae excidium, ut qui plurimum minimumque tradunt, anno trecentesimo nonagesimo quarto.
2.I   Condita civitate quam ex nomine suo Romam vocavit haec 10 fere egit. multitudinem finitimorum in civitatem recepit, centum ex senioribus legit, quorum consilio omnia ageret, quos senatores nominavit propter senectutem. . . .

                                        Breviarium I.I.I–2.I

I.I.I   Τῆς Ῥωμαϊκῆς βασιλείας ἐν προοιμίοις οὐδὲν ἐγένετο μεῖόν τε καὶ ταπεινότερον· τῇ δὲ κατὰ μικρὸν αὐξήσει καὶ ταῖς ἀεὶ προσθήκαις κατὰ τὴν οἰκουμένην ἅπασαν οὐδὲν οὔτε μεῖζον οὔτε δυνατώτερον ἡ μνήμη τῶν ἀνθρώπων φέρει· ταύτης τὴν πρώτην κρηπῖδα   5

45. For consideration of these factors, see W. Den Boer, 'Rome à travers trois auteurs du quatrième siècle', *Mnemosyne* 21 (1968), 255, 276, and Reichmann, 62.

46. See Reichmann (n. 10), 62–82, for a detailed stylistic analysis of the entire translation. J. Irmscher reports (*Byzantinoslavica* 16 [1955], 361–5) that an excellent study of Paeanius' translation is contained in a book very difficult to obtain – Διονύσιος Ν. Τριβόλης, *Eutropius historicus* καὶ οἱ Ἕλληνες μεταφρασταὶ τοῦ *Breviarium ab urbe condita* (Athens 1941), x, 194.

47. Text of Eutropius and Paeanius, here and below, from Droysen.

κατεβάλετο ῾Ρωμύλος· ὃς ἐκ ῾Ρέας Σιλβίας, οὕτω
καλουμένης ῾Εστιακῆς παρθένου, τῷ ῎Αρει συνελθούσης,
ὡς ὁ πολὺς κατεῖχε λόγος, ἐκ διδύμου γονῆς σὺν
2 ἀδελφῷ ῾Ρέμῳ προῆλθεν εἰς φῶς· οὗτος ὀκτωκαίδεκα
γεγονὼς ἔτη βίον τε ἔχων τοῖς ποιμέσι συλληστεύειν   10
ἐλάχιστόν τι πολίχνιον ἐπὶ τοῦ ὄρους τοῦ Παλλαντίου
κατεστήσατο πρώτῃ τοῦ Μαΐου μηνὸς ἔτει τρίτῳ
τῆς ἕκτης ὀλυμπιάδος· τῆς δὲ ᾿Ιλίου καταστροφῆς
κατὰ τοὺς τὸ πλεῖστόν τε καὶ ἐλάχιστον παραδεδωκότας
ἔτει τετάρτῳ καὶ ἐννενηκοστῷ καὶ τριακοσιοστῷ.   15
2.1 Οἰκίσας δὲ τὴν πόλιν καὶ καλέσας αὐτὴν ἐξ ἑαυτοῦ
῾Ρώμην, πρῶτον μὲν πολὺ πλῆθος ἐκ τῶν περιοίκων
εἰσεδέξατο, ἔπειτα δὲ τοὺς προβεβηκότας εἰς ἡλικίαν
ἐκλεξάμενος τούτους ἐπέστησε τοῖς λοιποῖς ἡγεμόνας
τῶν πρακτέων, σενάτωρας αὐτοὺς καλέσας κατὰ τὴν   20
᾿Ιταλῶν φωνήν· ἐπειδὴ σένης ἐκεῖνοι καλοῦσι τοὺς
γέροντας· σύγκλητον δὲ ῞Ελληνες ἐκάλεσαν τὸ
συνέδριον, ἐκ τοῦ πρότερον μὲν τοὺς βασιλεύοντας
μετὰ δὲ ταῦτα τοὺς ὑπάτους συγκαλεῖν τε αὐτοὺς ἐπὶ
τὰς βουλὰς καὶ τῶν ψήφων ποιεῖσθαι κυρίους. . . .   25
ΠΑΙΑΝΙΟΥ ΜΕΤΑΦΡΑΣΙΣ ΤΗΣ ΕΥΤΡΟΠΙΟΥ
ΡΩΜΑΙΚΗΣ ΙΣΤΟΡΙΑΣ 1.1.1–2.1

The Greek translation reproduces the basic sequence of ideas
from the Latin text but alters the original syntax considerably. The
first sentence of the Latin text is expanded into four independent
clauses in the Greek, but both Latin and Greek versions open with
the words *Romanum imperium*: Τῆς ῾Ρωμαϊκῆς βασιλείας, which is
given appropriate emphasis by appearing in first position. The
Greek version also maintains the neat contrast of *minus . . . amplius*
(lines 1 and 2) in an expanded and more emphatic form (μεῖόν τε
καὶ ταπεινότερον line 2; οὔτε μεῖζον οὔτε δυνατώτερον line 4).
Although the Greek text reflects these features from its Latin
original, it demonstrates independent literary and stylistic features
as well. It is generally more expansive and leisurely in tone than the
Latin text. The Greek text, for instance, removes the bald, abrupt
sentence which begins paragraph two in the Latin and absorbs it
into a complex sentence similar to those of paragraph one. Careful
word choice and arrangement produces alliteration in line 17
(πρῶτον μὲν πολὺ πλῆθος ἐκ τῶν περιοίκων) and an interesting
repetition of the καλ-, κλη- root in lines 20–25.

Paeanius is obviously conscious that he writes for an audience
ignorant of Roman institutions and Latin vocabulary. Thus,

Roman gods acquire their equivalent Greek names (*Martis* line 4: Ἄρει line 7; *Vestalis* line 3: Ἑστιακῆς line 7) and the 'Palatine Mountain' (line 6) recalls, by orthographical implication, a supposed connection with Pallantium in Arcadia (τοῦ ὄρους τοῦ Παλλαντίου line 11).[48] The Roman-style date *XI Kal. Maias* (line 7, April 21 in modern reckoning)[49] is not correctly translated by Paeanius' πρώτῃ τοῦ Μαΐου μηνὸς (line 12); either Paeanius mistranslated, thus demonstrating that even well-educated Greeks were unfamiliar with some Roman cultural references, or he correctly translated a Latin exemplar which lacked the numeral *XI*. In the case of an important Roman institution like the Senate, which Eutropius explains in terms of a Latin etymology (line 14), Paeanius repeats the etymological discussion (line 20) and glosses it by mentioning the Greek term for Senate, συνέδριον, and by discussing the origins of a parallel Greek institution, the σύγκλητον. Although the contents of the Latin text may have prompted this excursus on the Greek political assembly, it is an independent feature of the translation, designed solely for the Greek-speaking audience. In sections of the translation not quoted here, Paeanius occasionally improves upon the historical content of his Latin original with supplementary information from Cassius Dio.[50]

Paeanius generally translates freely, but in quoting a passage from Vergil he adopts a very literal style:

quin etiam per litteras occultas Aurelianum ita fuerat deprecatus, ut inter alia versu Vergiliano uteretur: eripe me his invicte malis.   *Aeneid* vi.365
φασὶ γοῦν αὐτὸν γράμμασι λαθραίοις παρακεκληκέναι τὴν ἀρχὴν ὑποδέξασθαι καὶ τὸ ἔπος ἐνθεῖναι τοῖς γράμμασιν, ὃ πεποίηκεν ὁ Βεργίλλιος ἐκ προσώπου Παλινούρου πρὸς τὸν Αἰνείαν 'ἐξάρπασόν με τούτων ἀήττητε τῶν κακῶν'.

                                                    Breviarium ix.13.1

The introduction to the Vergil quotation typifies Paeanius' free,

48. Explained by Pausanias, *Description of Greece* viii.43.2. For further passages, see Henricus Stephanus, *Thesaurus Graecae Linguae* (Paris 1842–7), *s.v.* Παλλάντιον.

49. See Alan E. Samuel, *Greek and Roman Chronology: Calendars and Years in Classical Antiquity* (Munich 1972), 154–5.

50. Ernest Schulze, 'De Paeanio Eutropii Interprete', *Philologus* 29 (1870), 298; Reichmann (n. 10), 78.

literary style of translation, for he supplements the Latin original by identifying the quotation's speaker and addressee.[51] Paeanius translates the Vergil quotation itself, however, in a very literal manner – without meter, word for word, in precisely the same order as the Latin original. This is the style of the juxtalinear texts, but in an extreme form. For all their fidelity to the Latin original, even the juxtalinear texts made minor adjustments in cases of extreme hyperbaton. Paeanius, however, changes nothing from Vergil's original. He demonstrates a pious regard for the Latin text, preserving it like a treasured museum piece with as little 'restoration' as possible. This contrasts sharply with his attitude toward Eutropius' narrative, which he freely rewrites and expands, serving as an *alter ego* for Eutropius himself and becoming a contributor to, as well as translator of, the *Breviarium* in its Greek edition.

IV. The Greek version of Jerome's *Vita Hilarionis*

During the fourth century, Christian works were translated from Latin to Greek in increasing numbers.[52] Many of these Greek versions have perished, but several early translations of Jerome's *Life of Hilarion* survive, probably because the saint's biography, set in Palestine and Egypt, remained interesting to many Greek readers in the East. Jerome himself reports that the *Vita Hilarionis* was among a number of his works translated from Latin to Greek by his friend Sophronius:[53]

Sophronius, vir adprime eruditus, 'laudes Bethlehem' adhuc
puer et nuper 'de subversione Serapis' insignem librum composuit,
'de virginitate' quoque ad Eustachium et vitam Hilarionis
monachi opuscula mea in graecum sermonem elegantissime
transtulit, psalterium quoque et prophetas, quos nos de hebraeo   5
vertimus in latinum.

De Viris Illustribus 134

51. The fact that neither Vergil nor the two characters from the *Aeneid* are further explained or identified implies that Paeanius expected his Greek audience to be familiar with the basic outline of the *Aeneid* and with the name of Vergil.
52. Dekkers (n. 7), 195–9, 203, 205.
53. Text from Wilhelm Herding, *Hieronymi de Viris Illustribus Liber* (Teubner 1924). I have deleted Herding's semicolon after *monachi* (line 4) because I think it suggests a misleading construction of the passage.

Of these tracts and translations written by Sophronius before the end of the fourth century[54] all have perished, except – perhaps – his translation of the *VH*. Three Greek versions of the *VH* survive;[55] the question before us is whether one of these can be attributed to Sophronius. The most recent editors of the texts observe that the three versions are completely independent from one another and were probably made at different times and places to satisfy different audiences.[56] Two versions are very literal; the third is translated more freely and is the only one that can be dated. Since the free version of the *VH* was apparently used by Sozomen in composing his *Ecclesiastical History* (before A.D. 444), it must have appeared sometime during the late fourth or early fifth century.[57]

Its recent editors deny, however, that this version could be the translation by Sophronius which was known to Jerome. They argue that the Greek translator must have used a Latin text of the *VH* which contained many interpolations typical of Latin manuscripts; from this they conclude that the translation must have been made at a point late in the textual tradition of the Latin *VH*.[58] Although the editors recognize that their line of reasoning contradicts the evidence of Sozomen, they do not question their assumption that the free version is actually a literal and exact translation, albeit of an interpolated exemplar. As we have already seen, Paeanius' translation of the *Breviarium* demonstrates that fourth-century Greek translations from Latin were not always literal and that their innovations were purposefully designed for a Greek audience. If, therefore, we can demonstrate that the discrepancies between the free version of the *VH* and Jerome's Latin text serve the tastes and requirements of a Greek audience, we may discard the theory of a heavily interpolated (and therefore late) Latin exemplar and suggest that the free version of the *VH* may indeed be Sophronius' translation.

54. *De Viris Illustribus* was written in 392/3 (Timothy David Barnes, *Tertullian: A Historical and Literary Study* (Oxford 1971), 235).

55. Ruth French Strout, 'The Greek Versions of Jerome's *Vita Sancti Hilarionis*', in *Studies in the Text Tradition of St Jerome's Vitae Patrum*, ed. William A. Oldfather with comments by Grundy Steiner (Urbana, Ill. 1943), 307.

56. Strout and Steiner (n. 55), 308, 446.

57. Parallel passages in Paul Van den Ven, *S. Jérome et la Vie du moine Malchus le Captif* (Louvain 1901), 105–6; discussed by Strout *et al.* (n. 55), 309–11.

58. Steiner commenting in Strout (n. 55), 310–11.

To illustrate the relationship of the free version to Jerome's original, I quote their opening sections:[59]

Scripturus vitam beati Hilarionis, habitatorem ejus invoco
Spiritum sanctum: ut qui illi virtutes largitus est, mihi
ad narrandas eas sermonem tribuat, ut facta dictis exaequentur.
Eorum enim, qui fecere, virtus (ut ait Crispus) tanta habetur,
quantum eam verbis potuere extollere praeclara ingenia.   5
Alexander magnus Macedo, quem vel arietem, vel pardum, vel
hircum caprarum Daniel vocat, cum ad Achillis tumulum pervenisset:
Felicem te, ait, juvenis, qui magno frueris praecone meritorum:
Homerum videlicet significans. Porro mihi tanti ac talis viri
conversatio vitaque dicenda est, ut Homerus quoque si adesset,   10
vel invideret materiae vel succumberet. Quamquam enim sanctus
Epiphanius Salaminae Cypri episcopus, qui cum Hilarione plurimum
versatus est, laudem ejus brevi epistola scripserit, quae vulgo
legitur . . .
                                             Vita Sancti Hilarionis, Prologue

1 Τοῦ μακαριωτάτου καὶ φίλου τοῦ Θεοῦ Ἱλαρίωνος τὴν
  πολιτείαν ἀναγράφεσθαι μέλλων, ταῖς ἐκείνου πρεσβείαις
  τὸν Κύριον παρακαλῶ ὥστε διὰ τοῦ ἁγίου πνεύματος
2 αὐτοῦ δοθῆναί μοι λόγον, ἵνα δυνηθῶ πρὸς ἀξίαν τὰς
  ἐκείνου ἀρετὰς διηγήσασθαι, καὶ κατὰ μίμησιν τοῦ ἁγίου
  βίου αὐτοῦ εὐθυνόμενος τῇ τοῦ Κυρίου χάριτι τῆς αἰωνίου   5
3 καταξιωθῶ σωτηρίας. Τοσαύτη γάρ ἐστιν ἡ τοῦ ὁσίου
  ἐκείνου ἀνδρὸς πρὸς Κύριον παρρησία, καθὼς ὁ μακάριος
  δοῦλος τοῦ Χριστοῦ Κρίσπος ἡμῖν διηγήσατο, ὡς
  πάντα λόγον καὶ ἔπαινον ἀνθρώπων ταῖς τῶν πράξεων   10
4 αὐτοῦ ἀρεταῖς καλύπτεσθαι· ὅθεν εἰ καὶ μὴ πρὸς
  ἀξίαν ταύτας ἀναγραψόμεθα, ἀλλ' ὅμως ἐπὶ πέρας
  ἄγειν τὴν τοιαύτην ἡμῶν πρόθεσιν τῇ τοῦ Κυρίου
  χάριτι σπουδάζομεν, τὰς πνευματικὰς ἀριστείας τοῦ
5 ὁσίου ἐκείνου ἀνδρὸς ἀποκαλύπτοντες. Εἰ γὰρ   15
  Ἀλέξανδρος, ὁ τῶν Μακεδόνων βασιλεύς, ὁ ἐν τῷ
  ἁγίῳ προφήτῃ Δανιὴλ

59. The 'free version' exists in two recensions – a fragmentary, rather more literal one, and a complete one quoted here. The relationship between the two recensions of the 'free version' is a vexed problem – see Van den Ven (n. 57), 142–8, and Strout (n. 55), 335–7. Because the complete recension alone agrees with Sozomen in two peculiar interpretations of Jerome's text (see Strout (n. 55), 309–10), I am quoting it to exemplify late fourth- early fifth-century translation here.
Jerome text from H. Hurter, *Vitae S. Pauli, S. Hilarionis et Malchi Monachorum*, Sanctorum Patrum Opuscula Selecta, 48 (London 1885). Greek text from Strout (n. 55), 347–8. Role of manuscript M (containing interpolations from the more literal recension of the free translation) discussed by Strout on pp. 341–3.

PV   M (= Rec. 1)
                    χαλκὸς ἢ πάρδαλις ἢ τράγος αἰγῶν
                    συνήθως ἀποκαλούμενος καὶ
πάντων μᾶλλον τῶν πρὸ αὐτοῦ βασιλέων ἕως ἄκρον τῆς   20
6 οἰκουμένης μεγαλυνθείς, ὅς, φασίν, ἐπὶ τὸν τάφον τοῦ
  Ἀχιλλέως γενόμενος τὴν πολεμικὴν ἐκείνου ἀνδρείαν
7 θαυμάζων εἶπεν· εὐτυχὴς εἶ παρὰ πάντας τοὺς ἥρωας
  ἄνδρας, ὦ νεώτερε, ὅτι τοιαύταις εὐφημίαις λόγων
  καὶ παρ' Ὁμήρου καὶ παρὰ πολλῶν σοφῶν ἡ πολεμική   25
8 σου ἀκαταμάχητος ἀνδρεία κηρύσσεται, πόσῳ μᾶλλον
  ἡμῖν πρέπον τῆς ἀληθείας κήρυκας γενομένους τὴν
  σεμνὴν καὶ ἐπέραστον τοῦ θεοφιλοῦς τούτου ἀνδρὸς
9 διηγήσασθαι πολιτείαν, ἧς καὶ ὁ ἅγιος Ἐπιφάνιος ὁ
  ἐπίσκοπος Κύπρου ἱκανοῦ χρόνου αὐτόπτης γενόμενος,   30
  πρὸς ὄνησιν τῶν μανθανόντων σχεδὸν πασῇ τῇ οἰκουμένῃ
  ταύτην ἐκήρυξεν·
                    ΒΙΟΣ ΤΟΥ ΟΣΙΟΥ ΠΑΤΡΟΣ ΗΜΩΝ ΙΛΑΡΙΩΝΟΣ, Prologue

The translator understood Latin idiom well. He has correctly represented the future sense of *scripturus* (line 1) with the participle μέλλων (line 2), and he has idiomatically interpreted *vulgo* (line 13) with σχεδὸν πασῇ τῇ οἰκουμένῃ (line 31). The Greek translation reflects the sequence of ideas and devout tone from its Latin original but innovates in matters of style and syntax. The translator adds pious adjectives (to *Hilarionis* Latin line 1 and Greek line 1, and to *Crispus* Latin line 4 and Greek line 9), he changes the emphasis of the first sentence by placing a different word in first position (*scripturus* line 1, focusing attention on Jerome as hagiographer; τοῦ μακαριωτάτου line 1, focusing on Hilarion), and he expands and spiritualizes a simple purpose clause (*ut facta dictis exaequentur* line 3) into the hope that he might worthily describe Hilarion's virtues and gain salvation by imitating them (Greek lines 4–7). By making these additions and alterations the translator effects stylistic changes in the Greek version but simultaneously maintains and intensifies the pious tone of the original Latin text. He may be building upon the image suggested by *extollere* (line 5) with καλύπτεσθαι (line 11) and ἀποκαλύπτοντες (line 15), but the word play he develops on 'covering' and 'discovering' is the translator's innovation. The sentence structure of the Greek version is in general more elaborate and hypotactic than the Latin original's; one huge, luxuriant Greek sentence (lines 15–31) subordinates within itself three Latin sentences (lines 6–14).

The translator has changed the substance of the passage as well as its style in order to make it more acceptable and appealing to a Greek-speaking audience. These changes center on the portrayal of Alexander, Achilles, and Homer. In each case, the translation presents a more favorable and extensive picture of these revered figures than the Latin original does. Jerome describes Alexander in bestial terms drawn from the Book of Daniel (lines 6–7);[60] the translator replaces or supplements this portrait with an imperial description which also occurs in Daniel (lines 20–1).[61] Jerome quotes Alexander at the tomb of Achilles in a terse sentence which recalls Cicero's version of the incident (line 8);[62] further, he mentions but briefly the great name of Homer in a parenthetical author's note (lines 10–11). The translator attributes to Alexander a short but graceful eulogy of Achilles; this eulogy specifically mentions Homer in company with other authors (lines 23–6).[63]

60. Cf. Daniel 7:6 ὀπίσω τούτου ἐθεώρουν καὶ ἰδοὺ ἕτερον θηρίον ὡσεὶ πάρδαλις, καὶ αὐτῇ πτερὰ τέσσαρα πετεινοῦ ὑπεράνω αὐτῆς, καὶ τέσσαρες κεφαλαὶ τῷ θηρίῳ, καὶ ἐξουσία ἐδόθη αὐτῇ.
Daniel 8:5 καὶ ἐγὼ ἤμην συνίων καὶ ἰδοὺ τράγος αἰγῶν ἤρχετο ἀπὸ λιβὸς ἐπὶ πρόσωπον πάσης τῆς γῆς καὶ οὐκ ἦν ἀπτόμενος τῆς γῆς, καὶ τῷ τράγῳ κέρας ἀνὰ μέσον τῶν ὀφθαλμῶν.
Daniel 8:21 καὶ ὁ τράγος τῶν αἰγῶν βασιλεὺς Ἑλλήνων· καὶ τὸ κέρας τὸ μέγα, ὃ ἦν ἀνὰ μέσον τῶν ὀφθαλμῶν αὐτοῦ, αὐτός ἐστιν ὁ βασιλεὺς ὁ πρῶτος. (Text from Joseph Ziegler, ed., *Susanna, Daniel, Bel et Draco*, in *Septuaginta Vetus Testamentum Graecum* 16.2 [Göttingen 1954].)
61. Cf. Daniel 8:9–11 καὶ ἐκ τοῦ ἑνὸς αὐτῶν ἐξῆλθε κέρας ἓν ἰσχυρὸν καὶ ἐμεγαλύνθη περισσῶς πρὸς τὸν νότον καὶ πρὸς τὴν δύναμιν·
10 ἐμεγαλύνθη ἕως τῆς δυνάμεως καὶ ἀπὸ τῶν ἄστρων, καὶ συνεπάτησεν
11 αὐτά, καὶ ἕως οὗ ὁ ἀρχιστράτηγος ῥύσηται τὴν αἰχμαλωσίαν, καὶ δι' αὐτὸν θυσία ἐρράχθη, καὶ ἐγενήθη καὶ κατευοδώθη αὐτῷ, καὶ τὸ ἅγιον ἐρημωθήσεται·
Daniel 8:23–5 καὶ ἐπ' ἐσχάτων τῆς βασιλείας αὐτῶν πληρουμένων τῶν ἁμαρτιῶν αὐτῶν ἀναστήσεται βασιλεὺς ἀναιδὴς προσώπῳ καὶ
24 συνίων προβλήματα. καὶ κραταιὰ ἡ ἰσχὺς αὐτοῦ, καὶ θαυμαστὰ διαφθερεῖ καὶ κατευθυνεῖ καὶ ποιήσει καὶ διαφθερεῖ ἰσχυροὺς καὶ
25 λαὸν ἁγίων. καὶ ὁ ζυγὸς τοῦ κλοιοῦ αὐτοῦ κατευθυνεῖ· δόλος ἐν τῇ χειρὶ αὐτοῦ, καὶ ἐν καρδίᾳ αὐτοῦ μεγαλυνθήσεται καὶ δόλῳ διαφθερεῖ πολλοὺς καὶ ἐπὶ ἀπωλείας πολλῶν στήσεται καὶ ὡς ᾠὰ χειρὶ συντρίψει. (Text from Ziegler.)
62. Cf. Cicero, *Pro Archia* 24 . . . cum in Sigeo ad Achillis tumulum astitisset: *O fortunate*, inquit, *adolescens, qui tuae virtutis Homerum praeconem inveneris!* Et vere . . . (Text from N. H. Watts, ed., *Cicero: The Speeches* (Cambridge, Mass. 1935].)
63. Alexander's words at the tomb of Achilles are reported by Plutarch (*Vita Alexandri* 15.4) and Arrian (*Anabasis of Alexander* 1.12.1–2). The translation reproduces neither of these versions exactly, but offers some verbal parallels with

Moreover, Jerome integrates the Alexander anecdote with the subject of Hilarion by observing that even Homer would find the virtues of Hilarion an overwhelming subject (lines 9–11); this small but pious slur against Homer's reputation has disappeared from the Greek version, while the translator concentrates instead upon the outstanding inspiration and worthy subject matter which Hilarion provides to an author (lines 26–9).

It is necessary for the translator to cope with Latin cultural references in lines 4–5, where Jerome mentions the historian Sallust (*Crispus*, line 4) and quotes from his writings (*eorum enim . . . praeclara ingenia* lines 4–5, from *Catiline* 8.4). The translator treats this quotation exactly as he treats Jerome's own prose, expanding it and interpreting it freely (lines 7–11). He displays none of the exquisite regard for an author's exact words which Paeanius demonstrated in translating Eutropius' *Aeneid* quotation. The existence of juxtalinear Vergil texts indicates that fourth-century Greeks knew the *Aeneid*, but there is no evidence that they also knew Sallust's writings. The free manner in which Jerome's translator renders this quotation from Sallust implies some unfamiliarity with the *Catiline*; either the translator himself did not recognize the quotation or he felt free to recast it because he doubted his audience would recognize it. In identifying 'Crispus' for a Greek audience, the translator applies an epithet (ὁ μακάριος δοῦλος τοῦ Χριστοῦ Κρίσπος lines 8–9) which shocks the modern reader with its blatant inaccuracy; it leads him to doubt seriously the translator's competence and to reject flatly the suggestion that this free version could possibly be Sophronius' translation, approved by Jerome himself as '*elegantissime*'. The epithet is, however, not so bizarre and inaccurate as it might at first seem. 'Blessed slave of Christ' expresses the translator's conviction that Sallust was an instrument of God's will; because Sallust's writings are moralistic and critical of the (pagan) society which surrounded him, a Christian might indeed say that Sallust served as God's

the passage from Arrian: . . . τὸν Ἀχιλλέως [ἄρα] τάφον ἐστεφάνωσε· καὶ εὐδαιμόνισεν ἄρα, ὡς ὁ λόγος, Ἀλέξανδρος Ἀχιλλέα, ὅτι Ὁμήρου κήρυκος ἐς τὴν ἔπειτα μνήμην ἔτυχε . . . (Text from E. Iliff Robson, ed., *Arrian* 1 [Cambridge, Mass. 1961].) It is entirely possible, of course, that the translator drew his version of Alexander's speech from a Greek source now lost to us; the career of Alexander was an extremely popular topic in the ancient world (see Lionel Pearson, *The Lost Histories of Alexander the Great* [New York 1960], 1–21).

spokesman in pre-Christian Rome. The epithet does not imply that the translator thought Sallust a Christian; in this period, δοῦλος can be used of an *unwitting* instrument of God (cf. Theodoret Cyrrhensis, *I Tim.* 6:11, Migne *PG* 82 col. 825). Thus interpreted, ὁ μακάριος δοῦλος τοῦ Χριστοῦ is a characterization congenial with Jerome's own views on Sallust and on certain other pagan authors.[64] Jerome cited Sallust frequently in his own writings and clearly admired him (*nobilis historicus, in Eccl.*, p. 430, Migne *PL* 23 col. 1109; *auctor certissimus, Onomastica Sacra*, ed. Lagarde no. 117, line 12). Moreover, Jerome expresses the idea that pagan authors could reveal Christian truths when he finds *partem vasorum domus Dei* in the writings of Plato and the Stoic philosophers (*Comm. in Danielem* 624). Jerome's famous justification for Christians studying pagan literature (*Epistle 70*, to Magnus) inspired scholars to use antique learning for Christian purposes throughout the Western Middle Ages.[65]

The singular epithet applied to Sallust is, in my opinion, no impediment to identifying this translation as Sophronius'. The preceding discussion illustrates, moreover, that the discrepancies between Jerome's original text and this version of the *VH* are the sorts of expansions and explanations which Paeanius used and which are acceptable in a fourth-century free translation. The question of the translator's identity remains. Van den Ven has demonstrated that the same translator produced both the free version of the *VH* and a Greek translation of Jerome's *Vita Malchi*.[66] These translations bear certain characteristics consonant with what Jerome tells us about his friend and translator Sophronius (see above), and Van den Ven has argued that Sophronius translated both texts. The translator has made learned additions to his texts, cited and explained Biblical passages, and added to the *VH* a speech based on Jerome's *Epistula ad Eustochium*, a work which Jerome tells us was translated by Sophronios.[67]

64. Arthur Stanley Pease, 'The Attitude of Jerome Towards Pagan Literature', *Transactions and Proceedings of the American Philological Association* 50 (1919), 163–6, esp. p. 164 n. 105.

65. Ernest Robert Curtius, *European Literature and the Latin Middle Ages*, trans. Willard Trask (New York 1953), 40; Jean Leclerq, *The Love of Learning and the Desire for God*, trans. Catharine Misrahi (New York 1961), 120–1.

66. Van den Ven (n. 57), 110–21.

67. Van den Ven (n. 57), 129–38.

Jerome, speaking generally of his friend's translations, characterized them approvingly as 'very elegant' (*elegantissime*). The free
version of the *VH*, with its fluid and elegant expansions into good
idiomatic Greek, can justly qualify for such praise; it can properly
claim Sophronius for its author. Indeed, Sophronius' translation
represents an improvement over the Latin original from the
viewpoint of a Greek-speaking, literate, and devout Christian
audience. Sophronius' rather florid style would appeal to rhetoric-
sensitive readers far more than Jerome's spare sentences; his
positive presentation of Alexander, Achilles, and Homer would
suit Greek readers conscious of their Hellenic heritage far better
than Jerome's comments on these revered figures. The translator's
presentation of 'Crispus' as a (pre-Christian) teacher of Christian
values would tell a pious Christian audience what they really
needed to know about an otherwise unfamiliar but obviously
moralistic author. In short, Sophronius' version of the *VH*, like
Paeanius' translation of the *Breviarium*, is an edition as well as a
translation, made with the requirements and preferences of a
particular Greek-speaking audience in mind.

V. Eusebius' translation of the Edict of Toleration

The fourth-century ecclesiastical historian Eusebius of Caesarea
relied chiefly on Greek sources for the history of the Western as well
as the Eastern Church;[68] he also used some Latin sources. At two
points in his narrative, Eusebius claims that he himself translated
Latin legal documents into Greek, evidently confident of his own
abilities as a translator and doubtful that his Greek audience could
read Latin for themselves.

The first of these translated documents had in fact been quoted
in Latin by Eusebius' Greek source, Justin Martyr (*Apology* I.68):[69]
τούτοις ὁ μὲν δηλωθεὶς ἀνὴρ αὐτὴν παρατέθειται τὴν Ῥωμαϊκὴν
ἀντιγραφήν, ἡμεῖς δ' ἐπὶ τὸ Ἑλληνικὸν κατὰ δύναμιν αὐτὴν
μετειλείφαμεν, ἔχουσαν ὧδε· (*Historia Ecclesiastica* IV.8.8). Regret-

68. Bardy (n. 4), 129–30.
69. Passage cited by Adolf von Harnack, 'Die griechische Übersetzung des
Apologeticus Tertullians', *Texte und Untersuchungen* 8.4 (1892), 1. Text from
Eduard Schwartz, ed., *Eusebius Werke*, vol. II.1: *Die Kirchengeschichte*, Die
griechischen christlichen Schriftsteller 9.1 (Leipzig 1903).

tably, we cannot compare Eusebius' translation with the original Latin text, because that text has perished.[70] The second translated document, the famous Edict of Toleration,[71] survives, although somewhat truncated, in Lactantius' *De Mortibus Persecutorum* 34.1:[72]

> . . . Et iam deficiens edictum misit huiuscemodi:
>
> 1 «Inter cetera quae pro rei publicae semper commodis atque
>   utilitate disponimus, nos quidem uolueramus antehac iuxta
>   leges ueteres et publicam disciplinam Romanorum cuncta corrigere
>   atque id prouidere, ut etiam christiani, qui parentum suorum   5
>   reliquerant sectam, ad bonas mentes redirent, siquidem quadam
>   ratione tanta eosdem christianos uoluntas inuasisset et tanta
>   stultitia occupasset, ut non illa ueterum instituta sequerentur,
>   quae forsitan primum parentes eorundem constituerant, sed pro
>   arbitrio suo atque ut isdem erat libitum, ita sibimet leges   10
>   facerent quas obseruarent, et per diuersa uarios populos
>   congregarent . . .»

> viii.17.2 . . . αὐτίκα γοῦν ἔργου τῷ λόγῳ παρηκολουθηκότος,
>   ἥπλωτο κατὰ πόλεις βασιλικὰ διατάγματα, τὴν
>   παλινῳδίαν τῶν καθ' ἡμᾶς τοῦτον περιέχοντα τὸν
>   τρόπον·
>
> 3 [An introductory reference to Galerius and his titles follows.
>   Since its Latin counterpart does not survive, I shall bypass this
>   portion of the edict and proceed to the section also preserved in
>   Latin by Lactantius.]
>
> 6 Μεταξὺ τῶν λοιπῶν, ἅπερ ὑπὲρ τοῦ χρησίμου καὶ   5
>   λυσιτελοῦς τοῖς δημοσίοις διατυπούμεθα, ἡμεῖς μὲν
>   βεβουλήμεθα πρότερον κατὰ τοὺς ἀρχαίους νόμους
>   καὶ τὴν δημοσίαν ἐπιστήμην τὴν τῶν Ῥωμαίων

70. Rufinus' Latin version of this document is simply a translation back into Latin of Eusebius' text (Timothy David Barnes, 'Legislation Against the Christians', *Journal of Roman Studies* 58 [1968], 37 n. 55 citing Schanz-Hosius, *Gesch. der röm. Litt.* III.3. [1922]).

71. After quoting the Edict in Greek (*HE* viii.17.3–10), Eusebius remarks at §11 ταῦτα κατὰ τὴν Ῥωμαίων φωνήν, ἐπὶ τὴν Ἑλλάδα γλῶτταν κατὰ τὸ δυνατὸν μεταληφθέντα, τοῦτον εἶχεν τὸν τρόπον (ed. Schwartz). The phrase κατὰ τὸ δυνατὸν is interpreted by Harnack (p. 1) as evidence that Eusebius translated this edict himself. This is also the interpretation of two modern translators, Gustave Bardy ('*selon que nous avons pu*', *Eusèbe de Cesarée, histoire ecclesiastique* [Paris 1958]) and G. A. Williamson ('the original Latin, which I have turned into Greek to the best of my ability', *Eusebius, the History of the Church* [Baltimore 1965]).

72. Latin text from J. Moreau, ed., *Lactance, de la mort des persécuteurs* (Paris 1954). Greek text from Schwartz.

ἅπαντα ἐπανορθώσασθαι καὶ τούτου πρόνοιαν
ποιήσασθαι ἵνα καὶ οἱ Χριστιανοί, οἵτινες τῶν   10
γονέων τῶν ἑαυτῶν καταλελοίπασιν τὴν αἵρεσιν,
εἰς ἀγαθὴν πρόθεσιν ἐπανέλθοιεν· ἐπείπερ τινὶ
λογισμῷ τοιαύτη αὐτοὺς πλεονεξία κατειλήφει
7 ὡς μὴ ἕπεσθαι τοῖς ὑπὸ τῶν πάλαι καταδειχθεῖσιν,
ἅπερ ἴσως πρότερον καὶ οἱ γονεῖς αὐτῶν ἦσαν   15
καταστήσαντες, ἀλλὰ κατὰ τὴν αὐτῶν πρόθεσιν καὶ
ὡς ἕκαστος ἐβούλετο, οὕτως ἑαυτοῖς καὶ νόμους
ποιῆσαι καὶ τούτους παραφυλάσσειν καὶ ἐν διαφόροις
διάφορα πλήθη συνάγειν . . .

Historia Ecclesiastica VIII.17.2–7

As an example of Latin prose, the opening section of the Edict of Toleration is notable for its complex, highly subordinated sentence structure (i.e. the twelve lines quoted here represent a single Latin sentence) and for a tendency to use co-ordinated, double expressions (e.g. lines 2–3 *commodis atque utilitate*; line 4 *leges veteres et publicam disciplinam*; lines 7–8 *tanta . . . voluntas invasisset et tanta stultitia occupasset*; lines 9–10 *pro arbitrio suo atque ut isdem erat libitum*; lines 10–12 *ita sibimet leges . . . populos congregarent*). Eusebius' translation retains these two features of the original Latin text. The Greek sentence follows the structure of the Latin one almost exactly, sometimes proceeding in a word-for-word correspondence with the original text (e.g. line 2 *inter . . . pro*: line 5 Μεταξὺ . . . ὑπὲρ; lines 3–5 *nos quidem . . . corrigere atque*: lines 6–9 ἡμεῖς μὲν . . . ἐπανορθώσασθαι καί; lines 5–7 *ut etiam christiani . . . tanta eosdem*; lines 10–13 ἵνα καὶ . . . αὐτούς). The verbs of the Greek translation derive their moods according to the requirements of Greek syntax, but their tenses in the indicative correspond in a generally consistent manner to the tenses of the Latin: a Greek present represents a Latin one (e.g. line 3 *disponimus*: line 6 διατυπούμεθα), a Greek imperfect a Latin one (e.g. line 10 *erat*: line 17 ἐβούλετο) and a Greek perfect represents the Latin pluperfect (e.g. line 3 *volueramus*: line 7 βεβουλήμεθα; line 6 *reliquerant*: line 11 καταλελοίπασιν). The pluperfect indicative at line 9, *constituerant*, appears in a Greek periphrastic tense, however (lines 15–16 ἦσαν καταστήσαντες). Because Eusebius has successfully translated the Latin pluperfect elsewhere, it is unlikely that the periphrasis results from some sort of misreading or mistranslation on his part. Instead, I suspect that he chose it for variety and for the interesting play of sound in ἦσαν καταστήσαντες. In lines 18–19 Eusebius develops a play on words in Greek which is only suggested in the Latin text: *diversa varios*: διαφόροις διάφορα. The translation is a careful representation of the Latin original, but it is not a mechanical *calque* from it. Eusebius occasionally represents a Latin idiom closely in Greek (e.g. line 6 *ad bonas mentes redirent*: line 12 εἰς ἀγαθὴν πρόθεσιν ἐπανέλθοιεν), but he also incorporates Greek expressions which please him (e.g. the alliterative πρόνοιαν ποιήσασθαι lines 9–10 for *id providere* in line 5) or which correctly represent a rather difficult and oblique Latin idiom (e.g. line 10 *ut isdem erat libitum*: line 17 ὡς ἕκαστος ἐβούλετο). Although the structure of the Greek passage parallels the Latin closely, at line 18 Eusebius has chosen to co-ordinate two verbs (ποιῆσαι καὶ τούτους παραφυλάσσειν) in the manner so typical of this passage, rather than to subordinate the second verb as happens in the Latin version (line 11 *facerent quas observarent*). The degree of Eusebius' independence from the Latin text is especially evident in line 13. Here, Eusebius drops the noun from *eosdem christianos* (line 7) and lets the pronoun αὐτούς suffice; he also condenses the two clauses *quadam ratione . . . invasisset* and *tanta stultitia occupasset* (lines 6–8) by representing both subjects with πλεονεξία and both verbs with κατειλήφει. It is possible, of course, that factors other than Eusebius' free choice influenced the form of line 13 – Eusebius may have had an illegible or faulty Latin text to translate, or the Greek text may be a truncated version of Eusebius' original translation, abridged through subsequent damage or scribal error. I think it unlikely that Eusebius was unable to translate line 13 exactly, since the syntax and vocabulary are both straightforward; he may, however, have chosen to suppress an insult against the Church and believers by casting it in less specific terms than the Latin original. In all, the translation is a competent and even stylish witness to the fact that Eusebius could read and translate Latin very well if and when he chose to do so.

VI. Eusebius and the Greek version of Tertullian's *Apologeticus*

Eusebius quotes from chapters 2–5 of Tertullian's *Apologeticus* in five separate sections of the *Historia Ecclesiastica* (II.2.4ff., 25.4; III.20.9, 33.3; v.5.6) and twice in the *Chronicle*, using, he admits, a

Greek version of the *Apologeticus* made by an unnamed translator (cf. line 4 of the Greek text below).[73] To illustrate how Eusebius integrated this translation into his narrative, I shall compare the first two passages of the *HE* which contain parts of the Greek *Apologeticus* with the corresponding section of the Latin original.[74]

5.1 Ut de origine aliquid retractemus eiusmodi legum, vetus erat decretum, ne qui deus ab imperatore consecraretur nisi a senatu probatus. Scit M. Aemilius de deo suo Alburno. Facit et hoc ad causam nostram, quod apud vos de humano arbitratu divinitas pensitatur. Nisi homini deus placuerit, deus non erit; homo 5
2 iam deo propitius esse debebit. Tiberius ergo, cuius tempore nomen Christianum in saeculum introivit, adnuntiatum sibi ex Syria Palestina, quod illic veritatem ipsius divinitatis revelaverat, detulit ad senatum cum praerogativa suffragii sui. Senatus, quia non ipse probaverat, respuit; Caesar in sententia 10 mansit, comminatus periculum accusatoribus Christianorum.
3 Consulite commentarios vestros; illic reperietis primum Neronem in hanc sectam cum maxime Romae orientem Caesar-
[iano
gladio ferocisse. Sed tali dedicatore damnationis nostrae etiam gloriamur. Qui enim scit illum, intellegere potest 15 non nisi grande aliquod bonum a Nerone damnatum.

Apologeticus 5.1–3

11.2.4 . . . ταῦτα Τερτυλλιανὸς τοὺς Ῥωμαίων νόμους ἠκριβωκώς, ἀνὴρ τά τε ἄλλα ἔνδοξος καὶ τῶν μάλιστα ἐπὶ Ῥώμης λαμπρῶν, ἐν τῇ γραφείσῃ μὲν αὐτῷ Ῥωμαίων φωνῇ, μεταβληθείσῃ δ᾽ ἐπὶ τὴν Ἑλλάδα γλῶτταν ὑπὲρ Χριστιανῶν ἀπολογίᾳ τίθησιν, κατὰ λέξιν τοῦτον ἱστορῶν τὸν τρόπον 5
5 > ἵνα δὲ καὶ ἐκ τῆς γενέσεως διαλεχθῶμεν τῶν τοιούτων νόμων, παλαιὸν ἦν δόγμα μηδένα θεὸν ὑπὸ βασιλέως καθιεροῦσθαι, πρὶν ὑπὸ τῆς συγκλήτου δοκιμασθῆναι. Μάρκος Αἰμίλιος οὕτως περί τινος εἰδώλου πεποίηκεν Ἀλβούρνου. καὶ τοῦτο ὑπὲρ τοῦ 10 ἡμῶν λόγου πεποίηται, ὅτι παρ᾽ ὑμῖν ἀνθρωπείᾳ δοκιμῇ ἡ θεότης δίδοται. ἐὰν μὴ ἀνθρώπῳ θεὸς ἀρέσῃ, θεὸς οὐ γίνεται· οὕτως κατά γε τοῦτο ἄνθρωπον
6 θεῷ ἵλεω εἶναι προσῆκεν. Τιβέριος οὖν, ἐφ᾽ οὗ τὸ τῶν Χριστιανῶν ὄνομα εἰς τὸν κόσμον εἰσελήλυθεν, 15

73. Harnack (n. 69) tentatively identifies the translator as Julius Africanus (pp. 23–35); Sickenberger rejects this suggestion ('S. Julius Africanus', *RE* x [1919], col. 117).

74. Latin text from Henricus Hoppe, ed., *Quinti Septimi Florentis Tertulliani Apologeticum*, Corpus Scriptorum Ecclesiasticorum Latinorum 69 (Leipzig 1939). Greek text from Schwartz.

ἀγγελθέντος αὐτῷ ἐκ Παλαιστίνης τοῦ δόγματος τούτου,
ἔνθα πρῶτον ἤρξατο, τῇ συγκλήτῳ ἀνεκοινώσατο,
δῆλος ὢν ἐκείνοις ὡς τῷ δόγματι ἀρέσκεται. ἡ δὲ
σύγκλητος, ἐπεὶ οὐκ αὐτὴ δεδοκιμάκει, ἀπώσατο·
ὁ δὲ ἐν τῇ αὐτοῦ ἀποφάσει ἔμεινεν, ἀπειλήσας   20
θάνατον τοῖς τῶν Χριστιανῶν κατηγόροις. <
    τῆς οὐρανίου προνοίας κατ᾿ οἰκονομίαν τοῦτ᾿ αὐτῷ
πρὸς νοῦν βαλλομένης, ὡς ἂν ἀπαραποδίστως ἀρχὰς
ἔχων ὁ τοῦ εὐαγγελίου λόγος πανταχόσε γῆς διαδράμοι.

Historia Ecclesiastica ii.2.4–6

ii.25.3 ... ἐνέδει δ᾿ἄρα τοῖς πᾶσι καὶ τοῦτ᾿ ἐπιγραφῆναι αὐτῷ,   25
    4   ὡς ἂν πρῶτος αὐτοκρατόρων τῆς εἰς τὸ θεῖον εὐσεβείας
        πολέμιος ἀναδειχθείη. τούτου πάλιν ὁ ῾Ρωμαῖος
        Τερτυλλιανὸς ὧδέ πως λέγων μνημονεύει
            > ἐντύχετε τοῖς ὑπομνήμασιν ὑμῶν, ἐκεῖ εὑρήσετε
        πρῶτον Νέρωνα τοῦτο τὸ δόγμα, ἡνίκα μάλιστα   30
        ἐν ῾Ρώμῃ, τὴν ἀνατολὴν πᾶσαν ὑποτάξας, ὠμὸς
        ἦν εἰς πάντας, διώξαντα. τοιούτῳ τῆς κολάσεως
        ἡμῶν ἀρχηγῷ καυχώμεθα. ὁ γὰρ εἰδὼς ἐκεῖνον νοῆσαι
        δύναται ὡς οὐκ ἄν, εἰ μὴ μέγα τι ἀγαθὸν ἦν, ὑπὸ
        Νέρωνος κατακριθῆναι. <   35
    3   ταύτῃ γοῦν οὗτος, θεομάχος ἐν τοῖς μάλιστα πρῶτος
        ἀνακηρυχθείς, ἐπὶ τὰς κατὰ τῶν ἀποστόλων ἐπήρθη
        σφαγάς ...

Historia Ecclesiastica ii.25.3–5

Eusebius' introduction to the *Apologeticus* is particularly interesting. As mentioned above, he admits that he is quoting a Greek
translation of Tertullian's original Latin work, but he offers no
information about the translator or the context in which he found
the translation. Instead, Eusebius focuses upon Tertullian and
upon the qualities which make the Roman author a reliable source
for legislation affecting the early Church. Eusebius' statement that
Tertullian was a jurist and a senator (lines 1–3) is unsupported by
Western sources and presumably without historical value; he
probably deduced it from the text of the *Apologeticus* itself.[75] This
information is consistent, however, with Eusebius' general tendency to exalt the status of early Christians,[76] and it serves to
recommend Tertullian's authority as a source for legislation and
Eusebius' perspicacity in quoting him.

Eusebius claims that he has quoted Tertullian exactly (line 5

75. Barnes, *Tertullian* (n. 54), 25.
76. Barnes, *Tertullian* (n. 54), 25.

κατὰ λέξιν),[77] and a comparison of the Latin and Greek texts suggests that this is probably so, since the translation corresponds to the original almost word-for-word. The exception in line 18, where the Greek δῆλος . . . ἀρέσκεται offers a paraphrase of the technical legal expression *cum praerogativa suffragii sui* (line 9), may, of course, be Eusebius' (rather than the translator's) substitution for some legal expression in the older Greek version. In general, the translation is a pleasing example of Greek prose style, and, although it stays close to the Latin original, it contains no awkward Latinisms.[78]

The second section of the translation as quoted by Eusebius contains an egregious error. The translator has misconstrued the expression *cum maxime* (line 13) and, as a result, forced the sentence into an exaggerated portrayal of Nero's victories in the East (line 31), apparently interpreting *orientem* as a reference to Corbulo's successful Armenian campaign concluded in A.D. 63.[79] Eusebius evidently did not check the translation against a Latin text, nor did he attempt to correct or to explain the misleading impression conveyed by the translation that Nero conquered the entire East. He simply copied it verbatim, rejecting the role of contributing editor or corrector. Eusebius' respectful use of the *Apologeticus* translation implies that this literal translation acquired for him the full authority of Tertullian's own words; it suggests the power and prestige of the literal translation style.

Some years before writing the *HE*, Eusebius had used two passages from the *Apologeticus* translation in compiling his *Chronicle*.[80] I quote the section based on *Apol.* 5.22 (see *HE* II.2.6. above) to illustrate how Eusebius used the translation in this terse and abbreviated work:[81]

77. Eusebius quotes *Apol.* 2–5 exactly in the five passages of the *HE* where he uses it, summarizing only once at *HE* v.5.6 = *Apol.* 5.6 (Harnack, p. 9).

78. The style and accuracy of the translation are discussed in detail by Harnack (n. 69), 18–22.

79. For a discussion of Corbulo's activities, see Edward T. Salmon, *A History of the Roman World from 30 B.C. to A.D. 138*[3] (London 1957), 192–4, and B. H. Warmington, *Nero: Reality and Legend* (New York 1969), 93–7.

80. For relative date of the *Chronicle*, see Eduard Schwartz, 'Eusebius von Caesarea', *RE* VI (1909), col. 1376. *Apologeticus* passages recognized by Harnack (n. 169), p. 27 n. 1. See *HE* II.2.6 = *Chronicon Paschale* 229[d] (430,18), ad Olym. 203,3; *HE* III.33 = Syncellus 346[d] (655,8), ad Olym. 221.

81. Text from Rudolf Helm, ed., *Eusebius Werke* vol. VII: *Die Chronik des*

Πόντιος Πιλᾶτος περὶ τοῦ Χριστοῦ καὶ τοῦ Χριστιανῶν
δόγματος ἐκοινώσατο Τιβερίῳ Καίσαρι κἀκεῖνος τῇ
συγκλήτῳ ʽΡώμης. τῆς δὲ μὴ προσιεμένης Τιβέριος
θάνατον ἠπείλησεν τοῖς χριστιανοκατηγόροις (τοῖς
Χριστιανῶν κατηγόροις, Cedrenus) ὡς ἱστορεῖ Τερτυλλιανὸς ὁ ʽΡωμαῖος.

Chronicon Paschale 229 d

Although Eusebius has abridged and slightly rearranged the original translation, the *Chronicle* preserves unmistakable traces of its wording. ἐκοινώσατο ... κἀκεῖνος τῇ συγκλήτῳ (lines 2–3) reflects the translation's τῇ συγκλήτῳ ἀνεκοινώσατο (line 17). Eusebius has expanded a phrase in the translation (ἀπειλήσας θάνατον τοῖς τῶν Χριστιανῶν κατηγόροις line 20–1) into an independent clause (Τιβέριος θάνατον ἠπείλησεν τοῖς χριστιανοκατηγόροις [τοῖς Χριστιανῶν κατηγόροις Cedrenus] lines 4–5), shifting θάνατον forward in the clause apparently for emphasis. The abbreviated style of the *Chronicle* does not allow Eusebius to quote Tertullian exactly or in full, but he mentions Tertullian as his source (line 5) and paraphrases the words of the translation with care, as if they possessed Tertullian's own cachet.

VII. Latin literary influence on Greek technical treatises

Two technical writers of the fourth century, Apsyrtus and Anatolius, demonstrate some acquaintance with Latin literary sources. Apsyrtus, born in Clazomenae, lived in Prusa and Nicomedia and served as staff veterinarian with the armies of Constantine in the Danube region.[82] While in the army, Apsyrtus must have used Latin;[83] his writings also indicate some familiarity with the language. He uses Latin technical terms (e.g. σκαῦρος: *scaurus*, 'with deviating hoof', *Hippiatrica* 14.4), sometimes qualifying such terms as ῥωμαϊστί.[84] Excerpts from his manual on the care of horses and mules are preserved by the *Hippiatrica*, a ninth or

Hieronymus, Die griechischen christlichen Schriftsteller 47 (Berlin 1956), p. 400 ad Jerome Olym. 203.

82. For a full discussion of Apsyrtus' career and writings, see Eugene Oder, 'Apsyrtus', *Veterinärhistorisches Jahrbuch* 2 (1926), 121–36. I am unconvinced by Gudmund Björck's complicated attempt to place Apsyrtus in the third century (*Apsyrtus, Julius Africanus et l'Hippiatrique grecque* (Uppsala Leipzig 1944), 7–11).

83. Zilliacus (n. 3), 126–31; Jones, *Empire* (n. 5), 989; Trahman (n. 3), 46–9.

84. *Hipp.* 1, *Hipp. Berol.* 2.1, 51.1, 52.1; *Hipp.* 2, *Hipp. Paris* 225.

tenth-century Byzantine compendium.[85] A section of this manual
bears some resemblance to a passage from Columella, raising the
possibility that Apsyrtus may have translated the Latin agricultural work or used an existing Greek translation of Columella.[86]
Any analysis of the relationship between Apsyrtus and Columella
is complicated by the fact that Apsyrtus' text survives only in
excerpts. Scholarly opinion considers these excerpts a fairly
accurate reflection of what Apsyrtus wrote, in that the redactor
may have abridged Apsyrtus' original text, but he neither added
his own supplements to it nor changed its original wording.[87]
Apsyrtus' discussion of the stud donkey incorporates part of
Columella's long discourse on the breeding of mules and hinnies
(VI.37.1–11);[88]

VI.37.5 . . . Itaque commodissimum est asinum destinare mularum
　　　　　generi seminando, cuius, ut dixi, species experimento est
　　　6　speciosior. Verumtamen ab aspectu non aliter probari debet,
　　　　　quam ut sit amplissimi corporis, cervice valida, robustis ac
　　　　　latis costis, pectore musculoso et vasto, feminibus lacertosis,　5
　　　　　cruribus compactis, coloris nigri vel maculosi. Nam murinus
　　　　　cum sit in asino vulgaris, tum etiam non optime respondet in
　　　7　mula. Neque nos universa quadrupedis species decipiat, si
　　　　　qualem probamus conspicimus. Nam quemadmodum arietum
　　　　　　　　　　　　　　　　　　　　　　　　　　　　　　　　[quae sunt
　　　　in linguis et palatis maculae, plerumque in velleribus agnorum 10
　　　　deprehenduntur: ita si discolores pilos asinus in palpebris

85. Date discussed by Reinhard Froehner, 'Die berliner Prachthandschrift der
griechischen Hippiatrika', in *80 Jahre H. Hauptner 1857–1937* (Berlin 1937), 25; also
Eugen Oder and Carl Hoppe, *Corpus Hippiatricorum Graecorum* II (Leipzig 1927), vi.
　86. Although Columella claims to have consulted *magna porro et Graecorum turba*
(1.1.7), I consider it unlikely that the similarities between the text of Apsyrtus and
of Columella derive from a Greek source common to them both because
Columella appears to have relied primarily upon Latin sources. (Kappelmacher,
'L. Iunius Moderatus Columella', *RE* x [1919], cols. 1060–1). Apsyrtus may have
encountered material from Columella in the writings of Eumelus of Thebes, a
third-century author often quoted by Apsyrtus. (Oder and Hoppe (n. 85), II,
viii–ix). See, for example, *Hipp. Berol.* 86.8 = Columella VI.17.1; *Hipp.* 68.4 = Col.
VI.30.1; *Hipp.* 107.3 = Col. VI.30.3. Other examples may be traced through Oder
and Hoppe indices: I, 454 and II, 342.
　87. Max Ihm, 'Die Hippiatrica', *Rheinisches Museum* 47 (1892), 315; Froehner
(n. 85), 24. Weber (n. 10), pt. 2 p. 7, doubts that the redactor's work can be
separated from Apsyrtus'.
　88. Latin text from E. S. Forster and Edward H. Heffner, edd., *Lucius Junnus
Moderatus Columella, On Agriculture* (Cambridge, Mass. 1954). Greek text from
Oder and Hoppe I.

aut auribus gerit, sobolem quoque frequenter facit diversi
coloris, qui et ipse, etiam si diligentissime in admissario
exploratus est, saepe tamen domini spem decipit. Nam interdum
etiam citra praedicta signa dissimiles sui mulas fingit ...   15

De Re Rustica vi.37.5–7

14.1   Ἄψυρτος Καριστανίῳ Φρόντωνι χαίρειν. σπουδαίως
ἔχοντός σου ἐν τῇ ἱπποτροφίᾳ καὶ ζητοῦντος, ἐκ τίνων
δεῖ καὶ ποταπῶν τὸ ὀχεῖον ποιεῖσθαι, ἀναγκαῖον εἰδέναι
σε καὶ τοῦτο ...

[Apsyrtus then describes several conditions which disqualify a stallion for
breeding purposes: a congenital eye defect, a sluggish disposition, an
undescended testicle, and varicose veins.]

2   Εὔχρηστον εἰδέναι τοῖς ποιουμένοις τὴν σύστασιν ἐκ τοῦ   5
ἱππικοῦ καὶ ὀνικοῦ ζῴου, ὅτι δεῖ ὑπάρχειν τὸν ἀναβάτην
ὄνον μέγαν τῇ ἕξει, καὶ πολὺν τῇ περιοχῇ τοῦ σώματος,
τὴν κεφαλὴν μεγάλην ἔχοντα καὶ μὴ ἱππώδη, πρόσωπον
[ὡσαύτως,
καὶ τὰς ἐν αὐτῷ γνάθους καὶ χείλη μεγάλα, ὀφθαλμοὺς μὴ
μικροὺς μηδὲ κοίλους, μυκτῆρας μεγάλους, ὦτα μὴ μικρὰ   10
μηδὲ κλαμβά, αὐχένα πλατύν, μὴ βραχύν, στῆθος ὡσαύτως
πλατὺ καὶ σαρκῶδες, μεμυωμένον, στερρὸν πρὸς τὸ
ὑπομένειν τὰ ὑπὸ τῆς ὀργῆς λακτίσματα, ὠμοπλάτας, μεγάλας,
καὶ τὰ ὑποκάτω τούτων, ἐπάνω δὲ τῶν γονάτων παχέα καὶ
σαρκώδη καὶ ἰσχυρὰ καὶ ὡς μάλιστα διάστασιν ἔχοντα.   15
δεῖ γὰρ αὐτὸν ἐν τῇ ἐπιβάσει τὴν ὀχευομένην εὐπερίληπτον
ἔχειν.

3–4   [Apsyrtus describes further the physical characteristics of a male
donkey desirable for breeding purposes: a straight spine and
back, even shoulders, good body markings, a trim belly, small
flanks, broad hams, a tapering tail, firm thighs, well-propor-
tioned genitals, proper legs and hoofs, and a ringing voice.]

5   τῇ χρόᾳ δὲ καλοὶ οἱ λαμπροὶ καὶ οἱ πορφυρίζοντες καὶ ἐν τῷ
προσώπῳ λευκοὶ καὶ οὐ φαιοί. πάντων δὲ καλλίονες οἱ μέλανες,
καὶ μὴ πολιὰν ἔχοντες τὴν κοιλίαν ἀλλ' ὁμόχρωμον. εἰ δὲ τύχοι   20
τὸ ἐντὸς τοῦ στόματος μέλαν ἔχων καὶ τὴν γλῶσσαν, πρόδηλός
ἐστιν ὅμοια γεννήσων. τοὺς δὲ λευκοφάρους, οὓς καλοῦσι
μάρονας, μὴ παραλαμβάνειν μηδὲ ποιεῖσθαι ἐξ αὐτῶν τὸ
ὀχεῖον. χρόᾳ γὰρ ἄτιμοι ὡς ἐπιτοπολὺ γίνονται ἐκ τούτων.

Hippiatrica 14.1–5

Apsyrtus preserves features of Columella's text in sections two
and five. The adjective εὔχρηστον (line 5) reflects *commodissimum*
(line 1) in its sense, in its construction with an infinitive
complement, and in its commanding first position. Apsyrtus' list of
physical attributes desirable in the stud donkey includes several

mentioned by Columella and retains the order established by Columella: large body (l. 4 *amplissimi corporis*, l. 7 πολὺν τῇ περιοχῇ τοῦ σώματος), sturdy neck (l. 4 *cervice valida*, l. 11 αὐχένα πλατύν), muscular chest (l. 5 *pectore musculoso et vasto*, ll. 11–12 στῆθος . . . στερρόν), brawny upper legs (l. 5 *feminibus lacertosis*, ll. 13–15 ὠμοπλάτας μεγάλας . . . καὶ ἰσχυρά), and black coat (l. 6 *coloris nigri*, l. 19 πάντων . . . οἱ μέλανες) not grey (ll. 6f. *Nam murinus . . .*, ll. 22f. τοὺς δὲ λευκοψάρους . . .). Like Columella, Apsyrtus mentions the animal with spotted mouth and tongue (ll. 9f. *nam quemadmodum . . .*, ll. 20f. εἰ δὲ τύχοι), although he does not attribute the condition to rams nor develop the topic as Columella does.

Throughout this passage, however, Apsyrtus deviates freely from Columella's text. He omits some items in the list of a good donkey's characteristics (ll. 4–5 *robustis ac latis costis*, l. 6 *coloris . . . - vel maculosi*) and adds a great deal of material. On one occasion, he may have borrowed from another section of Columella (ll. 12–13 πρὸς τὸ ὑπομένειν τὰ ὑπὸ τῆς ὀργῆς λακτίσματα explains why a broad chest is a desirable trait in a donkey and may reflect Columella's description of a good donkey's temperament at VII.1.2, *plagarum et penuriae tolerantissimus*). At other times, Apsyrtus adds material either from an unidentified source or from his own experience (ll. 8–11, donkey's head and facial characteristics; l. 15, desirability of widely spaced legs; sections 3–4, general body characteristics, including some already discussed; ll. 18–20 observations on coat color).

Apsyrtus' text departs from Columella's to a greater extent than we have observed in any of the free translations examined so far. The free translation deviated from the original text only to improve and enhance it in the eyes of Greek readers; the free translator recognized and respected the integrity of the work he translated. Apsyrtus, however, has gone much further toward creating a new text. He has organized the material in it according to his own plan, and, citing no sources by name, he has become the ultimate authority for the information he presents in this passage. Portions of his text are in effect translated elements from Columella's work, but the original text has been fragmented to such an extent that its translated parts no longer reflect the Latin literary whole. It is this failure to recognize and respect the integrity of a

Latin source text which separates Apsyrtus from the 'free' translators and, by contrast, more clearly defines the nature of their work.

The fourth-century authority on farming, Vindanius Anatolius of Berytus, demonstrates some acquaintance with Latin literature in the excerpts of his agricultural treatise preserved by the *Geoponica*, a tenth-century Byzantine compendium.[89] Anatolius attributes information twice to Vergil and three times to Varro;[90] however, his versions of the original texts are so vague or so altered in detail that they apparently derive from earlier Greek agricultural writers who cited Vergil and Varro, both of whom were still recognized and respected in the fourth century.[91] Anatolius' chapter on farm craftsmen resembles a section from Varro in its general outlines, although Varro's name is not mentioned.[92] The emphasis of Anatolius' text and its details, however, differ too much from Varro to be considered even a free translation. In Anatolius' agricultural treatise, as in Apsyrtus' veterinary one, Latin literary influence is perceptible and elements of translation may be isolated. In these technical treatises, however, the relationship between Greek text and Latin literary source responds more readily to the investigations of the *Quellenforscher* than to the analyses of the student of translations.

VIII. Problematic translations

There are tantalizing reports which associate fourth-century Greek translations from Latin with the writings of Cyprian, bishop of Carthage, and Athanasius, patriarch of Alexandria. In the case of Cyprian, Rufinus describes how Macedonian heretics circulated examples of Cyprian's letters in Constantinople to support their own views.[93] Although Rufinus does not specify whether these letters circulated in Latin or in Greek translations, Greek versions

---

89. Date discussed by John L. Teall, 'The Byzantine Agricultural Tradition', *Dumbarton Oaks Papers* 25 (1971), 40.

90. R. H. Rodgers, 'Varro and Virgil in the *Geoponica*', *Greek, Roman and Byzantine Studies* 19 (1978), 278–80.

91. Rodgers (n. 90), 278–9, 280.

92. Rodgers (n. 90), 281–2, 283.

93. Rufinus, *De Adulteratione Librorum Origenis* 12.

of several letters do survive.[94] No evidence, however, connects these translations either to the Macedonian heretics or to the fourth century. Bardy's suggestion[95] that Chrysostom quoted briefly from a Greek version of Cyprian rests upon a supposed parallel between the two texts which is too vague to be significant.

Because Athanasius lived and wrote in the West, it seems likely that he himself might have translated the Latin documents which he quotes in Greek.[96] Only circumstantial evidence supports this supposition: Athanasius knew Latin, he presents two different versions of the same document at different points, and he labels a translation 'the best possible'. Nowhere, however, does he admit translating Latin documents into Greek. The translations could be Athanasius' – or they could be official chancery versions. Such an ambiguity places them outside the scope of this study.

Conclusion

The relatively small number of Greek translations discussed here should not lead us to conclude that they represent a rare phenomenon. Scholars in late antiquity and in the Middle Ages apparently did not consider Greek translations from Latin literature particularly unusual, as the case of Gelasius of Caesarea illustrates. The great Byzantine scholar Photius asserts (*Bibliotheca* cod. 89) that Gelasius translated into Greek an original Latin text by Rufinus; Rufinus' text is actually a translation of Gelasius' Greek original.[97] The fact that a medieval scholar who knew ancient literature very well nevertheless committed an error of this sort indicates that a Greek translation from Latin seemed to him a perfectly plausible literary phenomenon. Indeed, the few translations included in this study very likely represent only a part of the

94. For location of these Greek texts, see Hans von Soden, *Die Cyprianische Briefsammlung*, Texte und Untersuchungen 25.3, n.s. 10 (Leipzig 1904), 181, and Dekkers (n. 7), 197.

95. Bardy (n. 4), 138.

96. Bardy (n. 4), 131, Dekkers (n. 7), 199.

97. The priority of Gelasius' Greek text over Rufinus' Latin one was established by Ernest Honigmann, 'Gélase de Césarée et Rufin d'Aquilée', *Académie royale de Belgique, Bulletin de la classe des lettres et des sciences morales et politiques* 40 (1954), 123–8. Bibliography of the controversy available in Friedhelm Winkelmann, 'Zu einer Edition der Fragmente der Kirchengeschichte des Gelasios von Kaisareia', *Byzantinoslavica* 34 (1973), 193 n. 2.

total output in the fourth century. For purposes of our discussion, we have demanded a double portion of benevolence from tradition and history, because we must possess both the original Latin work and its Greek translation. It is not at all surprising that there are only a few such literary pairs, given the low survival rate of Greek and Latin literature in general.

This group of translations permits us to make several observations about translators and translations from Latin to Greek. The translators whom we know by name (Paeanius, Sophronius, and Eusebius) were not Hellenes from mainland Greece, but rather Greek speakers from the eastern Mediterranean,[98] a cosmopolitan area where Greek culture predominated but influences from other traditions existed as well.[99] Apsyrtus, who knew Latin veterinary literature in some form, and the anonymous Egyptian schoolmasters who translated the juxtalinear texts also belong in this group of Greek speakers from outside Greece proper who were eager to promulgate Latin literature. The translations themselves demonstrate that the translators attained a generally high level of proficiency in Latin, although the majority of readers were apparently not interested in studying the Latin language itself, since there are only a few juxtalinear texts in our sample. The range of subject matter and genre selected by translators is broad (poetry, oratory, history, hagiography, theology, law) and suggests that the appeal of Latin literature was not confined to any particular occupational, religious, or ethnic audience, but touched a great variety of groups in the Greek-speaking world – Christians, Roman history buffs, Egyptian compatriots of St Hilarion, etc. The presence of Latin culture in the Greek world was clearly more extensive and varied than modern views of Graeco-Roman cultural relations have traditionally allowed.

These translations enable us to characterize in terms of ancient practice the two styles of translation recognized in antiquity – *verbum e verbo* and *sensum de sensu*. The *verbum e verbo* style performed two

98. Paeanius was a native of Antioch (A. H. M. Jones, J. R. Martindale, and J. Morris, *Prosopography of the Later Roman Empire*, vol. I A.D. 260–395 [Cambridge 1971], *s.v. Paeanius*); Sophronius apparently came from Egypt (Van den Ven (n. 57), 140–1); Eusebius was a native of Caesarea in Palestine (Karl Bihlmeyer and Hermann Tüchle, *Church History* I, trans. Victor E. Mills [Westminster, Md. 1958], §75.1).

99. This point has been made by Dekkers (n. 7), 227.

distinct functions. In the juxtalinear teaching translations, the exact equivalence between Latin and Greek words provided a grammatical explanation of the Latin text for the Greek-speaking student. In the remaining literal translations (Paeanius' line from the *Aeneid*, Eusebius' Edict of Toleration, and the anonymous *Apologeticus* quoted by Eusebius), the *verbum e verbo* style enabled the translator to preserve the very words of a highly revered text uncontaminated by translator's explanation or expansion. These three texts deserved such respectful treatment for various reasons: the Edict was associated with the Emperor Constantine and the Roman State, the *Aeneid* occupied an important place in Roman literary and imperial tradition, and the author of the *Apologeticus*, Tertullian, was a prominent Father of the Church. Eusebius' care in quoting the *Apologeticus* translation exactly, including its errors, suggests that he regarded this *verbum e verbo* translation with the same respect which the original Latin text of Tertullian would have commanded. The translator who chose the literal style expressed his own reverence for the original work and may have found his translation regarded with similar respect by his audience. Although the *verbum e verbo* style required the translator to adhere strictly to the original text, there was still some room for creativity. The juxtalinear Vergil translation on parchment and Eusebius' translation of the Edict of Toleration incorporate niceties of style and of vocabulary choice which distinguish them as works of literature in their own right.

In the *sensum de sensu* translation, the creative translator comes into his own. To Paeanius and Sophronius, translating *sensum de sensu* meant providing a virtual exegesis of the original text, tailored to the needs, interests, and aesthetic standards of a cultivated Greek-speaking audience. These 'exegetical' translations are almost – but not quite – new literary creations. They comprehend the integrity of the original Latin work and depart from its pattern only to make changes which the translator sees as improvements. In contrast, Apsyrtus' *Hippiatrica* plunders a Latin text and displays the spoils in a new literary context of the translator's own making.

The *Fourth Eclogue* translation shares characteristics with both the *verbum e verbo* and *sensum de sensu* styles. Like the *verbum e verbo* translations, it remains very close to the sequence of ideas and even to the sentence structure of the original text; its elegant vocabulary is typical of an 'artistic' literal translation like Eusebius' Edict and the juxtalinear Vergil parchment. Like the *sensum de sensu* translations, however, the Eclogue translation appeals deliberately to the literary tastes of its Greek audience because it is in meter. The translator achieves the most striking feature of *sensum de sensu* translation, its exegetical character, by very subtle means; he redefines and refocuses the original, rather than adding phrases or whole passages as Paeanius and Sophronius do. The Eclogue translator's ambivalent approach, both *verbum e verbo* and *sensum de sensu*, is the key to understanding his intention. Because the translator seems to work *verbum e verbo*, he fosters the illusion of approaching the original Latin text while in reality producing a thorough-going exegesis of that original. The Greek *Fourth Eclogue* encompasses the standards both of literal and of exegetical translation. It provides a striking demonstration of how a skillful translator wielded the tools of his trade.

The empress and the poet: paganism and politics at the court of Theodosius II

ALAN CAMERON

The names of the poet Cyrus and the Empress Eudocia have always tended to be linked. They were indeed the two most celebrated poets of the court of Theodosius II – and its two most conspicuous political casualties. In the past their fall has generally been seen as the collapse of a movement to liberalize the increasingly intolerant Christian culture of the age. This paper offers an alternative interpretation, beginning with the career and personality of Cyrus.

I. Panopolis

Like so many Greek poets of the fourth and fifth centuries of our era, Fl. Taurus Seleucus Cyrus Hierax (to give him his recently discovered full name) was not born at one of the traditional cultural centres of the Graeco-Roman world, but in Upper Egypt.[1] His home town was Panopolis. Cyrus was indeed by no means the first or last poet to be produced in such a seemingly unpromising spot. The most famous of his fellow townsmen, and an approximate contemporary of Cyrus,[2] was the remarkable Nonnus, perhaps the most influential Greek poet since Callimachus. The wily Pamprepius, philosopher, magician and adventurer as well as poet, was born there on 29 September 440,[3] just

1. For a useful collection of the sources see O. Seeck, *RE* xii, 188–90 – though he was not justified in identifying the Cyrus of 'Antiopolis' mentioned by Photius (*Bibl.* cod. 279, p. 536a Bekker) with our Cyrus. The corrupt place name points to Antinoopolis or Antaeopolis rather than Panopolis, and the context in Photius suggests a fourth-century writer (cf. *CQ* (1970) 120, and T. Viljamaa, *Studies in Greek Encomiastic Poetry of the Early Byzantine Period* (*Comm. Hum. Litt. Soc. Sci. Fenn.* 42.4, 1968), 30). Most of the literature since Seeck is quoted in D. J. Constantelos' (inaccurate and uncritical) study 'Kyros Panopolites, Rebuilder of Constantinople', *GRBS* 12 (1971), 451–64, and see too now T. E. Gregory, 'The Remarkable Christmas Homily of Kyros Panopolites', *GRBS* 16 (1975), 317–24, and G. Dagron, *Naissance d'une capitale* (Paris 1974), 267–72, 315–16. The first three names were revealed by the inscription published in *Jahres. Akad. Wien* 44 (1959), Beibl. 283–4; the last by an unpublished Vienna papyrus kindly shown me by R. S. Bagnall and K. A. Worp. See now *PLRE* ii, Cyrus 7, pp. 336–9.

2. See below, p. 235–9.

3. The precision thanks to his horoscope, identified by A. Delatte, *Bull. de la Classe des Lettres de l'Académie de Belgique* 9 (1923), 58f., cf. Keydell, *RE* xviii.3, 408f.

three months before Cyrus entered upon his consulship. About a century earlier the poet and grammarian Horapollon was born at Phenebith, a village in the nome of Panopolis.[4] And it was somewhere in the Panopolite nome, it seems, that Triphiodorus was born, rather earlier still.[5] And though the prolific and widely travelled Anastasian poet Christodorus came from Coptus himself, his family too seems to have originated in Panopolis.[6] From the general area we may add Andronicus of Hermupolis[7] and Olympiodorus of Thebes, better known now as a historian and diplomat, though on his own description a 'poet by profession'.[8] Poetry had seldom been so profitable as in the early Byzantine world,[9] and no doubt there were dozens of lesser Panopolitans, unknown to us, who followed in the footsteps of such luminaries, travelling from city to city in the search for fame and fortune.

The names of two such men have been rescued for us on a papyrus newly published by Gerald M. Browne.[10] It is a petition addressed to the Catholicus of Egypt by one Aurelius Ammon, a scholasticus of Panopolis and son of a local priest, concerning some

See also E. Livrea, 'Pamprepio ed il. *P. Vindob.* 29788 AC', *ZPE* 25 (1977), 121–34, and R. C. McCail, *JHS* 98 (1978), 38–63, arguing that Heitsch xxxv.1 dates from 479.

4. See my entry in *PLRE* I.

5. Keydell, *RE* vii.A.1, 178. The startling discovery of *P. Oxy* 2946 shows that Triphiodorus wrote in the fourth or even third century, and not after Nonnus as had been previously assumed (see my *Claudian* (Oxford 1970), 478–82). He bears one of the theophoric names (after the goddess Triphis) 'strictement localisés à Panopolis et dans ses environs immédiats' (V. Martin, 'Relève topographique des immeubles d'une metropole', *Recherches de Papyrologie* 2 (1962), at p. 60).

6. His father was called Paniscus, another theophoric name localized at Panopolis: V. Martin, *l.c.* For another Paniscus from Panopolis see G. M. Browne (cited n. 10 below), p. 192.

7. *PLRE* I, *s.v.*

8. *PLRE* II, *s.v.*

9. For a collection of material on poetry as a profession and its professionals at this period, see my 'Wandering Poets', *Historia* 14 (1965), 470–509. Add the poet/doctor Heraclides of Egyptian Memphis and the poet/teacher Cleobulus, another Egyptian, both correspondents of Libanius (*PLRE* I, 215–16, 418). See too D. T. Runia, *Historia* 28 (1979), 254–6.

10. 'Harpocration Panegyrista', *Illinois Classical Studies* 2 (1977), 184–96. I am most grateful to Dr Browne for showing me this important document before publication. It is exciting to know that it is only the first of a small archive of documents relating to Ammon and his family, to be published by Browne, L. Loenen, J. F. Oates and W. H. Willis: see already Willis, *ICS* 3 (1978), 140–51, and *Actes du XVe congrès de Papyrologie*, Brussels 1977 (1978).

slaves of his brother Aurelius Harpocration, a travelling panegyrist, and his nephew (son of another brother) 'Apollo the poet'. Ammon refers to his brother's wanderings 'from place to place, from Greece to Rome and from Rome to Constantinople, having gone round most of the world from one city to another telling of the victories of our triumphant emperors and everywhere performing his royal panegyrics', adding that he 'managed the affairs in the illustrious cities of Greece'. Ammon's description does not make it quite clear whether, like his nephew, his brother was a poet rather than just a rhetor, though in view of the dominance of the poetic panegyric in fourth- and fifth-century Egypt this seems likely. An earlier letter, shortly to be published by William H. Willis, claims that Harpocration 'dined daily' with the emperor. The obvious temptation to identify him with the Egyptian poet and rhetor Harpocration known to Libanius, another traveller who had worked for a while in Constantinople, has to be resisted. Libanius' correspondent was still alive in 363,[11] whereas Ammon's brother was evidently dead by the date of his petition, 9 December 348. Harpocration is a widespread Egyptian name, but we ought not perhaps to rule out the possibility that the two poets were related, in which case both might have been Panopolitans.

No less worthy of our attention is one humbler figure who returned to his native city after his wanderings: a certain Ptolemagrius, who had once served 'in the wars of Caesar' and in his old age threw open to the public his gardens in Panopolis, perhaps some sort of religious foundation. Here he placed (at least) two decorated pillars, covered all over with a curious series of Greek poems in a variety of metres.[12] Schubart and Wilcken dated them to the second or third century A.D., Milne and Wilhelm to the reign of Augustus. Whether the poet be Ptolemagrius himself or a professional hack, 'some dim forerunner of Nonnus in the town',[13]

11. *PLRE* I, *s.v.*

12. C. B. Welles, 'The Garden of Ptolemagrius at Panopolis', *TAPA* 77 (1946), 192–206, and (with an important regrouping of the fragments) A. Wilhelm, 'Die Gedichte des Ptolemagrios aus Panopolis', *Anz. Österr. Akad. d. Wiss., phil.-hist. kl.* (1948), no. 22, 301–26; see too now E. Bernand, *Inscriptions métriques de l'Egypte gréco-romaine* (Paris 1969), no. 114, and (criticizing Bernand and offering a new text) W. Peek, *ZPE* 10 (1973), 239–45.

13. Welles, p. 196, and Peek, p. 244, are for the hired poet, but Wilhelm, p. 326, argues that the highly personal tone of the poems points strongly to Ptolemagrius himself as the author.

here we have Greek verse (reasonably correct if somewhat homely in tone) being written in Panopolis, for a local audience, perhaps as early as the first century of our era. Earlier still, in the fifth century B.C., Panopolis (then Chemmis) had been singled out by Herodotus[14] as the only city in Egypt prepared to adopt Greek customs (this, he was told, was because Perseus was born there).

It is clear that by the fourth century Panopolis must have become something of a centre of Greek culture. There is good reason to believe that a number of important 'wandering' papyri were found at or near Panopolis, notably the Bodmer codex containing Menander's *Aspis, Dyscolus* and *Samia*.[15] There must have been good schools, good libraries, and (above all) traditions in which a Greek poet could take legitimate pride. No doubt many of our band would have echoed the proud boast ascribed to Nonnus in the following epigram, probably designed for the title page of a copy of his *Dionysiaca:*[16]

Νόννος ἐγώ· Πανὸς μὲν ἐμὴ πόλις· ἐν Φαρίῃ δὲ
ἔγχεϊ φωνήεντι γονὰς ἤμησα Γιγάντων.

I am Nonnus; Panopolis was my native city; but it was in Alexandria that I mowed down the crop of Giants with speaking sword.

There may well be much truth in Browne's claim that 'Being a center of Hellenic culture, Panopolis was also the focal point of pagan intellectual reaction against Christianity.'[17] A generation after Cyrus we find two most militant pagans in Pamprepius and – until his conversion – Horapollon. But the 'hellenic' traditions of Panopolis are not the whole story. It was also a deeply Christian city, a city of monks and saints. Just across the Nile stood the White Monastery, presided over for so many years by the redoubtable Shenoute. If we leave this side of Panopolitan culture out of account, we shall never reach a true understanding of such a characteristically Byzantine personality as Cyrus, poet and courtier, civil servant and builder, bishop and hagiographer. A closer look at his many-sided activity may help to provide an introduction to some of the subtle cultural tensions of his age, tensions

14. Herodotus II.91: see A. B. Lloyd, 'Perseus and Chemmis', *JHS* 89 (1969), 79f.
15. E. G. Turner, *Greek Papyri*[2] (Oxford 1980), 52–3, 201.
16. *AP* ix.198, with A. Wifstrand, *Von Kallimachos zu Nonnos* (Lund 1933), 166–8. 17. *ICS* 2 (1977), 192.

usually submerged in modern works beneath crudely polarized stereotypes, pagan and Christian, 'classical culture' and 'simple piety'.

II. Career

How Cyrus gained his first steps on the ladder we do not know, but it is a fair guess that (as often happened at this period) it was by the recital of an appropriate poem that he first drew attention to himself. We hear that the Empress Eudocia, herself a poetess of modest attainments, admired his work,[18] and we shall be examining below what appears to be a fragment from a panegyric on her husband, the Emperor Theodosius II.

By March 439 (and perhaps as early as 437) he was prefect of Constantinople, and by December 439 praetorian prefect of the East too. The literary sources explicitly confirm the surprising implication of the law codes that he held both prefectures concurrently, an extraordinary (if not, as often claimed, unprecedented) accumulation of offices.[19] At a date unknown he was included in the then very select band of patricians,[20] and finally, in 441, raised to the ordinary consulship.

Despite the sour remark of a later and humbler servant in the *officium* of the praetorian prefecture that 'poetry was all he knew anything about',[21] Cyrus proved to be one of the most efficient, active and popular of Theodosius' ministers. He restored and beautified the city, improved its nocturnal illuminations and completed its fortifications. He was the first praetorian prefect to issue his decrees in Greek, a move which in an age of mushrooming bureaucracy may well have done something to make the administration seem less remote to the Greek-speaking mass of the population.[22] We may readily believe that Theodosius was

18. *Suda*, κ. 2776 (of which more below).

19. See *PLRE* I, *s.v.* Limenius 2.

20. A. H. M. Jones, *Later Roman Empire* III (Oxford 1964), 155 and T. D. Barnes, *Phoenix* 29 (1975), 167–8, both oddly omitting Cyrus (there seems no reason to disbelieve Malalas, p. 361 and the *Suda* entry on this point, both presumably from Priscus).

21. John Lyd., *de magg.* ii.42.

22. See G. Dagron's interesting study 'Aux origines de la civilisation byzantine: Langue de culture et langue d'État', *Revue historique* (1969), 23–56. On the illuminations, see Barry Baldwin, 'Priscus of Panium', *Byzantion* 50 (1980), 45.

displeased (and Cyrus himself embarrassed) when on one occasion the people clamoured all day in the circus: 'Constantine founded the city, but Cyrus has restored it'.[23]

In Cyrus' own words, fortune had smiled too brightly on him.[24] In the autumn of 441, at the height of his power and fame, he was suddenly stripped of all his offices and consigned to the inhospitable bishopric of Cotyaeum in Phrygia. Nothing daunted, the resourceful and likeable prefect managed to win over a congregation that had lynched its last four bishops, and ruled his see in peace and popularity till Theodosius' death in 450, whereupon he retired to Constantinople and lived out his days in good works.

There are four different categories of source for the life of Cyrus:

(1) His poems (§ IV and V).

(2) The near contemporary biography of St Daniel the Stylite (§ X).

(3) The law codes, which supply some firm dates: namely that he was prefect of Constantinople between March 439 and January 440 and praetorian prefect of the East between December 439 and August 441.

(4) What I have called the 'literary' sources, in fact entries in chronicles (only Malalas, the *Paschal Chronicle* and Theophanes have independent value) and the entry for Cyrus in the *Suda* lexicon (κ.2776).

Now there are a number of close parallels in both content and language between these chronicle and *Suda* entries (note particularly the mistaken claim of both Malalas and *Chron. Pasch.* that Cyrus held both prefectures for four years), and there can be little doubt that they derive ultimately from a well-informed common source. The only detailed account of this period is the history of Cyrus' younger contemporary Priscus of Panium, described by Bury as 'the ablest Roman historian between Ammianus and Procopius'.[25] And the Paschal Chronicler happens explicitly to name 'Priscus the Thracian' as his authority for Cyrus.

It would not be profitable to analyse these versions in detail, but it should be observed that, where they differ, it is the *Suda* entry

23. Dagron, *Naissance d'une capitale*, 315.

24. οὐκ ἀρέσκει μοι τύχη πολλὰ γελῶσα (Malalas, p. 361).

25. J. B. Bury, *Later Roman Empire* II[2] (London 1923), 418: in general see now the brief characterization in H. Hunger, *Die Hochsprachliche profane Literatur der Byzantiner* (Munich 1978), 282–4; *PLRE* II, p. 906; Baldwin (n. 22), 18–61.

that should be presumed to reflect the original text of Priscus more faithfully. For the chroniclers abbreviate, embellish and all too often garble their sources, the later compounding the errors of the earlier, whereas historical entries in the *Suda* are normally copied direct from the excerpts from the original texts made under Constantine Porphyrogenitus.

The point may neatly be illustrated by the variations for the name of Cyrus' bishopric. Malalas (and *Suda* Θ.145, copied directly from him) gives Cotyaeum, whereas the *Paschal Chronicle*, Theophanes and later chroniclers give Smyrna.[26] Fortunately we have decisive independent confirmation of Cotyaeum in the *Lives* of both Daniel (§X) and Menas (§IX), not to mention the fact that (as Constantelos pointed out) another man is attested as bishop of Smyrna at the time. But it is clearly wrong to say (with Constantelos and Gregory) that Malalas differed from Priscus. For Malalas no less than the Paschal Chronicler drew (ultimately) from Priscus, and if Priscus had really written the incorrect Smyrna, it is highly improbable that Malalas would have been in a position to correct him – or that the later chroniclers would have reverted to Smyrna. The explanation is surely that Priscus wrote Cotyaeum, which was correctly copied by Malalas, closest in time to Priscus, but somehow misread by the Paschal Chronicler (equally inexplicably, he distorts the name of the Empress Eudocia's father from Leontius to Heracleitus), whose Smyrna infected all the later tradition. Even, it might be added, later texts of Malalas: the Slavonic version[27] not only gives Smyrna but interpolates the gloss 'Smyrna belonged to the eparchate of Lydia under the proconsul of Asia.' In the light of this ultimately total elimination of the true name from the chronicle tradition it is particularly striking (and reassuring) to see that the *Suda* entry for Cyrus (κ.2776) gives Cotyaeum.

Another illustration is provided by the variation over the date and place of Cyrus' death. Both Malalas and the Paschal Chronicler say that he remained in Cotyaeum till his death, the latter dating it to 450. We now know from the *Life of Daniel* that in

26. In future I shall not give individual references for chronicle entries that can easily be located under the appropriate year in the standard edition.

27. *Chronicle of John Malalas, Books viii to xviii*, translated by M. Spinka and G. Downey (Chicago 1940), 83.

450 Cyrus resigned his bishopric and returned to Constantinople, where he lived till the reign of Leo. It is hardly credible that Priscus could have been so misinformed about so celebrated a resident of the capital during his own lifetime as to kill him off in Phrygia 20 years too soon. And if we look carefully at *Suda* κ.2776, we find that it says that Cyrus went to Cotyaeum and 'lived on' (παρέτεινε) till the reign of Leo. We need not assume that Priscus placed his death *in* Cotyaeum, but it is easy to see how the false assumption came to be made. The question of the mistaken date must be postponed till the wider discussion of the chronology of Cyrus' fall in §XI.

One last shortcoming of the chronicles. According to Malalas (and again *Suda* Θ.145), Cyrus 'succeeded to the power' of the eunuch chamberlain Antiochus and was himself succeeded by another eunuch chamberlain, Chrysaphius. Lippold[28] was prepared to prolong Antiochus' hold on power (which dated from Arcadius' death in 408) right up to Cyrus' rise *ca* 439, but this seems incredible in itself, and the more so since our other sources place his deposition 20 or more years earlier, connecting it either with Pulcheria's assumption of power in 414 (of which more below) or Theodosius' marriage to Eudocia in 421. *PLRE* accepts that the city prefect Cyrus addressed in a law of 426 (*CTh* ii.7.5) is our Cyrus, and by implication connects this appointment with Antiochus' fall 'in the 420s'. But even granting him the prefecture, the word Malalas uses is δυναστεία, which in the context clearly means supreme power rather than just high office, and Cyrus certainly did not rise to supreme power in the 420s.

The explanation is simple. Insufficient notice has been taken of the peculiar character of this part of Malalas' account of the reign of Theodosius II. Just like the long, timeless section on the Empress Eudocia (§XII), this section does not even purport to offer a consecutive narrative: it is merely an enumeration of the 'favourite ministers' who dominated the weak emperor throughout his reign, namely Antiochus (408–414/21), Cyrus (439–41) and Chrysaphius (441–50). As we shall see later, there was no all-powerful favourite during the long ascendancy of Pulcheria (from *ca* 414 to the rise of Cyrus), but, given the limited purpose of this chapter, Malalas did not feel obliged (if he noticed) to comment on the gap in his sequence.

28. *RE* Suppl. XIII (1972), 154.

So there is no evidence here to warrant dating Cyrus' rise to power earlier than the late 430s (as the law codes imply). Since he lived till *ca* 470, he would have been exceptionally young for the city prefecture in 426, and the long hiatus before his next tenure would be surprising. We must surely either correct the date of the law (e.g. from Theodosius' XII consulship, 426, to his XVII, 439), or conclude that it is a different Cyrus.

III. Works

To the circumstances and causes of Cyrus' dramatic fall we shall return in §§V and XI. Let us first take a look at his poetry, in the judgment of contemporaries his chief title to fame. Even a hostile critic had to admit that it was still being read with admiration a century after his death, and Evagrius brackets him with Claudian. As late as the tenth century he was still remembered as 'the great poet'.[29] But virtually none of the abundant contemporary poetry of the fourth to sixth centuries has survived, and Cyrus was no luckier than the rest.

The few fragments and trifles that have come down to us are no sufficient basis for fair criticism. We do not even have any titles for his major poems, though it is reasonable to conjecture that they were mostly panegyrics on Theodosius and Eudocia, epithalamia and the like on lesser members of the court, epics on the emperor's wars, and perhaps the odd mythological poem (though a purely mythological poem might have stood a better chance of survival, to judge from the preservation of such works by Triphiodorus, Nonnus, Colluthus and Musaeus).[30] In short, a Greek Claudian. It is in fact paradoxical that, when Claudian is the unique Latin example of a veritable school of Greek contemporary poets, we have no single complete Greek 'original' with whom to compare him. At the very lowest estimate, Cyrus' poems would surely have cast a flood of light on the intrigues of Theodosius' court.

There are seven poems in the Anthology ascribed to a Cyrus: *AP* vii.557; ix.136; ix.623; ix.808–9; ix.813; xv.9. Editors have assumed

29. John Lyd., *de magg.* ii.42; Evagrius, *HE* i.19 (with my Claudian, 7f.); lemma to *AP* ix.136.

30. On the repertoire of the professional poet see *Historia* 14 (1965), 477–84.

that all are by Cyrus of Panopolis. It seems to me virtually demonstrable that only two are likely to be from his pen.

The only two that could plausibly have been referred to Cyrus of Panopolis had they been transmitted anonymously are xv.9 and ix.136. They are ascribed in *AP* to 'Cyrus the poet' and 'Cyrus the ex-consul' (ἀπὸ ὑπάτων), as is ix.813 in *APl* (anon. in *AP*). Now one of the trickiest problems to confront the scholars who (by their lights) laboured hard to ascribe the several thousand poems of the *Anthology* to their rightful authors was that so many bore the same names. If (by our lights) they were often unsuccessful and careless, they did at least do their best to distinguish homonyms. On the face of it, I would suggest, 'Cyrus the poet' and 'Cyrus the ex-consul' are two different poets, as carefully distinguished as one could wish. Cyrus of Panopolis did indeed reach the consulship, but this was by no means his principal or most obvious claim to fame.

We can go further. *AP* ix.813 commemorates a statue of the Empress Sophia, wife of Justin II, *ca* 566/7. If it is correctly referred to Cyrus the ex-consul, then he cannot be Cyrus of Panopolis, who died before the accession of Zeno in 474. Editors are normally chary of accepting Planudean ascriptions that conflict with those of *AP*, but (as Gow's careful study has shown), while ascriptions in *AP* are generally speaking more reliable, they are not invariably so.[31] There are many cases where *AP* is incorrect or defective and *APl* preserves a true or plausible ascription.

The modern reader, who sees 813 on the same page of his text of *AP* as 808 and 809, will naturally suspect that it was from 808–9, whether deliberately or through inadvertence, that Planudes took his ascription for 813. The force of this argument is much weakened by the fact that in *APl* the three epigrams are divided up between three separate chapters.[32] In any case why should he have ascribed 813 to this otherwise quite obscure Cyrus but none of the other adjacent late epigrams which he included (e.g. 811, 820–2)? 813 is one of four epigrams (ix.658–9, 812–13) which celebrate the refurbishing of the Great Praetorium by a certain Domninus under Justin II; 658 and 659 are ascribed (in *APl* as well as *AP*) to Paul

31. *The Greek Anthology: Sources and Ascriptions*, Hell. Soc. Suppl. Papers 9 (London 1958).

32. See the indications in Beckby's *app. crit.*, together with his 'Übersicht über die Planudea', IV², 583–5.

the Silentiary and Theaetetus Scholasticus, two of the contributors to Agathias' *Cycle*.[33] One or other of these names would have been a much more obvious guess.

The ascription to Cyrus would in fact have been a very foolish guess for anyone (hardly Planudes) who thought that he was Cyrus of Panopolis (presumably the reason editors have rejected it). Yet it can in fact be shown to be a very plausible ascription nonetheless, for a reason Planudes is unlikely to have worked out for himself. The two remaining poems ascribed to a Cyrus are vii.557 and ix.623.[34] vii.557 occurs in what appears to be a direct excerpt from Agathias' *Cycle* (550–614).[35] It is true that at the beginning of the sequence there is a definite intruder (554, by Philip of Thessalonica), but *prima facie* 557 is the work of a contributor to Agathias' *Cycle*. *AP* ix.623 too occurs in a *Cycle* sequence (ix.614–33). Not so pure an excerpt, it must be admitted,[36] but it would be implausible to insist that in both cases the Cyrus poem was an intruder. And no less implausible to assume (as editors do) that Agathias included poems by Cyrus of Panopolis. His purpose, as he himself describes it in the preface to his history,[37] was to collect together *contemporary* epigrams. None of the known contributors can be shown to have written before the reign of Justinian.[38] In the light of Planudes' ascription for ix.813, we may surely now conclude that Cyrus the ex-consul was a contributor to Agathias' *Cycle* early in the reign of Justin II.

This leaves only ix.136 and xv.9 for Cyrus of Panopolis, to which we may add (on the word of an almost contemporary writer) i.99 (see §X). In addition, there is the possibility (a thin one) that he should be credited with one of the several papyrus fragments of epico-panegyrical poetry from Egypt datable to this period. Viljamaa has recently claimed it as 'probable' that Cyrus wrote the so-called 'Blemyomachia' (Heitsch xxxii).[39] But it would be idle to

33. *JHS* 86 (1966), 21.

34. Both 'Cyrus the poet'. The fact that I shall be assigning both to Cyrus the ex-consul does not affect the distinction in principle between the two poets; it is hardly surprising that they should be confused from time to time.

35. See the analysis in Mattsson, *Untersuchungen zur Epigrammsammlung des Agathias* (Lund 1942), 12 n. 1.

36. Unless all the Agathian poems on baths stood together in the *Cycle*; several are anonymous, which need not prove them un-Agathian.

37. P. 425f. Keydell.

38. *JHS* 86 (1966), 6f.

39. *Greek Encomiastic Poetry*, 49.

pretend that the data at our disposal are more than consistent with such a hypothesis – and barely that if we look a little more closely at our evidence for invasions by the Blemyes. Assuming (which I for one cannot) that the 's.iv/v' date usually allotted the papyrus is precise enough to exclude the invasion of 291,[40] we have a choice between those of 441 and 452[41] (assuming, which we cannot, that there were no others we happen not to have heard of). Now 441, the year of Cyrus' fall, though possible, is rather on the late side for Cyrus, unless both campaign and poem fall early in the year. And though it might seem attractive to identify the general Germanus of C *recto* 75 with the Germanus sent to Africa against the Vandals in 441,[42] in fact this effectively rules him out of a campaign against the Blemyes in the same year. If the identification holds, then the poem more probably refers to the campaign of 452, when Cyrus was otherwise employed in Cotyaeum. Even among poets whose names we happen to know, Ammonius, author of an epic on the fall of Gainas in 438[43] (and from his name probably an Egyptian), is at least as good a candidate. And if we may assume an earlier campaign and perhaps (though not necessarily) a different Germanus, the best candidate of all is certainly Olympiodorus,[44] who is known to have had personal contacts with the Blemyes. The papyrus was actually found in his native Thebes.

IV. Panegyric

We pass (at last) to what little we have of what Cyrus did write. First xv.9, presumably a fragment from a panegyric on Theodosius rather than an independent poem in its own right (as the lemma[45] implies):

πάντα μὲν Αἰακίδαο φέρεις ἀριδείκετα ἔργα
νόσφι χόλου καὶ ἔρωτος·[46] ὀϊστεύεις δ' ἅτε Τεῦκρος,

40. E. Stein, *Histoire du Bas-Empire* I (Bruges 1959), 67.
41. Stein, p. 291 and 352.   42. *PLRE* II, *s.v.* Germanus.
43. See below, p. 255.
44. As recently argued by E. Livrea, 'Chi è l'autore della "Blemyomachia" (P. Berol. 5003)?', *Prometheus* 2 (1976), 97–123, with a full stylistic and metrical analysis. Add now Livrea's commented edition, *Anonymi fortasse Olympiodori Thebani Blemyomachia (P. Berol. 5003)*, Beiträge zur klass. Philol. 101 (1978).
45. ἐγκώμιον εἰς Θεοδόσιον βασιλέα.
46. Perhaps the only place where *Laur.* 32.16 (L) preserves the truth. P has

ἀλλ᾽ οὔ τοι νόθον ἦμαρ· ἔχεις δ᾽ ἐρικυδέα μορφήν
τὴν Ἀγαμεμνονέην, ἀλλ᾽ οὐ φρένας οἶνος ὀρίνει·
ἐς πινυτὴν δ᾽ Ὀδυσῆι δαΐφρονι πᾶν σε ἐΐσκω,
ἀλλὰ κακῶν ἀπάνευθε δόλων· Πυλίου δὲ γέροντος
ἶσον ἀποστάζεις, βασιλεῦ, μελιηδέα φωνήν,
πρὶν χρόνον ἀθρήσεις τριτάτην ψαύοντα γενέθλην.

All the famous deeds of Achilles are yours, except for his wrath and his love; you draw the bow like Teucer, but are no bastard; you have the great beauty of Agamemnon [cf. *Iliad* 3.169], but wine does not disturb your mind; in prudence I liken you to the cunning Odysseus, but without wicked deceit; and, O King, you distil a honey-sweet speech equal to the old man of Pylos [Nestor], before you see Time touching the third generation.

A number of studies have illustrated in detail the debt of Claudian's panegyrics to the precepts of the rhetoricians, and T. Viljamaa has now done the same for what we possess of the Greek contemporary poetry of the period. So it will not be necessary to quote parallel or precept for the extended use of 'favourable comparisons'.[47] Theodosius has all the virtues and none of the vices of the greatest Homeric heroes. More interesting (if no more unusual) to remark the fact that the exempla are drawn exclusively from Homer. Had they been historical they would almost certainly have been drawn from the period before Alexander; no jarring 'modern' note must be allowed to intrude on the 'classical' illusion.[48]

Yet the fact that the exempla are commonplace does not mean they have nothing to tell us. The allusion to Teucer's marksmanship in line 2, for example, can be paralleled by several passages in Claudian, where there is similar emphasis on Honorius' skill with or enthusiasm for the bow or javelin.[49] Hunting was and was long to remain the favorite relaxation of Byzantine emperors.

νόσφι λοχαίου καί, which editors have repaired by omitting the καί. But a 'clandestine love' (on Scyros) is hardly Achilles' greatest flaw, and one need only consult *LSJ s.v.* λοχαῖος 1 to see how poorly attested this meaning is. L's χόλου καί (not even mentioned by Buffière) not only introduces the notorious wrath; we can now see where P's καί came from as well as its λοχαίου; λοχαίου is an almost perfect anagram of χόλου καί, a sort of copying error very fully documented (on the Latin side) by Housman, *Manilius* i, liv f. Having done this, the scribe then wrote the καί again properly in its proper place.

47. Viljamaa, *Greek Encomiastic Poetry*, 115–16, commenting on this poem.
48. Cf. *Claudian*, 356.   49. *Nupt. Hom.* 5f.; *Fex. Hon.* i.13f.

The concluding comparison, with Nestor, can again be paralleled from Claudian, who does his best to claim for the wretched Honorius the eloquence that was so important in the Byzantine world.[50] But there is something more solid here as well. Theodosius is said to be like Nestor in eloquence but not in years. Not to have seen 'time touching the third generation' surely means not to have yet had grandchildren. Now Theodosius' only surviving daughter Eudoxia (born in 422) celebrated a long-planned match with Valentinian III on October 29, 437. Their first child, Eudocia, was born in 438, their second, Placidia, in 439 or 440.[51] How could Cyrus have made his remark about three generations *after* the birth of Eudocia – or indeed after the marriage, for people would have started to think in terms of grandchildren from that moment?[52]

It might be argued that Cyrus' words need not have been intended to refer directly to a third generation in Theodosius' family; Homer's words on Nestor, which Cyrus must have had in mind, do not actually specify his own grandchildren:

τῷ δ' ἤδη δύο μὲν γενεαὶ μερόπων ἀνθρώπων
ἐφθίαθ', οἳ οἱ πρόσθεν ἅμα τράφεν ἠδ' ἐγένοντο
ἐν Πύλῳ ἠγαθέῃ, μετὰ δὲ τριτάτοισιν ἄνασσεν.

A. 250–2

Even so, it is hard to believe that Cyrus would have gone out of his way to emphasize the emperor's youth in precisely this way if time had in fact already touched the third generation in his own family. If he had wanted to compliment Theodosius on his youth, he could easily have done so in a different way (so young to be a grandfather ...). I suggest then that Cyrus' panegyric was written a year or so (at least) before the marriage; *ca* 435, perhaps. That is to say well before his rise to fame and high office.

V. Bucolic

AP ix.36, once more presumably a fragment (though with such an unusual poem it is difficult to be sure):

50. Cf. *Claudian*, 385–6.
51. Bury, *LRE* I[2], 251.
52. As illustrated, for example, by Claudian's Epithalamium on Honorius and Maria: cf. *Claudian*, 100–1.

αἴθε πατήρ με δίδαξε⁵³ δασύτριχα μῆλα νομεύειν,
ὡς κεν ὑπὸ πτελέῃσι καθήμενος ἢ ὑπὸ πέτρης⁵⁴
συρίσδων καλάμοισιν ἐμὰς τέρπεσκον ἀνίας.
Πιερίδες, φεύγωμεν ἐϋκτιμένην πόλιν, ἄλλην
πατρίδα μαστεύσωμεν· ἀπαγγελέω δ' ἄρα πᾶσιν,
ὡς ὀλοοὶ κηφῆνες ἐδηλήσαντο μελίσσας.

Would that my father had taught me to pasture shaggy flocks, so that, sitting beneath the elms or a rock blowing on my pipes, I might beguile my cares. Muses, let us flee this well-built city, let us seek another land; I say to you all, that the baneful drones have destroyed the bees.

The lemma tells us that this is a lament (θρῆνος) of 'the great poet' when he was about to leave the city in exile, a lament addressed 'to the gate of the acropolis' (the latter detail, which can hardly have been invented, presumably derives from a source independent of the poem as we have it).⁵⁵ If we are to believe this, Cyrus declaimed these lines publicly before leaving Constantinople in 441. But they are more than just a lament.⁵⁶

In the first place, while it is certainly not true bucolic, whether in dialect or style, there is an unmistakable bucolic flavour to the poem. This is the more interesting in that (excluding drama) pastoral is the one major Hellenistic genre that is conspicuous by its absence in early Byzantine times. The only comparable work known to me is another 'epigram' in the *Anthology*, ix.361, in fact a 24-line hexameter description of spring, ending:

εἰ δὲ φυτῶν χαίρουσι κόμαι, καὶ γαῖα τέθηλεν,
συρίσδει δὲ νομεύς, καὶ τέρπεται εὔκομα μῆλα,
καὶ ναῦται πλώουσι, Διώνυσος δὲ χορεύει,
καὶ μέλπει πετεεινά, καὶ ὠδίνουσι μέλισσαι,⁵⁷
πῶς οὐ χρὴ καὶ ἀοιδὸν ἐν εἴαρι καλὸν ἀεῖσαι;

If the foliage of plants rejoices, and the earth flourishes, and the shepherd

---

53. μ' ἐδίδαξε, P and Plan: I think it more likely that Cyrus avoided the elision, as did Nonnus in the two passages (*Dion.* xvi.321 and xx.372) discussed below. P. Waltz (Budé ed. *ad loc.*) very rashly 'corrects' both Nonnus passages to μ' ἐδίδαξε.

54. πέτρης P, πέτραις Plan.

55. For the Acropolis of Constantinople, Janin, *Constantinople byzantine*² (Paris 1964), 304–5.

56. On the rhetorical lament in late poetry, see Viljamaa, pp. 118f.

57. The metaphor is explained (significantly enough a fifth-century poet) by Christodorus, *AP* ii.343, where a μέλισσα is described as κηρίον ὠδίνουσα μελισταγές.

pipes, and the fleecy flocks disport themselves, and sailors sail, and Dionysus dances, and the birds sing, and the bees bring forth, how should a singer too not sing beautifully in the spring?

The poem is ascribed in *AP* to Meleager, and though there are still scholars who cite it as the work of the anthologist from Gadara, there can be no doubt that Gow and Page were correct to omit it from their edition of his *Garland*.[58] Wifstrand had already pointed out the features in style and treatment that indicate a late imperial date.[59] Wilamowitz once casually ascribed the poem to Cyrus;[60] hardly a suggestion to be taken seriously,[61] but a fine example of that uncanny flair of his which, even when it overshot the mark, at least pointed in the right direction. The same sort of generally bucolic theme in a generally un-bucolic style. Most of the poem is in fact a rhetorical description having more in common with Pamprepius' *Description of a Spring Day*[62] than with Theocritus.

What then is the inspiration of Cyrus' poem? Vergil's *Eclogues*, according to Beckby and G. Luck.[63] Taken by themselves, the parallels they cite are hardly sufficient to establish their case. For example, Beckby cites *Ecl.* x.35–6, when Theocritus vii.86f.,[64] unquestionably Vergil's source, is actually closer to Cyrus' words – though not nearly so close as two passages of Nonnus. Whether Cyrus copied Nonnus or Nonnus Cyrus (see below), for the main form of the line it is certainly Theocritus rather than

---

58. *Hellenistic Epigrams* II (Cambridge 1965), 593, without comment.

59. *Von Kallimachos zu Nonnos* (1933), 168–9 (not quoted by Gow and Page).

60. As quoted by Knaach, in Susemihl, *Gesch. d. griech. Literatur in der Alexandrinerzeit* II (Leipzig 1892), 559 (cf. Wifstrand, *Von Kall.*, 168 n. 2).

61. There seems no good reason to doubt that the author's name was Meleager. The lemmatist who supplied this name can hardly have been intending a serious ascription to the famous Meleager, and (*pace* Stadtmueller) a mechanical corruption seems very unlikely.

62. So after all, it seems, the poem should be called; Maas' attempt to set the scene in autumn (supported by Wifstrand, *Von Kall.*, 191–3, and accepted by Heitsch) is probably mistaken: see Alan Griffiths, 'Alcman's Partheneion', *Quad. Urbin.* 14 (1972), 17 n. 29. Against, however, see Livrea, *ZPE* 25 (1977), 124–5.

63. See Luck (reviewing Beckby) in *Gnomon* (1961), 781.

64. '*atque utinam ex vobis unus vestrique fuissem/ aut custos gregis . . .*'/ αἴθ᾽ ἐπ᾽ ἐμεῦ ϳωοῖς ἐναρίθμιος ὤφελες ἦμεν/ ὥς τοι ἐγὼν ἐνόμευον ἀν᾽ ὤρεα τὰς καλὰς αἶγας/ . . . τὸ δ᾽ ὑπὸ δρυσὶν ἢ ὑπὸ πεύκαις . . . It is Nonnus who supplies the crucial detail of the father teaching (below).

Vergil that Cyrus had in mind here, for it is thence he derives his δασύτριχα.[65]

Curiously enough, neither Beckby nor Luck adduced the two arguments that lend real plausibility to their suggestion. First, although in the late Republic or early Empire it would be almost unthinkable for a Greek poet even to read, much less imitate a Latin poet, by the late Empire the situation had changed. For the first time Greeks found it necessary to learn Latin for career purposes,[66] and as a consequence some at least gained some knowledge of Latin literature. An ever increasing number of Latin literary papyri are turning up from late Roman Egypt,[67] and it has long been realized that a number of late Greek (especially Egyptian) poets were familiar with Latin poetry.[68] If the case of Quintus of Smyrna is still *sub judice*,[69] Nonnus' debt to Ovid has been put beyond reasonable doubt in a full and acute recent discussion by J. Diggle.[70] Harpocration visited Rome, though we have no means of knowing whether the panegyrics he performed there were in Latin rather than Greek. Claudian was exceptional in that he composed as well as read in both languages.[71]

Olympiodorus too visited Rome, and although there is no evidence that he composed in Latin, he certainly knew the language. He actually quotes a few Latin words in his *History* and, more interesting still, was so impressed by the size of the mansions of the nobility there that he broke out into verse:

εἷς δόμος ἄστυ πέλει· δόμος ἄστεα μύρια κεύθει.

One house is a city; a city conceals many cities.

W. Gernentz duly listed this passage among a series of texts illustrating the material splendour of Rome,[72] but quoted no

65. *Vox propria* of goats in Greek bucolic (correctly restored by Reiske in Simmias, *AP* vi.113.1; 11 times in Nonnus).

66. *Historia*, 14 (1965), 494f.; cf. *Claudian*, 19–21.

67. R. Cavenaile, *Corpus Pap. Lat.* (Wiesbaden 1958), 7–117; cf. *Historia* 14 (1965), 495.

68. *Historia*, *l.c.*, and cf. Barry Baldwin, 'Vergilius graecus', *AJP* 97 (1976), 361–8.

69. F. Vian, *Recherches sur le Posthomerica de Q. de S.* (Paris 1959), 95f., with R. Keydell, *Gnomon* (1961), 278.

70. *Euripides Phaethon* (Cambridge 1970), 180–200.

71. See my *Claudian*, ch. 1 and *passim*.

72. 'Laudes Romae' (diss. Rostock 1918), 50.

parallel for the precise comparison of an aristocratic mansion to a city. There is in fact an exact parallel, Ovid, *Fasti* vi.641–2, on the house of Vedius Pollio:

> urbis opus domus una fuit, spatiumque tenebat
> quo brevius muris oppida multa tenent.

If Nonnus knew and imitated Ovid, why should not Olympiodorus?

Cyrus' decision when praetorian prefect to issue his own rulings and to permit testaments to be made in Greek is hardly likely to reflect a personal unfamiliarity with or dislike of Latin. Given that Greek was the first and in most cases only language of the majority of the population in the Eastern cities, it was inevitable that Latin should gradually retreat before Greek at an official level. Cyrus' measures are only one official stage in a long process.[73]

In principle, then, it is quite reasonable to assume that Cyrus knew Latin. And if he had read any Latin poetry at all, then (as the numerous Vergil papyri confirm) he is bound to have read Vergil. Now the other factor which is Vergilian rather than Theocritean in Cyrus' poem (in fact quite the most interesting thing about it altogether) is his use of the pastoral mode for contemporary political comment.

Cyrus does not even pretend to write as a genuine pastoral poet. He makes it clear that he is a city dweller, who does not so much yearn for the country (as might the pastoral neatherd obliged, like Corydon in *Ecl.* 1, to visit the city) as wish that he had been brought up a countryman instead. He does not envisage country life as a serious possibility for himself, even as an exile, but affects to recognize its virtues. In fact, it is not so much country life he yearns for as the (supposed) ability of the pastoral poet to forget his woes in song (a hint at Cyrus' own woes). Cyrus *is* a poet (cf. the address to the Muses in l. 4), but he cannot use his poetry this way. When he leaves the πατρίς (meaning Constantinople) he has been expelled from, the other πατρίς he must seek is another city, Cotyaeum, not the countryside. And when he calls the city he is

73. Constantelos (*GRBS* 12 (1971), 454) was quite wrong to see Cyrus' influence in the establishment of more Greek than Latin chairs in the 'university' of Constantinople in 425 (further below), long before Cyrus had any influence at the Eastern court. In any case, three rhetors and ten grammarians in Greek in a basically Greek-speaking city is hardly excessive.

leaving ἐϋκτιμένη, 'well-founded', this is more than a stock Homeric epithet for any city; we can hardly doubt that Cyrus' purpose was to evoke his own very substantial contributions to the beautification and fortification of that particular city.[74]

It is surely from Vergil that Cyrus got the idea of using pastoral conventions in this way. This, rather than just the verbal parallels, is why I am prepared with some confidence to derive Cyrus' contrast between the man who is forced to leave his 'native land' in exile and the happy neatherd from *Ecl.* i. 3–5:

> nos *patriae* fines et dulcia linquimus arva:
> nos *patriam* fugimus; tu, Tityre, lentus in umbra
> formosam resonare doces Amaryllida silvas.

Since Cyrus was on the point of leaving to become a bishop, and given the wide currency of the metaphor, it is hard to doubt that the lack of instruction in 'herding flocks' to which line 1 alludes was meant to evoke his new destiny at Cotyaeum.

In the last two lines Cyrus addresses his readers (listeners) directly, cloaking his parting shot in another piece of rustic imagery: the 'bees' are the honest and industrious Cyrus, the 'baneful drones' are those who have ousted him from the emperor's favour, the sinister eunuch chamberlain Chrysaphius and his henchman Nomus, the master of offices. The imagery is carefully chosen. For not only were drones seen as evil parasites from Hesiod on; given the obvious reference here to Chrysaphius, their lack of proper function in the community neatly suggests the eunuch. If Cyrus was writing with Vergil in his mind, then it would be tempting to derives the bees and drones from *Georgic* 4.

But it is the political use of the pastoral mode rather than knowledge of this or that poem of Vergil that matters. Hardly a distinguished but certainly an unusual and sophisticated poem.

VI. Nonnus

P. Friedlaender, in his canonical study on the still controversial date of Nonnus,[75] discussed the technique of Cyrus' verse at some

---

74. It will be remembered that it was to Constantine the founder of the city that the people compared Cyrus in the circus.

75. *Hermes* (1912), 43–59.

length. Cyrus was uninfluenced either by the extravagantly strict metrical practice of Nonnus (note for example the proparoxytone line ending at xv.9.6 and the hiatuses at xv.9.1 and 5)[76] or by the characteristic Nonnian stylistic idiosyncrasies that so haunted his disciples (e.g. the fantastic coinages, the repetitions, the periphrases and use of pregnant nouns as adjectives). Our 2-line fragment from the *Gainea* of Ammonius, recited in 438,[77] likewise contains an un-Nonnian elision. And even a somewhat younger contemporary of Cyrus such as Proclus (410–85) shows no Nonnian influence in his hymns.[78] Eudocia's verse too is 'pre-Nonnian'. By the end of the century, however, there was undoubtedly a veritable Nonnian school (Christodorus, Colluthus, Musaeus, Pamprepius and countless anonymous epigrammatists), a group of poets 'united by an agreement to write by the same striking rules'.[79]

Friedlaender made the rather simplistic assumption that Nonnus could be neatly slotted in between the last datable poet who does not show his influence and the first who does. It was on this basis that he settled on the reign of Anastasius (491–518).

It would now be generally conceded that subsequent papyrus finds point to a terminus nearer 450.[80] If the panegyric on the Athenian grandee Theagenes (Heitsch xxxv.4) is indeed by Pamprepius (as seems probable) then it was presumably written between 473 and 476, during his stay in Athens.

If Keydell's restoration of line 37 of the equally Nonnian Heitsch xxxiv is to be accepted, then that poem too would date from around 470. And since Christodorus' earliest poems can be shown to date from not long after 480,[81] he was perhaps a closer contemporary of Pamprepius than hitherto supposed. R. C. McCail has recently assigned Heitsch xxxv.1 to 479.[82] J. Golega

76. The un-Nonnian correption λοχαίου ἔρωτος at xv.9.2 is removed by L's more acceptable χόλου καὶ (καί *in priore brevi omnes dactyli libere admittunt*, Keydell, *Nonni Dion.* i (Berlin 1959), p. 41*, §18).

77. Friedlaender, *Hermes* (1912), 50.

78. See the useful edition and commentary by E. Vogt (Wiesbaden 1957).

79. Gordon Braden, *The Classics and English Renaissance Poetry* (Yale 1978), 70, in a brilliant study of Musaeus.

80. Between 450 and 470 according to F. Vian, *Nonnos de Panopolis: Les Dionysiaques* i (Paris 1976).

81. As I shall be arguing elsewhere.

82. *JHS* 98 (1978), 38f.–though I have my doubts. I am still inclined to

argued that the ps.-Apollinarian paraphrase of the Psalms, which certainly shows Nonnian influence, was written in the 460s. The case is not watertight but it is plausible.[83] We can hardly rule out the possibility of a new papyrus find that will take us a decade or so earlier still.

There are three other objections to Friedlaender's assumption. First, just because most poets who write after Nonnus succumbed to his hypnotic spell, it does not follow that all did (e.g. Proclus). Second, how long need we allow between the publication of the *Dionysiaca* and the earliest Nonnian disciples? One possibility is that Nonnus himself was the teacher in Panopolis who formed the forerunners of his 'school' in person, in which case no long interval would be required. But although many poets of the age were teachers, the most able and successful (Claudian, Cyrus himself, Olympiodorus, Pamprepius) usually (and understandably) scorned so lowly and unrewarding a profession. If Nonnus was not a teacher (and *AP* ix.180 at least implies that he was living in Alexandria rather than Panopolis when he wrote the *Dion.*), then we need a little longer for his style and metric to establish their sway. Pamprepius, clearly as steeped in Nonnus as any of the later Nonnians, was born in 440 and so learning his craft with the *grammaticus* in the early to mid 450s. I would submit that on our present evidence 450 is about the latest possible date for the *Dionysiaca*. Golega's study of the paraphrase of St John has supplied strong (though not decisive) support for the traditional ascription to Nonnus.[84] Its christology fairly clearly puts it after 431. If

accept that items 3 and 4 in E. Heitsch, *Griech. Dichterfragmente d. röm. Kaiserzeit*[2] (1963), xxxv are by Pamprepius. Viljamaa's attempt to ascribe the poems to Christodorus seems particularly misconceived (*Greek Encomiastic Poetry*, 54–7). If the arguments in favour of Pamprepius are not impregnable, Christodorus is the merest guess. If I had to guess, I should try Colluthus' for xxxv.1 (known by title only, from *Suda s.v.*). It is difficult to see how Viljamaa can find evidence for an *Isaurica* (Christodorus', though Pamprepius wrote one as well) when the Roman enemy named is the Persians (αὐχένα γα[ῦ]ρον Ἄρηος Ἀχαιμεν[ιδ . . .] 1 *recto* 14). I would suggest that πτολίεθρον ἀμ[. . . at *ib.* 22 be restored Ἀμ[ιδαίων . . .], introducing a reference to the recapture of Amida in 505 (Bury, *LRE* ii[2], 14), which, as Anastasius' only success against the Persians, is likely to have featured prominently in Colluthus' poem (known at least to have been written under Anastasius).

83. *Die homerische Psalter* (Ettal 1960), with Keydell in *BZ* 54 (1961), 379–82.

84. *Studien über die Evangeliendichtung des Nonnos von Panopolis* (Breslau 1930); cf. too Keydell, *RE* xvii, 917–20.

Nonnus is the author, it is probably the later of the two works, whether we assume an intervening conversion or merely that the *Dion.* was a product of his less pious youth. If he is not, then we have a further Nonnian poem to fit in before ps.-Apollinarius and Musaeus, both of whom had certainly read it. The *Dion.* surely dates from the second rather than the third quarter of the century.

The third objection is that *contemporaries*, whose own style had already been formed before they read Nonnus, might well not be much influenced by him. Cyrus, born *ca* 400, is surely a contemporary rather than predecessor. It has long been noticed that there is one striking parallel between a poem of Cyrus and Nonnus. With *AP* ix.136.1 (αἴθε πατήρ με δίδαξε . . .) compare *Dion.* xvi.321f. and xx.372f. In the first passage Pan expresses the wish that he too knew how to make wine (so as to get reluctant women drunk, of course):

αἴθε πατήρ με δίδαξε τελεσσιγάμου δόλον οἴνου.

In the second (even closer to Cyrus, whose second line begins ὥς κεν . . .) Lycurgus wishes that he knew about fishing as well as warfare:

αἴθε πατήρ με δίδαξε μετὰ κλόνον ἔργα θαλάσσης,
ὥς κεν ἀεθλεύσοιμι . . .

With Friedlaender, I feel bound to rule out Maas' suggestion of a common bucolic source.[85] It is hard to believe in any such hypothetical poem offering anything as close as the threefold verbal, thematic and structural parallelism between these passages of Cyrus and Nonnus, both prominent poets, on any hypothesis close contemporaries and even fellow-citizens. Whichever was the later of the two may surely be presumed to have read the earlier. Thus the hypothesis of a lost common source is in principle less probable than a direct connection one way or the other between Cyrus and Nonnus.

Friedlaender argued that Cyrus would not have been likely to imitate two not especially striking lines of Nonnus, whereas

85. *Deutsche Literaturzeitung* (1910), 2588. It is in fact now possible to quote an interesting parallel from a poem which cannot from its subject matter be later than its papyrological dating to the third century; Page, *Gr. Lit. Pap.*, 130.22, οὕνεκα κεῖνα πατήρ σε διδάξατο, ταῦτα δὲ Μοῦσαι. Close, but lacking the αἴθε (highly characteristic of Nonnus: see Peek's *Lexicon*, *s.v.*) and the structural parallelism.

Nonnus might be expected to recall the opening of such a highly personal poem of Cyrus. But such questions cannot be decided on grounds of probability. Nor is it decisive that Cyrus shows no other Nonnian influence. Clearly he is not one of those whose style, metric and vocabulary alike were formed on a solid diet of Nonnus in the schoolroom. Suppose, for example, the *Dionysiaca* had appeared in the 420s, when Cyrus was already a fully-fledged and practising poet. We should not expect it to have affected his style as a whole, particularly since he can hardly have had much time for poetry during at any rate the later 430s. What we might expect is the occasional echo, perhaps only in Cyrus' later work. *AP* ix.136 can be placed firmly in autumn 441, and if the latest plausible date for the *Dion.* is *ca* 450, then the priority of Nonnus is more than a serious possibility.

If the ps.-Apollinarian paraphrase of the Psalms does indeed date from the 460s, we would have an interesting parallel. For while it contains a certain number of verbal echoes of Nonnus, it does not show the influence of his metrical innovations, which might be held to suggest that its author (apparently an Egyptian) was, like Cyrus, an approximate contemporary, whose metrical practice had been established before he read Nonnus. There is more than a chance that Cyrus is the earliest extant reader of Nonnus, the first in a long line.

VII. The Christian

In my study 'Wandering Poets' published in 1965, influenced by the undoubted tenacity of paganism among the Egyptian poets of the fourth and fifth centuries, I made the mistake of accepting the allegation of his enemies that Cyrus was a pagan. Soon after, W. E. Kaegi went so far as to call Cyrus a 'pagan philosopher', suggesting that it was not till he reached his bishopric in Phrygia that he was finally forced to accept Christianity.[86] The recent discussion by Constantelos does at least take it for granted that Cyrus was a Christian, but without adequately arguing the point or exploring the relationship between his Christianity and the 'profound

86. 'The Fifth Century Twilight of Byzantine Paganism', *Classica et Mediaevalia* 27 (1968), 266.

attachment to Greek culture' which Constantelos is so concerned to stress.

There are three substantial arguments in favour of Cyrus' Christianity – over and above what must surely be conceded to be the general improbability of a known or even seriously suspected pagan being appointed to a bishopric.

First, there is the celebrated church of the Theotokos that he built in Constantinople. Though not directly attested before the early seventh century, there is no call to doubt Theophylact Simocatta's firm attribution to our Cyrus. To Janin's dossier[87] should be added two epigrams by John Geometres,[88] an eleventh-century writer but a monk of the church and so more likely than most to be well informed. According to the first:

Κῦρος μέν σε δόμησεν, ἔθηκε δὲ κῦρος ἁπάντων,
δεσπότις ἡμετέρη, τῶν ἐπὶ γῆς θαλάμων.
ἔνθεν ἐπορνυμένη Βυζαντίδος ἀμφιπολεύεις
κύκλον ὅλον, χαρίτων νάμασι πληθομένη.

Cyrus built this house for you, Our Lady, and made you supreme over all worldly halls [i.e. other churches]. Rising thence [i.e. from Cyrus' church] you guard the whole circuit of Byzantium, abounding in springs of grace.

The 'whole circuit' of Constantinople that the Virgin is said to patrol must be an allusion to Cyrus' completion of the circuit of the city walls. By the fifth century the fast swelling population of the city had far outgrown the original Constantinian fortifications, and early in the reign of Theodosius II the praetorian prefect Anthemius saw to the construction of new walls about a mile to the

---

87. *Les églises et les monastères*[2], *La géographie ecclésiastique de l'empire byzantin* III.1 (Paris 1969), 193–5; to which add too the story of the advice given to a woman with a sick child there in *Miracula S. Artemii*, 12 (written between 660 and 668), published by A. Papadopoulos-Kerameus, *Varia Graeca Sacra*, *Transactions (Zapiski) of the Historical-Philological Faculty of the University of St. Petersburg* 95 (1909).

88. Cramer, *Anecd. Paris.* IV (Oxford 1839–41), 305, reprinted with no indication of the author in *Anth. Graeca* III (ed. Cougny, 1890), i. 355–6, with some improvements by Piccolos, *Suppl. à l'Anthol. grecque* (Paris 1853), 138. In the second of the two poems P's nonsense word εὐερίην was improved by Piccolos to ἠερίην, a popular word in late epic (e.g. 58 times in Nonnus), yielding a possible though rather trite sense (a ladder to heaven could not but be 'lofty' or 'aerial'). I propose the palaeographically neater and (for the Virgin) more appropriate εὐιέρην, 'very holy', likewise well attested in late poetry (e.g. Paul Sil., *H. Soph.* 143; *Ambo* 175; *Orph. Hy.* 7.2,12; 77.10).

west of the old ones.[89] Anthemius' fortifications were landward only; so long as the Mediterranean remained a Roman lake, what need was there of seaward protection? But the sudden rise of the Vandal navy changed all that (see below), and in 439 Cyrus filled in the seaward gaps in the new city walls.[90]

Eight years later, in 447, the landward walls were severely breached in an earthquake, and, this time under the threat of Hunnic invasion, repaired in record time by the praetorian prefect Constantine.[91] Constantine's activity was commemorated by two epigrams still to be read on the Rhesion gate and by a third from the Xylokerkos gate.[92]

It is not altogether surprising that already in Byzantine times the activity of the two latter prefects was confounded, but less pardonable that the confusion should be perpetuated by modern scholars. It is to be hoped that we have heard the last of the 'Cyrus Constantine' who performed only one operation on the walls, having taken the second name after his 'conversion'.[93] Careful study of the evidence leaves no room for doubt that Anthemius built (in 413) and Constantine repaired (in 447) the land walls, while Cyrus (in 439) completed the two gaps left by Anthemius in the seaward sides of the promontory.

So when our epigram says that the Virgin guards κύκλον ὅλον, this is a very precise allusion to Cyrus' achievement in completing the circuit of the walls. It is interesting to compare the account of *Chron. Pasch., s.a.* 439, where Theodosius is said to have ordered τὰ τείχη κύκλῳ γενέσθαι ἐν ὅλῳ τῷ παραθαλασσίῳ Κωνσταντινοπόλεως.

89. B. Meyer-Plath and A. M. Schneider, *Die Landmauer von Konstantinopel* II (Berlin 1943).

90. Meyer Plath/Schneider II, 152f. There is some evidence that the area enclosed by these walls was originally called Eudocopolis after the empress: D. J. Alexander, *The Oracle of Baalbek* (Washington 1967), 80–2.

91. For the date, Meyer-Plath/Schneider II, 153.

92. *CIL* iii.734 = *ILS* 823; the Greek inscription was included in the *Anthology* as *AP* ix.691, with the reassuringly accurate lemma εἰς πόρταν τοῦ Ῥησίου [Ῥηγίου, less correctly Plan.] ἐν Βυζαντίῳ. See now the full new publication of these and the other inscriptions on the Rhesion gate by I. Ševčenko, *ZRVI* (1970), 1f., with pl. 1.

93. See A. van Millingen, *Byzantine Constantinople* (London 1899), 50. P. Sherrard has recently claimed (*Constantinople* (London 1965), 11) that Cyrus built a triple line of walls in 439 'across the five-mile landward base of the promontory in order to defend the new suburbs' – apparently confusing Cyrus and Anthemius.

The fact that Geometres links the completion of the walls with the Theotokos' protection of the city is not enough in itself to prove that Cyrus did his building in or after 439, but in view of the brief period of his power, it is not likely to have been much before then and cannot have been much after.

Now the dedication of a church to the Theotokos *ca* 439 is not to be interpreted as a casual expression of piety. Cyrus cannot have been unaware of the controversy over the application of the title Theotokos (i.e. 'mother of God', with all that implied, rather than simply 'mother of Christ') to the Virgin that had threatened to split the Eastern church in the early 430s. Nestorius, appointed patriarch of Constantinople in 428, had 'outraged popular piety by emphatically and repeatedly rejecting the term Theotokos',[94] meeting with vigorous opposition from Cyril, the unscrupulous patriarch of Alexandria. The orthodoxy of the term was firmly established by the Council of Ephesus in 431, but the underlying issues remained, to reappear in a different form in what was to be known as the Monophysite controversy. It would be an exaggeration to ascribe actively polemical or partisan aims to Cyrus' foundation. The actual Theotokos issue had been settled decisively enough by the late 430s, and it is not likely that Nestorius had ever had much popular support in Constantinople. Nevertheless, at the very least we can hardly deny that Cyrus took an interest in the great christological controversies of his age. He certainly does not emerge as a 'pagan philosopher', a cultivated intellectual above the petty squabbles that divided the church. Such issues mattered to Cyrus, as they mattered to most Christians of the day, and he made no secret where he stood.

The potent Byzantine motif of the Theotokos as the supernatural protectress of Constantinople does not surface in extant literature before the reign of Heraclius.[95] It might seem natural and prudent to conclude that it was Geometres who imported it into his account of Cyrus' foundation of the 430s. But the idea must have been evolving for some time before, on our fragmentary record, it bursts forth in full flower in the context of the Avar siege of 626, and the fact that a prominent figure like Cyrus built a major

94. W. H. C. Frend, *The Rise of the Monophysite Movement* (Cambridge 1972), 16.
95. See Averil Cameron, 'The Theotokos in Sixth-century Constantinople', *Journal of Theological Studies* 29 (1978), 79–108.

church of the Theotokos *and* fortified the city at a moment of potential danger is just the sort of coincidence that might have provided a stimulus. It is tempting to conjecture that the dedication to the original foundation might already have adumbrated the basic concept: or even that Geometres might have been copying an original dedication by Cyrus himself.

VIII. The Theologian

It was one thing for a busy administrator and man of letters to build churches – but quite another to find himself drafted overnight, and probably for life, to an obscure and dangerous bishopric in Phrygia. He was apparently (and understandably) reluctant to show himself at once to his new congregation, who began to suspect that perhaps he *was* a pagan. Cyrus was in turn doubtless aware of the fate of his last four predecessors. Eventually, on Christmas day 441, he was forced to deliver his first sermon. It was deemed sufficiently remarkable to be preserved in its entirety:[96]

'Brethren, let the birth of God, our saviour, Jesus Christ be honoured by silence, because the Word of God was conceived in the holy Virgin through hearing only. To him be glory for ever and ever. Amen.'

The brevity, not to say impatience of Cyrus' discourse certainly suggests a man who has not altogether warmed to his new role. But they are not the words of an unbeliever, or even of a theological innocent. It would be quite wrong to see here the cynicism of an intellectual contemptuous of theological subtleties. Certainly the people of Cotyaeum did not think so, for they were delighted, and gave Cyrus their blessing.

Brief though it is, Cyrus' sermon is full of interest. In the first place, as one would expect from a champion of the Theotokos, he explicitly calls Christ 'God' at the moment of the incarnation.

Secondly, the entreaty that Christ's birth 'be honoured in silence' (σιωπῇ τιμάσθω) is not an idiosyncratic request by Cyrus, but a direct quotation from the *Monachicus* of Evagrius of Pontus, a collection of sayings for anchorites written in the 380s or 390s.[97] It is perhaps a little surprising to find Cyrus reading a work like this

96. Malalas, p. 361, corrected from Theophanes, p. 97, 11f. I quote Bury's translation (*LRE* 1², 228; cf. too Gregory, *GRBS* (1975), 318).
97. J. Quasten, *Patrology* III (Westminster, Maryland 1960), 169, 172–3.

(of which only a few fragments survive). More probably he learned of this particular saying of Evagrius from the same source as ourselves: Socrates, who quotes it (with approval of Evagrius' common sense) in his *Ecclesiastical History* (iii.7), published, in Constantinople, as recently as 439.[98]

Lastly, the conception of the Virgin 'by hearing alone'. The theory that the Virgin actually conceived Christ *aurally* (i.e. by simply hearing the words of the Holy Ghost) was in Cyrus' day one of the latest attempts to solve an age-old embarrassment. There can be no doubt where he got it:[99] Proclus, archbishop of Constantinople from 437 to 447. Proclus developed the idea in the same way in his sermon against Nestorius of 428 or 429: 'Just as the serpent injected the poison through disobedience (παρακοή), so the Word entered in through obedience (διὰ τῆς ἀκοῆς εἰσελθών) and took upon himself humanity' (*ACO* 1.1.i.103, cf. 107; compare his *Oratio III de incarnatione*, *PG* lxv.708). Here too, as in Cyrus' sermon, the theme is used to emphasize the virtue of passive and expectant acquiescence.

In my own earlier account of Cyrus' first meeting with his flock, unaware of this background, I remarked that they 'were evidently too taken aback to lynch him'. The truth is, of course (as Gregory has pointed out), that the moment Cyrus' congregation heard these words they realized that he was a follower of Proclus and so a safe anti-Nestorian. Indeed, we may go a little further. It was surely less to the innate unruliness of the people of Cotyaeum that his four unlucky predecessors owed their violent ends (or even to the length of their sermons) than to their *Nestorianism*. The trouble here had presumably been a succession of heretic bishops. What we might almost call the folk motif of the jealous king and the wronged minister has so shaped our tradition as to suggest that Cyrus was being sent to certain death, saved only by a desperate display of resourcefulness. In all probability he was never in any serious danger so long as he offered prompt reassurance of his orthodoxy. Proclus himself, as patriarch, will certainly have been consulted about the appointment of a new bishop within his jurisdiction,[100]

---

98. See further below, p. 265f.

99. See Gregory, *GRBS* 16 (1975), 321-4.

100. Jones, *Later Roman Empire* II (1964), 891, quoting an example of the people of Caesarea asking Proclus for a new bishop.

and it is hardly surprising that Cyrus should have been duly prepared and well received.

IX. The Hagiographer

Poet, administrator and finally bishop: Cyrus had always been quick to adapt and exploit challenging new circumstances. It was not long before he discovered what his congregation at Cotyaeum lacked, and, being a literary man, he was able to fill the gap. He gave them a martyr of their very own.

Little is known of the Egyptian saint Menas, martyred (it was said) at Alexandria under Diocletian, and that little is confined to Egypt and Nubia. Or it was, until a curious legend about him was invented, centering (of all places) on Cotyaeum in Phrygia, where he is represented as performing the actions of the soldier martyr St Gordius of Caesarea. The Passion of St Menas is in fact an obvious and total fiction, based on St Basil's *Life* of Gordius.[101] It is not often that one can provide an answer to the questions of date, authorship and motive in the case of a hagiographic fiction like this. The credit for doing so goes to the Bollandist Paul Peeters, who saw that all pointed to Cyrus.[102]

As Peeters observed, it is difficult to deny some connection between the following three facts: (a) One of the earliest cult centres of St Menas in Egypt was at Panopolis, Cyrus' home town. (b) Cyrus became bishop of Cotyaeum 'dans des conditions assez spéciales, qui devaient l'inviter à faire un effort d'imagination'.[103] (c) St Menas was transformed out of the blue into a martyr of Cotyaeum, where he had been until then totally unknown.

So what we want is a Greek-speaking Egyptian who lived in Cotyaeum. Cyrus fits the bill to perfection. Not merely does the versatile ex-poet and prefect now emerge as a hagiographer. We can see that, for all his 'hellenic culture' and theological expertise, for all his worldly success in cosmopolitan Constantinople, with a fashionable church of the Virgin to his credit, Cyrus never forgot the local saint whose legend he had known as a boy back home in

---

101. P. Franchi de' Cavalieri, 'Hagiographica', *Studi e Testi* 19 (Rome 1908).
102. *Le tréfonds oriental de l'hagiographie byzantine*, Subsidia Hagiographica 26 (Brussels 1950), 32f.
103. Peeters, p. 40.

Panopolis. One is reminded of the pillars Ptolemagrius erected in his garden at Panopolis, where, engraved in the Egyptian style above the Greek inscriptions, are a series of Canopic jars, 'representing fourteen of the more notable Egyptian gods and goddesses'.[104]

There is no need in such cases to see 'conflict' or even 'tension' between the two worlds; no need either to talk of a 'thin veneer of hellenism', as though it was in some way less genuine than the local culture. Before as after the victory of Christianity, it was perfectly possible for a man to live in both worlds at once without discomfort. And never more so than in the Byzantine age, when the breakdown by Christianity of the 'internal frontiers between the learned and the vulgar' makes it impossible to draw any sharp distinction between upper and lower class culture. 'In the fourth and fifth centuries', as Momigliano has recently remarked, 'there were of course plenty of beliefs which we historians of the twentieth century would gladly call popular, but the historians of the fourth and fifth centuries never treated any belief as characteristic of the masses and consequently discredited among the élite.'[105] This is very much a feature of Christian rather than pagan culture. We may contrast the pagan neoplatonists of Athens, perpetuating their tiny and exclusive sect by desperate intermarriage between a few families,[106] quite unable (or rather contemptuously unwilling) to communicate their truths to the masses. Not the least remarkable thing about Cyrus, and not the least proof of his unquestioning Christian piety, is that he made a *good* bishop of Cotyaeum, beloved by his flock, able to communicate with them on the same level.

It is characteristic of this 'classless' Christian culture that the dominating figure in the everyday world of Byzantium was, not the Roman governor or the lord of the manor, not even the local bishop, but the holy man, normally a total illiterate but respected equally by all classes alike, from the humblest peasant right up to

104. Welles, *TAPA* 77 (1946), 192–3.

105. A. Momigliano, 'Popular Religious Beliefs and the Late Roman Historians', *Studies in Church History* 8 (1971), 17–18 (= *Quinto contributo alla storia degli studi classici* (Rome 1975)), 92.

106. H. D. Saffrey, *REG* 67 (1954), 297f.; cf. *Proc. Camb. Phil. Soc.* (1969), 20.

the emperor himself.[107] And it is to Cyrus' dealings with one of the most important of all the early Byzantine holy men, Daniel the Stylite, that we fittingly turn to conclude his story.

X. Daniel

The outline is best told in the words of the Anonymous who wrote St Daniel's *Life*:[108]

In the meantime there came to the Saint one Cyrus, an ex-consul and ex-praetorian prefect. He was a very trustworthy and wise man who had passed through all the grades of office owing to his extreme sagacity. But late in life he suffered from a plot hatched by Chrysaphius, the Spatharius, and was sent as bishop to a small town, namely to Cotyaeum in Phrygia, and realizing the treachery of Chrysaphius he yielded so as not to bring his life to a miserable end. After the death of the Emperor Theodosius he divested himself of his priestly dignity and resumed his secular rank and so continued to the end of his life, for he lived till the reign of Leo of most pious memory. He used to distribute all his belongings to the poor. This man Cyrus had a daughter called Alexandria who was afflicted by an evil spirit, and he had brought her to the holy man Daniel when the latter was still at the foot of the hill in the church, and thanks to the intercessions of the archangels and the tears and prayers of the holy man the Lord freed her from the demon within seven days. Consequently from that time forth the two men had a passionate affection for each other (§31).

So when Cyrus came and found that the column had been erected, he enquired who had placed it and hearing that it was Gelanius, the steward at the imperial court, to whom the lands also belonged, at first he was indignant that Daniel should have allowed this to be done by one who had shown him such insolence. 'Should I not far rather have been allowed to do this, if anything else was wanted?' Then the Saint began to beg and beseech him saying, 'All people everywhere proclaim your good will towards me; I accepted this column from Gelanius in order that I might not offend him. The God Whom I serve will recompense you with good things according to your faith.' And after giving him his blessing he dismissed him (§32) . . .

On the following day there happened to come the elder daughter of Cyrus, the eminent man of whom we have already spoken, and she had an evil spirit; and after staying some time in the enclosure she obtained

107. Peter Brown, 'The Rise and Function of the Holy Man in Late Antiquity', *JRS* 91 (1971), 80f.

108. I quote from the version in E. Dawes and N. H. Baynes, *Three Byzantine Saints* (Oxford 1948), made from the text published by H. Delehaye in *Anal. Boll.* 32 (1913), 121–229, reprinted in his *Les Saints Stylites* (Brussels 1923), 1–94.

healing through God. After his daughter had been freed from the demon and returned to her home, the most distinguished man, Cyrus, whom we have often mentioned, came giving thanks to God and to the Saint and asked to be allowed to put an inscription on the column. Though the just man did not wish this to be done, yet being hard pressed by Cyrus and not wishing to grieve him, he allowed him to do it. So he had carved on the column the following lines:

> 'Standing twixt earth and heaven a man you see
> Who fears no gales that all about him fret;
> Daniel his name. Great Simeon's rival he;
> Upon a double column firm his feet are set;
> Ambrosial hunger, bloodless thirst support his frame
> And thus the Virgin Mother's Son he doth proclaim.'

These verses are still inscribed on the column, and thus preserve the memory of the man in whose honour they were written (§36).

Now the *Life* of St Daniel is considerably more authoritative than Cyrus' *Life* of St Menas. Daniel was born in 409 and died after thirty-three years and three months on his pillar, in 493.[109] We may guess that Cyrus was in his late thirties or early forties at the height of his career (the *Life* says his disgrace came 'late', ὀψέ ποτε), which would suggest a date of birth *ca* 400. His second visit to Daniel's pillar took place (as we shall see) in or after 462, which accords perfectly with the general statement that he lived 'till the reign of Leo' (457–74). He probably died somewhere in the region of 470, about 25 years before Daniel. The author of Daniel's *Life* was a younger follower; 'I will put down truthfully', he claimed (§1), 'everything I heard from the men who were the Saint's disciples before me and I will also relate truly all the things I saw with my own eyes.' General considerations of probability combined with the detail and accuracy of his information suggest that he wrote very soon after the Saint's death, that is to say before, perhaps well before 500.[110]

It has not (I think) been pointed out in support of so early a date that §91 must have been written, not only before the death of Anastasius, but probably very early in his long reign (491–518). Daniel apparently prophesied that Zeno's successor would (a) 'turn aside from that love of money which according to the Apostle

109. *Life* §101, with Delehaye, *Anal. Boll.* 32 (1913), 227.
110. So, in general terms, Delehaye, *Anal. Boll.* 32 (1913), 225. It is presumably by mere oversight that H. G. Beck, *Kirche und Theol. Literatur im Byz. Reich* (Munich 1959), 411, assigns the *Life* to the early seventh century.

(I *Tim.* vi.10) is the root of all evil' and (b) 'throughout his reign grant peace and confidence to the most holy churches and to the order of monks'. Now the two reproaches that were to stick most firmly to Anastasius' name were – miser and heretic. In 511 violent protest from the people and monks against his attempted 'monophysitation' of worship in the capital all but cost him his throne, and his removal of the Chalcedonian patriarch Euphemius as early as 496 must have seemed a disturbing sign.[111] Indeed, the so-called Oracle of Baalbek, a recently published apocalyptic work, perhaps written as early as 503, which treats Anastasius' reign as setting off the chain of events that will lead to the end of the world, singles out two shortcomings above all others: his hatred of the poor and his hatred of the godfearing.[112] It is theoretically possible that, when the biographer claims Daniel's prophecies fully borne out in Anastasius, he is being ironic, but this would seem totally out of character. Much simpler to make the reasonable assumption that he put together the great man's life straightaway after his death, when the financial and religious policies of Anastasius still seemed to contrast very favourably with Zeno's.

So the biographer may have written within 30 years of Cyrus' death, able to question people who knew him personally, if not to meet him himself.

It will not be necessary after Delehaye[113] and Baynes[114] to underline the excellence of the abundant historical information contained in the *Life*. It is enough for our present purpose to remark that Cyrus is correctly given as 'ex-consul and ex-prefect', the information about the plot against him is eminently plausible (see §XI), and his bishopric is given as Cotyaeum (with the more reliable branch of the chronicle tradition, confirmed now by the evidence of the *Life* of St Menas), not Smyrna. But we must look

111. See (for example) Bury, *LRE* I², 436f.; P. Charanis, *Church and State in the Later Roman Empire* (Madison 1939), or C. Capizzi, *L'imperatore Anastasio I* (Rome 1969), 100f.

112. P. J. Alexander, *Oracle of Baalbek* 19, with Alexander's excellent commentary (see pp. 83, 95–7, 104) and the few extra remarks in C. Capizzi, 'L'imperatore Anastasio I e la Sibilla Tiburtina', *Orient. Christ. Per.* 36 (1970), 377–406 (with whom I agree that πτωχοί in the passage quoted above means poor in general rather than beggars in particular).

113. *Anal. Boll.* 32 (1913), 225–9.

114. 'The Vita S. Danielis Stylitae', *Engl. Hist. Rev.* 40 (1925), 397–402, and in the notes (pp. 72–84) to Dawes and Baynes, *Three Byzantine Saints* (n. 108).

rather more carefully at the context of Cyrus' two visits to Daniel.

It was in September 460 that Daniel first ascended his first column.[115] Unfortunately he did not bother to ask the permission of the *castrensis* Gelanius, who owned the land where it stood, and Gelanius protested (§27) to the emperor and patriarch (this is the 'insolence', ὕβρις, to which Cyrus alluded in §32). The biographer carefully and correctly notes at this point that Gennadius was now patriarch, since the 'blessed Anatolius [mentioned as patriarch in §17] had already gone to his rest' (Anatolius died in July 458). Gelanius' first attempt to dislodge Daniel was greeted by a miraculous hailstorm that ruined his vineyard, but then, to avoid further awkwardness, Daniel agreed to let Gelanius provide him with a new pillar (whether or not still on Gelanius' land is not stated). It is implied that the whole transaction took only two or three weeks ('the next morning', 27; 'not many days later', 29; 'the following day' . . . 'for a week', 30), and Cyrus' first visit ('in the meantime', 31) took place before the new pillar was ready: presumably then in October or (at latest) November 460. Though it should be noted that this was not the first meeting of the two men. Daniel had already cured Cyrus' daughter Alexandria on some earlier occasion (he had previously spent nine years in a haunted church at the bottom of the hill).

The second visit is dated very firmly to the 'following day' (§31) after a consultation by the princess Eudoxia, freshly returned from Vandal captivity in Africa (§30): that is to say, some time in 462.[116] There is in fact a minor problem here, but first we must turn to the original text of the epigram translated above, p. 248):

Μεσσηγὺς γαίης τε καὶ οὐρανοῦ ἵσταται ἀνήρ,
πάντοθεν ὀρνυμένους οὐ τρομέων ἀνέμους.
λιμῷ δ' ἀμβροσίᾳ τρέφεται καὶ ἀναίμονι δίψῃ,
ἴχνια ῥιζώσας κίονι διχθαδίῳ·
τοὔνομα ⟨μὲν⟩ Δανιήλ, ⟨μεγάλῳ⟩ Συμεῶνι δ' ἐρίξει,
υἱέα κηρύσσων μητρὸς ἀπειρογάμου.

This poem is transmitted (a) anonymously in *AP* (i. 99) and (b) in all three versions of the *Life* of Daniel; that is to say (using Delehaye's *sigla*,[117]) (i) the original text (LVOP), (ii) the epitome

115. Delehaye, p. 227.   116. Bury, *LRE* i², 334.

117. I quote the *sigla* Delehaye used for his edition of 1913 (and 1923), not those of his article 'Une épigramme de l'Anthologie grecque (i, 99)', *REG* 9

(R) and (iii) the metaphrastic reworking (divided into two groups, M and N, according to whether they preserve (M) or omit (N) the first five words of line 1). For the fairly numerous trifling variants and corruptions I refer to the full apparatus compiled by Delehaye. Delehaye.

No one source preserves the poem entire. LORN omit the first five words of line 1. For line 5 MSS have only Συμεῶνι δ' ἐρίξει, Συμεὼν δ' ἐρίξει or (worse) Συμεὼν δὲ ρίξη. It was no doubt a text such as this in his exemplar that caused the scribe of *AP* to omit the whole line, leaving a blank space. It is Delehaye's P alone (*Par. gr.* 1451, s.xi) that preserves as much as τοὔνομα Δανιήλ, Συμεῶνι δ' ἐρίξει. Delehaye's supplements,[118] if not inevitable, are as close as we are likely to come.

The most interesting textual question is the order of the lines. All MSS of the *Life* (except V) give the poem as printed above. *AP* and V[119] (which is probably influenced here by *AP*)[120] alone reverse the order of lines 3 and 5. It is not surprising that all editors of *AP* have loyally stuck to the order of their *codex unicus*; but even Delehaye submitted to the vulgate without question, so that all printed texts of the poem give the lines in the sequence 1,2,5,4,3,6. This seems to me improbable on two quite separate counts. First, on *a priori* grounds. There is no external or internal indication in any MS of the *Life* (except V) that these two lines are out of order. *AP*, on the other hand, altogether omits one of the two. Now is it not easier to see how the scribe of *AP*, while worrying about the defective or missing line in his exemplar, might have come to put his blank line in the wrong place, than to explain why all the many MSS of the *Life* (which cannot, even in the earliest version,[121] be

(1896), 216–24. Waltz and Beckby used only the earlier study, based on a less thorough study of the extant MSS.

118. Suggested to him by T. Reinach (*REG* 9 (1896), 223). E. Kurtz's ἀγαύῳ after ἐρίζει involves a most improbable violation of Hermann's bridge and an unattractive correption for a poet of such reputation and skill.

119. So Delehaye stated in *REG* 9 (1896), 223; his edition is silent on the point.

120. It is commoner than might be imagined for a copyist to check a quotation in his exemplar with another source (see M. L. West, *Textual criticism and Editorial Technique* (Stuttgart 1973), 10–11), especially if it featured in a well-known anthology (*AP* is of the tenth (see *GRBS* 12 (1971), 339f.), V of the twelfth century). My suggestion is supported by the fact that V alone shares with *AP* the obviously correct λιμῷ in l. 3 against the unmetrical trivialization τρόφη of all the other *Life* MSS (see n. 122 below).

121. As Delehaye saw, the four MSS of the 'original' *Life* already diverge so

derived from a common archetype) should have reversed the order of two lines?

The second consideration is the structure of the poem. Line 1 dramatically puts before our eyes a man – unnamed – suspended between earth and heaven; line 2 shows him braving winds from all quarters (vividly described in §§47 and 52–3 of the *Life*); line 4 graphically pictures his feet rooted to the pillar (for the pitiful state of his feet see §§28, 44, 72, 82, 98). What we want between 2 and 4 is another line depicting some further feature of the saint's demeanour or sufferings on the column. In short, line 3 as printed above: 'he is nourished by heavenly hunger and angelic thirst' (that is to say, the hunger and thirst that tormented him did not need satisfying in the ordinary human way).[122] A statement of his name and master (Symeon the Stylite, whose tunic Daniel wore – §§22, 52) seems intrusive in such a context. Nor does the proclamation of Christ seem as closely linked to his hunger and thirst as the participle κηρύσσων ought to imply. On the other hand, after four lines describing the marvel of Daniel's penance, a down to earth conclusion identifying the prodigy and explaining his motives is entirely appropriate and homogeneous: 'his name is Daniel, his model the great Symeon, his purpose to proclaim the son of the Virgin mother'.

Earlier editors were troubled by διχθαδίῳ (l. 4). Hence Boissonade's διχθάδια (with ἴχνια, i.e. both feet).[123] The *Life* has revealed that the text is sound. Daniel's perch was exceptional in

widely from each other that at times they represent two different redactions of even this version.

122. Cf. *Suda*'s excellent gloss: ἀναίμονι δίψῃ· τουτέστιν ἀγγελικῇ· αἷμα γὰρ οὐκ ἔχουσιν οἱ ἄγγελοι, καθὸ οὐδὲ ἐσθίουσι. The ἀπήμονι of *AP* (and one *Life* MS) is a stupid trivialization of what is still a difficult phrase even if this (already Homeric) sense of ἀναίμων is recognized; stupid, because it would be both false and insulting to suggest that any aspect of the terrifying tortures to which Daniel subjected himself was 'painless'. The τρόφη of all *Life* MSS but V (see n. 120) is likewise a weak (and unmetrical) trivialization of the paradoxical λιμῷ τρέφεται (λιμῷ is of course guaranteed by the chiastically balancing δίψῃ). The combination of ἀπήμονι and the defective line 5 (p. 251) show that the *AP* version derives from a MS source (presumably a *Life* of Daniel), not the original pillar (which still existed in the tenth century; see n. 124).

123. '*non in duplici columna pedum plantis quasi radicitus inhaerescentibus stabat fanaticus heros, sed in una columna binis pedum plantis*' (quoted in the notes to the Didot ed.). It is not quite clear to me what Stadtmueller's διχθαδίως was supposed to mean.

that it did indeed rest on a 'double column' (§§44, 47, with the MSS varying between διχθάδιος and διπλοῦς in both passages). §47 describes how during a storm the pillar 'was torn from its supports on either side by the violence of the winds and was only kept together by the iron bar which held the two columns in the middle'.

It is nice to have διχθαδίῳ illustrated in so striking a fashion, but it is here nevertheless that our minor problem (so far unnoticed) arises. §36 of the *Life* implies that Cyrus wrote his epigram for Daniel's second column, the one erected by Gelanius in 460. But the double column was the third one, a gift from the emperor. It is apparently the third (and final) column the biographer actually has in mind, for he remarks that the inscription could still be read there when he was writing (ἕως νῦν); and of course it must be the third, double column to which the epigram itself refers.

An inconsistency or inaccuracy somewhere, to be sure, but hardly serious enough to cast doubt on the ascription of the poem to Cyrus. The biographer relates the laying of the foundations for the third column (38) almost immediately after the visit of Cyrus' daughter (36), and although we have no exact date for Daniel's move to his new and final home (accomplished by means of a plank laid across the top of the two pillars), he was certainly there before the great fire of 465 (44–5). And it should be remembered that it is only the visit of Cyrus' daughter that is expressly dated to 462. It is perfectly possible that her cure was not immediate and her father's gratitude not manifested till after the erection of the new column. Even supposing that Cyrus did originally write for the second column, it is likely enough that, rather than see his handiwork demolished with the old column[124] and the new one lack an inscription, he would have done the job again for the new column.

Oddly enough editors of the *Anthology* have treated the ascription of the poem to Cyrus as though it were merely a conjecture of Père Delehaye.[125] In fact, of course, it was explicitly and circumstantially made by the near contemporary author of the *Life* of Daniel.

---

124. To judge from the fuss Gelanius made about the first column, it seems likely that both the earlier columns would have been demolished once Daniel had vacated them. Certainly by the tenth century there seems to have been only one (*V. Lucae Stylitae* 7, *Patr. Or.* xi.2 (1914), p. 195).

125. So too even Baynes, *Three Byz. Saints*, 78 ('Delehaye suggested . . .').

Delehaye simply observed that it was strongly supported by the fact that Cyrus was a well-known poet. More strongly still, I would suggest, by the fact that the biographer, a man of simple culture to judge from his style, shows no knowledge that Cyrus was a poet, and thus had no reason to pick Cyrus rather than some other admirer of his master.

The poem as a whole is quite worthy of Cyrus and the last line positively characteristic of him. Père Delehaye remarked of this line that it was 'probablement un écho des querelles théologiques du temps', adding that 'Saint Daniel, ardent défenseur de la foi orthodoxe, ne manqua aucune occasion de prêcher au peuple, accouru au pied de la colonne, le Fils de la Vierge, Dieu et homme tout ensemble'.[126] Now Daniel's orthodoxy is beyond question; his intervention in 476 was instrumental in causing Basiliscus to withdraw his monophysite *Encyclical*.[127] Nevertheless, his was an 'impenetrable' orthodoxy, guaranteed, not by frequent christological disputation, but by his obvious personal holiness and his 'dogged defence of his status as a total stranger in a faction-ridden city'.[128] Those who tried to test his orthodoxy (no easy task, since he spoke only Syriac) were told not to seek out things too high for them, to read the Scriptures and Fathers, and to believe in the Trinity (90). Even in 476 Daniel resolved the crisis less by threatening Basiliscus than by playing the honest broker, so that monophysite emperor and chalcedonian patriarch alike could end up prostrated in front of him, neither side losing face in reconciliation.[129]

The Virgin is barely mentioned in the *Life*, and never with any emphasis. I would suggest that the last line of Cyrus' epigram, while in no sense inappropriate to Daniel, nevertheless in its emphasis on the mother of Christ reflects the preoccupation with the Theotokos which we have found to be characteristic of Cyrus himself.

XI. Downfall

The sons and grandsons of Theodosius the Great were a feeble

126. *REG* 9 (1896), 224.
127. §§70.; cf. Frend, *Rise of the Monophysite Movement*, 165, 172.
128. Peter Brown, *JRS* 91 (1971), 92.   129. Brown *JRS* 91 (1971), 93.

crew. The story of their reigns is largely the story of the struggle for the power behind their thrones. In the case of Arcadius and Honorius these intrigues can to some extent be reconstructed, thanks to the political poems of Claudian and the contemporary tracts of Synesius. For the long reign of Theodosius II (408–50) we have little more than bald entries in chronicles, allusions in theological works and guesswork to go on.[130] It is here above all that the historian most laments the loss of Cyrus' poetry.

An example of the undercurrents that it is bound to have mirrored is perhaps to be found in the only historical epic of the reign for which we have a title and author's name, though the text itself is unfortunately lost: the *Gainea* of Ammonius, recited in the emperor's presence (so Socrates informs us) in 438. Gainas was a barbarian *magister militum* who had seized power at Constantinople in 400 and been killed the next year. These events were described at the time in a lost epic by one Eusebius Scholasticus and less directly evoked in two extant texts of more lasting significance, Synesius' *de regno* and *de providentia*. Now the contemporary poetry of the age normally concerned itself strictly with the very latest deeds and aspirations of its heroes – which is evidently the main reason it has so completely perished. Its appeal was so ephemeral, and after a few years the very names and events could barely be made out beneath the hyperbole and classicizing periphrasis. Why should any poet seek to revive the saga of Gainas 37 years after the event? The answer is surely that Ammonius had a contemporary purpose, the same one that had animated Synesius at the time: the danger of an overpowerful barbarian element in the army. For some while after Gainas' fall barbarians were vigorously eliminated from high commands, but by the 430s they had returned in large numbers.[131] In the event they were still loyal, but it is not difficult to believe that there was some anxiety nevertheless, of which (I suggest) Ammonius was a spokesman. Gainas stood for the rising military dynasty of Ardabur, Areobindus, Plinthas and Aspar, which it might have been impolitic to criticize too openly.

On the whole, however, despite minority and incapacity in the

---

130. There is no comprehensiv{e modern study, but see A. Lippold's excellent article 'Theodosios II' in *RE* Suppl. xiii (1972), 125–208.

131. Jones, *Later Roman Empire* i (1964), 181–2; for more details, A. Demandt, 'magistri militum', *RE* Suppl. xii, 747f.

ruling house, power remained firmly in the hands of the civil authorities. At the beginning of the reign the prefect Anthemius (408–14) seems to have been in control. From 414 till perhaps 427 (an unprecedented tenure) the *magister officiorum* Helio seems to have been, in Jones' words, 'effective prime minister'.[132] Pulcheria exercised considerable influence from perhaps as early as 414, when she was proclaimed Augusta, and as time passed Eudocia too came to play a part, supported by her brothers and (later) Cyrus. And there were always the eunuchs. The fascinating list of bribes allegedly distributed round the court *ca* 413 by Cyril of Alexandria is no doubt an excellent guide to those who counted then: top of the list comes the chamberlain Chryseros, with 100 lbs. of gold, then several with 50, including the wife of the praetorian prefect (though not the prefect).[133] Finally, from *ca* 439 almost up to Theodosius' death in 450, there was the baneful chamberlain Chrysaphius and his creatures, the 'drones' of *AP* ix.136.

It may have been by reciting his poetry in a Byzantine drawing room that Cyrus first caught the attention of Eudocia, but it was more practical qualifications than this that brought him to the summit of political power between 439 and 441.

Constantelos has attempted to link Cyrus' fall directly with the fall from grace of Eudocia, and to this end he places them both in the same year, 443. In the year at least he is certainly mistaken. And though there was a common factor in the two catastrophes, it was not 'Christian hellenism' but Chrysaphius. In the late 430s, when we may presume Chrysaphius conceived his grand design, there was strong competition: Pulcheria, Eudocia and Cyrus, to whom we might perhaps add Paulinus the *magister officiorum*, a central figure in the later Eudocia legend and no doubt a figure of some consequence in real life too. During a period of not more than two or three years all four were eliminated. It was not till shortly before Theodosius' death in 450 that Pulcheria managed to regain control, and the execution of Chrysaphius was one of the first acts of the new emperor Marcian, whom Pulcheria took as her consort.

A precise chronology or at any rate sequence of these successive eliminations is essential for our purpose, and it has yet to be won. The utmost confusion reigns in all the standard works. We may

132. *Later Roman Empire* i, 179.
133. *Acta Conc. Oec.* i. iv. 223–4.

begin with the one absolute date that can be fixed with something approaching certainty: Cyrus' fall.

Our sources state what one would in any case have assumed: that Cyrus' fall was sudden; he was relieved of his prefectures and despatched to Cotyaeum without delay. Constantelos, basing himself on Priscus' statement[134] that Cyrus held both prefectures for four years concurrently and noting that he did not hold both before December 439, infers that he continued to hold both till late 443. He overlooked the fact that already by February 442 another man is attested in the praetorian prefecture, one Thomas, and another again, Apollonius, between August 442 and May 443.[135] There can be little doubt that Cyrus was relieved of his prefecture soon after the last date he is attested in office, namely 18 August 441. Soon after, because his first sermon in Cotyaeum was delivered on Christmas day, by which time (it is implied) he had already been there at least a week or two. Presumably Christmas 441; his property was confiscated, so no long delay for arranging his affairs is likely to have been needed – or granted. He probably left Constantinople around September 441, pausing only to declaim *AP* ix.136.

It is in fact demonstrable that Cyrus did *not* hold both prefectures concurrently for four years, since his praetorian prefecture can be no less tightly circumscribed at the other end. His predecessor, Florentius, was in office till 26 November 439,[136] so Cyrus cannot have begun his tenure more than a week before his first attestation, on 6 December. So he held the praetorian prefecture for not much more than 20 months altogether. What is perfectly possible is that he held the *city* prefecture for four years; he is not attested in the office before 23 March 439, but no predecessor later than 435 is known,[137] so he might easily have been appointed in late 437, that is to say, counting back four years from his fall, in or soon after August 441.

One further indication has recently come to light. Two dated papyri survive from Cyrus' consular year. The first, of 4 September

134. *Chron. Pasch.*, p. 588 = Priscus, fr. 3a, Müller *FHG* iv. 73.

135. Seeck, *Regesten der Kaiser und Päpste* (1919), 373; and see now the fasti in *PLRE* ii, p. 1250.

136. *PLRE* ii, Florentius 7.

137. *PLRE* ii, p. 1256. *PLRE* improbably suggests (ii, p. 339) that the figure four 'must refer to the combined total of years in the two posts'.

441, is dated 'in the consulship of Fl. Cyrus Hierax'; the second, of 6 December 441, is dated by the postconsulate of the preceding year.[138] Now it was normal to date by the postconsulate of the preceding year until the new consular names were announced, which by the mid fifth century was often quite late in the year. But a careful recent study by R. S. Bagnall and K. A. Worp has shown that there is never an overlap of more than a few days between the use of the two dating formulas in any given year.[139] Scribes were apparently more prompt and uniform than has often been supposed in adopting the new formula once it became known. The overlap of more than three months between these two papyri is by far the longest known. An error of some sort is always possible, but the obvious explanation (as Worp has already suggested) is that the later scribe deliberately reverted to the postconsular dating after Cyrus' fall. There was certainly no *damnatio memoriae*. Cyrus' name appears in all surviving consular fasti, eastern and western alike, and in a papyrus of 442 dated by his postconsulate. But it would not be surprising if people had played safe in the period of uncertainty immediately following his dramatic removal from all his offices. If so, then Cyrus was on his way to Cotyaeum by (at latest) November 441.[140]

Now for Eudocia and Paulinus. The legend is well known.[141] Theodosius gave Eudocia an apple of remarkable size which she presented to Paulinus, unwell at the time, who unwittingly gave it back to Theodosius; when questioned, Eudocia swore under oath that she had eaten it. There may be some kernel of truth in the story (it is dated to Epiphany, when people did give each other presents), but its most disquieting feature is less (as often supposed)

---

138. *P. Vindob. G.* 16775, to be published by K. A. Worp in *Festschrift 100 Jahre Papyrussammlung Wien* (= *CPR* ix) (Vienna 1983); *P. Mil.* i.64, as corrected by Bagnall and Worp in *ZPE* 28 (1978), 226–7.

139. *Bulletin of the American Society of Papyrologists* 17 (1980), 27–36, though their remarks there on 441 are to be corrected in the light of Worp's forthcoming discussion of *P. Vindob. G.* 16775.

140. Bagnall objects that scribes did not normally exercise such discretion, but this was a moment that might have seemed to call for discretion. Compare the discussion of the confused consular datings of a later period of uncertainty (475–8) in *P. Köln III* (Cologne 1980), 152, pp. 131–3.

141. Malalas, pp. 356–8, variously embroidered or abbreviated in later chronicles.

the 'folk-motif' of the apple[142] than its evident exculpatory purpose. The exaggerated picture of a jealous husband overreacting to a friendly gesture by an innocent wife to an ill friend suggests uglier rumours. That such rumours were indeed current at the time is proved by Nestorius' remark, written in exile *ca* 451, that 'the demon, the prince of adultery, threw the queen into shame and disgrace.'[143] And the identity of the man was seemingly supplied by the dramatic execution of Paulinus. For the moment, our only concern is with the date.

The *Paschal Chronicle* puts the whole saga in 444 (the much later Cedrenus apparently a year earlier, in 443). Marcellinus records just Paulinus' execution (with no mention of Eudocia) under 440. Some have been quite happy to dissociate the fates of Eudocia and Paulinus (Seeck, for example, who rejected the legend in its entirety, and thought that it was solely out of 'excess of piety' that Eudocia went to live in Jerusalem). But whatever the truth, the basis for the identification of Paulinus as the man in the affair must surely have been an approximate synchronism – hardly a gap of four years – between his execution and Eudocia's departure.

On the face of it, we have a choice between Marcellinus' 440 and the *Paschal Chronicle*'s 444, and other things being equal one would ordinarily prefer the earlier and more reliable Marcellinus. Paradoxically enough, however, a surprising number of modern writers have rejected both, opting for 443, at any rate for Eudocia's departure. The virtually worthless authority of Cedrenus on such a point has been thought to find support in a mistaken numismatic argument.

A. A. Boyce[144] drew attention to a series of *solidi* bearing the date 'IMP XXXXII COS XVII', i.e. 443, struck for Theodosius II, Pulcheria, Eudocia, Galla Placidia, Eudoxia the younger (daughter of Eudocia and Theodosius) and Valentinian III, that is to say the whole imperial house. According to Boyce Eudocia's coins are very scarce, a scarcity (she supposes) 'due to some special

---

142. See, A. R. Littlewood, 'The Symbolism of the Apple in Byzantine Literature', *Jahrb. d. Österreich. Byz. Gesell.* 23 (1974), 33–59.

143. *The Bazaar of Heracleides*, translated by G. R. Driver and L. Hodgson (Oxford 1925), p. 379 (=p. 331 tr. F. Nau, 1910).

144. 'Eudoxia, Eudocia, Eudoxia: Dated Solidi of the Fifth Century', *American Numismatic Society Museum Notes* 6 (1954), 134–42.

circumstance', which she takes to be Eudocia's departure for the Holy Land. There are two flaws in the argument.

In the first place, *all* the imperial ladies are sparsely represented in this issue (as J. P. C. Kent, who has surveyed all the available evidence for the forthcoming *Roman Imperial Coinage* x, has kindly informed me). The fact that there may (or may not) be marginally more extant specimens of Eudoxia simply does not warrant the conclusion 'that the mint was neglecting Eudocia while paying court to Eudoxia'.

The second objection is that Eudocia did *not* leave court in disgrace; the official version was that the empress was going on another pilgrimage (even the chronicles say that she left at her own request), and whatever the rumours, no-one would have been tactless enough to deprive her of any honour to which her rank entitled her (who could tell when she might return to court, favour and power?). The break came in 444, when (as Marcellinus again records) she killed (both Marcellinus and Priscus[145] say in person) an agent of Theodosius who had killed two of her clerics (a strange affair, of which one would like to know more). She was at once deprived of her imperial retinue (*regiis spoliata ministris*). Whether or not her face ever appeared on the imperial coinage after 444, clearly an issue of 443 is quite irrelevant to the question of her standing before then.

So we are back where we started with the choice between Marcellinus' 440 and the Paschal Chronicler's 444. And over and above the intrinsic superiority of Marcellinus, the apparent precision of the Paschal Chronicler's date is seriously undermined by the fact that his entry comprises the whole saga, from Epiphany apple to Eudocia's death and burial at Jerusalem in 460. Now it is not uncommon for a Byzantine chronicler to go beyond his year's limit (in either direction) in order to round a story off, and (as Romilly Jenkins has noted) he would often date 'a series of events to the year of its last recorded event'.[146]

The conflict under discussion is the more interesting in that Marcellinus and the Paschal Chronicler (as has long been realized) share a common annalistic source for this period.[147] It was not,

145. Priscus fr. 8, Müller, *FHG* iv. 94 (top).
146. *DOP* 19 (1965), 92.
147. The parallel entries in the *Chron. Pasch.* are helpfully printed in parallel

however, from this source that the Chronicler took his Eudocia saga but, word for word, from Malalas. Unfortunately, however, Malalas tells the whole story continuously without a single date. If his annalistic source had, like Marcellinus, given him two possible pegs on which to hang his story, the execution of Paulinus in 440 and Eudocia's activity at Jerusalem under 444, the chronicler is more likely than not to have chosen the latter. It is significant that Marcellinus concludes his entry for 444, like this entry in the *Paschal Chronicle*, with a statement that Eudocia remained at Jerusalem till her death. Theophanes too telescopes the affair with Paulinus, the departure for Jerusalem and the killing of Eudocia's clerics into one sequence – though in a 'flashback' under 450.[148]

Curiously enough, the dating of the same Paschal Chronicler's entry for Cyrus provides an exact parallel: it tells the story from his appointment as praetorian prefect (439) through his fall and sermon (441) right down to his death (in fact *ca* 470), all under one year – 450, the year of Theodosius' death. The *Chronicle*, like Malalas and Theophanes, says that Cyrus stayed at Smyrna till his death, mistakenly, since we know that he retired to Constantinople. We have already seen that *Suda* κ. 2776 says that he went to Cotyaeum and lived till the reign of Leo. I suggest that the original text of Priscus correctly recorded that he remained at Cotyaeum till the death of Theodosius, and then returned to Constantinople where he remained till his own death under Leo. It is not difficult to see how a carelessly abbreviated version of this could have suggested that Cyrus died at Cotyaeum in the same year as Theodosius, *viz.* 450. In all probability this is why the whole story is entered under the year 450. So the main elements in the story, Cyrus' fall and sermon, have been displaced by nine years so as to fit in a continuous account of his whole career told in the form of an obituary hung on a date for his death that is some twenty years in error. Who would have dared to suspect so extensive a double

columns in Mommsen's edition of Marcellinus in *Chron. Minora* II, *MGH Auct. Ant.* II (1894) – thereby misleading the unwary (e.g. Constantelos, p. 453 n. 10) to think that Marcellinus himself wrote in Greek!

148. There is hardly a single event of these years correctly dated in Theophanes: see the lists of his errors in (e.g.) O. J. Maenchen-Helfen, *The World of the Huns* (Berkeley 1973), 112–13 and C. Mango, *Byzantine & Modern Greek Studies* 4 (1978), 119–20. See too B. Croke, *GRBS* 18 (1977), 360.

displacement if we had no independent evidence for the dates of Cyrus' fall and death?

So, quite apart from the general and conspicuous superiority of Marcellinus in points of chronology, the *Paschal Chronicle* cannot even in principle be supposed to 'confirm' (as Bury thought) a precise date of 444 for the first element in the Eudocia saga, the execution of Paulinus. In the entry for Cyrus we should have been similarly mistaken in inferring that his promotion to praetorian prefect (439) belonged in the same year as his fall (441) – or even that the Chronicler intended to suggest this.

Bury's main argument in favour of 444[149] was based on a misinterpretation of the passage of Nestorius quoted above. On the last page of the *Bazaar of Heracleides* Nestorius lists some disasters that followed his deposition in 431:

For immediately, as indeed you are persuaded, you have first seen that death has carried off the daughter of him who was then reigning, and thereafter, you see, the demon, the chief of adultery, who cast down the empress with insult and contumely. Again you see that the cities of Africa and Spain and of Musicanus[150] and great and glorious islands – I mean Sicily and Rhodes and many other great ones – and Rome itself have been delivered over as spoil unto the barbarian Vandal.

Bury seems to have thought that the first allusion was to Theodosius' *sister* Arcadia, who died in 444, thus providing a 'context' that pointed to 444 for the second allusion too. In fact there can be no doubt that Nestorius meant daughter, since, on the evidence of Marcellinus, once doubted but clearly now borne out by Nestorius, the emperor's younger daughter Flaccilla did indeed die 'immediately' after Nestorius' deposition in 431.[151] As for the Vandals, they had been causing trouble for years, but what Nestorius had in mind was not mere trouble but judgments of God. He must surely have been thinking of the wave of panic that swept the Mediterranean world on the news of the Vandal capture of Carthage in 439, leading to Cyrus' completion of the circuit of the walls of Constantinople that same year and the repair of the city

149. *LRE* I[2], 230 n. 4.

150. Presumably this name is corrupt, though see L. Abramowski, *Untersuchungen zum* Liber Heraclidis *des Nestorius, CSCO* 242, *subsidia* 22 (Louvain 1963), 129.

151. As recognized by E. W. Brooks, *BZ* 21 (1912), 96 – and indeed by Bury a few pages earlier, p. 220 n. 3.

walls of Rome next year. In 440 the Vandals launched a massive naval expedition against Sicily, and Rome itself feared invasion. In 441 Theososius sent an armada, but a Hun invasion caused him to recall it and the situation was stabilized by a treaty in 442.[152] So Nestorius, by far our earliest source (*ca* 451), placed what he describes quite bluntly as the empress' adultery *between* the death of Flaccilla in 431 and the Vandal panic of 439/41. For what his evidence is worth it certainly points to 440 rather than 444.

The decisive text has scarcely ever been cited in this connection: the precious *Suda* entry κ.2776, whose Priscan credentials and reliability were established in §II. After stating that it was Eudocia who was Cyrus' patron, the excerpt goes on to say that Cyrus was 'plotted against' and made bishop of Cotyaeum (the correct see, thus pointing to the original text of Priscus) 'while she was absent from the palace and living in the East, in Jerusalem'. Not her first visit in search of relics, firmly datable to 438–9,[153] and so inescapably her second. Since we have now established that Cyrus fell from power in autumn 441, it follows that Eudocia must already have left for the Holy Land by then. Without more of the original context, it is impossible to tell whether Priscus' point was that the 'plot' against Cyrus was laid the moment Eudocia was out of the way, or merely that, when the plot was laid, perhaps some time after her departure, she was not there to protect him. There was never the slightest reason to question Marcellinus' 440 for Paulinus' execution, and it now receives implicit confirmation from two independent contemporaries, Nestorius and Priscus. We need and perhaps should not suppose that Eudocia left immediately or even soon after the execution. Since there was no public scandal, it is likely that both Eudocia and Theodosius would have wanted a decent interval to avoid feeding rumour by too obvious a synchronism. Perhaps 441 then rather than 440.

That leaves only the question of Pulcheria's departure from court. Here, despite very different accounts in modern works, there is no real room for doubt. The role of Chrysaphius emerges clearly from the two well-known stories told by the chronicles.[154] In the

152. Stein, *Histoire du Bas-Empire* I (1959), 324–5.

153. Marcellinus, *s.a.* 439.2, and Socrates, *HE* vii. 47.

154. Theophanes, p. 98 de Boor; John of Nikiu, *Chron.* 87; Nicephorus Callistus xiv. 47.

first, Chrysaphius points out to Eudocia that while Pulcheria had her very own grand chamberlain, she, the emperor's wife, did not. Theodosius ruled that Pulcheria had been born in the purple and for long acted as his regent; she therefore deserved a privilege which must, regrettably, continue to be denied to Eudocia. A setback for the eunuch, claimed Père Goubert,[155] echoing Theophanes. How so? He had brilliantly succeeded in sowing the seed of discord between two ambitious and sensitive women, simply by drawing attention to a tiny, but significant detail of protocol. Result: two disgruntled Augustas and an emperor beginning to see less creditable motives behind their conduct than he had hitherto suspected.

Next we hear how Chrysaphius put into Eudocia's head the suggestion that Pulcheria be consecrated a deaconess. This time Theodosius was prevailed upon to agree but, forewarned by the patriarch, Pulcheria anticipated her fate by retiring to the Hebdomon palace, a mile or so outside the Theodosian wall – after first sending her chamberlain to Eudocia.

There seems no reason to disbelieve at least the outlines of this picture, or at any rate the relative chronology it implies. The chroniclers are agreed that it was Eudocia whom Chrysaphius used against Pulcheria – the natural tactic in the situation. In addition Theophanes represents Theodosius, on discovering in 450 that Chrysaphius had betrayed him, blaming all his troubles on Eudocia for driving Pulcheria from the palace.[156] Since Eudocia left court at latest in summer 441 and possibly more than a year before then, Pulcheria's defeat would seem to fall in 439 at latest.

Many modern writers, however, have been misled by the fact that Theophanes gives the name of the patriarch who is supposed to have warned Pulcheria of her impending consecration as Flavian, not patriarch till 446. But this is simply one of Theophanes' all too frequent blunders, for the same entry that names Flavian as patriarch also gives Eudocia (by then five years in Palestine) her usual role in the story. It has also been felt that so central a figure in the ecclesiastical politics of the age cannot have been out of circulation for a whole decade, and her 'disgrace' is

155. 'Le rôle de Sainte Pulchérie et de l'eunuque Chrysaphios', *Das Konzil von Chalkedon*, ed. A. Grillmeier and H. Bacht I (Würzburg 1951), 307.
156. P. 101, 32 de Boor.

often put at only two or three years, 447–9.[157] Yet it is a mistake to see Pulcheria's retirement to the Hebdomon as a disgrace. Not for nothing had she spent a lifetime in the subtle and deadly intrigue of the Byzantine court. She knew her brother and recognized her match in Chrysaphius. All that happened was that she anticipated the sort of fate that soon overtook Eudocia and Cyrus by voluntarily withdrawing far enough from court to keep out of danger while staying close enough to remain in touch. If she left her chamberlain behind we may be sure that she took her secretaries with her, to maintain her extensive correspondence with leading churchmen and the Western court (where she continued in high esteem), waiting for Chrysaphius to overreach himself. Her tactics paid off, and she had completely regained her ascendancy by the time of Theodosius' sudden death on 28 July 450.

It has not (I think) been noticed that the relative standing of the two empresses at the beginning and end of the decade is illustrated in two contemporary documents, the ecclesiastical histories of Socrates and Sozomen. Both continued Eusebius to 439; Socrates published in that very year (vii.48), Sozomen (who drew heavily on Socrates) between 443 and the death of Theodosius, his dedicatee. Now Sozomen offers a fulsome eulogy of the wisdom and success with which Pulcheria directed affairs during Theodosius' minority (ix.1; cf. 2–3), but does not mention Eudocia. Socrates praises Eudocia (vi.21; 47), but does not mention Pulcheria. Both silences are surely significant.

There is one particular omission in Sozomen's account of the regency. Whether or not Pulcheria 'took over the government' in 414 when she was only fifteen, Arcadius died in 408, when she was nine (and Theodosius seven). Between 408 and 414 power had been in the hands of the praetorian prefect Anthemius, whose son Isidorus was prefect of the city in 410–12. Whatever the reason for Sozomen's failure to mention the *de facto* regency of Anthemius, which he must have known of from Socrates (see below), he would hardly have so exaggerated and expanded Pulcheria's role as her brother's sole mentor if, at the time he wrote, her rival Eudocia had taken over and driven her from court. On the other hand, if Pulcheria had still been in charge when Socrates wrote in 439, it seems incredible that he could have given an account of the

157. E.g. Goubert, p. 312.

regency which named *only* Anthemius, praising him as 'the most prudent man of his time'. It follows that Socrates wrote *after* Pulcheria's retirement, which must therefore have taken place by 439, and that Sozomen wrote after her return to favour and power in 450.[158]

Now Socrates' long eulogy of Theodosius in vii.22 (which in contrast to Sozomen ix.1 again does not mention Pulcheria) lays its heaviest emphasis on the emperor's clemency. When asked why he never inflicted capital punishment on offenders he would reply: 'Would that it were possible to restore to life those who have died.' If a criminal was sentenced to death, he would invariably issue a pardon.[159] Even if we did not have Socrates' own word that he finished his book in 439, we should have been able to guess from this passage alone that he was writing before the dramatic execution of Paulinus in 440. More important, for Theodosius to have so spectacularly deserted the most publicized of his virtues (Marcellinus specifies that Paulinus was executed *iubente Theodosio principe*),[160] it looks as if he must indeed have done something particularly heinous. No other disgraced minister of the age suffered this penalty: the case of Cyrus the following year springs to mind. No wonder that people identified Paulinus – perhaps rightly – as the man behind the dark rumours about Eudocia.

There is one final touch. As we know from the dedicatory inscription to a church erected at Ravenna in or soon after 439, in addition to her daughters Eudoxia (b. 422) and the short-lived Flaccilla (d. 431), Eudocia also gave birth to a son called Arcadius. He is only otherwise mentioned in the dedicatory epigram to a calligraphic copy of the *Cento Probae* presented to Theodosius

158. This is surely put beyond doubt by the statement that it was because of Pulcheria that 'new heresies are not victorious in our own day' (ix.1.9). What can this refer to but Pulcheria's recovery of initiative in imperial religious policy in the last months of her brother's life, the initiative that led to Chalcedon? This could hardly have been written while the emperor himself was still inclined to Monophysitism. Indeed, it is surely because he was reluctant to embark on the embarrassing decade 440–9 that Sozomen cut short his history in the same year as Socrates.

159. Lippold (*RE* Suppl. XIII, 203) points out that some of Theodosius' laws prescribe the death penalty, but even so we cannot know how often it was carried out, and it seems clear that around the time Socrates was writing at least, the personal clemency of the emperor was a leading theme of imperial panegyric.

160. According to both Marcellinus and Theophanes (p. 99.27), Paulinus was taken to Cappadocia before being executed – as though to avoid publicity.

probably in the mid to late 430s, where it is implied that 'minor Arcadius' is still an infant.[161] Male children in the Theodosian house were normally soon elevated to the rank of Augustus: Arcadius senior at the age of 5 or 6, and even his younger brother Honorius when 9; Theodosius II himself when only 9 months. It is difficult to see how this longed for and late born heir could have reached even his teens without being either elevated (after which his name would have appeared in the headings of all imperial laws) or achieving more frequent and conspicuous mention in our sources. So in 440 he may only have been about five. Now as soon as the possibility of the empress' adultery had been admitted, an appalling corollary must inevitably have suggested itself: the emperor could no longer assume that he was the father of his heir. It is understandable that, staggering under two such blows, the credulous emperor should have reacted with unaccustomed ferocity. The further dilemma whether, given the rumours, the young Arcadius could continue to be treated as Theodosius' heir was providentially resolved by his early death. It may be more than accidental that Marcellinus and the *Paschal Chronicle*, usually meticulous in recording imperial births, pass over both the birth and death of this unfortunate prince. The embarrassing dates were perhaps removed from the official fasti on which they drew.

At last we can trace the successive stages of Chrysaphius' grand design. First he fostered and then skilfully exploited Eudocia's natural jealousy of her only slightly older sister-in-law's monopoly of influence over the malleable Theodosius. But once rid of Pulcheria, presumably after her return from the Holy Land in 439, Eudocia installed her own favourites; Cyrus in the key praetorian prefecture and Paulinus reappointed *magister officiorum*.[162]

There can have been few at the time who knew for certain whether Eudocia actually committed adultery with Paulinus, and we will certainly never know now. Her own deathbed denial and her husband's supposed homosexuality are scarcely decisive

161. *ILS* 818.3, with Dessau's note, and T. D. Barnes, *Phoenix* 28 (1974), 228. For the epigram see *Probae Cento*, ed. C. Schenkl, in *Poetae Christiani Minores, CSEL* 16 (1888), p. 568; I shall be discussing this poem in detail elsewhere.

162. Since Paulinus is recorded by the Code as *mag. off.* in 430 (Seeck, p. 357), he has often been described in 440 as *ex mag. off.*, but there seems no reason to question the clear implication of both Marcellinus and Malalas that he was in office again in 440 (no holder is recorded between March 435 and April 441).

arguments either way. Whatever its basis, the accusation provided a convenient pretext to get rid of her. Chrysaphius is not actually named in this connection, but who will have been better placed than a palace chamberlain to keep track of court rumours and the empress' visitors?

With Eudocia and Paulinus out of the way, that left only Cyrus, and the 'plot' that destroyed him is specifically laid at Chrysaphius' door by the well-informed *Life of St Daniel*.

It is usually stated roundly that Cyrus was accused of paganism or pagan sympathies, which is indeed the version of Malalas (ἐπλάκη ὡς Ἕλλην). The *Suda* entry for Theodosius II adds 'aiming at the throne' to paganism. But we have seen that these chronicle and *Suda* entries are all more or less simplified or garbled extracts from Priscus, and our other witnesses to the original account suggest a more nuanced picture. The *Paschal Chronicle* implies that it was Theodosius' 'wrath' at Cyrus' popularity that was his undoing. The idea that he might be a 'hellene' is represented later in the entry as a 'suspicion' of his new congregation at 'Smyrna' – a suspicion that was decisively scouted by the sermon discussed above. Theophanes perhaps reflects an even more modified version, in which the 'Smyrneans' merely suspected him of being ἑλληνόφρων, 'sympathetic to hellenic ways'. It would not be surprising if the people of Cotyaeum, who did not take easily to new bishops, had been dubious about the latest, a poet who had to be persuaded to give a sermon on Christmas day. It is true that Theophanes also claims that it was on the pretext of these same 'hellenic sympathies' that Theodosius deposed him, but emperors did not need 'pretexts'. It is unlikely that any formal accusation was made – or made public. The second allegation in Theophanes might be no more than a doublet of the first, a guess to supply the emperor with a motive.

No doubt Theodosius really was disturbed at the popular demonstrations in Cyrus' favour, demonstrations which Cyrus may have been vain enough to encourage and the significance of which Chrysaphius will easily have been able to exaggerate, reminding the emperor that this was the favourite of his faithless wife, hardly a safe man. Both Malalas and the *Paschal Chronicle* record that Cyrus drove around the city in his prefect's carriage. Since all prefects were entitled to do this, the implication is that

Cyrus did it to excess or in a particularly ostentatious way. If capital was made of his 'hellenic sympathies' (which were real enough), it can hardly have taken the form of a serious accusation of paganism. The statement in the *Life of Daniel* that Cyrus 'recognized Chrysaphius' plot and yielded, so as to avoid a wretched death', suggests rather that he was offered the chance of proving his Christianity by accepting ordination – a variation on the threat of consecration used against Pulcheria two years earlier, and on Eudocia's 'voluntary' second pilgrimage to the Holy Land of the year before. This 'penal' exploitation of the church is a notable development in Byzantine political warfare.

The fact that Cyrus was a Christian did not mean that he could ignore the danger of an accusation of paganism. For by Cyrus' day the Christian public at large had very little idea what paganism really meant. An accusation of paganism in fifth-century Byzantium was much like an accusation of communism in the United States in the 1950s: not easily defined, but evil and sinister beyond definition and (unlike the charge of heresy, another popular weapon) impossible to refute once made. The man accused did not need to look or behave like a pagan (however that was). It was widely believed (and must often have been the case) that the pagan, unlike the heretic again, concealed his paganism behind a carefully constructed façade of Christianity and good works. Anybody, even a patriarch (like Gregory of Antioch in 579),[163] might find himself accused of crypto-paganism. As for Cyrus' case, how better might the devil have advised him to conceal his true nature than by building a church of the Theotokos? It was well known that most Egyptian poets of the recent past had been pagans, many from Cyrus' own native Panopolis.

Cyrus was more vulnerable to such an accusation (however false) than most. Like Pulcheria and Eudocia before him, he saw that one way or another his days at court were numbered, and accepted the alternative that allowed him to extricate himself with life and dignity intact.

Seen in context, there can be no doubt that the opposition to Cyrus was essentially *political*, not religious. It tells us nothing about the failure of 'Christian hellenism', or about a discredited 'liberal' party at court. The story of Cyrus is not that of a pagan

163. John of Ephesus, *HE* iii.29f.

caught out at a Christian court; nor of a Christian torn between his faith and his classical culture. Cyrus himself seems to have known just where he stood. The problem was what other people thought, or (given enough ill will) could be made to think. It was long to remain a problem for Byzantine 'intellectuals' – who were often (like Cyrus) not really intellectuals at all in the modern sense.

XII. Eudocia

The age of Theodosius II was the first for many centuries in which literature had either received or looked for encouragement at court on a large scale. The court of Theodosius could indeed boast what Momigliano has called 'one of the most impressive intellectual circles of the ancient world'.[164] It has scarcely begun to be accorded the scholarly research it deserves, nor is this the place to do more than touch on such aspects as relate (or have been thought to relate) to Cyrus and Eudocia.

Historians continue to write of the 'circle of the Athenian Eudocia', implying (given Athens' reputation as a hotbed of paganism) a salon filled with paganizing litterateurs and neoplatonists.[165] At the very least, there is a conspicuous tendency to see her influence behind any cultural movement of the age, and to assume that she was motivated by a deep admiration of classical culture and a natural sympathy for highly educated pagans.[166]

Already in our first and fullest connected account of Eudocia's life, the chronicle of Malalas, everything has been gilded with an aura of romance: Athenais the sophist's daughter, driven out of house and home by her wicked brothers; the beautiful pagan who turned to Christ and became an emperor's bride; the imperial poetess who collected holy relics; and (finally) the tragic misunderstanding about the Epiphany apple and those last years dedicated to good works in the Holy Land.

There has been surprisingly little serious attempt to subject Malalas' account to a critical scrutiny. Some have been content to see only the imputation of adultery as legend. Others have frankly

164. *Quinto contributo*, p. 85.
165. H.-G. Beck's article 'Eudokia' in *RAC* 6 (1966), 844–7 is notably sober by contrast – though he takes Cyrus for a pagan (847).
166. Most conspicuously (e.g.) Bury, Constantelos, Holum.

preferred the Eudocia of legend to the Eudocia of history. Bury, for example, unwilling to believe that 'this amiable lady' could even have 'permitted' the death of the *comes* Saturninus, relegated to a footnote good evidence that she killed him herself.[167] Most recently, Kenneth Holum has announced that the entire story of the marriage is 'mostly fiction, including the notion that Pulcheria had anything to do with it'.[168]

His version is that in 414 Pulcheria threw off the influence of the 'traditionalist' party of Anthemius, which contrived briefly to regain its power over Theodosius in 421/2 by marrying him to a pagan sophist's daughter. The leaders of this party are held to be Eudocia's uncle Asclepiodotus, praetorian prefect of the East from 423–5, Anthemius' son-in-law, Procopius, *magister militum* from 421 or 422, and his son Isidorus, who is alleged to have 'reappeared in high office for the first time since 412 as praetorian prefect of Illyricum' in 423.[169] After the 'traditionalists' had lost power again, Pulcheria somehow acquired the credit for arranging the marriage. It will not be irrelevant to the central theme of this paper to set forth the weakness of this bold new reconstruction.

In the first place, there is simply no evidence that these men had anything in common, let alone opposition to Pulcheria. Anthemius' disappearance from the record in 414 after a long career is most plausibly explained by his death or retirement. The fact that Sozomen does not mention Anthemius does not in the least prove, as Seeck thought, that 'Pulcheria and those who admired her despised his memory'. Writing as he was more than 35 years after Anthemius left office, Sozomen may simply have suppressed Anthemius' regency so as to extend and magnify Pulcheria's. The fact that it was in 413 that she vowed herself and her sisters to virginity – a spectacular gesture for a 14 year old – need not imply that it was unwelcome suitors from Anthemius' family she was afraid of. If he had had such ambitions, he would certainly have married or at least betrothed her to a son or grandson well before the age of 14. The implication rather is that she took the vow because she knew that the loyal Anthemius was about to step

167. *LRE* I², 231 with n. 3.

168. 'Pulcheria's Crusade and the Ideology of Imperial Victory', *GRBS* 18 (1977), at pp. 169–70.

169. References in Holum, pp. 169–70, and see too the respective entries in *PLRE* II.

down. She may even have acted on his advice. As for Procopius, there is nothing to suggest that it was not Pulcheria herself who appointed him to his command. After all, Procopius' son, another Anthemius, later married Pulcheria's stepdaughter Euphemia (Marcian's daughter by a former marriage) and later still became emperor of the West.[170]

But the most serious objection of all is the very notion of 'traditionalists'. What Holum has in mind is the undoubted fact that Anthemius associated with poets and (as Socrates tells us) was very dependent on the counsel of the sophist Troilus of Side.[171] It has often quite arbitrarily been stated that Troilus was a pagan (e.g. by Bury and Stein), and Holum even expresses (quite unjustifiable) doubts about Anthemius' Christianity. There happens to be no evidence for the religious beliefs of Troilus, but we do know that he was a kinsman of the prolific Christian historian Philip of Side, and of his three pupils whose careers we can trace, two became bishops[172] and the third an ecclesiastical historian.[173] A close friend of both Troilus and Anthemius was Synesius, another 'hellene' who ended his days a bishop. Holum is guilty of the common oversimplification of identifying sympathy for classical culture with sympathy for paganism – and then assuming that paganism implies opposition to a Christian government. So this supposed hostility between Pulcheria and the 'party' of Anthemius is not personal or political but ideological: the inevitable clash between hellenic traditionalism and imperial piety.

In the course of his long reign Theodosius issued many laws forbidding pagan practices. It so happens that the mildest (*CTh* xvi.10.23) was addressed to the prefect Asclepiodotus in 423; which in this context means, after announcing that the crime merited execution, the law prescribed only exile and confiscation of property. It should hardly be necessary to point out that reluctance to execute pagans does not necessarily imply sympathy for paganism. But it might be worth recalling (a) that (as we have seen) reluctance to execute for any crime was one of the more

170. *PLRE* II, *s.v.* Anthemius 3.
171. *PLRE* II, *s.v.* Troilus 1.
172. Socrates, *HE* vii.12.10; 37.1.
173. His frequent complimentary references to Troilus and his knowledge of the careers of so many of Troilus' pupils strongly suggest that (as Valesius long ago conjectured) Socrates himself was a pupil.

publicized virtues of the emperor himself; and (b) that only two months earlier another law addressed to the same Asclepiodotus (*CTh* xvi.10.22) had opened: 'Although we are confident that no more pagans are left. . . .' So much for the 'traditionalist persuasion' of Asclepiodotus.

But the key element in Holum's reconstruction is of course the synchronism of this 'traditionalist' coup he has identified with the arrival of Eudocia at court: 'with her support these men were able to break Pulcheria's hold over her brother'.[174] That is to say, while rejecting almost every detail in the traditional account, he has accepted and built upon its one demonstrably legendary feature: Athenais the cultivated pagan.

Our earliest and soberest information on Eudocia's origins (written before even she left court) comes from Socrates, who merely states that she had received a thorough education from her father, the sophist Leontius, and was 'made a Christian' and baptized by the patriarch Atticus before the marriage.[175] In later sources,[176] from Malalas on, Leontius bears the rarer and more honourable title of philosopher, and Eudocia herself becomes, not merely well educated, but an expert in astronomy and geometry, not to mention every branch of literature and philosophy, Greek and Latin alike. Leontius' promotion is more than just academic snobbery; in Athens more than anywhere philosopher implied diehard pagan. A curious work of the eighth century presents a garbled story of seven pagan philosophers from Athens who came to Constantinople with Eudocia's brothers.[177] The public debate in the hippodrome between the philosophers and the emperor's entourage which ensues is so obscure that it is not even clear whether it is the Christians or the pagans who win. This particular story is clearly influenced by the visit of the seven (real) pagan philosophers from Athens to the Persian court under Justinian.[178] The only kernel of truth is the two brothers who came to share in their sister's good fortune (see below), but it nicely illustrates the progressive exaggeration of Eudocia's pagan origins.

174. P. 170.
175. *HE* vii.21.
176. Collected in A. Ludwich's *Eudociae Augustae, Procli Lycii, Claudiani . . . reliquiae* (Leipzig 1897), 3f.
177. *Parastaseis Syntomai Chronikai* 64 = T. Preger, *Script. Orig. Cpol.* i (1901).
178. Agathias, *Hist.* ii.30–1, with *Proc. Camb. Phil. Soc.* 195 (1969), 7–29.

Fortunately it is still possible to rescue authentic information about Leontius. That he was a sophist rather than a philosopher is borne out by Olympiodorus. In a curious fragment (fr. 28) Olympiodorus describes how he used his influence to secure the election of a certain Leontius to the official chair of rhetoric at Athens in 415.[179] Unless we are prepared to believe that two men called Leontius held chairs of rhetoric at Athens in the second decade of the fifth century, this must surely be Eudocia's father. If he had not held an official chair till 415, only shortly before his death (420 at latest, since Eudocia was married in June 421), either he had not till then been much of a success or he had previously been teaching somewhere else.

Then there is the list of professors at Alexandria around 400 that Damascius, the last Athenian scholarch, gives in his *Life of Isidorus*.[180] Immediately before the philosopher Olympius, who played a conspicuous role in the pagan persecutions of 391, Damascius gives a tantalizing character study of a man called Leontius (subject unspecified, at least in Photius' abstract): Leontius thought he had been clever, but after an unfortunate display of outspokenness 'went home', failing to win the fortune and security he had hoped for, losing his 'godloving piety', his soul completely destroyed. The last detail is a variation on a formula we find several times in Damascius, and undoubtedly refers to conversion to Christianity. Any reader of the *Life of Isidorus* will know how freely and frequently professors of this period moved between Alexandria and Athens, and whether or not Athens was the 'home' to which Leontius returned after the incident described, Damascius' itinerant professor might well be the Leontius who won the Athenian chair in 415.

If the identification here proposed of these three professors called Leontius is accepted, then a series of minor but significant details fall neatly into place.

Eudocia, like Cyrus, must have been born *ca* 400. So if her father had been teaching in Alexandria in the years before 415, this would

179. Müller, *FHG* iv.63, Fr. 28; for a translation and commentary see J. W. H. Walden, *The Universities of Ancient Greece* (New York 1912), 301–3, quoting the other sources on student hazing at Athens. See *PLRE* II, *s.v.* Leontius 6.

180. *Damascii Vitae Isidori reliquiae*, ed. C. Zintzen (Hildesheim 1967), p. 68, §46 (included in the index nominum as 'sophista?'). He is registered separately as Leontius 14, '? pagan sophist' in *PLRE* II.

explain why she is said to have studied grammar with two professors, Orion and Hyperechius,[181] neither of whom is known to have had any connection with Athens while both are known to have taught in Alexandria (Orion being firmly attested there as the teacher of Proclus *ca* 420).[182]

Olympiodorus too had connections among the academic circles of Alexandria. He was a friend of the philosopher Hierocles, the dedicatee of his book *On Fate*,[183] whereas the description of student hazing rites at Athens with which fr. 28 continues suggests the tourist on his first visit to Athens. Why then did he help Leontius? Perhaps because he had known and admired him in Alexandria.

There is another problem here. Olympiodorus remarks that the Leontius he helped was 'unwilling'. Why was he unwilling, and why did Olympiodorus help him to win the chair nonetheless? Of course the explanation may have been something quite routine, such as ill health, but another possibility is that the fresh convert was reluctant to resume a profession about which he may now have felt differently. Socrates tells us of a sophist (a former pupil of Troilus) who 'got religion' and repudiated his gaudy academic gown.[184]

Two further conclusions follow more relevant to the present enquiry. First, the Athenian sage of legend turns out to have taught rhetoric there for no more than three or four years. More intriguing still, in all probability he died a Christian. It is clear from Socrates that Eudocia was not yet a Christian when she was selected as Theodosius' bride, but it does not follow that she was brought up a thoroughgoing pagan.

How did the young orphan Athenais gain access to court in the first place? According to Malalas, she presented her petition against her brothers to Pulcheria under the guidance of two aunts (one on her mother's, the other on her father's side), and Pulcheria was so struck by her eloquence and beauty that she immediately began to groom her to be her brother's bride. It is easy to see why doubts might be felt here, given Eudocia's later rivalry with

181. Tzetzes, *Chiliades* 52 f., and see further below on Orion.
182. Marinus, *Vita Procli* 8.
183. Photius, *Bibl.* cod. 314 *init.*, with *Historia* 14 (1965), 476 n. 37.
184. *HE* vii.37; for the gown (worn by both professors and students), which features prominently in Olympiodorus fr. 28, see Walden (n. 179), 301f., and add (e.g.) Palladius, *Hist. Laus.* 37, p. 101.4 Butler.

Pulcheria. And we have now discovered that she may have had a powerful family friend at court already in the pagan Olympiodorus. Yet Olympiodorus may have been far from court at the time, gathering materials for his history in the West;[185] and it is not self-evident that he would have taken Eudocia's side in the family dispute.

It is conceivable that it was in order to heighten the later clash between Pulcheria and Eudocia that Pulcheria came to be represented as her sponsor, but there is no hint of the irony and/or ingratitude that such a purpose might have been expected to inject into the saga. The simplest and most reasonable explanation is that this is the way it really happened.

At least one important detail in Malalas' account has received conspicuous corroboration from a passage in the Syriac *Life of Symeon the Stylite*, which reveals that the prefect Asclepiodotus was Eudocia's maternal uncle.[186] Assuming this man had a wife, here is the maternal aunt of Malalas, and if he was accurate thus far, why not in the role she played in bringing Eudocia to court? Asclepiodotus was *comes sacrarum largitionum* early in 422 and ordinary consul for 423, perhaps even before his promotion to the praetorian prefecture, a meteoric rise from nowhere. It would not be surprising if he had been the first of Eudocia's kin to feel the benefit of the emperor's gratitude. The Valerius attested as *magister officiorum* in 434 is certainly to be identified with the brother Valerius whom Malalas credits with precisely that office; his ordinary consulship in 432 indicates a man with an unusual claim on the emperor's favour.[187] Although contemporary corroboration is still lacking, there seems no reason to doubt that the other brother Gessius did reach, as Malalas alleges, the more modest

185. On what is known of the dates and movements of Olympiodorus, see John Matthews, *JRS* 60 (1970), 79–97; Baldwin, *L'Ant. Class.* 49 (1980), 212–31.

186. *V. Sym. Syr.* 130–1 (*Texte u. Unters.* xxxii.4 174–5), giving his name as Asclepiades: the author's claim that Asclepiodotus was deposed for his leniency towards Jews is false or at any rate exaggerated (G. Downey, *History of Antioch in Syria* (Princeton 1961), 460–1). See too *PLRE* II *s.v.* Asclepiodotus 1.

187. *PLRE* II, *s.v.* Valerius 4. Whether or not he was ever a pagan; whether or not he was the governor of Thrace in 421 in a puzzling fr. (27) of Olympiodorus (cf. B. Croke, *GRBS* 18 (1977), 358–64); by the 450s he appears as one of the orthodox party at court urging Eudocia to abandon her monophysite friends in Palestine (Cyril Scyth., *V. Euthym.* 30, p. 47.12f. Schwartz).

position of prefect of Illyricum.[188] Paulinus too is correctly given as *magister officiorum* in 440. Tradition may well have heightened for dramatic purposes the original hostility and the subsequent reconciliation between Eudocia and her brothers, just as the emphasis on Paulinus' boyhood friendship with Theodosius heightens the poignancy of their final break, but the detailed framework is reassuringly accurate.

Pulcheria and her sisters might keep suitors at bay by a vow of chastity, but the dynasty had to be continued and sooner or later Theodosius was bound to marry. By 420, when he was 19, court receptions were no doubt already being packed with the presentable daughters of the rich and powerful. The best way to minimize the obvious risks was for Pulcheria to take the initiative and pick a girl herself. Though unexpected, Eudocia was by no means an unsuitable choice. Her beauty may or may not have been exceptional , but in wit and culture she must surely have sparkled among the dull Byzantine debs, and Theodosius was notoriously the most studious of emperors. It might have been a perfect match. Most important of all, however, from Pulcheria's point of view, socially and politically speaking, as a professor's daughter, Eudocia was a nobody. There was, to be sure, the odd brother and uncle to be briefly elevated to appropriate dignities, but no powerful clan to edge Pulcheria out of her control of her brother and the administration.

The only major stumbling block, given the notorious personal piety of Pulcheria and her sisters, must surely have seemed this paganism and preoccupation with pagan culture so emphasized in modern accounts. The answer must be that, on the one hand, the depth and tenacity of Eudocia's former paganism has been exaggerated; while on the other, Pulcheria was satisfied that her conversion was genuine and complete. And no ancient evidence suggests that she was wrong. It is only modern scholars who have consistently assumed that the conversion was nominal and that she remained a hellene at heart. Typical is the verdict of Charles Diehl:[189] 'C'était une éducation toute païenne qu'avait reçue Athenais, et le léger vernis de christianisme dont le patriarche para l'âme de la nouvelle convertie n'altéra guère sans doute les enseignements qu'avait reçue sa jeunesse.'

188. *PLRE* II, *s.v.* Gessius. 189. *Figures byzantines* I[10] (Paris 1925), 31.

In fact the cultural and family traditions of her Athenian origin seem to have meant rather little to Eudocia herself, however much they may have fascinated later centuries. We have seen that she may not even have lived in Athens very long, though it does look as if she was born there. The panegyric she delivered at Antioch in 439 closed with a line adapted from Homer:[190] ὑμετέρης γενεῆς τε καὶ αἵματος εὔχομαι εἶναι. On the face of it this might look like a claim to *Antiochene* blood, but two loyal sons of Antioch, Malalas and Evagrius, assure us that she was alluding to Athenian colonists who helped to found Antioch (Evagrius supplies a bibliography of 8 items on the subject, *HE* i.20). This piece of erudition would have been entirely pointless unless she had been born an Athenian. The people of Antioch erected statues to her and she responded with more material benefits. She seems never to have returned to Athens and never paid it any similar honours. Indeed she wrote a poem on the martyrdom of St Cyprian of Antioch which contains a very hostile account of the converted magician's days as a pagan priest at Athens (II.16f.).

The fact is that Eudocia seems to have adapted without discomfort or reserve to the pious practices of Pulcheria and her sisters. It may indeed have been in fulfillment of one of her new family traditions that in 439, in the company of St Melania the younger, she brought the remains of St Stephen from Jerusalem to Constantinople. For in 421 (according to a late tradition) Pulcheria had had the right hand of St Stephen brought to Constantinople, where she built a special chapel to house it. Even if this is legend, it is nonetheless significant (and securely attested) that the basilica of St Lawrence in which Eudocia deposited her relics in 439 was completed by Pulcheria in 453. Indeed it looks as if Eudocia's relics were deposited at the inauguration of Pulcheria's church – a conspicuous example of co-operation between the two empresses in the religious sphere.[191]

It was later generations who played up Eudocia's Athenian origins, partly, no doubt, because it was a good romantic story, but also so as to magnify the glory of the girl who rejected paganism

190. There is very little to be said for the old conjecture that the whole panegyric was in verse.

191. Holum, *GRBS* 18 (1977), 163, and see too Holum and G. Vikan, *DOP* 33 (1979) 127–32, for Pulcheria's chapel. See John Wortley, *GRBS* 21 (1980), 385, for the basilica of St Lawrence.

and her pagan family to serve Christ; who, having known both, quite literally preferred Jerusalem to Athens.

As for her 'cultural paganism', here too legend has improved on the more modest truth. Even her most enthusiastic modern admirer, F. Gregorovius (in his celebrated *Athenais* of 1882), admitted that she had no 'creative talent', but praised her highly as an 'artist of superior linguistic training'. Yet this, to judge from the 800 extant lines of her *Martyrdom of St Cyprian*, is precisely her weakest suit.[192] It is not just that, in company with one or two other late poets, she gets her quantities wrong (and badly wrong). She admits hiatus so freely as to show that she had no conception of the restrictions on its use that all other reputable hexameter poets of the age adhere to with only the slightest of variations. She constantly employs non-existent pseudo-epicisms (such as μεροπήων, δυσεβῆας, ἔλλιπα), and props up her halting lines not only with that age-old stopgap γε, but also κε(ν), evidently unaware of its conditional significance. More striking still, such barbarisms as οὐμόν for τὸν ἐμόν or τὸ ἐμόν (*T*. 452, 467) show that she did not even recognize οὐμός as a crasis of ὁ ἐμός. What could be more lukewarm than Photius' review of her paraphrase of the Octateuch (*Cod.* 183): 'worthy of admiration for a woman and a queen', whose diction was 'as correct as she could make it'? Compared with any other minor classicizing poet of the age, Colluthus for example, or Musaeus, impeccably correct in metre and language and full of allusions to earlier poets, Eudocia cannot but seem uncouth and ignorant – and that without the redeeming virtue of freshness and simplicity.

It is safe to say that no-one would ever have heard of so minor a poet as Eudocia if she had not become empress. But she did become empress, and it remains to consider what sort of literary patronage she exercised, first at Constantinople and then at Jerusalem.

XIII Christian Culture

The dominating literary preoccupation of the age was ecclesiastical history and hagiography:[193] Philip of Side, Socrates and

192. There is little to add to Ludwich's article 'Eudokia ... als Dichterin', *Rh. Mus.* 37 (1882), 206–25.

193. Momigliano, *Quinto contributo*, 88f.; see too L. Cracco Ruggini, *Athenaeum* 55 (1977), 107–26.

Sozomen, Palladius and Theodoret, not to mention the heretic Philostorgius. Sozomen dedicated his book to Theodosius, Palladius his *Lausiac History* to the chamberlain Lausus (otherwise known for his remarkable collection of pagan statues – another nice illustration of the cultural diversity of the age). Socrates too clearly wrote with an eye on favour at court.

The success of Olympiodorus and Cyrus tends to be explained on the assumption that Eudocia 'permitted pagan intellectuals' at court.[194] Yet Olympiodorus was a trusted imperial representative long before Eudocia arrived on the scene,[195] and while it is true that his history made no secret of his pagan sympathies, the fact remains that it was to Theodosius, not Eudocia, that he dedicated it. As for Cyrus, Greek poetry was not the only or the most important interest he shared with Eudocia. Like him she was a keen amateur theologian; like him she built churches; like him too she hobnobbed with stylite saints (St Symeon, Daniel's model and inspiration). We have already caught Cyrus and will soon find Eudocia reading Socrates. Eudocia's activities in the Holy Land, as described in the *Life of St Melania* (§§58–9), reveal her more in tune with the ideals of the *Lausiac History* and Theodoret's *Historia Religiosa* than classical poetry. Her own extant poetry (to which we shall be returning) is devoted to hagiography and biblical paraphrase.

Another supposed member of Eudocia's 'hellenic' salon is the grammarian Orion, of a priestly family from Egyptian Thebes and so presumably (though not inevitably) a pagan. He is known to have taught in Alexandria and Caesarea (in Palestine), but solely on the strength of the dedication of his gnomic anthology to Eudocia it has generally been assumed that he also taught at Constantinople.[196] Yet the manuscript that carries the dedication also calls Orion 'grammaticus of Caesarea'. The obvious inference

194. E.g. Kaegi, *Class. et Mediaevalia* 27 (1968), 266, and *Byzantium and the Decline of Rome* (Princeton 1968), 65–6.

195. I am not persuaded by Maenchen-Helfen that Olympiodorus' embassy to the Huns in 412–13 was undertaken as a representative of the Western rather than Eastern court (*World of the Huns*, 73–4). It is not as certain as Thompson once supposed that Olympiodorus dealt exclusively with the West; there are many digressions relating to the East (notably fr. 28): see Matthews, *Western Aristocracies and Imperial Court A.D. 364–425* (Oxford 1975), 383.

196. E.g. Wendel in *RE* XVIII, 1083f, Orion 3, assuming on the flimsiest of grounds that Caesarea in Cappadocia is meant.

is that it was while Orion was in Caesarea and Eudocia in nearby Jerusalem that he dedicated the book to her.

So not only was there no pagan grammarian at court; we can also see that Eudocia's life is not to be divided straightforwardly into a hellenic phase at court and a religious phase at Jerusalem. On the one hand she was still prepared to accept the dedication of a piece of traditional classical scholarship amidst her manifold ecclesiastical and charitable activities in the Holy Land. On the other, no less a figure than the Alexandrian patriarch Cyril dedicated a christological work to her at court. In 430 Theodosius reprimanded Cyril for writing separately to Pulcheria, Eudocia and himself in the hope of dividing the imperial household.[197] Evidently Cyril had expected Eudocia no less than Pulcheria to understand the theological issues involved and use her influence on the emperor. And Cyril was not a man to waste effort.

There is little indeed to be said for the assumption that Eudocia's withdrawal from court was a setback for the 'classical revival' she is supposed to have been promoting. In the first place, despite the fame of Eudocia and Cyrus as poets, the age of Theodosius was not conspicuous for its poetry. The only other poet we know (from the ecclesiastical history of Socrates) to have performed at court is Ammonius, and while the form and style were classicizing, the theme was not – and we cannot be sure that the treatment (like Socrates') was not frankly Christian. The same reservation applies to Eudocia's panegyric on the Persian victory of 422. Holum has argued that the war was undertaken on the initiative of Pulcheria.[198] If we abandon Holum's own unnecessary conjecture that Pulcheria's influence on Theodosius was 'broken' during the war by the 'traditionalists', then Eudocia emerges quite simply as the panegyrist of 'Pulcheria's crusade'. There is certainly no justification for assuming that she presented the victory in pagan rather than Christian terms. No mythological poet (e.g. Nonnus) can be assigned to her circle, and as for even Ammonius, it should be added that 438 was the year of Eudocia's first visit to the Holy Land, and depending on how late in the year he performed his *Gainea*, Eudocia may not have been in the audience.

It was the second rather than the first half of the fifth century that saw the great revival of classicizing (especially mythological)

197. *Acta Concil. Oec.* I.I.I.   198. *GRBS* 18 (1977), 162f.

poetry, in the wake of Nonnus. To name only those we know to
have been active in Constantinople, under Zeno there were
Aetherius, Panolbius and Pelagius; under Anastasius, Christodorus, Marianus of Eleutheropolis and perhaps Colluthus.[199] An
anonymous panegyric on (probably) Anastasius[200] states that
there were many 'sons of song' at court, as too does Priscian in his
Latin panegyric on the same emperor.[201]

In the second place, Eudocia's main personal contribution to the
cause of Christian hellenism was in all probability written in the
Holy Land, her biblical and hagiographical paraphrases: hexameter versions of the books of Zachariah and Daniel, an eight-book
sequence on the Octateuch, and three books on the martyrdom of
Cyprian of Antioch. Hitherto they have been assigned to her
hellenic or religious phase according to whether it is the hellenic or
religious element that the critic has chosen to stress. We need a
more rigorous criterion. It is particularly unfortunate that we have
no firm date for either of the other two biblical paraphrases of the
age. All that can be said of the Nonnian paraphrase of St John is
that it is later than 431 and earlier than the ps.-Apollinarian
paraphrase of the Psalms (which imitates it), of perhaps *ca* 461.[202]
Eudocia was active between *ca* 420 and 460. We might also add the
twin prose and verse paraphrases of the *Acta* of St Thecla (prose
only extant) of Basil of Seleuceia, who died *ca* 460.[203]

In an oft quoted passage whose relevance to this question seems
not to have been perceived, Socrates tells us in some detail (iii.16)
how, when the Apostate Julian forbade Christians to teach the
classics, the Apollinarii of Laodicea rewrote most of the Bible into
the various classical genres, the Pentateuch into hexameters, the
Gospels into Platonic dialogues and so forth. But Julian soon died
and these paraphrases 'are now of no more importance than if they
had never been written'. In the longest digression in the whole of
his history Socrates explains just why he thinks their neglect such a
good thing. An intelligent Christian, he reasoned, will read both
the Scriptures and Classical literature (Socrates himself had
enjoyed an excellent classical education); Holy Writ for its divine

199. For the less familiar names see *Historia* 14 (1965), 505–7.
200. See n. 3 above.
201. *Pan. Anast.* 160–1.
202. J. Golega, *Der Homerische Psalter* (Ettal 1960), 93f.
203. J. Quasten, *Patrology* 3 (1960), 528.

message, and the classics, in part for their educational value, in part to help us understand and refute at first hand the folly of the hellenes. The paraphrases of the Apollinarii were neither the one nor the other. It is for this reason that he makes what he is well aware is the provocative and paradoxical assertion that it was by divine providence that Julian died so soon; partly for the obvious reason, but partly too because his death allowed Christians to sharpen their minds on pagan philosophy once more.

Now the latter part of Socrates' work verges on imperial panegyric, and he certainly knew that Eudocia wrote poetry. If any of her paraphrases had appeared by 439 when his history was published, Socrates could not have failed to realize that his criticisms of the efforts of the Apollinarii took in the empress as well. So unless we are to suppose that his purpose was in fact to criticize her, we are surely bound to conclude that none of Eudocia's paraphrases had been published by 439.

We cannot so safely make the same assumption about the Nonnian paraphrase, since Socrates might simply not have heard of it (if he had we might expect him to have mentioned it, given his interest, remarkable in an ecclesiastical historian, in recent poets).

A decade later Sozomen gives even more detail about the Apollinarian paraphrases, adding Menandrean comedies, Euripidean tragedies and Pindaric odes to the list (v.18). For Sozomen, however, Apollinarius' work (he mentions only the elder Apollinarius) is 'equal in character, diction, style and structure to the books most celebrated among the hellenes'. 'If men did not admire antiquity and hold dear that which is familiar, they would (I think) praise the efforts of Apollinarius equally with the ancients and learn them by heart.'

It looks as if Socrates' forthright condemnation of these paraphrases sparked off fresh interest in them and a lively debate about their propriety and utility. They had been written for a didactic purpose at a moment when Christians were forbidden to teach the classics. That moment had long since passed and to that extent Socrates' criticisms were justified. But even in the Christian world of the fifth century they could be made to serve a valid purpose by those who were less sure than Socrates of the desirability of a first hand knowledge of pagan literature: to provide safe Christian 'classics' for those who still valued style as much as content.

It is surely against the background of this debate that all these paraphrases were written in the 20 years or so between *ca* 440 and 460. So Eudocia's paraphrases were not (as they are often represented) the attempts of a pagan sympathizer to seduce the faithful with classical culture. On the contrary, they were designed to *save* the pagan sympathizers among the faithful by providing them with acceptable Christian substitutes for the pagan classics.

It is even possible to assess Eudocia's place within the movement. The futility of attempting to determine priority between the *Martyrdom of Cyprian* and the paraphrase of St John by looking for traces of one in the other is immediately revealed by a comparison of their techniques. Eudocia (like ps.-Apollinarius a little later) followed her model as closely as possible with a minimum of embellishment and amplification. Nonnus (if he it was) treated his model with the utmost freedom, producing an elaborate rhetorical masterpiece in the high style scarcely inferior in its way to the *Dionysiaca*.[204] The difference goes deeper than his obvious superiority as a poet; though a serious Christian and even something of a theologian, the Nonnian poet evidently put a much higher premium than Eudocia on virtuosity and originality. There can be no doubt which approach posterity preferred.

The point may be illustrated further by the biblical Homer cento Eudocia edited. It is often said that she 'completed' a project begun by an unfortunately unidentifiable bishop called Patricius. It is true that l. 9 of her preface refers to Patricius' work as 'half-finished', but a careful reading of the rest will show that this is a literary judgment rather than a statement of fact. Patricius, she says, deserves the highest praise for his idea, but he did not 'tell the whole truth or keep the full harmony of the verses or use only lines from Homer'. She claims that she struck out what was 'not in order'. Apparently Patricius had been too free, adding words and lines of his own to link his Homeric tags together. True to her ideal of fidelity to model and self-suppression in sacred paraphrases, Eudocia went through Patricius' book 'harmonizing' his tags without the help of the superfluities.

204. There is much of interest on the character of the Nonnian paraphrase in both Golega's studies (see n. 84 and 202 above).

If this well-meaning but unimaginative pedantry is Christian hellenism, it was not a hellenism to which even the most bigoted could take exception. It is illuminating to find Eudocia taking Sozomen's side against Socrates' enlightened defence of the study of pagan literature.

I pass now to the last area in which the hand of Eudocia (and occasionally of Cyrus too) has been detected: the founding of the 'University' of Constantinople in 425.[205] Now in that year Theodosius established a number of professorial chairs in Constantinople: ten *grammatici* in both Greek and Latin; three orators in Latin and five sophists in Greek; and three further posts 'profundioris . . . scientiae atque doctrinae', two chairs of law and one of philosophy.[206] All were to be paid out of state funds and teach in the same specified lecture rooms attached to the Capitol. Unquestionably this is the nearest thing to a modern university known from antiquity and it is a landmark in the history of education. But we must beware of seeing it as a distinterested act of educational philanthropy inspired by a literature-loving empress – and not only because specific evidence for the connection is lacking.

The long preamble to the law explains in instructive detail the existing situation it was designed to remedy: not too few professors, but too many! All those who had hitherto been falsely arrogating the name of *magister* to themselves are forbidden to give public lectures in future, under penalty of 'infamy' and banishment. Only those who teach at the Capitol are to enjoy the tax immunities traditionally accorded to professors. The law does not specify what the new state supported professors were to be paid, but presumably less than successful private practitioners could earn, or they would not have been forbidden to take private pupils as well. No doubt many bad teachers were weeded out, but some celebrities with lucrative private practices, unwilling to accept the drop in salary, may have left – or refused to accept chairs in the capital.

A few weeks later another edict honoured with the *comitiva* of the first rank six Constantinopolitan professors (three grammatici, two

205. On which see most recently P. Lemerle, *Le premier humanisme byzantin* (Paris 1971), 63–4, with the criticisms of P. Speck, *BZ* 67 (1974), 385–93, and H. G. Beck, *Age of Spirituality: A Symposium*, ed. K. Weitzmann (Princeton 1980), 34–5.

206. *CTh* xiv.9.3; cf. xiv.1.53.

sophists and a lawyer), promising the same honour to any professor of proven ability and unimpeachable morals who taught in Constantinople for 20 years.[207]

The two edicts are linked in more ways than one. The first was designed to raise educational standards – but not by spending more public money on it. The second was an attempt to keep good professors, not by paying them more but by dangling the carrot of a reward in kind after 20 years' service. Not surprisingly it was not very effective. For all the attention and admiration these edicts have won, it has seldom been observed that, after as before, no really prominent or productive professor, whether in grammar, rhetoric or philosophy, held a chair at Constantinople. The only name in the honours list of 425 otherwise known to us is the grammarian Helladius, assuming that he is the grammarian recorded under Theodosius II by the *Suda*.[208] He is usually further identified with the pagan grammarian Helladius who fled from Alexandria to Constantinople after the destruction of the Serapeum in 391 and taught Socrates (*HE* v.16). Naturally this has been taken as yet further proof of Eudocia's concern for pagan scholarship. Yet even if this is the same Helladius (after 34 years), and even if he was still a pagan in 425 (which cannot be taken for granted), the most relevant factor is surely that he was the only professor in Constantinople with more than a local reputation.

It does no harm to suppose that Eudocia had been casting a professional eye on the state of education in the capital. Not that any emperor since Julian would have needed less prodding in this direction than the studious Theodosius II. It is only modern scholars who have sensed a gulf between the spiritual and literary interests of the imperial couple. It was Theodosius who commissioned a calligraphic copy of the *Cento Probae*, a life of Christ extracted from Vergil. Was it coincidence that Eudocia busied herself with its Homeric counterpart, or do we catch her sharing an interest of her husband?

Whatever a few bigots might recommend, not many Christians seriously believed that there was a genuine alternative to the traditional grammatical and rhetorical education. The measures of 425 are not likely to have brought much disquiet to the Christian population of Constantinople – or much reassurance to the few

207. *CTh* vi.21.1. 208. *PLRE* ii, *s.v.* Helladius.

remaining pagans. The main reason the state continued to support grammarians and sophists was to ensure an adequate supply of rhetorically trained candidates for the imperial administration and (increasingly) for the major bishoprics.[209] And the provision for chairs of law reflects the growth of the legal education so deprecated in sophistic circles. No doubt the new measures eliminated some inadequate teaching, but it is not so clear that they did much to raise standards or attract new talent. Their most obvious and significant consequence was to tighten state control of education. After 425 education in Constantinople was in effect the monopoly of a Christian government. If Eudocia was in any sense the inspiration behind the new measures, it was certainly not her purpose to reproduce in Constantinople the academic world of Athens.

It is curious that moderns have been so fascinated with the pagan rather than Christian elements in the culture of Cyrus and Eudocia. Given both the intrinsic power of classical culture and its entrenched position in the educational system, it is hardly surprising that pagan sympathies should long have lingered in academic circles and among the educated generally.[210] It would be interesting, to be sure, if the poets and sophists patronized by Anthemius had been pagans – but even more interesting if they had been Christians. It was after all the marriage between Christianity and classical culture – an uneasy, uneven but nonetheless enduring marriage – that was the defining characteristic and backbone of Byzantine civilization.

It is regrettable that there is not more first-hand information about this group, but we do have two witnesses of a sort: Synesius (who maintained a correspondence with both Anthemius and Troilus); and Socrates (apparently a pupil of Troilus). Synesius has often been the victim of precisely the sort of misinterpretation here under discussion: the hellene who became a Christian. In fact, for all his devotion to rhetoric and neoplatonism, there is no reason to doubt that Synesius was a Christian (of sorts) all his life.[211] And

209. We have already seen that two of even Troilus' pupils became bishops.
210. See the evidence collected by Kaegi in *Class. et Mediaevalia* 27 (1968), 243–78.
211. See H.-I. Marrou, 'Synesius of Cyrene and Christian Neoplatonism', in *The Conflict between Paganism and Christianity in the Fourth Century*, ed. A. Momigliano (Oxford 1963), 126–50.

we have already seen that Socrates, whose Christianity needs no illustration, was as convinced as Synesius of the educative power of classical literature and philosophy (the theme of Synesius' *Dion*). Now while we cannot infer that the hellenism of Anthemius and Troilus was like this, there are certainly no adequate grounds for assuming that it was even implicitly hostile to Christianity.[212]

This is not to deny the possibility that Pulcheria and her sisters disapproved of such secular tastes – or that Anthemius deprecated the transformation of the palace into a nunnery. But this might have seemed more a difference of style than an ideological gulf compared with the perils of heresy. Once we look at Eudocia's works and actions in the light here suggested, she surfaces squarely in the mainstream of mid fifth-century Christian culture. If there was a controversy about the utility of biblical paraphrases, it was not conducted between the pious and those with hellenic sympathies. On the contrary, it was an internal Christian debate, with Eudocia rejecting the 'liberal' Christian line of Socrates.

In recommending this approach to Eudocia and Cyrus, I am only following the emphasis of our sources. Not even the most enthusiastic ancient admirer of Eudocia's secular culture ventures to suggest that it compromised her faith after her baptism and marriage.[213] Her later rivalry with Pulcheria is seen by the chroniclers in personal rather than ideological terms. If it had been true that (as Diehl put it) 'dans les cercles demeurés attachés aux idées anciennes, le mariage de l'empereur avec la jeune Athénienne peut-il sembler comme une victoire du paganisme', it is surprising that (e.g.) it is not so represented by Damascius, who has so much to say about the womenfolk of the professors of Athens and Alexandria, and does his (implausible) best to claim pagan sympathies for the Western emperor Anthemius (467–72). It is true that we do not have Damascius' *Life of Isidore* complete, but we do have very full excerpts by Photius, who would certainly have reported any such allegations about Eudocia, whose works he had also read with care.

212. Not even the fact that it was (presumably) Anthemius who sent Olympiodorus on his embassies proves that it was his paganism rather than his ability and experience that Anthemius admired.

213. Her brief flirtation with heresy in Palestine was a different matter; fortunately for her reputation she was reconciled with Chalcedon before her death.

In the popular tradition Cyrus too was remembered less for his poetry than for his worldly achievements: the circuit of the walls, the nocturnal illumination of the city, the great church of the Theotokos. Like Eudocia, he was seen as the innocent victim of a jealous emperor. If there was any whisper of paganism at the time of his deposition, the mud did not stick. The biographer of Daniel (who may actually have known Cyrus) recalled him only as a wise and good man, a loyal friend of the saint. Like most educated people of the time, Cyrus and Eudocia valued their classical culture – but not above their Christianity. Their standing labels 'poet' and 'poetess' suggest a preoccupation with the literary traditions of the past which is only one side of the *Weltanschauung* of two very practical and contemporary figures. Rather than Christian hellenes, which implies an exceptional combination of talents and interests, it would be more appropriate to call them, in the full cultural sense of the word, Byzantines.

Pastiche, pleasantry, prudish eroticism: the letters of 'Aristaenetus'

W. GEOFFREY ARNOTT

Più volte Amor m'avea già detto: 'Scrivi,
Scrivi quel che vedesti in lettre d'oro.'

With the substitution of some less precious metal for Petrarch's
gold, these lines, which open his 93rd sonnet, would provide an
appropriate motto for the curious collection of fifty fictitious letters
contained in a single Greek manuscript copied in the south of Italy
about A.D. 1200 and now preserved (cod. phil. graec. 310) in the
Austrian National Library at Vienna.[1] This manuscript twice
identifies its epistolographer as one Aristaenetus, but in fact the
author's name is as uncertain as his birthplace and the dates of his
career.

Mercier[2] was the first scholar to observe that the first letter in the
collection was imagined by its author to have been sent by one
Ἀρισταίνετος to one Φιλόκαλος, and to suggest in consequence that
'*forsitan nomen inscriptum primae epistolae translatum ad auctorem huius
rhapsodiae.*' The genre of imaginative epistolography to which this
rhapsodia belongs appears to have been subject to a number of rules
about such things as the exploitation of earlier writers, the choice
and use of themes, and attitudes to sexual morality. One of the
rules concerned the naming of the fictitious correspondents. Three
kinds of name were tolerated. Real names from the historical and
literary past were affixed to some of the letters in order to add a
spurious touch of verisimilitude to the nostalgic evocation of a
more classical past. In Alciphron 4.1, for example, Phryne is the

---

1. Cf. A. Lesky, *Wien. Stud.* 70 (1957), 219ff.; H. Hunger, *Katalog der griechischen Handschriften der Österreichischen Nationalbibliothek* i (Vienna 1961), 402f.; O. Mazal, *Gutenberg-Jahrbuch* (1968), 206ff., and the *Praefatio* to his edition of the letters (Stuttgart 1970), v ff.; J. Irigoin, *Settimane di Studio*, Spoleto, 22 (1974–5), 437 and 455; O. Mazal, *ibid.* 451.

2. At the end of the *Ad Aristaenetum Notae* which accompany his editions of this author (Paris 1st ed. 1595 with some copies dated 1594 or 1596, 2nd ed. 1600, 3rd ed. 1610, 4th ed. 1639). Cf. also the prefaces to the editions by J. C. de Pauw (Utrecht 1736 and 1737), 3, and J. F. Boissonade (Paris 1822), vii. References to more recent discussions about the author's name are given in my review of Mazal's edition, *Gnomon* 46 (1974), 353f.

imaginary sender of a letter to her lover Praxiteles about his celebrated statue of her, and the same author's 4.16 has the courtesan Lamia writing to Demetrius Poliorcetes about their love affair. 'Aristaenetus' 1.5 is similarly imagined to be a letter from Alciphron to Lucian, thus paying a pretty compliment to literary predecessors whom the author often quotes or exploits in various ways. The second type of name was taken from the characters of later Greek comedy. Aelian's collection of *Rustic Letters* includes a run of ten where nearly all the fictive senders and recipients bear such names: Derkyllos and Opora (7, 8: from Alexis' *Opora*[3]?), Chremes and Parmenon (9), Lamprias and Tryphe (11, 12), Kallippides and Knemon (13 to 16: from Menander's *Dyskolos*[4]). Alciphron sometimes blurs the boundaries between these two types by combining them in the same letter; thus the dramatist Menander exchanges letters with the *hetaira* Glykera, one of his characters (4.18 and 19), in a situation which shows that by Alciphron's time the character was believed to have had a real-life, extra-dramatic existence.[5]

Most common of all, however, is a third type of name, invented specially for the occasion to suit the character or the situation of the imaginary sender and recipient. Such invented names normally have no more than a general appropriateness: Alciphron's fishermen, for example, are named after the sea and its weather, the coast, boats and fishing equipment, while his parasites tend to take their names from such things as meals, food and drink, tables and tableware, the desire to eat and the guzzling performance.

Yet sometimes there is a more precise connection between the invented names of the imaginary letter-sender and the language of the respective letter, and here the first letter in the 'Aristaenetus' collection becomes very relevant. For example, in the letter which is placed first by the majority of manuscripts and all modern

3. Cf. B. Warnecke, *Hermes* 41 (1906), 158f.; my own papers in *Rhein. Mus.* 98 (1955), 312ff., and *Proc. Cambridge Philolog. Soc.* 196 (1970), 8f.

4. Cf. Inga Thyressen, *Eranos* 62 (1964), 7ff.

5. Basic here is A. Körte, *Hermes* 54 (1919), 87ff., together with his article in *RE* XV (1931), *s.v. Menandros* 9, 712. The attempts to challenge Körte's arguments and to allege Glykera's historicity (W. Schmid, *Woch. Klass. Phil.* 36 (1919), 166f.; M. A. Schepers, *Mnemosyne* 54 (1926), 258ff.) seem to me unsuccessful. Cf. also J. J. Bungarten, 'Menanders und Glykeras Brief bei Alkiphron' (diss. Bonn 1967); P. M. Fraser, *Ptolemaic Alexandria* II (Oxford 1972), 873 n. 11; and K. Treu, *Schriften zur Geschichte und Kultur der Antike* 6 (1973), 207ff.

editors of Alciphron's collection (1.1), Εὔδιος (Fairweather) writes to Φιλόσκαφος (Loveboat) about the advantageous calm (χρηστὴν . . . τὴν γαλήνην) at sea that day, which enabled him to launch his little boat (σκαφίδιον) and catch a vast quantity of fish. The headings of Alciphron 3.1 and 3.2 have been erroneously changed around in the manuscripts,[6] for the imaginary writer of 3.1 is not Τρεχέδειπνος (Dinnersprint) but Ἐκτοδιώκτης (Six-chaser), who opens his letter with the grumble that the sundial's shadow hasn't yet reached the sixth hour, and he's starving. Similarly in 'Aristaenetus', letter 1.3 is ascribed to a Φιλοπλάτανος (Loveplanetree) and lovingly details the events of a *fête champêtre* held beneath the shade of spreading plane trees (line 3)[7], and the fictitious writer of 1.14 is Φιλοχρημάτιον (Lovemoney), who begins her letter with the remark that 'Neither can the pipe persuade the courtesan nor does one persuade harlots by the lyre, without cash (ἀργυρίου χωρίς)'.

The opening letter in the 'Aristaenetus' collection is imagined to be written by Ἀρισταίνετος (Bestpraiseworthy) to Φιλόκαλος (Lovefair), and it consists of an elaborate encomium of the beauty of the alleged writer's mistress; 'Aphrodite', it claims, 'adorned her fairest of all' (line 2). Clearly here, as in the other cases mentioned, the name of the imaginary letter-writer was invented[8] to suit the contents of the letter. It would be a curious and unparalleled coincidence if that invented name were also the actual name of the real epistolographer.[9] In all the other letters belonging to this

6. This was first noticed by Schepers; cf. A. S. Gratwick, *CQ* 29 (1979), 308f.

7. Letter and line references conform to those in Mazal's edition (above, note 1). On these names see also A. Lesky, *Aristainetos: Erotische Briefe* (Zürich 1951), 139.

8. Or perhaps taken from Lucian's *Dialogi Meretricii*, where two imaginary Aristaeneti are mentioned, one as father of a Charmides in 2.4, and the other as philosopher and tutor of a Clinias in 10. This work is a favourite quarry of 'Aristaenetus' (the borrowings are conveniently collected in Mazal's edition. p. 181), who copies a phrase from Lucian's first dialogue at 1.1.44–5, two passages from the third dialogue at 1.16.28–30 and 2.1.34–5 (while two of its expressions, ἀπογυμνοῦσα . . . τὰ σφυρά and ὑπερεπήνει τὸ εὔρυθμον, are echoed at 1.27.26–7 in a characteristic game of *imitatio cum uariatione*), a phrase from the ninth dialogue probably at 1.28.2–3 (where V's ἀπό ought to be retained, in view of Lucian's identical wording), while the proverbial expression ἡ ἀπὸ Σκυθῶν ῥῆσις is common to the tenth dialogue and 2.20.6–7.

9. In real life the name is found from the late fourth century B.C. onwards: cf. J. Kirchner, *Prosop. Att.* no. 1633; *RE* II (1896), 850–2 (ten entries in all, including the epistolographer).

tradition of fictive correspondence there is no example remotely comparable. Either all the names of the imagined correspondents are fictional (so in Alciphron, Aelian, Theophylactus Simocatta, and all the other letters of 'Aristaenetus'), or all the letters in a collection are imagined to be, as they really are, the author's own missives (as with Philostratus). Reality and fiction are never combined in a way that they would be if a real Aristaenetus were at the same time both author and imaginary sender of letter 1.1. Given these facts, only one explanation of the Vienna manuscript's attribution of its collection of letters to 'Aristaenetus' seems satisfactory. The name of the real author must have been lost or deliberately suppressed at some stage in the transmission.[10] Some copyist or scholar then, preferring a definite even if incorrect name to anonymity, looked quickly at the invented name of the imaginary sender of the first letter in his manuscript and probably with idle carelessness assumed it to be the real name of the author of the whole collection.

'Aristaenetus' thus becomes anonymous, a Byzantine shadow distinguished for modern readers by a soubriquet of convention which ought properly to be enclosed within inverted commas. The soubriquet may perhaps conceal the identity of a literary figure already known for other work accurately ascribed, or it may simply label the single surviving work of some Byzantine nonentity. Evidence to penetrate behind the mask and to establish even the date and place of composition with any degree of precision is inadequate. Letter 1.26 has a passing reference to a celebrated mime-dancer called Caramallus.[11] A mime of this name is praised in one of Sidonius Apollinaris' poems (23.268) written between A.D. 462 and 466, and John Malalas records (*Chronogr.* 15)[12] that a dancer from Alexandria with the same name was associated with the Greens in Constantinople around 490. These two references clearly do not concern the same mime-dancer at the two extremes of his career, for Malalas' Caramallus is still young; they must

---

10. It is always possible that the author's name was originally placed only at the colophon of the manuscript, and so was lost when an accident removed the final page or pages of the work, containing the end of letter 2.22 and any subsequent letters, from our tradition.

11. Cf. A. Lesky, *IIIe Congrès international des études byzantins* (Athens 1932), 85f.; and my brief discussion in *Gnomon* 46 (1974), 354.

12. Migne, *PG* 97.573 = *Corp. Script. Hist. Byz.* 386.

rather identify two different artists, perhaps of the same family but belonging to successive generations. In any case they define the limits within which the letters of 'Aristaenetus' were composed as 450 to 510, since the fame of mime-dancers at Byzantium was likely to have been ephemeral and not to have extended more than one generation after the climaxes of their careers.

A series of subsidiary arguments tallies with, although it does nothing to pinpoint more exactly, these dates. The letter which refers to Caramallus, for example, also mentions 'the older Rome, as well as the new one' (lines 22–3), thus placing the author firmly in the new world inaugurated by Constantine when he renamed Byzantium in 330 and honoured it with the title of the New Rome. Linguistic and rhythmical characteristics also tie the composition of the letters to the period when classical paganism was giving way to Byzantine Christianity. 'Aristaenetus' strove hard to imitate the Attic dialect of models like Plato and Menander, but as with so many writers of late antiquity his aim often fell far short of the target, and his Greek abounds with solecisms such as εἴθε with the future indicative (1.6.24–5, 2.2.13, 2.5.48–50, cf. 2.5.9–10), indefinite relative clauses with ἄν and the optative (1.15.51, 2.1.3, 2.2.18), and conditional protases where εἰ introduces a subjunctive (2.1.49, 2.7.28–9).[13] Such anomalies flood into Atticizing Greek from the time of Lucian on; εἰ with the subjunctive, for instance, is a characteristic construction of Lucian, the second Philostratus, and Achilles Tatius.[14] Rhythmical considerations also support a latish dating for 'Aristaenetus'. His letters are some of the earliest surviving works with accent-regulated clausulae. At the ends of sentences sequences of words with one or no unaccented syllables between the final and penultimate accents are avoided, and sequences with two or four such syllables are favoured. This fashion

13. Cf. T. Nissen, *Byz. Zeitschr.* 40 (1940), 10ff.; and my comments in *Gnomon* 46 (1974), 354f. Many of these anomalies were wrongly emended out of the text by nineteenth-century scholars such as Cobet and Hercher.

14. Cf. W. Schmid, *Der Atticismus* (Stuttgart 1887–97), I. 244, IV. 85 and 620; Nissen (note 13), 13. I take over here Schmid's identification of the second Philostratus as the author of the earlier *Imagines*, the *Life of Apollonius of Tyana*, the *Lives of the Sophists*, and a few other works. The best recent account of the family of the Philostrati is G. W. Bowersock, *Greek Sophists in the Roman Empire* (Oxford 1969), 2ff.

appears not to have been adopted before the fourth century A.D.[15]

One final point. Like his predecessors in the genre of the fictitious letter, 'Aristaenetus' quotes, adapts and exploits passages from earlier writers.[16] His favourite sources include several who were active Atticists in the second and third centuries A.D. (Achilles Tatius, Alciphron, Lucian, the Philostrati of the *Imagines* and the *Letters*, and Xenophon of Ephesus), but none datable to the fifth century or later.

II

In the Greek world letters in prose, written with no intent to deceive their readership about their true authorship or to foist upon some past celebrity the composition of their contents, but designed purely to dazzle and delight a jaded world, form an interesting, unassuming and doubtless also an undervalued little genre of their own. The earliest extant collections belong to the second and third centuries of our era, when Alciphron outshone rivals like Aelian and Philostratus,[17] and the tradition continued at least until Theophylactus Simocatta in the first half of the seventh century. 'Aristaenetus' comes about midway in time between Alciphron, 'the master of the style',[18] and the pitifully jejune Theophylactus; in quality, however, despite the savagery of some modern critics,[19] 'Aristaenetus' deserves to stand at least next to Alciphron.

In the Vienna manuscript the letters of 'Aristaenetus' are divided between two books, with 28 in the first and 22 (the last incomplete) in the second before the manuscript breaks off. The subject of all of them is love, or more precisely sexual passion. Nothing could be more titillating at the first approach, nothing

15. Cf. W. Meyer, *Gesammelte Abhandlungen zur mittellateinischen Rhythmik* II (Berlin 1905), 202ff.; Nissen (n. 13), 1ff.

16. See below, section III.

17. The relative dating of the trio is uncertain. On Alciphron, see especially A. R. Benner and F. H. Fobes' Loeb edition of the letters of Alciphron, Aelian and Philostratus (1949), 6ff.; on Philostratus, G. W. Bowersock (n. 14).

18. R. Hackforth and B. R. Rees, in *OCD*[2], *s.v. Letters, Greek* §6.

19. Yet when G. Cobet (*Mnemosyne* 9 (1860), 150) claimed '*delirabat Graecia et tristi senio repuerascebat quum talia legebantur et placebant*', his attack was directed rather at the subject-matter of 'Aristaenetus', with its clear acceptance of sexual immorality, than against faults of imagination or expression in the writer.

eventually more tedious than this deliberate limitation of subject-matter, but the author makes every effort to add variety to his themes. Apart from 1.10 and 1.15 (the stories of Acontius and Cydippe, and of Phrygius and Pieria respectively, where 'Aristaenetus' follows his source Callimachus in making the wedding night the sexual climax), the passions and escapades are entirely extra-marital,[20] but every imaginable variety of extra-marital situation is dredged up. Young men are infatuated with *hetairai* (e.g. 1.1, 1.3), but their passions may be unrequited (1.17) or rapaciously exploited (1.23, cf. 1.14); they fall for a maiden (2.2), a mother-in-law (2.8), somebody else's slave-girl (2.4), their father's concubine (1.13); they are desired in their turn by *hetairai* (1.22, 1.25), maidens (1.2), and a free woman of uncertain marital status (1.11). Adultery is a common theme (1.5, 1.9, 1.20, 2.22), with at least one outrageous variant where a widow is in love with her friend's husband, and her friend with the widow's male slave (2.15). One young man has a casual encounter with *hetairai* (1.4), another loves his wife and mistress simultaneously (2.11), a third is captivated by his own painting of a beautiful girl (2.10). A slave-girl is crazy about her mistress' lover (2.7), a music girl persuades the man who has given her a child to marry her (1.19), a free girl has an affair before her wedding (1.6). Even incest appears to be condoned (1.16).

To variety of theme must be added variety of treatment. Some letters are miniature romances (e.g. 1.10, 1.15), tales of intrigue (1.13, 1.19) or witty anecdotes (1.5), with narrative predominating; others consist largely of conversation (e.g. 1.4) or declamation (1.14); still others feature elaborate descriptions of a person (e.g. 1.1, 1.26, 2.21) or a scene (1.3). To these eleven examples the letter form is incidental, a mere excuse for the author to develop themes which could be transplanted into other genres such as the novel, declamations or Philostratean ἐκφράσεις without much alteration.

---

20. Even in 2.3 the newly wedded wife turns her thoughts away from the inattentive lawyer who has married her and threatens that 'another rhetor is going to look after my case' (lines 13–14). The rareness of the conventional 'Acontius and Cydippe' type of love story, where an innocent romance is sealed by marriage, is all the more surprising when two of the major sources of 'Aristaenetus' are considered: the Greek novel, and plays of the New Comedy like Menander's *Dyskolos*. The epistolographer plagiarizes their language, often too their situations; but he does not care for their nuptial climaxes.

Other letters, however, have a fictive epistolary purpose; 1.28, for instance, would not be out of place in a modern agony column, while 2.2 and 2.13 are love letters with ulterior motives, the start of a liaison and an excuse for inconstancy. The material admittedly is often hackneyed, often tricked out with τόποι from the rhetorical schools or literary tradition; 'Aristaenetus' nevertheless is at some pains to avoid the repetition of identical incidents or developments in different letters, although the very monotony of his subject-matter poses difficulties of its own. The number of ways, for example, in which a girl's pretty face and figure can be described within the conventions of Second-Sophistic literature is rather limited.

This emphasis on variety in an author who takes many of his stories, situations and phrases from earlier writers is easily explained. 'Aristaenetus' simply wishes to avoid boring his readers. One of his two main functions is journalistic in the modern sense: the provision of morally shocking but never pornographic light entertainment. His modern counterparts are the story-writers in romantic magazines, reporters who describe trials and scandals spiced with sex, and the aunties who give advice on personal problems in the popular press. It is a misfortune that his works stand in modern libraries cheek by jowl with the poems of Archilochus, the plays of Aristophanes and the philosophy of Aristotle, because dismissive critics are thereby induced to judge 'Aristaenetus' as if he were a serious but failed aspirant in the lists of high literature, rather than as a literatured entertainer whose work was probably designed to be read once, to while away the tedium of an idle hour in the salons of Byzantium.

We have no means of identifying precisely who his readers were intended to be, but I expect that few if any of them would have been experts in literature and rhetoric, able to draw up a genealogy for each τόπος or to name the source of each phrase or passage which 'Aristaenetus' had 'plagiarized' (to use a term whose validity will be examined in section III below) from earlier literature. Could 'Aristaenetus' perhaps have seen himself primarily as a populariser of the stories and wisdom of previous generations? Or was his role rather that of a problematist, teasing his readers and challenging them to identify the limits and the source of each 'plagiarism'?

Whatever the correct answer to these questions may have been, it need not conflict with the second function that the letters fulfil, the function of rhetorical display. This is far less attractive to most modern readers, but it deserves to be assessed in terms of the age when 'Aristaenetus' wrote. He is clearly a product of the rhetorical schools, a devotee of the florid Asianic style; his letters may be divertissements, but they are carefully written epideictic divertissements.

Rhetoric firstly forged his style,[21] which may aptly be summed up in the words which Menander the rhetor (if he really was the author of the work in question) used of a Philostratus: γένοιτο δ' ἂν καὶ ἀπὸ λέξεως ἐπιτετηδευμένης καὶ κεκαλλωπισμένης χάρις ἐν λόγῳ (*Rhet. Gr.* iii.411 Spengel). For 'Aristaenetus' this 'carefully artistic and embellished diction' means an abundance of adjectives and adjectival phrases in long, punctiliously structured sentences marked by interlacings, anaphora and a predilection for artificial antitheses where the δέ clause provides no real contrast to its μέν predecessor but rather repeats the idea in varied words: Λαΐδα τὴν ἐμὴν ἐρωμένην εὖ μὲν ἐδημιούργησεν ἡ φύσις, κάλλιστα δὲ πάντων ἐκόσμησεν Ἀφροδίτη (the opening words of the first letter). The result is an almost Apuleian *lactea ubertas* which quickly palls on those occasions when the writer's imagination is unequal to the richness of his style.[22] Repetitiveness indeed is the major fault of the 'Aristaenetan' style: a repetitiveness less of words than of ideas, despite the attempt to cloak it by changing the diction the second time round (e.g. 1.18.1–5: note the presence of five words meaning 'handsome' or 'desirable', three meaning 'young', three meaning 'you enjoy'; 1.24.10–12; 2.16.1–2). Pleonasm (e.g. 1.18.1 ὑπερευδαιμονεῖς . . . εὐτυχοῦσα, 1.13.24 πρῶτος . . . ἡγούμενος) is another variety of the same fault.

It is a second weakness of the same style that it does not always know when to leave well alone, but tends to add the extra detail which spoils rather than caps the total effect. At 1.3.58ff., for instance, 'Aristaenetus' closes an otherwise charming account of cups of wine being cooled by the water as they float along a ditch in the open country, with the detail that 'each of the cups as they

21. Cf. especially J. Pietzko, 'De Aristaeneti epistulis' (diss. Breslau 1907), 11ff.
22. Cf. Aristotle, *Rhet.* 3.3., 1405[b] 34ff.: τὰ δὲ ψυχρὰ . . . γίγνεται κατὰ τὴν λέξιν . . . ἐν τοῖς ἐπιθέτοις τὸ ἢ μακροῖς ἢ ἀκαίροις ἢ πυκνοῖς χρῆσθαι . . . ἀλλὰ δεῖ στοχάζεσθαι τοῦ μετρίου.

sailed on like merchantmen carried with it a leafy sprig of citron, and these formed sails for our goblets on their happy voyage'. This addition of the citron sprigs seems to me unrealistic, an extraneous device invented solely to create an analogy with the sails of tubby cargo-ships, and it would have better been left out.

Such faults are easy to exemplify, but they do not occur everywhere in the letters. That 'Aristaenetus' is uneven in the quality of his inventive imagination and also of the style that expresses it, nobody will deny. The letters in Book 2 of the collection are generally inferior to those in Book 1,[23] although 1.11 seems to me wholly banal,[24] while the narrative in 2.22 maintains the reader's interest as vigorously as the best examples in Book 1. At their worst the combination of reiterative floridness in the style and superabundant familiarity in the ideas may tend to counterbalance the procacious allure of the subject-matter and the effort at variety in the selection and organization of themes. The best letters however, have a lighter touch; a good observation here or an unexpected twist in the story there keeps the attention from flagging, while turgidity is replaced by a more economical elegance; 1.4, in which the imaginary writer neatly shows his Dr Watson of a companion how he can read a girl's character and intentions from her appearance and gestures, is a case in point.

The influence of rhetoric on 'Aristaenetus', however, extends far beyond diction, and indeed merits a detailed study to itself. Here a few brief illustrations must suffice; they may serve as a protreptic to other scholars. For example, some of the more elaborate narratives (e.g. 1.13, the doctor's diagnosis; 1.15, Phrygius and Pieria) are preceded by formal proems which consist largely of general maxims and are pointedly related to the subsequent narratives. The προοίμιον[25] of 1.13 discusses the relationship of chance (τύχη)

23. They also tend to portray more shockingly immoral situations. The two factors may be linked.

24. This judgment requires substantiation. In this letter a woman in love converses with her servant about the good looks of her inamorato. Hackneyed phrases (e.g. κάλλος γε καλόν line 12: cf. Theophilus fr. 12 Kock; Lucian, *De Dom.* 1) and verbal plagiarisms (ὑφ' ἡδονῆς παντοδαπὰ χρώματα . . . ἠφίει 25–6 comes from Plato, *Lysis* 222b) abound; rhetorical tricks such as anaphora (9–10, 14–16) and balanced clauses (16–18) bear witness to careful composition; but I search here in vain for any imaginative touch that might linger in the memory.

25. The word itself is actually used at the beginning of the letter (lines 5–6) to describe its opening section.

and skill (τέχνη),[26] and at the moment in the actual story when the doctor makes his diagnosis we are told that it was the result partly of chance, partly of skill (21–2). Again, several letters end with a relevantly pointed maxim (e.g. 1.13.74–5) or proverb (e.g. 1.17.31–2). Proverbs in fact are one of the most characteristic features of the 'Aristaenetan' letter;[27] their use had been approved by rhetoricians at least from the time of Aristotle (cf. *Rhet.* 3.11, 1413ᵃ), and 'Aristaenetus' does not restrict his choice to the more familiar examples, like 'a Cadmeian conquest' (2.6.18) or 'I've got a wolf by the ears' (2.3.21–2), but introduces many more recherché but vivid ones otherwise known only from the late paroemiographic collections,[28] such as 'teaching a dolphin to swim' (2.1.53) and 'she's a notice-board of the troubles that go with sex' (1.17.10–11).

And yet, when all is said and done, it is not when 'Aristaenetus' wears his rhetorician's cap and loads his letters with proverbs, rhetorical clichés, τόποι and εἰκόνες from the schools,[29] that he is at his most interesting. It would be absurd to claim that he had a gargantuan talent, but such skills as he did possess were characteristically deployed in fascinating ways. He used material from earlier writers without any demur, but the techniques with which he inserted the borrowed gems in the mosaic of his own text are continuously intriguing. He had a way of describing sexual activity that may not be unique to him but nevertheless remains entertaining today. And at times he gives evidence of a distinct wit and of an eye for the imaginative and significant detail. The remaining sections of this article will be devoted to these aspects of his craftsmanship.

III

There was nothing new about the unacknowledged exploitation of material from earlier literature at the time when 'Aristaenetus'

26. A hackneyed τόπος: cf. Agathon fr. 6 Nauck², 'Menander' monostich 740 Jäkel, and an anonymous epigram in *Anth. Pal.* 7.135.

27. Cf. especially D. A. Tsirimbas, *Platon* 2 (1950–1), 25ff.

28. 'Aristaenetus' may well have collected some of these from works now lost to us, such as some of the comedies of Menander.

29. Many of the most hackneyed τόποι are conveniently listed by J. Pietzko (note 21), 4ff.

wrote his collection. It appears to have been considered an inalienable feature of the genre of imaginary and imaginative letters right from the beginning. Aelian's *Rustic Letters*, written at the end of the second or the beginning of the third century, expropriate incidents, vivid phrases or even whole passages, and character names from a variety of earlier authors. His second letter borrows much of its opening sentence from Menander, *Georgos* 48–52; letter 4 is modelled on Aristophanes, *Acharnians* 995–8; 6 takes the names Callaras and Callicles and much of its material from Demosthenes' speech against Callicles (55);[30] 13 to 16 inclusive derive the names Kallippides and Knemon and a series of fine phrases from Menander's *Dyskolos*,[31] although here Aelian has attempted to alter some of the details in the Menandrean setting.[32]

Four hundred years after Aelian, the epistolographer Theophylactus Simocatta continued in the same tradition, quarrying tags and phrases particularly from Menander; πέτρας γεωργεῖν in letter 5 (Hercher's numeration) seems to derive from *Dyskolos* 4f., πέπονθα . . . τὴν ψυχήν in 15 is a tag perhaps taken from *Heros* 18, ῥαγδαῖος σκῆπτος in 24 may come from *Aspis* 402f., 27 rephrases *Georgos* 35ff., 29 copies *Georgos* 77f., 61 slightly alters *Epitrepontes* fr. 6 Körte, and 77 transforms rather more substantially *Heros* 16f.

Before the comparable practices of 'Aristaenetus' are considered, it will not be inappropriate to ask the question why this tradition of exploiting without any acknowledgement material from earlier, and particularly Athenian, authors attached itself so firmly to the epistolary genre. Part of the answer lies in the period when this genre first flourished, for prose writers of the Second Sophistic commonly followed the same practice, although their

30. Cf. E. L. De Stefani, *SIFC* 19 (1912), 8ff.

31. Cf. Inga Thyressen, *loc. cit.* in n. 4.

32. All these are proven sources. Other sources have tentatively been suggested for other letters: Isaeus' speech against Timonides (fr. 43 Thalheim) for 3 (De Stefani, *loc. cit.* in n. 30), Alexis' *Opora* for 7 and 8 (Warnecke and myself, *locc. citt.* in n. 3), Alciphron 2.1 for 11 (J.-R. Vieillefond, *Rev. Phil.* 55 (1929), 357: but there is some doubt whether Alciphron antedates, postdates, or is contemporary with Aelian; see n. 17 above). Other letters too may have sources now lost: e.g. Menander's *Thrasyleon* for 9 (the letter mentions a soldier of this name, while its main theme is the imaginary writer's ignorance of the real characters of *hetairai*: cf. Menander fr. 203 Körte-Thierfelder), and another play of later Greek comedy for 18 (many phrases in the letter, e.g. λάρου βίον ζῇ and Αἰγυπτίους τε καὶ Σύρους φαντάζεται καὶ περιβλέπει τὸ δεῖγμα, have the rhythm of comic iambics: cf. T. Kock, *CAF* iii.443, fr. 181).

strategy varied from the mild exploitation of tags, familiar quotations and first pages that we find in Lucian[33] to the more comprehensive and complex redeployments of 'Aristaenetus'. But a less superficial explanation lies in the nostalgia of the age for a more glorious past when Athens was the centre of civilization, Attic Greek the paragon of literary dialects, and its texts the venerated masterpieces whose piecemeal exploitation by writers such as 'Aristaenetus' was a mark rather of sincere homage than of plagiaristic deceitfulness. 'Aristaenetus' perhaps was not so obsessed with the Attic reverie as his predecessor Alciphron, whose letters attempt to evoke Athens in the fourth century B.C., a precise place and a precise time. 'Aristaenetus' is much less specific over place and period; his letters generally convey the impression of an unfocused past,[34] with the geography of his towns with their narrow alleys (1.2) and of his country meadows in summer (1.3) unspecified. Only rarely are peculiarly Attic features mentioned: a reference to Alcibiades' beauty (1.11.11–12), to the eleven police commissioners (2.22.14), and to the deme Alopeke (1.4.1).[35] Yet the nostalgia for the classical past is not diminished by the vagueness. It is revealed in the countless quotations from, and allusions to, Attic and Atticizing authors, in the often unsuccessful attempt to imitate the classical Attic dialect, in the general ambience of a world devoted to *hetairai*, the pursuit of love, and New-Comedy situations, in the frequent oaths by the pagan Greek gods, and in the scattered references to the heroes of Greek mythology.[36] At a time when Byzantine Christianity was transforming or rejecting the values of classical antiquity, 'Aristaenetus' is thus seen to be offering a valedictory hymn to paganism.[37]

If the answers suggested above to the question why 'Aris-

33. Cf. G. Anderson, *BICS* 23 (1976), 59ff.

34. Letter 1.26, with its references to the mime-dancer Caramallus and to the old and new Romes (see above, section 1 of this paper) is the unique exception here, being an evocation of the present or very recent past. Several letters, however, take for granted behaviour that would have been unthinkable in Athens during the fifth and fourth centuries B.C.: see A. Lesky (n. 7), 143f.

35. Cf. A. Lesky (n. 7), 44. The choice of the deme has some witty overtone: see below, section V of this paper.

36. E.g. Nestor (1.15.61–2), the Atreidae (1.17.28), Achilles (2.5.7), Theseus and Ariadne (2.13.6–8).

37. Yet it remains, curiously enough, a hymn very much of its own period: see below, section IV of this paper.

taenetus' and the other epistolographers so openly exploited material from earlier writers appear speculative and incomplete (they leave out of the reckoning, for example, an author's wish to parade the range and depth of his literary knowledge), the methods used by 'Aristaenetus' to weave this borrowed material into the texture of his letters are absolutely clear and at times both intricate and intriguing. In an earlier article[38] I examined these methods at some length, and here accordingly a brief summary will suffice.

Four types of exploitation can be detected. First, there is direct quotation from earlier writers either verbatim or with slight amendments to adapt the original to the epistolographer's own context, style and rhythm.[39] These quotations vary in length from brief phrases and commonplace tags to passages over seventy words long, like the extract from the fifth book of Plato's *Republic* (474 d–5 a) at 1.18.20–30. The second type of exploitation sheds a much more interesting light on the 'Aristaenetan' method of composition. When the epistolographer is directly transcribing a passage or phrase from an earlier author, he will characteristically scrutinize the surrounding context in his source for additional brilliancies to adorn other parts of the letter he is writing. In 1.2.22–4, for instance, he copies fifteen words (μεχρί up to ἐντεῦθεν) directly from Plato's *Symposium* (217 e), but earlier in the same letter (line 10) he has borrowed the vivid word ʒηλοτυποῦμεν from 213 d of the Platonic dialogue. The third type of exploitation couples straightforward copying with the typically Hellenistic practice of *imitatio cum uariatione*. It can conveniently be illustrated from letter 1.27.17–18, where 'Aristaenetus' describes a lover convinced that he himself is more beautiful than the girl he loves,

38. *GRBS* 14 (1973), 197ff., where I labelled this practice 'plagiarism'. This term, with its more modern pejorative associations, now seems to me excessively harsh and culturally unjustified. When writers like 'Aristaenetus' spatchcocked the brilliant ideas of hallowed predecessors into their own compositions, their policy was not the deceitful one of passing stolen peacock feathers off as their own plumage. Their unacknowledged quotations seem rather to be tokens of reverence for the cherished writings of past ages, whose memorabilia were, in the eyes of these later authors, too important to be left mouldering in forgotten contexts. Hence their reverent redeployment in fresh fields and contexts new.

39. 'Aristaenetus' occasionally alters the wording of his source in order to make it conform to the rules of his accent-regulated clausulae; for examples, see Nissen (n. 13), 1ff.

οἰόμενόν τε κάλλος ὑπὲρ κάλλους χαρίζεσθαι, μέγιστον ἀντὶ βραχέος. It was noticed long ago that the phrase κάλλος ὑπὲρ κάλλους χαρίζεσθαι appears to imitate a phrase in Plato's *Symposium* (218 e) which comes shortly after the passage copied in letter 1.2: ἀλλάξασθαι κάλλος ἀντὶ κάλλους. A sceptic might now well ask how we can be so certain that 'Aristaenetus' is deliberately varying the passage of Plato here; could the similarity not be a mere coincidence? The reply is provided by the surrounding text in both Plato and the epistolographer. The latter adds three words of explanation, μέγιστον ἀντὶ βραχέος, to his Platonic variation, and in this explanation the *word* ἀντί picks up Plato's ἀντί, and the *idea* of exchanging something valuable for something small comes from two lines later on the passage from the *Symposium*, ‘χρύσεα χαλκείων’ διαμείβεσθαι, where Plato in his turn cites Homer (*Iliad* 6.235f.). But this is not all. 'Aristaenetus' here also profits from the passage of Plato with his second type of exploitation, for *Symposium* 218 c contains the expression ἐραστὴς ἄξιος (transformed to ἀξιέραστος in line 12 of the letter), the verb χαρίζεσθαι itself (line 18), and 218 e has εὐμορφίας (εὐμορφίᾳ line 16 of the letter).

The fourth and last type of exploitation may at first sight seem not to deserve the stigma of such a name. Here 'Aristaenetus' simply takes an old story and retells it at least partly in his own words. In Book 1 the stories of Acontius and Cydippe (letter 10) and of Phrygius and Pieria (15) are taken from Callimachus' *Aetia* (cf. frs. 67–75 and 80–3 Pfeiffer[40] respectively), that of the physician and the boy who loved his father's concubine (13) from an allegedly historical incident linking Antiochus Soter and Stratonice first told perhaps by Phylarchus but later fictionalized by the novelist Heliodorus (4.7) and elsewhere,[41] and that of Melissarion (19) at least partly from the Hippocratic tract Περὶ φύσιος παιδίου (7.490 Littré = 55 Joly). In the three cases, however, where the 'Aristaenetan' source either wholly or partly survives, direct copying is demonstrably involved. Several phrases from the extant portions of Callimachus' elegiacs can be identified

40. But frs. 82.1–3 and 80.19–21 Pfeiffer should be joined together; see E. A. Barber and P. Maas, *CQ* 44 (1950), 96 and 168.

41. Cf. E. Rohde, *Der griechische Roman*[3] (Leipzig 1914), 55ff.; J. Mesk, *Rhein. Mus.* 68 (1913), 366ff., and *Wien. Stud.* 57 (1939), 166ff.; A. Lesky (n. 7), 151ff.; and my own paper (n. 38), 209f.

in letters 10 and 15,[42] while several lines of the Hippocratic tract, translated into the Attic dialect, can be recognized in letter 19 (lines 16 to 28).[43]

An interesting variant of this type is provided by some 'Aristaenetan' borrowings from drama. Here the epistolographer exploits a scene or a group of scenes from a particular play, extracting several ideas from the dramatic situation and a few examples of vivid phraseology, and then transmogrifies them into the related situation of his letter. Thus 2.3, the complaint of a young wife about her husband's neglect, incorporates ideas and language from Aristophanes' *Clouds*. The name of the unsatisfactory husband is Strepsiades (2.3.1), clearly taken from that of the hero of the play. The main substance of the wife's grievance against her husband is his lack of sexual interest in her (lines 2–3, 6–7, 10–11, 13–16); it is likely that the basic idea here derives from Strepsiades' early speech in the *Clouds* implying that his rich wife was too interested in sex (46–55).[44] 'Aristaenetus' opens this letter by describing his Strepsiades as τῷ σοφῷ ῥήτορι, and he goes on to emphasize the husband's preoccupation with lawsuits. *Clouds* 1206–11 gives the basic inspiration for all this (note ὦ Στρεψίαδες ... ὡς σοφός ... λέγων τὰς δίκας). Given the general background and methodology of 'Aristaenetan' exploitations, who can doubt that two instances of vivid phraseology, appearing only here in the letters, also derive from Aristophanes' play: προμνήστριαν (line 19, from *Clouds* 41) and δικορράφος (line 23, from δικορραφεῖν *Clouds* 1483)?

Other examples of this technique can be seen in letters 1.5 and 1.7 (where the source for some of the expressions and situations may be Menander's *Samia*), 1.22 and 2.12 (where the sources seem to be two of Menander's lost comedies), and 1.6 (where the source

42. On the relationship between 'Aristaenetus' 1.10 and Callimachus frs. 67–75 see especially, in addition to Pfeiffer's great edition, A. Dietzler, 'Die Akontios-Elegie des Kallimachos' (diss. Griefswald 1933), and my notes in *GRBS* 14 (1973), 207f., and *Mus. Phil. Lond.* 1 (1975), 15f.; on the relationship between 'Aristaenetus' 1.15 and Callimachus frs. 80–3 see additionally A. Barigazzi, *Prometheus* 2 (1976), 11ff.

43. Cf. my own paper, *GRBS* 14 (1973), 198ff.

44. Cf. Sir Kenneth Dover's note (his edition) on line 51.

is Euripides' *Hippolytus*).[45] This list would doubtless be extended if more of Greek drama, especially New Comedy, had survived.

Some additional points of considerable importance emerge from an investigation of the different ways in which 'Aristaenetus' exploits his sources. The wide range of these sources will be immediately obvious from the examples casually cited in this and other papers, although the modern researcher is handicapped in any attempt to make a rapid and accurate assessment by two impediments of different kinds. The loss of so much ancient literature makes it impossible to gauge exactly the epistolographer's debt to sources like Menander. It is highly likely that some of these lost works are exploited in the letters without any possibility of identification. And secondly the published lists of sources are neither complete nor conveniently organized.[46] Even so, it clearly emerges that the authors most frequently and extensively exploited by 'Aristaenetus' are Achilles Tatius, Alciphron, Homer,[47] Lucian, Menander, the Philostrati of the *Letters* and *Imagines*, and Plato. Many other writers, including the Attic tragedians, Aristophanes, Hellenistic poets, novelists other than Achilles Tatius, and the Ionic doctor who wrote Περὶ φύσιος παιδίου, are less often exploited. More striking than the range of authors used by 'Aristaenetus', however, is the depth of reading revealed by the exploitations. Many authors of the Second-Sophistic period try to pass themselves off as literary cognoscenti by quoting earlier writers with great frequency, but their parades of learning too often turn out to be shams and superficialities. A recent paper,[48] for example, has shown conclusively that Lucian's quotations tend to come second-hand from rhetorical anthologies or to be taken from the opening page or column of an original work. 'Aristaenetus', on the other hand, seems to know many works far more

45. The borrowings from drama in 1.5, 1.7, 1.22 and 2.12 are analysed in my paper (n. 38), 203ff.; on 1.6 and Euripides' *Hippolytus*, see below (the end of section III).

46. The apparatus of sources and parallels placed below Mazal's text is not complete, and it fails to make clear the distinction between verbatim copyings, loose adaptations, and tags (cf. *Gnomon* 46 (1974), 359f., and *Mus. Phil. Lond.* 1 (1975), 9ff.). Similar charges can be laid against Pietzko's dissertation (note 21); see K. Münscher, *Jahresbericht* 149 (1911), 130ff.

47. The quotations from Homer, however, are sometimes acknowledged (e.g. at letters 1.1.19 and 57f., 1.3.6–7 and 1.12.37–8).

48. G. Anderson, *loc. cit.* in n. 33.

deeply than that. His quotations are not confined to well-known tags or the first few lines of a book. This can be demonstrated very easily. Letters 10 and 15 of the first book put into prose form two stories (Acontius and Cydippe, Phrygius and Pieria) taken from the third book of Callimachus' *Aetia*. The fragmentary diegesis of the *Aetia* on a Milan papyrus shows that these two stories came in the later part of that third book, and the 'Aristaenetan' quotations, echoes and rephrasings of Callimachus clearly reveal that the epistolographer had a detailed knowledge of his verse source, as the following lists will show. The references to 'Aristaenetus' in each case precede the references to Callimachus, who is cited from Pfeiffer's edition (Oxford 1949):

Acontius and Cydippe.[49] 'Aristaenetus' 1.10.21–3 derives from Callimachus fr. 67, lines 1–3; 9–11 from 68; 14–20 from 70; 53–4 from 72; 59–61 from 73; 64–5 from 74; 81–95 from 75.10–31; 96–9 from 75.42–3; 106–10 from 75.44–9; 121–2 from 67.8. Compare also 1.10.25–7 and 36–8 of 'Aristaenetus' with the Diegesis, z1 (p. 71 Pfeiffer).

Phrygius and Pieria.[50] 'Aristaenetus' 1.15.33–4 derives from Callimachus fr. 80, lines 2–4; 37–42 from 80.5–9; 43–4 from 80.10–11; 49–51 from 80.12–13; 52–4 perhaps from 80.14–16; 54–6 from 80.18–19; 59–65 from 80.20–3; 67–8 perhaps from fr. 83.

Exploitations of other works, such as Menander's *Dyskolos*, are usually not confined to one or two letters, but scattered all through the collection, as the accompanying list will reveal. Here for convenience the references to the *Dyskolos* precede those to 'Aristaenetus':[51]

Dyskolos 62 perhaps in 'Aristaenetus' 1.6.15–16; 155 in 2.6.3–4; 193 in 1.24.12; 214 perhaps in 2.15.21; 310 in 2.18.3; 316 perhaps in 1.8.16; 341

49. Cf. the works cited in n. 42. I am not convinced that 'Aristaenetus' 1.10.12–13 owes anything to Callimachus fr. 69 Pfeiffer, as Mazal suggests in the apparatus of sources placed below his text.

50. Cf. n. 40 and the works cited in n. 42.

51. Cf. my note in *Hermes* 96 (1968), 384, and O. Mazal, *Studi classici in onore di Quintino Cataudella* II (Catania 1972), 261ff. Mazal's list of 'Aristaenetan' borrowings is considerably longer than my own, but several of his examples seem to me either insufficiently close in wording for direct copying to be probable (e.g. *Dyskolos* 46 and 'Aristaenetus' 1.4.30–1), or tags common to many comedies (e.g. the betrothal formula at 'Aristaenetus' 1.19.46–7, the curse ἐς κόρακας at 2.12.24, the exclamation ὦ δυστυχὴς ἐγώ at 1.10.64), or colourless banalities like ἑταίρας ἐρῶν (2.11.4). And ἐκτόπως ἐρᾳ (1.13.50, 1.22.13) owes nothing to *Dyskolos* 824 (ἀγαπῶ τ' ἐκτόπως); it is simply the normal expression in the fifth and sixth centuries A.D. (cf. Procopius, *Arc.* 1.17).

in 2.17.7–8; 345 in 2.17.8–9; 764 in 1.2.5; 788–90 perhaps in 2.8.3–5; 861–2 perhaps in 1.17.19–21.

For operations on so large a scale, 'Aristaenetus' must have known the *Dyskolos* well and in its entirety, and the same judgment holds for many of the other works which he exploited extensively.

One further point may be added here with protreptic intent. Every papyrus discovery of a hitherto unknown text may reveal a new source of 'Aristaenetan' exploitation. One scholar[52] has already argued that letter 1.21 contains echoes of the recently published verses of Archilochus on a Cologne papyrus. Even though in this case the alleged ties between the poet and the epistolographer appear to me highly uncertain,[53] the importance of scrutinizing each new papyrus for 'Aristaenetan' source material needs emphasis. And not only new papyri: exploitation of even the best-known classical texts still needs to be investigated by scholars. Letter 1.6, for example, in which a seduced girl writes about a conversation she has held with her nurse, owes a far greater debt to Euripides' *Hippolytus* than hitherto has been realized.[54] The links are five in number. First, in the letter as in the play a woman in love confesses her emotion to her nurse. Secondly, the woman swears the nurse to silence, and here the phraseology of 'Aristaenetus' (lines 3–4, ὀμώμοκεν ἡ τιτθή, ἡ δὲ παῖς . . .) may perhaps be intended to call to the reader's mind the notorious and often quoted tag of *Hippolytus* 612. Thirdly, the woman swears by Artemis (line 10) in a situation where otherwise there seems to be no occasion for picking out this particular goddess. Fourthly, the woman argues that although passionately in love, ἐσπούδακα σωφρονεῖν καθ' ὅσον ἠδυνάμην (lines 11–12), recalling Phaedra's words at *Hippolytus* 398f. Finally, the nurse in 'Aristaenetus' replies ἐπεὶ τὸ πραχθὲν οὐκ ἂν ἄλλως ἔχοι, τὰ δεύτερα παραινῶ, in a way very similar to the remark of the Euripidean nurse at *Hippolytus* 507f.

---

52. W. Theiler, *Mus. Helv.* 34 (1977), 56ff.

53. The source of the ideas in lines 14–18 of the letter is in my opinion more likely to have been a speech by a *hetaira* or a distraught lover (cf. the opening monologue of Diniarchus in Plautus' *Truculentus*) in a lost play of New Comedy.

54. In the notes appended to his translation (*op. cit.* in n. 7), 141f., A. Lesky draws attention only to the general similarity in situation between play and letter.

IV

In a writer whose central theme is heterosexual love in general and extra-marital liaisons with *hetairai*, slaves and other men's wives in particular, it is at first sight surprising to observe a certain reticence, almost prudery, with regard to the description of sexual activity. If 'Aristaenetus' really intended to celebrate the old pagan attitudes to sex at a time when they were being overthrown by the Pauline teaching of the New Testament, why did he not go the whole hog in his descriptions with predecessors like Archilochus, Aristophanes and Machon?

The squeamishness can be illustrated in two ways. First, when 'Aristaenetus' is exploiting a source that contains a detail which strikes him as lubricious, he cuts that detail out of his letter. In 1.19 his material comes from that Hippocratic tract Περὶ φύσιος παιδίου (7.490 Littré = 55 Joly).[55] The subjects of both letter and medical tract are courtesans; both have become pregnant. The medical writer advised his patient 'to jump up and down with her heels touching her buttocks; and she had already done this seven times when the "seed" dropped to the ground with a plop; and when she saw it she stared at it in amazement' (13.2). 'Aristaenetus' omits this passage from his letter. Admittedly he develops his account in a totally different way; his courtesan does not go in for an abortion, but bears her child and then uses it as a bait to attract its wealthy father to matrimony. Disgust at the noisome detail, however, in all probability played a part in the decision by 'Aristaenetus' to dispense with it, in view of the close parallel at letter 1.10.81–4, where the preliminaries to Cydippe's abortively planned wedding are being described.[56] Here the source is Callimachus' *Aetia*, as we have previously seen, but at this stage in the story the poet describes the local custom which made the bride spend the night before the wedding in bed with a παῖς ἀμφιθαλής (fr. 75, lines 1–9). This detail clearly shocked 'Aristaenetus', who substituted for it an acknowledged quotation from Sappho (fr. 71.6 Lobel-Page) and a description of the wedding-song outside the bridal chamber.[57]

55. Cf. my discussion in *GRBS* 14 (1973), 198f.

56. Cf. A. Dietzler (n. 42), 16ff. and 49, and my brief note in *Mus. Phil. Lond.* 1 (1975), 15f.

57. A cliché much overworked in Hellenistic literature and subsequently, especially when combined as here with the contrast between the happiness of the bridal procession and the grief of a funeral cortège (e.g. epigrams like Meleager

The second way in which the erotic prudery of 'Aristaenetus' is revealed has an interesting literary history. 'Aristaenetus' will describe with an eye for detail and sometimes with imaginative flair the various kinds of sexual foreplay in which his lovers indulge. They embrace and kiss passionately (2.16.18–19, 2.19.19–20), their lips pressed so hard against each other that the mouth is bruised (1.16.28–30, copied mostly from Lucian, *Dial. Meretr.* 3.2), or with the girl holding the man's ears (1.24.34–5). Another letter (1.25.14–23) tells first of wine-cups exchanged and kissed (an idea here probably condensed from Achilles Tatius 2.9.1–2), then of an apple[58] bitten by the man and tossed to the girl, who kissed it and pressed it under her stomacher between her breasts (the source here is Lucian, *Dial. Meretr.* 12.1). Women's breasts in fact play a large part in the sexual descriptions and narratives of 'Aristaenetus'. Swelling like quinces (1.1.37, 1.3.29–30: the image is taken from Leonidas 23 Gow-Page[59]), they thrust forward against the covering wrap (1.1.36–8). A bashful lover sees a little of his inamorata's breast carelessly uncovered (1.16.17–18). Breasts may be fondled, either as part of the foreplay (2.7.21–2, apparently 2.16.19–20) or as the prescribed limit of permitted cuddling (1.21.4–5).

And here too the prescribed limit of permitted description has been reached. 'Aristaenetus', in a highly conventional way, prefers to draw a veil over the subsequent love-making. Or rather, a series of different veils: for even in this area of taboos he aims at variety. Sometimes he closes his account before the bedroom is entered (e.g. 1.4); sometimes he interrupts his story with the coy admission that it would be improper to proceed further (1.2.22–3, taken from Plato, *Symposium* 217 e), or that the reader may supply the rest for himself (1.16.33–5). The sex act is never described, although in 2.7.25–6 the author's usual erotic constraints are relaxed so far as to allow mention of the concomitant gentle perspiration and rapid breathing. Here too the precise verb μέμικται is applied to the

123, Antipater 56, Erinna 2 and Philip 24 Gow-Page; Achilles Tatius 1.13, Heliodorus 2.1, Xenophon of Ephesus 3.6; Apuleius, *Met.* 4.33–5).

58. On the symbolism of the apple and its use as a love-token, see especially A. R. Littlewood, *HSCP* 72 (1967), 147ff., and P. I. Kakridis, *Hellenica* 25 (1972), 189ff.

59. Cf. my discussion in *GRBS* 14 (1973), 200.

act.[60] Elsewhere 'Aristaenetus' uses a conventional blend of oblique generalities (ἅπαντα πράττει 1.28.12, τὰ ἐπὶ τούτοις ἐδρῶμεν 2.4.23; cf. 2.7.18–19, taken from Lucian, *Dial. Meretr.* 6.4, and also 2.18.22–33), euphemisms (ἀπολαύω 2.5.50, 2.8.3, cf. 2.19.19; χαρίζομαι 2.19.17–18), metaphors ('sacrifice to Aphrodite' 1.24.35–6; 'heal one's sufferings' 1.27.34; συζυγία 2.22.6), and high-flown hints ('I displeased neither girl, finding an impromptu bedroom suitable to requirements'[61] 1.2.24–5; 'we competed with each other all night long, striving for the image of the better lover' 1.16.35–7, taken from Xenophon of Ephesus 1.9.9).

There is much here to compare, much to contrast, with the other erotic writers both in the epistolary tradition and elsewhere. Despite the allurements in his subject-matter, there is a total absence of crude pornography in 'Aristaenetus', and virtually no trace of coarseness. How far his canons of propriety were self-imposed, and how far dictated by his age and environment, we can no longer be wholly sure, although a partial answer will be suggested below. Only three passages, however, have I noted in the letters where 'Aristaenetus' seems to me to offend against these canons. His language is always free from vulgarity and underplays the physicality of the sex-act, except at 2.22.1, where an adulterer is described as προσεμβατεύοντα (so Mercier, for the manuscript's meaningless -εμματευ-). This verb appears nowhere else in Greek, but it may perhaps have been coined here by 'Aristaenetus' as an exotic on the analogy of comic usages like ἐπεβάτευον at Aristophanes, *Frogs* 48. Coarse *double entendres* are in general as foreign to 'Aristaenetus' as they are natural to writers like Aristophanes and Machon, but it is hard to believe that at 2.1.44–8, where in an elaborate εἰκών a woman is compared to a meadow (λειμών), the subsidiary sexual meaning of λειμών (the female *pudenda*: cf. Euripides, *Cyclops* 171) was entirely overlooked by the epistologra-

60. The compound συμμιγείην is used at 2.8.14, and the congeneric noun μῖξις at 1.21.14 and 2.19.24. These may have been the polite terms of the time; at any rate they are standard in Procopius half a century or more later (*Arc.* 1.17, 9.10, 15, 18, 25).

61. θάλαμον αὐτοσχέδιον εὑρὼν ἀρκοῦντα τῇ χρείᾳ. The source of this expression (unnoticed in Mazal's edition) is Alciphron 4.13.14, συνηρεφῆ τινα λόχμην εὕρομεν, ἀρκοῦντα τῇ τότε κραιπάλῃ θάλαμον.

pher.[62] Similarly at 1.17.5, as de Pauw was the first to observe, the word κῆποι ('gardens') appears to be deliberately chosen because it is capable of bearing the same subsidiary sexual meaning as λειμών (cf. Diogenes Laertius 2.116).

Apart from these lapses, 'Aristaenetus' is a polite amorist. He ranks with writers like Heliodorus and Menander the comic poet in vetoing the most intimate details of sexual description. The pseudo-Lucianic author of the *Amores* (§53) compares the pleasures of sex to a ladder whose rungs lead from the sight of the beloved to the act of love itself. In his descriptions 'Aristaenetus' halts on the rung where the man is allowed to fondle the girl's breasts. The lower half of the female body is forbidden territory. Here Alciphron (e.g. 4.13 and 14), Achilles Tatius (2.37), Longus (3.14 and 18) and the *Amores* (53) go both further and lower. The author of the last-cited passage in fact provides an exceptionally convenient yardstick against which to measure the techniques and the restraints of 'Aristaenetus'. Both writers reveal parallel interests in the ladder of sex, both coyly halt their accounts with remarks like 'what need to tell once more forbidden tales?' (*Amores* 53, quoting Euripides, *Orestes* 14). But pseudo-Lucian, in addition to describing caresses and parts of the body vetoed in this connection by 'Aristaenetus', ends his section by quoting from an unidentified comedy (fr. 798 Kock, *CAF* iii.548) a coarsely pointed *double entendre* which goes well beyond anything in 'Aristaenetus'.

At the same time, virtually every technique that has been exemplified for 'Aristaenetus' in this section can be paralleled from the works of those authors whom he habitually exploited. The coy admission that it would be improper to proceed further with his description, which on one occasion (1.2.22–3) he actually copied from Plato's *Symposium* (somewhat ironically, as we shall soon see), is closely parallel to Moschion's remark in Menander's *Samia* (47)

62. Here perhaps 'Aristaenetus' may have been copying or adapting a lost source (comedy? It was fond of εἰκόνες with elaborate word-play: e.g. Aristophanes, *Lysistrata* 574ff., *Frogs* 718ff.; Alexis frs. 45 and 278; Antiphanes fr. 240; Plautus, *Asinaria* 178ff., *Aulularia* 595ff., *Mostellaria* 84ff., *Poenulus* 210ff., 240ff., *Truculentus* 35ff.; cf. G. Monaco, *Paragoni burleschi degli antichi*, Palermo 1963) without full awareness of all its implications, but it is hardly conceivable that the most naive of adapters (and we have no evidence that 'Aristaenetus' was naïve) could have written ἡ κομὴ τῷ λειμῶνι ἐπακμάζει (2.1.46) in total ignorance of the phrase's ambiguous potential. Cf. also J. Henderson, *The Maculate Muse* (New Haven and London 1975), 136; and J. Glenn, *Class. World* 69 (1975–6), 435ff.

when describing his encounter with Plangon, ὀκνῶ λέγειν τὰ λοιπά; we may compare also Terence, *Eunuchus* 604–7 (a passage possibly, but not certainly, translated from the Menandrean original[63]), Lucian's *Dial. Meretr.* 5.4, Heliodorus 2.25, as well as the passage from the *Amores* just discussed. Parallels for the 'Aristaenetan' technique of dismissing the moment of climax with a vague generality are provided by Theocritus 2.143 (ἐπράχθη τὰ μέγιστα), Achilles Tatius 5.27.3 (ἐγένετο ὅσα ὁ Ἔρως ἤθελεν), and Longus 2.11 (εἰδότες δὲ τῶν ἐντεῦθεν οὐδέν). Sexual euphemisms like ἀπόλαυσις abound (e.g. Chariton 2.8, Longus 2.11, *Amores* 27), as do metaphors closely akin to the 'sacrifice to Aphrodite' at 'Aristaenetus' 1.24.35–6 (e.g. Achilles Tatius 2.19.1, 5.15.6, cf. 5.16.3, 5.27.4).

In one final respect, however, 'Aristaenetus' differs significantly from epistolographers like Philostratus, novelists like Achilles Tatius and Longus, and many of the writers he exploits. The love affairs which he describes are basically extra-marital, as has already been noted. Adultery and even incest (if that is the implication of the unspecified ἔρωτι . . . ἀπορρήτῳ at 1.16.1) appear to be condoned. Homosexuality, however, is totally excluded from the purview of 'Aristaenetus'. This may at first sight seem surprising when paederasty at least is tolerated in many and praised in some of his sources. For example, debates on the comparative merits of paederasty and heterosexual love occur in Achilles Tatius (2.35–8), Plutarch's *Dialogue on Love* (*Moralia* 750ff.), and the pseudo-Lucianic *Amores*. It is ironical that when 'Aristaenetus' copies that statement about the impropriety of continuing his description further (1.2.22–3) from Plato's *Symposium* (217 e), he takes it from a context in which Alcibiades uses the words to break off his story about the night he spent with Socrates.

Why did 'Aristaenetus' embargo homosexuality while cheerfully tolerating marital infidelity and perhaps even incest? His own private inclinations may have provided part of the answer, but it is possible that the age in which he wrote may have added its influence. At the end of the fifth century, when Christianity was

63. Cf. especially E. Fraenkel, *Mus. Helv.* 25 (1968), 235ff.; G. Williams, *Tradition and Originality in Roman Poetry* (Oxford 1968), 290f.; B. Denzler, 'Der Monolog bei Terenz' (diss. Zürich 1968), 36ff. and 128ff.; and W. Steidle, *Rhein. Mus.* 116 (1973), 340.

firmly established as the state religion, the attitudes of a nostalgic pagan were bound to be different from those of a writer in the heyday of the Second Sophistic. Could it entirely have been a coincidence that perhaps less than half a century after 'Aristaenetus', according to Procopius' *Secret History*, paederasty was banned by law (11.34–6) while adultery was allegedly flagrant and often condoned by the cuckolded husbands (17.24–6)?

V

A reasonable impression of some of the strengths and weaknesses of 'Aristaenetus' as a writer will already have been gained from the previous sections of this article. His subject-matter is restricted, but he aims at variety by diversifying his situations and by ranging from elaborate descriptions (with ἐκφράσεις and εἰκόνες) to narrative, anecdote, conversation and declamation. Like a hagiolater devoted to his relics, he incorporates into his letters brilliant phrases and passages copied from earlier writers whose compositions he appears to have venerated as masterworks from a more glorious age. At its worst, his richly ornate style can turn 'Aristaenetus' into an orotund euphuist. His quality is admittedly uneven. At his best, however, he is a highly entertaining and ingenious writer because of the flashes of imagination and wit which sparkle through his prose. It is not always easy or even possible to identify original marks of talent in him, given the expertise with which he absorbs alien material into his own work. In what follows, however, I have tried to isolate those flashes which are not second-hand.

In verbal games 'Aristaenetus' would not claim to be an Aristophanes, but his range is wider and his percentage of successes far higher than an earlier study of mine suggested.[64] Two of his *double entendres* have been stigmatized above for their uncharacteristic obscenity. The remainder are not offensive. Some are rather hackneyed; for instance, the play on ὀμφάκια in 2.7.21–2 (= here 1, unripe and so hard grapes; 2, hard breasts of an immature girl) is familiar from the epic poets of late antiquity (Tryphiodorus, 34; Nonnus, *Dionys.* 1.71 and 48.957).[65] Four others deserved to be

---

64. *Mus. Phil. Lond.* 1 (1975), 30 n. 13.
65. Cf. also lines 40–1 of the same letter, Σικελὸς ὀμφακίζει, . . . παρατρυγῶν

spotlighted, for they show a pretty wit. At 1.13.65 the verb
ἐκδοῦναι, which is properly used of the father 'giving in marriage'
his daughter (cf. LSJ *s.v.* ἐκδίδωμι, 2a), is here applied with
deliberate malice to a situation where a father is being asked 'to
hand over' his own concubine to his lovesick son.[66] At 2.16.2
πάρεδρον ἡδονήν has its normal meaning of 'a secondary pleasure',
but there is an amusing irony in the fact that the pleasure in
question was limited to a man's *sitting* demurely *next to* his mistress
when she in fact wishes him actively to make love to her. The third
and fourth examples exploit the techniques of unacknowledged
quotation with considerable imagination, if my interpretations of
the two passages are correct. At 2.16.21 the girl of the previous
example goes on to claim that her lover considers her to be εὐπειθῆ
καὶ ἑτοιμότατα προκειμένην. The last two words here seem to
parody Homer's stock phrase about food: ὀνείαθ' ἑτοῖμα
προκείμενα,[67] and their transposition to the different and mildly
improper context of an affair with a courtesan raises a smile. And
finally, at 1.18.30–2, where the fictitious writer and her courtesan
friends close the letter with the remark 'As for drinking wine, my
dear Dionysus, *that* we can look to ourselves, needing no lesson from
anybody else' (ἀλλοτρίου παραδείγματος μηδὲν δεηθεῖσαι), an
alternative meaning seems to be concealed in the final four words
of Greek: 'needing no further example from another writer (sc. to
quote without acknowledgement)'. Directly before line 30 of this
letter 'Aristaenetus' has quoted without acknowledgement and at
great length three passages of Plato: *Phaedrus* 240 d-e (lines 11–16 of
the letter), 240 c (17–19), and *Republic* 5.474 d–575 a (20–30). The
witty but ambiguous admission that follows the three quotations is
the only reference that 'Aristaenetus' makes in the whole collection
to his practice of quoting extracts from earlier writers, but even the
way in which he makes his admission, using a phrase that has one
application in terms of the fictitious writer and another in terms of
'Aristaenetus' himself, is probably derived from one of the sources

παιδισκάριον, developing a parallel theme equally hackneyed. The proverb
Σικελὸς ὀμφακίζεται, which occurs in the paroemiographic collections, is applied
to the theft of worthless objects; the *double entendre* on παρατρυγῶν goes back as far
as Aristophanes, *Peace* 1339–40; cf. Henderson (n. 62), 65 and 167.

66. Cf. also Plato, *Theaetetus* 151b, where the word-play is less biting.

67. The expression occurs fourteen times altogether in Homer (*Iliad* 9.91,
Odyssey 14.453, etc.).

he habitually exploited. The speech with which Getas closes Menander's *Dyskolos* contains an exactly parallel instance of ambiguity when the slave asks the audience to applaud if they have enjoyed 'the way we've triumphed over this troublesome humgruffin' (965f.: κατηγωνισμένοις / ἡμῖν τὸν ἐργώδη γέροντα), but these same words are also intended to mean 'the way we've acted the *Dyskolos* to the end' [68]

Like many Greek writers from Homer onwards, 'Aristaenetus' is fond of playing on the meanings of proper names. Here the opportunities were numerous and obviously easy, since many of the proper names were invented by the epistolographer to suit the situation.[69] Straightforward plays on a name's etymology often seem to us rather tedious, and call for little comment here (e.g. 1.3.73–4, Λειμώνη like a meadow; 1.10.14–22 the handsome Ἀκόντιος had wounded many hearts with love's arrows but now has himself felt one sting of love, μιᾶς ἀκίδος ἐρωτικῆς; 1.13.12–13 Πανάκειος an aptly named physician;[70] 1.19.35–7 Εὐτυχίδης as the name for a baby whose birth has resulted in good fortune for the mother; 2.20.35–6 Λύκων like a wolf[71]), but one passage has a special interest. At 1.4.1 'Aristaenetus' opens his letter with Ἱππίας ὁ καλὸς Ἀλωπεκῆθεν, copying the first three words from the opening of Plato's *Hippias maior* (281 a). The Platonic Hippias, however, is the sophist from Elis; his 'Aristaenetan' counterpart is a cunning young Athenian who knows how to interpret the ambiguous hints in a woman's behaviour, and the name of his deme, with its foxy association, is appropriate to his cunning.

Such games with words,[72] however, are only one small part of wit, of that perfect association of thought and expression which delights the reader sometimes by its aptness, sometimes by its unexpectedness. Here 'Aristaenetus', operating at the frequently undervalued level of literary entertainer, confidently holds his own. His narratives and anecdotes retain the attention because of

68. Cf. the commentaries of E. W. Handley and F. Stoessl, *ad loc.*

69. See section I, above.

70. Here 'Aristaenetus' is modifying the name which he found in his source (Heliodorus 4.7), Ἀκεσῖνος; cf. my earlier discussion in *GRBS* 14 (1973), 209f.

71. Cf. Theocritus 14.22ff. (on which J. Stern, *GRBS* 16 (1975), 55 has some interesting comments), and in modern Greek Kazantzakis' novel *Christ Recrucified*, ch. 3, where the priest of the village Lykovrissi is facetiously called 'the head wolf'.

72. For further examples, see my notes in *Mus. Phil. Lond.* 1 (1975), 14 (the word-game of the ambiguous anticipator).

their unexpected twists, their ingenuity, their well-observed and at times imaginative details. The tale of the clever doctor's diagnosis in 1.13 was already hackneyed when 'Aristaenetus' wrote his version of it, but its fascination remains because the writer handles its surprises so effectively: Panakeios' pretended decision to give up the case (lines 44–6), for example, and his substitution of his own wife for the father's concubine (49–52). The various stories and conversations abound with plausible details which produce an illusion of real life: the slave-girl's excuse for going downstairs in 2.4.13–14, that she needs to draw water from the well,[73] or the wife's panicky omission to pick up her cloak when beating a hasty retreat from a party in 1.5.9–14. Such details in the letters could easily be multiplied, and they are often the product of accurate observation of the minutiae of human behaviour. Letter 1.4 lists the various signs which enable an experienced man to identify a *fille de joie*,[74] and 1.15.42–8 the characteristic movements – touching the tassels of one's shawl with the fingertips, twisting the end of one's belt, shuffling the feet about on the ground, for instance – of respectable girls not knowing what to do in an embarrassing situation. The latter passage has its own special significance. The basic story of 1.15 is taken from Callimachus,[75] but only two of the signs in the 'Aristaenetan' catalogue are copied here from the poet (fr. 80, lines 10–11 Pfeiffer: references to blushing and turning the eyes away); the remainder are additions by 'Aristaenetus'.[76]

Accurate observation and plausibility of detail are not confined, however, to the narrative portions of the letters. Conversation and speech are also used extensively to create an air of verisimilitude, even though the language itself is tricked out with the artificialities of rhetoric. 'You puff out your cheeks like the son of a piper' says a woman to her conceited lover in 2.6.4–5; a *hetaira* who has been supplanted by a rival mentions to her ex-lover the kisses, embraces

73. The situation in Lysias 1.14 is remarkably parallel, but there is no evidence that 'Aristaenetus' used material from any of Lysias' speeches.

74. This passage and some others in 'Aristaenetus' (e.g. 1.14; 2.1.12–22), where a didactic function seems to be included, have obvious analogies with the didactic stretches in Roman love elegy and works like Ovid's *Ars Amatoria*. Cf. especially A. L. Wheeler, *Class. Phil.* 5 (1910), 28ff. and 440ff., 6 (1911), 56ff.

75. See n. 42 above.

76. They do not feature in other versions of the story (Plutarch, *Mulierum Virtutum* 16 = *Moralia* 253F; Polyaenus, *Strategemata* 8.35).

and breast-fondlings she had once permitted, and now, saying good-bye, she writes 'Don't ever, by the breasts and kisses of Thais, trouble me again' (2.16.25–6, cf. 18–20). Thais is the name of the successful rival.

Trivial words, when the spotlight of imagination is focused upon them, can take on unexpected potency. 'Aristaenetus' may not be a writer in the class of those story-tellers who, like Dickens, 'feel the story to its minutest point',[77] but often enough he can make a situation or a picture come alive with a flash of real wit, a vivid comparison, or a tiny detail of inspired observation which, like a pebble thrown into a still pond, sends the ripples out in ever-increasing circles. In 1.12.15–16 two lovers are sitting 'like the jackdaw always by the jackdaw's side'. The comparison introduces the Greek proverb whose English equivalent is 'birds of a feather flock together'; its application here, however, is unusual and unexpected, and its graphic appropriateness will be immediately seen by anyone who has watched pairs of jackdaws side by side on house gables. Letter 1.16 is on the whole a dull letter, but it quickens into life in its last two lines (37–8) with its memory of past delights: 'and when we made love and talked in flattery, half-completed words slipped out from our pleasure'. In 2.14.8–11 a lovers' quarrel had been mended, the girl went again into the man's room in tears of happiness, and 'touching the walls of the room I kissed my fingers for joy'.

The imagination is occasionally blended with a wry wit that still retains its power to amuse. In 1.20 a jailer has been guarding a convicted adulterer, who goes on to seduce the jailer's own wife; 'it's the ridicule, by Justice, that irks me, over and above the adultery – that I, a prison-guard and the captain of the warders, couldn't guard my own wife in the house' (lines 13–15). In 1.24 a girl is writing to her lover; 'when they criticized me loudly and enquired of me, "And who can love a man like that – no charm, loathsome, gawky?" . . . I replied "Who can? *I* can!" ' (26–29). The words that directly follow this quotation, with the appropriate change of gender, provide the perfect epitaph for 'Aristaenetus'

---

77. Cf. Q. D. Leavis, *Dickens the Novelist* (with F. R. Leavis, Oxford 1970), 42 and 50f.

and his amiable talents: ἔρρωσθε τοίνυν, ἔφην ἀναστᾶσα, καὶ συγγνῶτέ μοι ποθούσῃ.[78]

78. 'So good-bye,' I said as I got up, 'and pardon me for loving.'

This paper has benefited at several points from helpful suggestions made by Professor J. Winkler, to whom I am much indebted.

The date and purpose of the *Philopatris*

BARRY BALDWIN

Of unknown authorship, uncertain date, and debatable purpose, the *Philopatris* is one of the more curious documents to emanate from later antiquity. Its frequently peculiar language and its attempt to fuse traditional elements of the Platonic-cum-Lucianic dialogue with the newer demands of Christian orthodoxy conspire to make it a work of considerable interest to the student of late Greek literature.

No time need be spent defending Lucian against the charge of writing the *Philopatris*. Doubts were evinced at least as long ago as the Florentine *editio princeps* of 1496; they have prevailed ever since.[1] Three considerations rule out the satirist. First, the indifferent Greek, with its faltering syntax and confusion of dialects. Second, much of the piece is a cento of phrases and effects from genuine Lucianic works. Finally, the mention of an ἐξισωτής or *peraequator*, an official not attested before the reign of Constantine.[2]

The last two of these points are equally fatal to the notion, found occasionally in the older commentators,[3] that the dialogue predates Lucian. It has been assigned to around the time of Nero, on the basis of Triepho's claim (12) to have recently (πρῴην) had

1. Attached to the text of the *Philopatris* in the first edition of Lucian is the subscription οὗτος ὁ λόγος οὔ μοι δοκεῖ εἶναι τοῦ Λουκιανοῦ, apparently an editorial observation rather than an inheritance from the manuscripts. It recurs in very similar form in the Aldine editions of 1503 and 1522.

2. The earliest mention is by Eusebius, *Vit. Const.* 4.3 (*PG* 20.1152c), who describes their employment by the emperor as a novel way of pursuing justice in taxation. Other literary allusions furnished by lexica also belong to the fourth century: Basil, *Ep.* 198 (*PG* 32.713b); Greg. Naz., *Carm.* 2.1; 2.2 (*PG* 37.1451a, 1477a), along with the scholia to the latter of Cosmas Melodus (*PG* 38.469a, 473b). *Peraequatores* also feature in the Codes of both Theodosius and Justinian; cf. A. H. M. Jones, *The Later Roman Empire* (Oxford 1964), 3, 120–1. Reinach (cf. n. 10 below) oddly claims that the functions of the *peraequator* are 'postérieures au règne de Justinien'.

3. For whom, cf. Gesner's treatise below.

321

an encounter with the apostle Paul. But this is to impart to the dialogue a dramatic realism to which it does not pretend. For episodes from Greek history and mythology such as the blasting of Salmoneus (4), the deception of Croesus by the Delphic oracle (5), and Poseidon's rape of Tyro (6) are similarly brought in as events that happened πρῷην.

In 1714, Matthaeus Gesner advanced the thesis that the dialogue pertained to the age of Julian.[4] That, as will be seen, may be more of a possibility than is nowadays acknowledged. Unfortunately, Gesner dwelt too much on a facile equation between Lucian and the sophist of that name who is the recipient of a letter from Julian:[5] homonyms constitute no good argument,[6] and Gesner's dependence upon the point damaged his case accordingly.

The idea that the *Philopatris* is a Byzantine work originated in 1813 with C. B. Hase.[7] It quickly took root, thanks in part to the speedy adherence of Niebuhr,[8] and has held the field ever since. The whole issue then became a debate as to which particular period of Byzantine history did the dialogue belong, with the seventh and tenth centuries emerging as prime contenders.[9] Apparent precision and victory came in 1902 with the detailed study of Salomon Reinach,[10] who narrowed it down to the reign of

4. *De aetate et auctore dialogi Lucianei qui Philopatris inscribitur* (Jena 1714; revised versions Leipzig 1730, and Göttingen 1741), reprinted in the Bipontine edition of Lucian by Hemsterhuis and Reitz, 9, 559–605.

5. *Ep.* 197 (Bidez-Cumont). It is actually a note comprising two short sentences, establishing Lucian as a frequent recipient of the imperial correspondence, but furnishing no clue as to his beliefs or literary activity.

6. It is sufficient to record the presence of fourteen Christian Lucians in Smith-Wace, *Dictionary of Christian Biography* (London 1882). Julian's correspondent (presumably not a Christian) would fit the long-held belief that the *Philopatris* was an anti-Christian tract. However, especially since Reinach (n. 10, below), the dialogue has been very differently interpreted, a state of affairs that pays its own tribute to the incompetence of the author.

7. *Notices et extraits des manuscrits* (Paris 1813), 9, 121.

8. In the Preface to his Bonn edition of Leo the Deacon; cf. his *Kleine Schriften* (Berlin 1943), 2, 73–8.

9. The dialogue was ascribed to the reign of Heraclius by (most notably) A. Gutschmid, *Kleine Schriften* (Berlin 1894), 5, 434; W. Crampe, *Philopatris, ein heidnisches Konventikel des VII Jahrhunderts zu Konstantinopel* (Halle 1894). Cf. Krumbacher, *Gesch. Byz. Litt.* 461 for a bibliography of other nineteenth-century work on the dialogue.

10. 'La question du Philopatris', *Revue Archéologique* 93 (1902), 79–110, hereafter referred to by author's name.

Nicephorus Phocas, the spring of either 969 or 965. This dating has acquired almost canonical status,[11] although in point of fact, the arguments for it are few and weak. It is high time this was pointed out.

Reinach essentially rested his case on two items: a linguistic detail and an alleged historical allusion. On one occasion (9), the author of the dialogue employed the noun στρατηγέτης. Taking his wisdom from two predecessors,[12] and relying overmuch on the incomplete lexicon of E. A. Sophocles, Reinach maintained that this word did not enter Byzantine Greek until *ca* 950, adding that 'L'argument tiré du mot peut servir à confirmer la date que nous attribuons au *Philopatris* et pourrait même autoriser une plus basse.' Such confidence was never warranted. One can never be certain exactly when a word came into the language: the usual factor of lost works sees to that, as does (in the case of Byzantine literature) the lack of specialized editions and lexicons. And unfortunately for Reinach's argument, the word στρατηγέτης has come to light in an inscription from Miletus of 196 B.C.[13]

In c. 9 of the dialogue, Triepho tells Critias οἶδα γὰρ μυρίας διαμελεϊστὶ τμηθείσας 'νήσῳ ἐν ἀμφιρύτῃ, Κρήτην δέ ⟨τε⟩ μιν καλέουσι.' Reinach, developing the notion of Hase and Niebuhr, takes this to be an unequivocal reference to the recapture of Crete from the Saracens by Nicephorus Phocas in 961. Adduced in support is the *Acroasis*, a poem from the pen of Theodosius the Deacon, in which (58f.) Phocas is hailed for his slaughter of Saracen women.[14] A seductive notion, at first sight. Nevertheless, objections crowd in. The author of the *Philopatris* ends his work with eulogy of the emperor and his victories – why is the conquest of Crete not placed in that section instead of being tucked away in a mythological sequence? Also, Triepho follows up his account with

11. Accepted without discussion by M. D. Macleod in vol. 8 of the Loeb Lucian; and in (for instance) the muddled notice of the *Oxford Dictionary of the Christian Church* (1974), 1085.

12. J. Aninger, 'Abfassungszeit und Zweck des Philopatris', *Hist. Jahrb.* 12 (1891), 489; C. Stach, *De Philopatride* (Cracow 1897).

13. Dittenberger, *Syll.*³ 588. 60.

14. The poem is printed with the *History* of Leo the Deacon in the Bonn edition of 1828 (cf. *PG* 113). It should be remembered that the accounts of Phocas in Crete by Leo and Theodosius were unknown to Gesner and older scholars. In the present context, it is not too hair-splitting to observe that Theodosius describes the slaughter of Saracen mothers before their children, rather than of maidens.

the remark καὶ εἰ τοῦτο ἐγίνωσκον, surely a very poor way of signalling imperial triumph.[15]

Even if we grant the reference to Phocas, it would not guarantee that the dialogue belonged to his reign – the author might be looking back from a subsequent one. It has already been demonstrated that dramatic realism and chronological coherence are not features of the *Philopatris*.

There are other possibilities. The passage was once connected with barbarian activity around Crete and Rhodes in the reign of Claudius II,[16] which might be congenial to the thesis of Gesner. However, Zosimus (1.46), the source for this episode, asserts that the invaders 'achieved nothing worthy of record'. It might be thought unlikely (albeit with Zosimus one never knows) that he would put the slaughter of Cretan women into such a category. Gutschmid[17] produced a Syrian text as evidence for an attack on Crete in 623 by barbarians or pirates. Reinach rejected this alternative on the grounds that Triepho could not have shown the satisfaction he does at the massacre of Christian maidens: the victims must have been enemies of Byzantium – a reasonable point, except that it is difficult to find this satisfaction in the Greek. Triepho shows no more or less concern for the fate of the Cretan girls than he exhibits for the Gorgon, discussion of whom served to introduce the topic in the first place.

Triepho goes on to mention that the Cretans had shown him the tomb of Zeus, which Reinach took at face value: Triepho will have been on the island in the reign of Phocas as an official, and he could not have had the leisure in the troubles of 623 to be touring the sights of Crete. Most of this is nonsense. The tomb of Zeus was something that did much for the Cretan reputation for mendacity: it is a commonplace in Greek literature from at least the time of Callimachus.[18] Lucian himself often makes mock of the claim, in

15. Notice that Reinach translates both this and the following ἤγαγον as first-person singulars, whereas Macleod treats them as third-person plurals. The latter is probably right; even the author of the *Philopatris* can hardly have postluded the statement 'I have heard' with 'If I knew this'.

16. Cf. the Bipontine edition of Lucian, 9, 513–14, for this. Another theory there advanced, to the effect that Crete really refers to Gaza and Palestine, can be discounted.

17. *Loc. cit.* (n. 9).

18. *Hymn to Zeus*, 8–9.

one case in phraseology almost identical to that of Triepho.[19] This is the most likely inspiration for the author of the *Philopatris*. Furthermore, a Byzantine parallel for this kind of fake, or literary, autopsy is to hand. In the tenth century, Nicetas Magistros composed a Life of Saint Theoctista of Lesbos and, in the course of a description of the great church on the island, he inserted a personal-looking reference to examining a statue of Selene. In point of fact, he has simply thrown in a very close imitation of Achilles Tatius.[20]

This reference to the tomb of Zeus in the *Philopatris* is worth having for another reason: it helps to fill a long hiatus in such allusions between the fourth and eleventh centuries,[21] but it throws no light on the historical allusion in cause. Crete suffered a great deal in the Byzantine period and one hardly requires formal corroboration from history or chronicle to assume the frequency of atrocity. For obvious instances, many must have perished when the Saracens occupied the island in 826, or during the brief reoccupation of the island by the logothete Theoctistus in 843–4. The allusion of Triepho simply cannot be pinned down.

And it may well not refer to anything historical at all. The mention comes in a sequence of exclusively literary and mythological items (4–11). It is preceded by Athene and the Gorgon,[22] and postluded by Hera. Nothing precludes the notion that Triepho is alluding to the sacrifice of maidens in a Cretan ritual: the Minotaur very likely, or something to do with Britomartis.[23] True, on such a reckoning as this, the epithet μυρίας would be an exaggeration, but this is quite in the manner of the author. He had earlier (4) converted Zeus's hurling of Hephaestus from the

---

19. *Conc. Deor.* 7; cf. *Timon* 6; *Jup. Trag.* 45; *Philops.* 3; *De sacr.* 10.

20. For this, see Mango, 'Byzantine Literature as a Distorting Mirror', *Past & Present* 51 (1975), 7–8. Given this, it may be signal that he later (p. 18) hints at a doubt about Reinach's dating.

21. Sir Arthur Evans, 'Mycenaean Tree and Pillar Cult', *JHS* 21 (1901), 121, assembled a collection of references to the tomb, observing that there was a gap in the written records between Firmicus Maternus and Michael Psellus. This is wrong, if our dialogue belongs to the intervening period.

22. The Gorgon device would be known to any reader of Homer (and the author of the *Philopatris* incontestably was that), albeit he would not need to go further than Lucian, *De domo* 22, 25; *Dial. Mar.* 12.

23. Cf. R. F. Willetts, *Ancient Crete* (London 1965), 135–6, for Cretan rituals involving the death of females.

threshold of heaven into a jettisoning of 'all the gods'.[24] And with regard to the apparently contemporary nature of the Cretan episode, it will again be remembered that items from Greek mythology are presented in the dialogue as recent events.

Close scrutiny of the language reinforces suspicion that the virgins of Crete are simply one more in a literary sequence. The phrase διαμελεϊστὶ τμηθείσας is Homeric (*Od.* 9.291; 18.339); the *Philopatris* is crammed with epic tags. Another writer laid under obvious contribution by the author of the dialogue is Euripides. Striking, then, to find Triepho introducing his account of the Cretan massacre with the verb καρατομεῖν, for that is very reminiscent of *Alcestis* 1118, where the verb is used of the slaying of Gorgons, a context identical with this section of the *Philopatris*. Almost equally compelling is *Troades* 564–5: καράτομος ἐρημία νεανίδων.[25]

On all counts, the supposed reference to Nicephorus Phocas hardly stands up: its place in the dialogue suggests that it is just one of the agglomeration of mythological examples, and in terms of language, nothing more than a literary cento. With the passage eliminated as a contemporary allusion, Reinach's dating loses its foundations. There is no other clue so seemingly tangible – the general situation envisaged in the dialogue suits any number of periods.

That may be a depressing conclusion. However, it is not a complete surprise. A parallel is offered by the dialogue of Michael Psellus known as the *De operatione daemonum*. We obviously know the century in which it was composed, yet, as Cyril Mango has brilliantly demonstrated,[26] it contains not a single contemporary element and could easily be dated on internal grounds to not later than the sixth century. Mango's concluding description of this dialogue is worth quoting here, since it may well be found applicable to the *Philopatris*: 'On the one hand, it shows a close adherence to an antique literary genre which determines its form and its language. On the other hand, the time and setting that it

24. Compare the claim that Apollo destroyed ἑτέρους μυρίους along with Croesus and the Salaminians (5). Cf. the peculiar reference (13) to the *Birds* of Aristophanes as ποιημάτια.
25. Cf. *Rhesus* 586.
26. *Art. cit.* (n. 20), 12–14.

evokes are neither antique nor medieval, but those of the Early Christian Empire.'

If it can be shown that literary pastiche and allusive imitation of classical texts are the prime ingredients of the *Philopatris*, the search for contemporary allusion and historical precision will be accordingly restrained. The style was what mattered. To this end a brief commentary on the dialogue is here offered – brief, albeit fuller on the author's literary debts than anything published hitherto.[27] It will be borne in mind that what follows below is in addition to the many literary tags and quotations explicitly indicated as such by the author of the dialogue.[28] Various matters pertaining to the content of the piece can also be handily subsumed under this section.

1. βυσσοδομεύεις ἄνω καὶ κάτω περιπολῶν κερδαλεόφρονι ἐοικὼς κατὰ τὸν ποιητήν ὦχρος τέ σευ εἷλε παρειάς. The first part of this is imitated from *De calumn.* 24: ὡς ὁ ποιητής φησί, βυσσοδομεύει τὴν ὀργήν. The Homeric tag is parodied in *Jup. Trag.* 1.

δυσχεραίνεις καθ' ἡμῶν ἢ ἐκκεκώφωσαι. Modelled, as Macleod notes, on *Navigium* 10.

ἔτι ἀναπεμπάзω τοὺς ὕθλους. Perhaps derived from *Gallus* 5: ἔτι ἀναπεμπάзῃ τὸν ὄνειρον; cf. *Necyomant.* 12: τὰς ἀκοὰς ἀποφράττω; cf. *De Calumn.* 8: ὦτα ἀποφράττων. ἐπὶ κεφαλῆς σκοτοδινήσας; closely paralleled by *Philops.* 24: ὡς μὴ σκοτοδινιάσας ἐμπέσοιμι ἐπὶ κεφαλήν.

The petrifaction of Niobe, mentioned here and later in the *Philopatris* (18, 27), may have been suggested to the author by *Somnium* 14; *Pro imag.* 27.

2. ἐμβρόντητοι ποιηταί. Cf. *Timon* 1 for the phrase and the sentiment.

ἀλλὰ λῆρος πάντα γέγονεν ἐπί σοι. For this phrase, or almost identical versions, cf. *VA* 9; *Timon* 1.

27. Macleod, whose Loeb text is here followed, has some valuable notes on the author's sources, but he misses many of the thefts from Lucian and elsewhere. The annotations in the Bipontine edition are vigilant, but incomplete and often inaccurate as to references.

28. In the following commentary, these will simply be signalled, without quotation. References to Lucian are by title only, to avoid constant iteration of his name.

οὐ μικρὸν οὐδὲ εὐκαταφρόνητον πρᾶγμα ἀνακυκλεῖς. Quoted verbatim from *Navigium* 11.

παροπτέος ἢ ἀμελητέος. Taken directly from *Timon* 9.

ταυρηδὸν ὑποβλέπειν. Probably inspired by Aristophanes, *Ranae* 804 (where the simple verb rather than the compound is employed); Aristophanes is an author paraded more than once in the *Philopatris*; or by Plato, *Phaedo* 117b.

καταπεσὼν Τριεφώντειον πέλαγος κατονομάσῃς ὡς καὶ Ἴκαρος. Very similar to *Icarom.* 3: καταπεσὼν Μενίππειόν τι πέλαγος ὥσπερ τὸ Ἰκάριον.

ἃ γὰρ ἀκήκοα . . . μεγάλως ἐξώγκωσέ μου τὴν νηδύν. This conceit recurs near the end of the dialogue (27); see the detailed note there. In both cases the source is *Philops.* 39.

Critias blames his condition on what he had heard from the 'thrice-accursed' σοφιστῶν, a word which requires some comment. It is not all that common in Byzantine Greek. Sophocles registered only its application to Christ by Lucian in the *Peregrinus*. It is omitted from Lampe's *Patristic Greek Lexicon*. Two scholia to Lucian (*Gallus* 18: Rabe 92.3; *Rhet. Praec.* 1: Rabe 175.4) found it necessary to explain the term. A notice in the *Suda* (s 814 Adler) reproduces the scholia to Aristophanes, *Nubes* 331 and 1111. A writer of the period postulated by Reinach might have been expected to say 'Hellene' instead. Its presence here could conceivably suggest an earlier date, though it may just as well be there in its pejorative context to enhance the Lucianic tone.

3. πόσος κορκορυγισμὸς καὶ κλόνος τὴν γαστέρα σου συνετάρασσε. Imitated from Aristophanes, *Nubes* 386–7; ἐταράχθης τὴν γαστέρα καὶ κλόνος ἐξαίφνης αὐτὴν διεκορκορύγησεν.

κνήμην γαστέρα. Cf. *VH* 1.22: ἐν ταῖς γαστροκυνημίαις. The author continues with Zeus's pregnant head and a register of odd births and transmogrifications. Very similar lists can be seen in *De salt.* 57; *Philops.* 3; *Dial. Deor.* 9; cf. pseudo-Lucian, *Halcyon* 3.

In this section, there is also an imitation of Plato, *Phaedrus* 230b, employed for the setting of the dialogue under plane-trees, and a quotation from *Odyssey* 13.228.

4. Triepho expresses the fear that Critias is under a spell, that might turn him into a door or pestle (ὕπερον) – a clear reminis-

cence of *Philops.* 35, where enchanted door-bars, pestles, and brooms materialize.²⁹

Zeus is said to have been hymned by the poets as Τιτανοκράτωρ and Γιγαντολέτης. As Macleod saw, the author has been reading *Timon* 4, the unique source for these epithets. To this same dialogue, which is one of those most frequently mined by the author of the *Philopatris*, is owed the phrase Σαλμωνέα ἀντιβροντῶντα; cf. *Timon* 1.

κύκνος οὗτος ἐγένετο καὶ σάτυρος δι' ἀσέλγειαν, ἀλλὰ καὶ ταῦρος. A common enough motif, of course: compare, for example, the first line of *AP* 9. 48 (Anon.), Ζεὺς κύκνος ταῦρος σάτυρος χρυσὸς δι' ἔρωτα. The noun ἀσέλγεια, here substituted for the poet's ἔρως, and its cognates are favourites with our author.³⁰

Triepho's joke that Zeus was lucky, when manifesting himself as a bull, not to have been set to plough is appropriated from *Conc. Deor.* 7.

The Olympians' dinner with the Ethiopians is obviously inspired by Homer, but in this jesting context probably owes something also to the treatment in *Jup. Trag.* 37; cf. *De Sacr.* 2.

πώγωνα τηλικοῦτον ἔχων. For the phrase, see *Dial Deor.* 5, where Zeus is denounced by Hera for his facial hispidity. Similarly with the divine insobriety: the epithet ὑποβεβρεγμένος here employed is fastened upon Dionysus and Priapus in *Dial. Deor.* 23.

Incidentally, if one believes that the author's phraseologies were intended to reflect contemporary matters, the hirsute Zeus might be taken to allude to Constans II, son of Heraclius, who received the sobriquet Pogonatus.³¹ In view of the dating by some scholars of the *Philopatris* to the seventh century, this was worth noticing. So also is the *hapax legomenon* ἐνεργοβατοῦσαν, used of sex changes by Critias in his register of miracles (3), for the concept of ἐνέργεια in regard to the natures of Christ was pressed for a while by the Patriarch Sergius in the reign of Heraclius. Compounds with the suffix –βατέω are a favourite of our author, as will be seen. It is just

29. Observe that both authors have the rarish neuter form ὕπερον. For such magical apparitions, cf. H. H. Davis, 'Some Ancient Brooms and their Symbolism', *Class. Bull.* 34 (1957), 1–3 (ignoring the *Philopatris* item).

30. For the noun and its cognates in Lucian, cf. H. Betz, *Lukian von Samosata und Das Neue Testament* (Berlin 1961), 199 n. 3.

31. On whom, cf. E. H. Brooks, 'Who was Constantinus Pogonatus?', *BZ* 17 (1908), 455–62.

possible that he coined a new one in order to make fun of some contemporary notion.

τὰ δὲ τοῦ ἀετοῦ ... αἰσχύνομαι καὶ λέγειν. A combination of *Conc. Deor.* 8: μηδὲ περὶ τοῦ ἀετοῦ εἴπω and *ibid.* 10 (of Egyptian deities): αἰσχύνομαι γάρ ... The balance of the present sentence in the *Philopatris*, τὸ κυοφορεῖν καθ᾽ ὅλου τοῦ σώματος, is reproduced almost verbatim from *Dial Deor.* 9: ὅλος ἡμῖν κυοφορεῖ καὶ πανταχόθι τοῦ σώματος.

5. Apollo is described as προφήτης ἄριστος καὶ ἰητρός. Compare Aristophanes, *Plutus* 11 (of Apollo): ἰατρὸς ὢν καὶ μάντις ὥς φασιν σοφός. Conceivably the source for our author here; the *Plutus* was the most popular of Aristophanes' plays in Byzantine times.[32]

The subsequent coupling of the Croesus and Salamis oracles occurs in *Jup. Trag.* 20, 28, 45, where they are linked and made a reproach to Apollo.

6. Poseidon is introduced with an Homeric tag, as noted by Macleod. He is then adorned with the epithet σεισίχθων, which is not Homeric; Pindar, *Isth.* 1.76 could be the source. The selection of the rape of Tyro to exemplify the villainy of Poseidon is no doubt owed partly to the mention of her father Salmoneus a little earlier, partly to the Lucianic use of the incident both for reproach and jest: *Dial. Mar.* 13; *VH* 2.3.

The author of the dialogue also exploits sexual episodes for the condemnation of Hermes (7) and Hera (11); and there is prurient speculation about the virtue of the Gorgon (9). At first blush, a typically early Christian puritanism towards the Greek classics, yet the treatment is equally Lucianic in language and theme.[33]

7. Triepho rejects the topic of Hermes with the curt μή μοι (i.e. 'Do not speak of him'). The idiom is Aristophanesque: *Nubes* 83 (of Poseidon), 433 (with Dover's note); *Vesp.* 1179. For Hermes as the pander of Zeus, cf. *Dial. Deor.* 24, where this is his sole and detailed complaint.

8. The Homeric line about sacrificing thighs of bulls and goats (*Il.* 1.40–1) is paraphrased for comic purposes; cf. *De sacr.* 3, where it features in a mock lament.

32. The author of the dialogue might also have consulted Herodotus on the subjects of Croesus and Salamis; if so, that could explain his sudden slide into Ionic dialect.

33. Cf. Betz (n. 30), 199–201, for an exposition of this.

9. Critias (not the militantly Christian Triepho, notice) swears by the Unknown God of Athens. There is no need to add to Norden's classic treatment and the other vast literature on this subject. The celebrated reference by Paul (*Acts* 17.23) is patently relevant, here and in the last section of the dialogue where Triepho comes out with the same oath. Nevertheless, one should not overlook Philostratus, *Vit. Ap.* 6.3.5, where the Athenian taste for erecting altars to unknown gods is commended.

11. Triepho berates Hera for her ἀσελγεστάτης μίξεως, alluding to the famous sequence with Zeus in *Iliad* 14. This was a favourite topic with Christian moralists, who make much of Hera's alleged act of *fellatio* – hence, no doubt, Triepho's superlative adjective.[34]

In this same sentence, Triepho employs a rare (for the *Philopatris*) dual, ἐκ ποδοῖν καὶ χεροῖν, which is derived from Homer (cf. *Il.* 15.18f. for this particular one).

12. Triepho urges Critias to embrace Christianity in a welter of literary pastiche. He begins with a hexameter, thus: ὑψιμέδοντα θεόν, μέγαν ἄμβροτον οὐρανίωνα. That looks Homeric, though it should be noticed that all the epithets are regularly applied to God by Patristic authors.[35] Then comes a reference to the Trinity, with its components painstakingly spelled out. All of this is rammed home by the Euripidean τοῦτον νόμιζε Ζῆνα, τόνδ᾽ ἡγοῦ θεόν. According to taste, this use of Euripides to clinch the merits of Christianity will seem clever, comic, or clumsy. The line in question is a fragment from a lost play; our author will have got it from *Jup. Trag.* 41, where it is used in a mock philosophical seminar. The emphasis on the nature of the Trinity might be thought to reflect a period when it was necessary to combat monophysite or other heresies.

A brief ridicule of Pythagorean numerology follows, along the lines of *VA* 4.

Triepho resumes his 'conversion' of Critias. As before, he kicks off with a scrap of verse, σίγα τὰ νέρθε καὶ τὰ σιγῆς ἄξια. Reinach[36] absurdly referred to this as 'un vers d'Euripide'. Macleod reasonably describes it as an unidentified comic line (it is immediately

34. The cognate noun (for which, cf. n. 30 above) is employed in a spirited denunciation of the act by Theophilus of Antioch, *Ad Autol.* 3.8 (*PG* 6.1133b).

35. Lampe's *Patristic Greek Lexicon* furnishes examples.

36. He apparently (it is the most charitable explanation) misread a note in the Bipontine edition of Lucian, 9, 517.

postluded by a paraphrase of Aristophanes, *Nubes* 145). Given Triepho's hexametric effort just above, and the predilection of the *Philopatris* for opening sections with σίγα or similar injunctions,[37] it is possible that the line is of the author's own devising. Alternatively, there may be some recollection of *Jup. Trag.* 3, where the line θάρσει, τὰ νέρθεν ἀσφαλῶς ἔχει θεοῖς parodies Euripides, *Phoenissae* 117.

Now comes perhaps the only well-known section of the dialogue. Triepho describes his meeting with, and conversion by Γαλιλαῖος ἀναφαλαντίας ἐπίρρινος εἰς τρίτον οὐρανὸν ἀεροβατήσας. Almost every word clamours for comment. First, Γαλιλαῖος. This epithet (not used by Lucian in the *Peregrinus*) inevitably recalls the language of the Emperor Julian. It was a detail that attracted Gesner, and led Reinach to content himself with the simple observation that 'peut-être l'auteur du *Philopatris* avait-il lu Julien'. There is more to say than that. The epithet appears as early as Epictetus,[38] a hostile witness; it is found as late as the twelfth-century Byzantine satire *Timarion*, a manifestly Lucianic concoction.[39] According to Lampe,[40] it is invariably used in a hostile fashion. A curious term, then, for Triepho to employ – unless, that is, the author was intending to ridicule the Christians.

The Galilaean in question is generally regarded as Paul rather than Christ on the basis of the allusion to the third heaven (cf. *Second Corinthians* 12.2), and the description of him as big-nosed, since he is so endowed with this quality in *Acta Pauli et Theclae* 3. One might subjoin that Triepho's account is something of a parody of Paul's own conversion on the road to Damascus.[41] It should nevertheless be noted, since the point has hitherto been neglected, that a passage in John Damascene[42] applies the epithet ἐπίρρινος to Christ.

The aerobatic quality of the Galilaean no doubt owes something

37. Cf. 7, 11, 22, 27.
38. *Discourses* 4.7.6.
39. See the account of H. F. Tozer, 'Byzantine Satire', *JHS* 2 (1881), 233–70.
40. Apart from Julian, he cites *Martyrium Theodoti* i.31 (ed. F. de Cavalieri, *ST* 6 (1901), 80.15), and Manes' application of the term to the orthodox, in *Ep. Add.* (*PG* 86.904a). Julian's practice was commented upon by Greg. Naz., *Or.* 4.76 (*PG* 35.601b).
41. Though see Betz (n. 30), 53–7, for the theme of divine epiphany in Lucian and other Greek writers, secular and Christian.
42. *Ep. ad Theoph.* (*PG* 95.349c).

to Socrates in the *Nubes* (225), especially as that play had been referred to just previously in Triepho's speech. However, cf. *Bis Accus.* 33; *Philops.* 12. The conceit is later used of the prophets of doom (24, 25), and is generally worked to death in the dialogue.

For the word ἀναφαλαντίας, cf. *Timon* 47.

Triepho is rescued by the Galilaean ἐκ τῶν ἀσεβῶν χώρων; cf. for the phrase *VH* 2.17; *De Luctu* 8.

13. λέγε ... διὰ φόβου γὰρ ἔρχομαι. Quoted verbatim (with the slight change of λέγε for λέξον) from Euripides, *Orestes* 757.

An acknowledged extract from the *Birds* of Aristophanes follows, after which Triepho describes the creation of the Universe in a medley of phrases from Old and New Testaments; cf. Macleod for the details.

14. λέγε ... ἐγὼ δὲ μαθητιῶν ..., urges Triepho sarcastically, as Critias attempts to expound the theory of Fate. He is, unsurprisingly in view of the author's use of the play in the preceding section, echoing *Nubes* (182–3): καὶ δεῖξον ... μαθητιῶν γάρ.

The ensuing seminar on Fate consists almost entirely of quotations from Homer.[43] This is perhaps a telling indication that the author is more concerned to show off his intimate knowledge of Homer than to engage in a substantive debate.

A reference at the end of this section to 'the heavenly books of the good' is presumably inspired by *Revelations* 20.16 ('written in the Book of Life').

17. The opening words Εὖ πάντα ἀνακυκλεῖς are perhaps imitated from *Nigrinus* 6: ἀνακυκλῶ πρὸς ἐμαυτὸν τὰ εἰρημένα.

In reply to Critias' question as to whether even the deeds of Scythians are noted in heaven, Triepho asserts Πάντα γε, εἰ τύχῃ γε χρηστός, καὶ ἐν ἔθνεσι. Macleod adduces *Acts* 14.27 for this. Theme and language are in fact a compound of Julian, *In Gal.* 106b, and *Jup. Trag.* 42. Notice also that ἔθνος, here translated by Macleod as 'Gentiles', frequently refers in Patristic prose to pagans.[44]

In the eclectic fashion of the author, quotations follow from

43. Macleod provides the references; it may be added that a couple of these Homeric lines are quoted in *Apol.* 8.

44. See Lampe for examples. What nuances (if any) the author of the dialogue intends is usually impossible to say. The adjective χρηστός, for instance, could be suggestive; cf. Betz (n. 30), 210 n. 1. And it is tempting to see κατηχούμενος in the present section as equivalent to the Christian term catechumen. Until, that is, one observes it in *Jup. Trag.* 39; *Asin.* 48.

Aristophanes (*Nubes* 833–4) and *Psalms* 104.2. After these, he slumps into a misquotation of *Nubes* 86 and an unmetrical parody of *Iliad* 9.313.[45] Recovering himself, our author proceeds to quote *Iliad* 9.191 (also adduced in Lucian or pseudo-Lucian, *Amores* 5, 54), and to echo passages from *Acts* and *Romans*.

20. The unsavoury old prophets Charicenus and Chleuocharmus are now brought on parade. To attempt to identify them with historical personages, or even a particular period, is futile. Their main characteristic is the welter of Lucianisms which accompanies them. The opening phrase in the section, Καὶ δὴ πολλοὺς παραγκωνισάμενος ἧκον, is (with the exception of a change of tense in the main verb) taken verbatim from *Jup. Trag.* 16; cf. *Timon* 54; *Pisc.* 34. The ensuing description ὑπέβηττε μύχιον, ἐχρέμπτετο is lifted without alteration from an identical context in *Gallus* 10. Another theft is the colourful τριβώνιον ἔχων πολύσαθρον ἀνυπόδετός τε καὶ ἄσκεπος τοῖς ὀδοῦσιν ἐπικροτῶν, almost every word of which is from a combination of *Cataplus* 20 and *Icarom.* 31. A little later (21) the expression ἐν ἀκαρεῖ τῆς νυκτός is paralleled by Aristophanes, *Plutus* 244: ἐν ἀκαρεῖ χρόνου, which in turn is on display in *Timon* 3, 23; *Asin.* 37. In the following paragraph (22), the sentence οἱ δὲ ἀνεκάγχασαν ἅπαντες ὡς ἀποπνιγέντες ὑπὸ τοῦ γέλωτος καὶ τῆς ἀμαθίας μου κατεγίνωσκον combined *Jup. Trag.* 31 with *Philops.* 8, with hardly a word changed. Finally, the phrase δριμὺ καὶ τιτανῶδες ἐνιδών is imitated directly from *Icarom.* 23; cf. *Catapl.* 3; *Philops.* 30.

Apart from these linguistic items, some matters of content require discussion. Charicenus promises the advent of someone, perhaps a new emperor, who will cancel arrears of taxation, pay off creditors, and take care of rents. With regard to the first of these, both language and theme suit Julian, who boasts of his remissions (*Misopogon* 365b; *Ep.* 73), and who is commended for them by Ammianus (25.4.15). But needless to say, it would suit many other emperors too, in terms of propaganda if not in fact.

The content here is again tinted with literary reminiscence; τὰ χρέα τοῖς δανεισταῖς ἀποδώσει καὶ τά τε ἐνοίκια . . . is quite similar in phraseology and context to *Saturnalia* 15.

---

45. Though in the latter case, it should be pointed out that there is a close paraphrase of this line in prose in *Apol.* 6. Conceivably the author of the *Philopatris* was doing the same thing.

The promised saviour will also τοὺς εἰραμάγγας δέξεται μὴ ἐξετάӡων τῆς τέχνης. At least, that is what the manuscripts have. Macleod, calling it *faute de mieux*, prints Gesner's εἰρηνάρχας. Various possibilities offer. The manuscript reading is a *hapax legomenon*, which need not disqualify it: there are a number of otherwise unattested words in the *Philopatris*.[46] Rohde[47] in fact retained it in the belief that it meant gold Persian coins debased by Phocas. A fiscal flavour is plausible enough, given the tone of the rest of the sentence, but the allusion to Phocas depends, of course, on the dating of the dialogue earlier criticized. Possibly the reading is a corruption of a technical term: many such in Byzantine Greek are transliterated or adapted Latinisms. *Aer-* something would suit a monetary context. So would that notorious Byzantine system of taxation, the ἀλληλέγγυον. Could the manuscript reading be a corruption of something to do with this? If so, the passage would relate most easily to Basil II, who compelled the wealthy to pay this for the poor. And it would provide a *terminus post quem non* of sorts for the dialogue, since abolition of the *allelengyon* is credited to Constantine VIII and Romanus III Argyrus.[48]

Alternatively, the disputed word may have nothing to do with money. A reference to diviners or seers could be got out of the Greek, by means of a compound of ἀερ- and the verb μαγγανεύω, for instance. We have seen how addicted to aerobatic wise men the author is, and the verb is common in Lucian; an old reference to *aeromantis* by Varro (*ap.* Serv., *Aen.* 3.359) may be subjoined. The general context is not inappropriate to such an allusion. On balance, however, a financial meaning probably remains the more likely.

Chleuocharmus advertizes the prophecies of a shaven-headed sage from the mountains who showed him the putative saviour's name in hieroglyphic writing in the theatre. A little later, Crato the *peraequator* asseverates that the prophecies will come to pass in the month of Mesori. Do these two Egyptian details indicate an Alexandrian setting for the dialogue? Probably not. They could simply be there to give a requisite touch of exoticism to the

46. I have noticed the following: παλαιστέω, παρεισοδεύω, πολύωτος, ἐνεργοβατέω, and the editorial restorations διενειλέω and ἐξερρινέω.

47. *BZ* 13 (1896), 6.

48. For the sources and a discussion, cf. Ostrogorsky, *History of the Byzantine State* (2nd English ed., 1968), 307, 322.

utterances, and hieroglyphic writing can be linked with the use of works of art and hippodrome inscriptions, amongst which was the obelisk of Theodosius I, by seers.[49] Certainly, an Alexandrian setting is hardly consonant with the earlier maritime description (3), which by its content clearly suits Constantinople.

The cropped sage demands caution. Tonsures inevitably evoke monks and Byzantium: one can see that process at work in a scholiast on Lucian, *Bis Accus.* 20, where a shaven Stoic occasions the comment 'Just like the monks nowadays' (Rabe 139.28). Priests of Isis were also shorn.[50] The detail is of no help in determining the date of the dialogue – it may be nothing more than a conventional detail, taken over from the tonsured seer in *Philops.* 34. A comparable case in this same section is ἀνυπόδετος.[51] Notice also Critias' words concerning dreams and debts. Macleod sees a possible parody of the Lord's Prayer, but we need look no further than the opening of Lucian's *Gallus* and/or Theocritus (?) 21.67: μὴ σὺ θάνῃς λιμῷ καὶ τοῖς χρυσοῖσιν ὀνείροις.

In the next sequence, Critias is conducted through gates of iron and over bronze thresholds, up many stairs into a golden-roofed palace likened by the author to that of Menelaus described by Homer. There he meets a crowd of doomsayers, with whom he debates and remonstrates.

This section (23–6) has been adduced for historical allusions. In his introduction to the *Philopatris*, Macleod suggests that the prophets of doom may be monks. Later on, he proposes that they could be prisoners of Phocas, here criticized for being unpatriotic. This is on the basis of the iron gates and bronze thresholds, since there is an obvious echo of Homer's description of the prison for rebellious gods in the abyss of Tartarus (*Il.* 8.15); there is a similar effect in pseudo-Lucian, *Amores* 32.

Likewise, the golden-roofed palace has been taken to allude to the palace of the Patriarch at Constantinople, a centre for treacherous and intriguing monks.[52] In reality, we have merely a conflation of literary effects, typical of the *Philopatris*. The author is not concerned with Byzantine prisons (would any of these, it may

49. For this point, cf. Crampe (n. 9), 20, and Reinach, 95 n. 2, citing Codinus, *De signis* 52.

50. Cf. R. E. Witt, *Isis in the Graeco-Roman World* (London 1971), 167.

51. On this quality, cf. Dover's edition of *Nubes*, xxxix.

52. Reinach, 96–7.

be asked, have golden roofs?) or patriarchal palaces, but with showing off his Homeric expertise. The juxtaposition of prison and palace betokens ineptitude rather than symbolism – if, indeed, he intended any recollection of the tartarean abyss: the same detail is exploited in the context of luxury by pseudo-Lucian, *Cynic* 9.

Literary effects abound in this whole section. Comparing his admiration of the building to that of Telemachus in the *Odyssey*, Critias calls the latter 'that young islander'. So does Lucian, twice: *De domo* 3; *Scythian* 9. The doomsayers question Critias in Homeric lines about his origin. They have downcast heads and pale faces. The former is a standard detail in this type of satire; it can be seen in Ar., *Nub.* 186 and in Persius (3.80), from whom it is adapted by Jerome of monks.[53] The pallor is also found in the Aristophanic caricature (*Nub.* 103), a line which Theocritus re-applied to a Pythagorean (14.5). Having waxed Homeric (and the tag τίς πόθεν εἶς ἀνδρῶν probably is owed to its use in *Icarom.* 24), the prophets of doom now come out with the menacing statement δυστοκεῖ γὰρ ἡ πόλις, which happens to be a direct quote from Aristophanes, *Ran.* 1423. A little later (25), there is another borrowing from this play: ὥσπερ πρῖνος ἐμπρησθείς (859). Other phrases appropriated from Lucian are ῥαγδαίους ὑετούς (*Timon* 3), ταραχαὶ τὴν πόλιν (*Nigrinus* 29), and διάτορον ἀνεβόησα (*Gallus* 1). Critias' string of questions about meteorological disasters owes a palpable debt to *Icarom.* 25–6. His likening of their prophecies to old women's follies is reminiscent of *Alexander* 15. Here, and with the ensuing promise by the doomsayers to spend ten days ἄσιτοι καὶ ἐπαγρυπνοῦντες, there is a composite effect of Lucian and Gregory Nazianzenus. For Zeus is ἄγρυπνος καὶ ἄσιτος (*Bis Accus.* 2), and the phraseologies of the *Philopatris* are strikingly similar in part to Gregory, *Or.* 5 (*In Julianum* 2), 163 (*PG* 35.693b): οἱ τοῖς γραϊδίοις συγκαθεζόμενοι καὶ συμψάλλοντες, οἱ ταῖς μακραῖς νηστείαις ἐκτετηγμένοι, καὶ ἡμίθνητες, οἱ μάτην ἀγρυπνοῦντες, καὶ ταῖς παννυχίοις στάσεσι παραληροῦντες. And finally, when the soothsayers grin, the description of this act (οἱ δὲ σεσηρὸς ὑπομειδιῶντες) is almost identical to *Amores* 13.

27. Triepho breaks in at last to silence his companion. Situation and language are reminiscent of the comparable moment of

53. Cf. D. S. Wiesen, *St Jerome as a Satirist* (Ithaca 1964), 88, 98, for Jerome's frequent use of the motif.

interruption at *Lexiphanes* 16. The narrative of Critias has made Triepho feel swollen and pregnant. It was earlier noted that Critias was in the same condition at the beginning of the dialogue: there, a recollection of *Philops.* 39 was noted. The *Philopatris* now expands motifs and allusions. Triepho goes on: ἐδήχθην γὰρ τοῖς παρὰ σοῦ λόγοις ὡς ὑπὸ κυνὸς λυττῶντος. καὶ εἰ μὴ φάρμακον ληθεδανὸν ἐμπιὼν ἠρεμήσω, αὕτη ἡ μνήμη οἰκουροῦσα ἐν ἐμοὶ μέγα κακὸν ἐργάσεται. Of this, the first sentence is closely imitated from *Nigrinus* 38; the second contains two turns of phrase (φάρμακον ληθεδανόν and μνήμη οἰκουροῦσα) taken from *Philops.* 40.

There is more than linguistic debt here. This is the antepenultimate section of the *Philopatris*. It has purloined these phrases from the conclusions of the *Nigrinus* and *Philopseudes*. Those Lucianic pieces recommend philosophical wisdom as the only cure; the *Philopatris* offers the Christian equivalents, the Lord's Prayer and (perhaps – see below) a doxology. None of this structural similarity is likely to be a coincidence.

Along with the Lord's Prayer, Triepho recommends τὴν πολυώνυμον ᾠδήν – presumably a doxology, as Macleod suggests. The phrase, however, is derived from *Philops.* 17 (employed of an Arab spell).[54]

Enter Cleolaus in a flurry of tags from Homer and tragedy, all noted by Macleod. A late, brief entry into a dialogue by a third character is a common enough motif: Sopolis in the *Lexiphanes* may stand as an easy example. The function of Cleolaus is to terminate the duologue, and bring news of imperial victories. For the latter purpose, he is given a short cento of tragical lines and half-lines, slightly reminiscent of Aeschylus, *Septem* 794, in their opening. The Persians and Susa have fallen, it is claimed, and Arabia is next. Triepho develops the theme in the last speech of the dialogue, hoping for the crushing of Babylon, Egypt, and the Scythians. These geographical details have been exploited for the dating of the *Philopatris*: all but Egypt are said to be consonant with the achievements of Nicephorus Phocas.

Not for the first time, such assertions overlook the literary element. Reinach[55] states dogmatically that Babylon stands for

54. Cf. *Dial. Mer.* 4.5, and Betz (n. 30), 154 n. 4, for other parallels from Lucian and elsewhere.

55. Reinach, 88, followed, albeit with decent caution, by Macleod.

Bagdad, the Scythians for Russians or Bulgarians. As for Egypt, it is presumed that Phocas was planning to invade it. None of this survives analysis. True, Babylon is used of Bagdad by (for example) Cedrenus, but Anna Comnena applies it to Cairo;[56] in Constantine Porphyrogenitus, Bagdad is τὸ βαγδάδ. More to the point, Babylon is used of Persia quite regularly by early Byzantine authors. In *AP* 16.63 (on a statue of Justinian in the hippodrome), the poet celebrates ὁλλυμένην Βαβυλῶνα, a phrase identical with that used by Triepho in the *Philopatris*. The conceit is not restricted to Greek writers; Corippus' laudations of Justinian and Justin II exhibit it.[57] Poetic uses of Babylon are also discernible in Claudian.[58] Relevant also is Lucian, *De merc. cond.* 13, where the expression Βαβυλῶνα εἴληφας is proverbial for gaining the pinnacle of ambition.

The same principle obtains in the case of Scythians, a term notoriously used of Huns and other barbarians in earlier writers. Poets and historians are equally guilty.[59] *AP* 16.62, a companion to the piece mentioned above, applied the term to the conquests of Justinian; so does Agathias, in his Preface to the *Cycle*. As for Egypt and Arabia, they are nothing but standard *exempla* for the bounds of empire.[60] The mention of them in the *Philopatris* is of no use for dating.

Critias prays for αἱ ἡμέραι τοῦ αὐτοκράτορος, and Triepho gives thanks for the blessings τοιούτου κράτους; both references to the unnamed emperor might be thought somewhat cool, even unenthusiastic. The term αὐτοκράτωρ may be a little inconvenient for the Nicephorus Phocas date since, as a single title for the emperor, it began to go out after the famous novel of 629 in which Heraclius introduced that of Basileus. Soon afterwards, from that time, in official language, Autokrator is commonly employed as a supplementary title to Basileus.[61] By the time of Codinus, the three regular forms of addressing the emperor are Basileus, Despotes,

56. *Alexiad* 11.7; 12.1; cf. G. Buckler, *Anna Comnena* (Oxford 1929), 418 n. 2.

57. *Laud. Just.* 3.279 (with Stache's note).

58. References and discussion in Alan Cameron, *Claudian: Poetry and Propaganda at the Court of Honorius* (Oxford 1970), 347.

59. Cf. Averil Cameron, *Agathias* (Oxford 1970), 82.

60. See Alan Cameron (n. 58), 345.

61. See L. Bréhier, 'L'origine des titres impériaux à Byzance', *BZ* 15 (1906), 161–78, and Ostrogorsky (n. 48), 106–7 (summarizing his 'Autocrator i Samodrzac', *Glas Srpske Akad.* 164 (1935), 95–187 – inaccessible to me).

339

and Kyrios.[62] The point is inconclusive, since Autokrator might have been chosen to honour (or discreetly criticize?) a warlike emperor, but it should be noticed.

The *Philopatris* ends with the proverbial 'Hippocleides doesn't care': an overtly Lucianic flourish, especially as the satirist had used the phrase to conclude a dialogue.[63]

The foregoing commentary has made one thing plain: the *Philopatris* is a cento of phrases and tags from Lucian and elsewhere. This basic ingredient offsets all attempts to find an internal clue to the date of the piece; at the risk of tedium, the point must be exemplified one last time. Three passages in the dialogue have some thematic similarities with sections of the *Chronographia* of Michael Psellus: criticism of astrologers (*Chron.* 5.19–20); refutation of the theories of Fate found in the works of the Hellenes (*Chron.* 7.41); ridicule of the pretentions of the Naziraeans, including the aerobatic motif (*Chron.* 6.19–9). It might be argued on this basis that the *Philopatris* is reflecting Byzantine themes. However, it has been seen that in all three cases our author's main concern was literary pastiche.

A last word on language and style. The dialogue is written in unclassical Greek, at least when the author is not imitating the classics, but that in itself does not constitute a decisive argument for a date of the kind advanced by Reinach and company. One doubts that any age had a monopoly on graceless language, and a glance at an early Byzantine chronicle (that of Malalas, for obvious example) will reveal what was possible by the sixth century. Also, scrutiny of the piece discloses the absence of the commonest aspects of Byzantine Greek.[64] No argument here, then, for any particular period.

If it could be shown that the *Philopatris* had a definite purpose, it might be possible to assign it plausibly to some particular period, even reign. But as we have seen, there is no agreement over this.

62. *De offic.* 17 (*PG* 157.161b).

63. Namely the *Apology*; cf. also *Heracles* 8. Another detail that might be considered an open tribute to Lucian, in view of the latter's *Pseudologistes*, is the use of ἀποφράδι ἡμέρα (23).

64. Notably absent are such things as: latinisms (with the possible exception of εἰραμάγγας); 'objective phrases' (cf. Averil Cameron (n. 59), 75–88); οἰκεῖος = personal pronoun; ἐς with the accusative for ἐν with the dative; superlatives in a simple or comparative sense.

The older view was that it was an attack on Christianity; Reinach and others have tended to reverse that notion.[65] Macleod sensibly calls its purpose uncertain, suggesting that the first part is 'a light-hearted attack on contemporary humanists who had excessive enthusiasm for classical culture', whilst the second half 'is more serious and appeals to all patriots to support the emperor in his great campaigns'.

Given all this, some remarks on the structure of the piece are in order. Dialogue in its Platonic and Lucianic forms was a popular genre throughout the entire Byzantine period[66] and hence, on that simple reckoning, the *Philopatris* could have been produced at any time. As it stands, the title is a double one: *Philopatris or Didaskomenos*. This may amount to nothing more than another Lucianic flourish; a number of the satirist's pieces have alternate titles. Philopatris would appear to be a piece of self-advertizement for the author, to be taken along with the hint at poverty and hopes for suitable imperial largesse expressed in the final section.[67] Critias is generally taken to be the Didaskomenos, since he is given instruction in the Trinity, which suits one interpretation of the dialogue. However, he gives Triepho as much if not more information on many other matters, and leads the way in patriotism at the end. Neither character has a clear edge.

The name Critias was perhaps chosen to impart a Platonizing air to the piece,[68] and it may also suggest an identification of this character with the most vehement critic of mythological folly, Lucian himself. Perhaps the author uses the figure of Lucian *kritikos* both to assail modern enemies and also to show that the shrewd and critical pagan could come to appreciate the truths of Christianity. That all the characters except Triepho have names with similar initials (Critias, Crato, Charicenus, Chleuocharmus,

65. For a survey of opinions, with the secondary literature, see Reinach.

66. Cf. Mango (n. 20), 10, for this.

67. The author here displays his customary ineptitude. Apart from the cool-looking reference to the emperor, he has earlier (17) ascribed a house and servants to Critias, not to mention his long-standing friendship with the *peraequator* Crato.

68. In view of his frequent references to the petrifaction of Niobe, it is just conceivable that his name evokes the statue-maker Critius (Critias in some manuscripts and thus printed by Jacobitz, albeit not by Macleod in his *OCT*) mentioned in *Rhet. Praec.* 9.

Cleolaus) may be due to some fancy of the author's, or simply unconscious repetition.

Triepho is a very rare name – indeed, some older commentators wished to alter it to Tripho or Trupho. There was a philosopher called Tryphon in the third century,[69] and one also recalls Typhos from the *De providentia* of Synesius, but in view of his theological emphasis on the Trinity, it seems likely that the name was intended to connote the Trinity and his devotion to it ('Three-in-one').

The two characters are in certain ways interchangeable. Both speak in the same medley of literary tags and echoes, pagan and Christian. They both apply the image of painful pregnancy to themselves (2, 27). Triepho advises Critias to spit out his follies, μή τι κακὸν πάθῃς (2); later (18), Critias reverses the quotation upon his comrade. More signally, both swear by the Unknown God of Athens. The author makes the philhellene Critias do this first, even before he has been instructed in the Trinity. This is perhaps a sign of the author's relative indifference to consistent characterization, just as he is insouciant about the imagined physical world in which the conversation is supposed to be taking place: noted earlier were the mixture of details of the setting – variously evoking Constantinople, Athens, and Egypt – and the business of Critias' poverty. Evidently the fundamental convention of the *Philopatris* is not realism with its requirement of spatio-temporal consistency, but donnish conversation in a library of the mind. The method focuses on an admired feature of cultivated discourse in all ages – the apt quotation – and simply makes this the primary mode of speech. The ultimate case of this tendency is the cento.

With respect to the purpose of the dialogue, it may or may not be significant that the work is anonymous:[70] an attack on Christianity in any Byzantine period after Justinian's time would presumably have to be. By contrast, if the *Philopatris* belonged to the reign of Julian, one might have expected a name. However, the point cannot be pressed too much. There is more than one reason why a work might come down from antiquity in anonymous form.

The author's attitude towards Christianity is problematical. Apart from the Trinity, and the occasional details such as an oath by the Son of the Father and the injunction to use the Lord's

69. See *PLRE* (Cambridge 1971), 924.
70. As is the *Timarion*.

Prayer, there is very little of substance concerning the creed. The name of Christ is never used, our author prefers to talk about Galilaeans and the Unknown God.

The approach could be taken to suggest a situation in which Christianity was too powerful to require a detailed defence and by the same token, it might smack of indifference, if not contempt – in fact, not unlike the *Peregrinus.*

As Reinach and others have observed, an attack on pagans makes no sense after the sixth century or thereabouts, for the good reason that there were no pagans as such to attack. A Julianic date might look attractive here, or the reign of Justinian, for obvious reasons, and the references to the external enemies and frontiers would suit either of these. So might the choice of a *peraequator* to be Critias' friend, since we have seen that that official is best attested in these two periods.

But this is no sure solution either. The dangers, real or supposed, of excessive interest in Hellenism were a Byzantine theme.[71] Witness, for easy example, the warnings of men like Pachomius in the eighth century or Psellus in the eleventh, not to mention the vicious elegiac poem penned against Leo the Philosopher by a pupil, Constantine the monk, the content of which has some affinity with that of the *Philopatris.*[72]

For all the reasons put forward in this paper, it is hard to classify the dialogue as specifically anti-Christian or anti-pagan. In my opinion, the purpose, in so far as it may be said to have one, is simply to mock both – an attitude that would be as Lucianic as its language, style, and structure. Up to a point, it could have been congenial to Julian, who was quite willing in his *In Galilaeos* to admit that many Hellenic myths were incredible and monstrous.[73] Equally, it would suit a military-minded emperor with no interest in learning or culture, which is precisely the description of Basil II given by Psellus.[74] On all counts, the *Philopatris* is curiously hard to pin down. Its multiple re-impersonations of classical authors is a

71. For a survey of cases, with references, cf. S. Runciman, *Byzantine Civilisation* (London 1961), 226.

72. The poem can be read in *PG* 107.1xi–ii. It counters Hellenism with the Trinity, emphasizes the sexual side of mythology along with deceptive oracles and the like, but admits the seductiveness of Hellenic culture for the unwary.

73. *In Gal.* 44a–b.

74. *Chron.* 1.29.

technique which makes it virtually impossible (for us at least) to locate and follow a single argumentative intent. To see it as essentially a literary pastiche and uncommitted mockery may best suit its magpie structure. Nor can its date be settled. There is a case for the time of Julian, of Justinian, or anything subsequent. For the current confidence in the reign of Nicephorus Phocas, however, there is no warrant.